Geography and the Urban Environment

GEOGRAPHY AND THE URBAN ENVIRONMENT

Progress in Research and Applications

Editors

D. T. HERBERT

Department of Geography, University College of Wales, Swansea

and

R. J. JOHNSTON

Department of Geography, University of Sheffield

Editorial Advisory Board

Geography and the Urban Environment

Progress in Research and Applications

Volume I

Edited by

D. T. HERBERT
Reader in Geography
University College of Wales, Swansea

and

R. J. JOHNSTON
Professor of Geography
University of Sheffield

JOHN WILEY & SONS
Chichester · New York · Brisbane · Toronto

Library of Congress Cataloging in Publication Data:

Main entry under title:

Geography and the urban environment.

Includes index.
CONTENTS: v. 1. Progress in research and applications
1. Cities and towns—Addresses, essays, lectures.
2. Anthropo-geography—Addresses, essays, lectures.
3. City planning—Addresses, essays, lectures.
I. Herbert, David T. II. Johnston, Ronald John.
GF125.G46 301.36 77-13555

ISBN 0 471 99575 4

Photosetting by Thomson Press (India) Limited, New Delhi and
printed and bound in Great Britain by The Pitman Press Ltd., Bath.

For

Aled and Nia Wyn Herbert
and
Chris and Lucy Johnston

List of Contributors

KAREN L. AVERY	*Department of Geography, Bunche Hall 1255, University of California, Los Angeles, California 90024, U.S.A.*
MICHAEL BATTY	*Department of Geography, University of Reading, Whiteknights, Reading, RG6 2AF, England*
WILLIAM A. V. CLARK	*Department of Geography, Bunche Hall 1255 University of California, Los Angeles, California 90024, U.S.A.*
ALAN G. GILBERT	*Department of Geography, University College, Gower Street, London, WC1E 6BT, England*
LEONARD GUELKE	*Department of Geography, University of Guelph, Guelph, Ontario, Canada*
DAVID T. HERBERT	*Department of Geography, University College of Swansea, Singleton Park, Swansea, Wales*
HENRY W. IRVING	*Department of Geography, The University, Hull, HU6 7RX, England*
RONALD J. JOHNSTON	*Department of Geography, University of Sheffield, Sheffield, S10 2TN, England*
PAUL L. KNOX	*Department of Geography, The University, Dundee, DO1 4HN, Scotland*
ANDREW MACLARAN	*Department of Geography, Trinity College, University of Dublin, Dublin 2, Ireland*
PAT NINER	*Centre for Urban and Regional Studies, University of Birmingham, J. G. Smith Building, Birmingham, B15 2TT, England*

PETER M. WARD — *Department of Geography, University College, Gower Street, London, WC1E 6BT, England*

CHRISTOPHER J. WATSON — *Centre for Urban and Regional Studies, University of Birmingham, B15 2TT, England*

Contents

Preface

This series is a direct lineal descendant of our two-volume collection *Social Areas in Cities* (Wiley, London, 1976), both in origin and in general format. In each case, the impetus came initially from the publishers, who encouraged us to develop our ideas first for the original collection and then for the series. While *Social Areas in Cities* stands as a piece of work in its own right, this series, *Geography and the Urban Environment*, runs parallel to other Wiley series concerned with the Industrial Environment and with Resource Management. We are grateful to our publishers for ideas and constant encouragement.

At a time when complaints of an information overload are becoming increasingly frequent, any new series needs a distinctive purpose and a clear defence. Ours is that there is a proven need for a set of volumes which are intermediate to the purpose of an academic journal—with its focus on research reports—and the fully-fledged research monograph. There are many large research projects for which a monograph is not a viable end-product, particularly in the current state of the publishing market, and yet which would suffer in impact and penetration if subdivided for report into several journal papers. This series of volumes aims to provide an avenue for the publication of substantial reports on major pieces of research; authors will be given sufficient space to set their research in its context, to report their methodologies and findings in detail, and to draw the appropriate conclusions from their results.

Further, there are research areas in which many separate pieces of work have already been reported—and in which potential exists for further research—for which a single general review would perform a signal service to those not centrally involved but sufficiently interested to require updating on progress in these areas. Finally, there are now many changes in the orientation of geographical work, involving various ideological, philosophical, and methodological perspectives which require discussion and debate. Each issue of this series will contain at least one or two essays of this latter kind and will allow an ongoing debate on theory and method within urban geography.

In establishing the series, therefore, we are following the lead set in several other disciplines of publishing, approximately once per year, a volume of major essays which portray the 'state of the art' with regard to particular major themes. In restricting the current series to Geography and the Urban Environment, we are recognizing the existence of a major focus in geographical work upon the urban area. This focus has provided a diversity of studies of the city by human geographers which include the analysis of the regional urban system, of the city as a territory with distinctive component parts, and of urbanization as a process with both economic and social ramifications. Our brief is specialized in its specification of the urban environment, but it is one which we shall interpret in a catholic manner. As the series evolves, the varied content of individual volumes—with their mix of research monographs, important reviews of critical research areas, and contributions to the methodological/philosophical/ideological debate—will be linked longitudinally and will mirror the changing nature and practice of urban geography over time. The intended audience is teachers and researchers in higher education and senior undergraduates (primarily, though, not exclusively geographers), and those practising planners concerned with the problem of the urban environment.

This first volume illustrates by its contents the nature of the intended development. To set the scene, we have contributed an editorial essay which provides a brief outline of the history of urban geography and an evaluation of the current situation in the subject. This is followed by what we hope will be the first of a series of major contributions to the debate on method in urban studies in which Leonard Guelke presents an argument against the use of logical positivism in urban geography—an argument which runs counter to the dominant trend of the 1960s—and examines the alternative approaches, including that of idealism.

The next two chapters illustrate admirably the two major purposes of these volumes. In the first, Michael Batty presents a detailed review of modelling for planning purposes, giving not only a logic for the approaches taken but also, through a detailed example, a clear statement of the inputs, outputs, and intermediate processing stages of such models. He is followed by Bill Clark and Karen Avery, who introduce their analysis of a large volume of migration data in Amsterdam, using entropy-based measures, with a review of migration studies. Apart from their value as reviews, both of these contributions stand out for their clarity of exposition of methods and thus provide an invaluable service for those who wish to follow comparable lines of research in the future.

The chapter by Paul Knox and Andrew MacLaran also has a strong empirical content, although the topic and techniques stand in some contrast to the modelling themes of the previous two chapters. Attempts to measure and monitor the quality of life and social well-being have been numerous in recent years, and in their introduction the authors examine this emerging literature. A detailed analysis of the city of Dundee provides the case study and the empirical core of the chapter which, in particular, closely examines the roles of subjective values and perceptions in the context of the overall problem of measuring satisfaction with the urban environment. Another research field which is reasonably well established in the social sciences in general, but which has received relatively little direct investigation by geographers, is discussed by Henry Irving. While geographers have analysed some kinds of interaction, such as shopping behaviour and migration, in considerable detail, social interaction and the concept of friendship have received scant attention. Irving, with reference to his own researches in parts of rural England, in Hull, and in Los Angeles, examines the problem of measuring social interaction and the relative roles of both spatial and non-spatial variables. Social interaction is characterized as a key social process which has important links with the concept of community in the urban environment.

The last two chapters in this volume have the common theme of housing. Alan Gilbert and Peter Ward examine the question of housing in a Latin American context, with objectives which include an assessment of the housing response and the differing needs of socioeconomic groups. The key question of the nature of housing provision for the urban poor of these countries is examined in detail and with particular reference to research experience in a number of specified areas. While at all times stressing the diversity within Latin America and the special features of individual countries, Gilbert and Ward also seek to identify important common elements evident in housing markets, in their temporal change and in policies pursued towards them. Chris Watson and Pat Niner, with a similar brief in a British context, draw upon their considerable experience of housing research to present a balanced view of the nature of the housing market and of contemporary trends and policies. The need for balance is particularly evident in research into housing, where individual consumers, institutional managers, societal constraints, and the structural context must all be seen as facets of a complex and dynamic situation.

In producing this first volume we are indebted to a number of people, most particularly, of course, the authors, all of whom met our deadlines and provided us with a relatively simple editorial task. For this first volume the time constraint was acute and our policy of turning to potential contributors who were already well established in their fields has been amply justified. Numerous secretaries, cartographers, and technicians similarly have helped move the project along and Ann Barham has provided an excellent index. In continuing the series we are grateful to our editorial board—Larry Bourne, Bill Clark, Risa Palm, and Don Parkes—for their help and advice. To all, our thanks. Now that the nature of the series becomes clearer and its possibilities as an outlet for major pieces of research become obvious, it is our hope that potential authors will turn to *Geography and the Urban Environment* as a vehicle for publication, and all offers of help will be gladly received and sympathetically considered.

Chapter 1

Geography and the Urban Environment

David T. Herbert and Ronald J. Johnston

General statements about the nature of an academic discipline, or of some subfield of a discipline, rarely serve a useful purpose, and already the geographical literature contains plenty of review material regarding the course of recent developments. General texts on the evolution of geographical thought continue to appear (James, 1972) and the *Progress in Geography* series (now reformed into the journals *Progress in Human Geography* and *Progress in Physical Geography*) has monitored developments in the discipline over a number of years. Nevertheless, as an introduction to this new series, both in defence of its conception and to indicate its philosophy, some outline of its nature and orientation seems desirable. Our task here, therefore, is to review the development of geographical interest in various aspects of the urban environment, setting our comments within the wider history and sociology of this and related social sciences. Our purpose is to describe, and neither to predict nor to constrain, except in very broad terms, the content of this and succeeding volumes.

Urban geography has been a popular element in the academic field of geography during the last two decades or so. Whereas in the early 1950s a separate course on urban geography at an English-speaking university was quite exceptional (Johnston, 1969), today the absence of such a course would be equally remarkable; indeed, in many institutions students can opt for a group of courses treating different aspects of the urban environment. It is probable that the rapid growth of interest in the subject, a period during which urban geography was the most fashionable option for undergraduates and the most favoured research area for postgraduates, is now coming to an end. Alongside urban problems are those focused on environmental concerns in the public consciousness and the increased interest in these can be recognized in student activities. Urban geography, however, is now a well-established subdiscipline which continues to attract students and practitioners in considerable numbers and the volume of published work remains large. Ideas, methods, and attitudes within the subject remain vital and the focus of much debate.

A strength of urban geography in recent years has been the breadth of its terms of reference. It is not a systematic branch of geography, focused on a particular, well-defined subject matter (as, for example, is industrial geography);

rather it is a very catholic field of study. The core of its analysis is a central concern with a particular phenomenon—the urban settlement—and increasingly urban geographers are widening their intellectual brief to encompass whatever approaches from within the social sciences advance understanding of the operation of that phenomenon. From the outset, therefore, urban geography has an integrative and interdisciplinary role; hence the title of this series and the introductory essay. Such integration does not mean that there is not usually a focus in any piece of work on a single systematic theme within the urban environment, whether it be the commercial land-use pattern, the mosaic of social areas, or the journey to work. Nor does the suggestion of an integrative function imply the traditional holistic approach of 'classical' regional geography; a geography of *the* city, or of *a* city, has a limited function which few care to pursue.

Our general philosophy, therefore, is that geographical study of the urban environment is catholic, in the themes which it follows, in the stimuli which it reacts to from society and from other disciplines, in the techniques which it employs, and in the ideologies within which it is shaped. All of these themes, stimuli, techniques and ideologies have varied in their relative importance as geographical interest in the urban area has grown. In this essay, we outline the main trends in these variations, looking at urban geography within its environmental context and indicating the major themes which this series will be developing.

THE ENVIRONMENT OF GEOGRAPHICAL STUDY

Any attempt to trace and explain developments in the study of urban areas by geographers must do so in the context of the broader discipline of human geography. As emphases in the discipline have changed over time, so these have been reflected in urban geography; indeed, research concerned with urban settlements and urban problems has, particularly in the last few decades, to a disproportionate extent been the initiator of many new emphases which have subsequently diffused through the wider discipline. On a broader methodological front, the emergence of new paradigms and the relative retreat of others into the shadows provides the scenario against which the development of urban geography has taken place. At this contextual scale, events over the whole developing field of knowledge are relevant.

Disciplines rarely evolve in isolation; there is a strong and often unsuspected parallelism in the stages through which they proceed and in the variety of stances which they encompass. Sources of this parallelism are undoubtedly various. Sometimes a single major published work or scientific advance can be identified as the obvious source of ideas; the debate on geographical determinism and the formulation of an environmental paradigm, for example, can only be fully comprehended by reference to Darwinian theories of evolution (Stoddart, 1966). More commonly, however, new paradigms emerge from gradual and accumulative shifts of position and their influence has differential effects on individual disciplines, both temporally and in scale of impact. Despite this interrelated quality of the total field of knowledge and the inevitability of some measure of contact, diffusion, and resultant communality, human geography, far more than most other disciplines, occupied a self-imposed academic cocoon for the early decades of this century, within which the majority of practitioners avoided contact with much of the wider world of scholarship. Evidence for this isolation is provided by the avoidance of explicit theory and of any systematically developed attempt at generalization, following the discrediting of environmental determinism. During this long time period a number of paradigms dominated geographical study.

Classical, modern, and contemporary

There have been several detailed studies of the development of geographical thought (Freeman, 1961; James, 1972; Wrigley, 1965) and no attempt is made here to replicate them. James (1972) identified three main periods, labelled classical, modern, and contemporary, into which the development of geography as a studied discipline could be divided, and it is against a chronological background of this kind that the emergence of paradigms can be traced. Progress has not been even, particular paradigms do not belong neatly to individual time phases, and some phases have been more productive than others. Although some concepts have become completely outmoded and subsequently discarded, the process of development has characteristically been one of addition and modification rather than of rejection and replacement—an evolutionary rather than a revolutionary sequence of change. Of the three phases identified by James, the first two are closely associated with particular paradigms—even individual scholars—while more recently it is the proliferation of both which has become typical. Wrigley (1965), in discussing the classical phase of geography, distinguished between the pre-nineteenth century writers, who dealt with geographical facts in a haphazard and unsystematic way, and the key figures of von Humboldt and Ritter, who introduced new qualities to the classical school. These included the careful assembly of detailed factual data, the search for laws which gave coherence to accumulated material, and the investigation of how the physical environment affected the functioning and development of society.

James identified the year 1859 as the end of the classical period. This was the year in which von Humboldt died and for James he was the last of the 'universal scholars'—actors on an academic stage at a time when, as Wrigley has suggested, it was pointless to distinguish between those who were geographers and those who were not. The modern period of geography emerged in the latter half of the nineteenth century with the satisfaction of conditions necessary for the development of an academic field of study. James nominated three such sets of conditions: first, a body of concepts acceptable to members of the profession; second, specialized university departments offering advanced training; and, third, a career structure. Geographers from the newly established departments in

German universities played a major role in the earlier part of the modern period. Hartshorne (1939, 1959) has shown that their view of geography as a chorological science—areal differentiation—was not new when it was developed by Hettner, who elaborated Richthofen's concept of chorology into a paradigm for geographical study. As James (1972, p. 226) writes:

> With geography, its unity is its method ... it proceeds from the viewpoint of spatial variations. The goal of the chorological point of view is to know the character of regions and places through comprehension of existence together and interrelations among the different realms of reality and their varied manifestations and to comprehend the earth's surface as a whole in its actual arrangement in continents, larger or smaller regions and places.

Hettner's paradigm did not remain unchallenged for long; others sought definition by subject matter rather than by method—the rigidity and determinism of geography were under attack by the end of the nineteenth century. The French school, whose central character was Vidal de la Blache, provided a powerful and largely alternative set of concepts for the development of geography. From it emerged, in particular, a greater emphasis upon man rather than nature and the establishment of the idea of regional studies. The modern phase established geography as a university discipline but did not give it a rigorous conceptual base. The role of the contemporary period has, by contrast, been more varied and, though marked to date by the proliferation of techniques and increasing quantification, it has not yet seen the general acceptance of an overall paradigm of the subject; indeed, the likelihood of this happening has receded.

Against this broad canvas of development and historical change, a number of paradigms can be identified which have tended to dominate particular phases but the fortunes of which have risen and fallen over time. All are still represented in the contemporary phase; there are no 'paradigms lost'. While new ones have been added, the old have rarely been totally discarded, if only because of the conservatism of scholars whose life-spans are generally longer than the periods of intense activity in the paradigm within which they were socialized as academic geographers.

Exploration, environmentalism, and regionalism

The 'exploration' paradigm belongs most clearly to the early and classical phases in the development of geographical thought. Its characteristic features were the charting of unknown places and the gathering of basic facts on spatial phenomena. This activity motivated the early observers and the map-making tradition in geography; it also inspired the explorers themselves, who actually discovered new lands. Von Humboldt was himself an explorer of considerable fortitude, of course, and his systematic methodology for the gathering of specimens and maintenance of records set high standards of data collection. With declining necessity for further factual detail of this kind, the exploration paradigm is now of little direct relevance to academic geography, although its spirit persists in organizations like the Royal Geographical Society. Debate on 'exploration' or 'fact-finding' approaches, in a narrower definitional sense, continues, however. Within the broad field of urban geography, for example, Harvey (1973) has argued that we have more than enough data and that our work is characterized by an inability to handle such data in ways which advance understanding of the city. To him, further data collection is counterproductive. To Bunge, on the other hand, we have little, if any, of the right kind of data which enables a proper evaluation of the conditions of human society, and to counter this he has launched geographical expeditions in Detroit and Toronto to provide the needed data (Bunge, 1973; Bunge and Bordessa, 1975).

Environmentalism as a paradigm has a long and somewhat chequered history in geographical study. It can be found within the classical period when there was an awareness of the need to investigate the ways in which the physical environment affects the functioning and development of societies; it moved into a central position with the advocacy of geographical determinism in its most strident form in the last part of the nineteenth century. Within the general paradigm of environmentalism a variety of stances has been adopted, none of which is capable of being sustained with any degree of conviction. Determinism, possibilism, and probabilism have all been advocated, and in many ways the modern ecosystem approach, which draws upon general systems theory and stresses the essential harmony of man and nature and indeed the inadvisability of recognizing dichotomies rather than ranges of individual elements, is the direct inheritor of the environmentalist approach.

As a paradigm, the regional concept presents many faces to modern geography. It inherits in some ways the fact-finding tradition of the exploration ethos and in others the synthesis of man and environment which was present in classical geography and found full expression in environmentalism. Regional studies may involve the identification of homogeneous regions, the description of segments of the earth's surface, and the specialized regional monographs. As Vidal de la Blache developed his approach to the 'pays' of France he emphasized his study of landscape, but the synthesis of man and land was strongly evident in his writing (Wrigley, 1965, p. 8): 'The area within which an intimate connection between man and land had grown up in this way over the centuries formed a unit, a region, which was the proper object for geographical study'. There have been many variants of the regional concept. The 'landschaft' concept has always been difficult to interpret, but demanded study of those phenomena which could be observed on the surface of the earth and of landscape as the totality of such observations. In all of this work, the focus has been on human artifacts—on farms and fields, hedges and houses—rather than on human beings; the landscape is taken as a palimpsest of human activity, the study of which is virtually ignored, as indeed it still is in much historical geography. As a paradigm the regional concept has proved durable. Regionalization, an important tool in economic and urban geography, has an objective statistical methodology but is conceptually inherited from regionalism. The regional study as the ultimate synthesis of systematic geographical specialisms now has little academic credibility, but the teaching of regional geography remains a significant part of the discipline.

Contemporary paradigms

If the classical period in the development of geographical thought was really only dominated by one paradigm, that of exploration, and the modern period by two, environmentalism and regionalism, then the contemporary phase, dating really only from the early 1960s, has already provided several major new blueprints. It has inherited environmentalism and regionalism, which remain worthy of scrutiny and are capable of reformulation, and it has already added the substantial model-based paradigm of spatial analysis. Chorley and Haggett presented the case for such a new approach with their analysis of the geometrical qualities of spatial data and their advocacy of more numerical and model-based analyses (Chorley and Haggett, 1967, p. 34): 'In general we feel that geometrical analysis offers a logical, consistent and geographically more relevant alternative to the "element orientated" approach with its inevitable tendency to subdivide geography and force it outwards towards the relevant external systematic disciplines'. As a paradigm, with an associated set of methodologies and techniques, spatial analysis has recently dominated contemporary geography, generating a voluminous research literature. Other philosophies, which may become more dominant in the contemporary period, are as yet in an embryo state and are not firmly established. Behavioural geography is one expression of a wider contemporary interest in phenomenology in the social sciences as a whole, whereas reactions against positivism and functionalism as prevailing philosophies also find their parallels in other disciplines. An increased interest in conflict as opposed to consensus theories and a move towards a Marxist position have found footholds in human geography as elsewhere.

Identification of broad time phases in the development of geographical thought, and of the major paradigms which have emerged, sets the very general context within which the appearance of a subdiscipline can be viewed. It is against this kind of background, and particularly in relation to the types of work which dominated the classical and modern periods, that the relative isolation of geography from other fields of knowledge can best be understood. A focus on landscape, particularly on the artifacts of human occupance, for example, rather than on people themselves, ensured that human geographers were following blind-alleys rather than open-ended avenues of progress. This followed the discrediting of earlier geographical theories, notably that associated with environmental determinism, and a failure to replace them with sounder alternatives. Regionalism produced its own diversions and, as Davies (1972, p. 34) remarked, 'To consider the region as the culminating core of geography is to elaborate the doctrine of the unique'. Mackinder's (1919) heartland theory, which attempted to relate sources of power to global geography, was embraced by Haushofer (James, 1972, p. 240) and translated into the *geopolitik* of Nazi Germany as the art of using geographical knowledge to give support and direction to the policy of the state. In the United States, Hartshorne was preaching the Hettnerian doctrine of areal differentation, which gave prominence to an idiographic approach to the uniqueness of place, while Sauer and his disciples, with major contacts in anthropology, focused attention on the description of changing cultural landscapes. In Britain, historical geography, whose scholarship involved cross-section descriptions linked by narratives of change, was important, alongside the regional description tradition which emphasized the linkages between natural environments and human responses.

Although this work covered a wide range of phenomena and adopted a variety of stances, two themes stand out. First, it was very largely oriented to rural rather than to urban areas, despite the importance of the latter in the societies under review; and, second, the focus was on the land as the stage on which human actors performed and placed their artifacts rather than on the inhabitants themselves. This is not to say that there were not exceptions, for some geographers were looking at towns within the established paradigms. Notable examples of such work are Dickinson's (1929, 1933; see also Smailes, 1946) early studies of the urban sphere of influence as a region, and also his (1945) study of town plans. These were isolated urban foci in a traditionally rural-centred discipline, however, perhaps because the rural ethos was strong in the class backgrounds, even the geographical backgrounds, of the geographers of the modern phase.

WAR, CONTACTS, AND 'NEW GEOGRAPHIES'

After the Second World War, a number of changes occurred in the geographical discipline, several of them reaching their *apogee* in the United States between 1955 and 1960 and in Great Britain a few years later. Again the origins of these are many and varied. Important among them was probably the war itself, the organization of which involved geographers working in teams with members of other disciplines (Ackerman, 1945, 1958) and thereby becoming aware of the current methods, interests, and issues beyond the narrow horizons of the few other subjects—anthropology, geology, history—with which they had maintained some contact. This was indeed a period of major change in many social science disciplines. Economics, for example, had passed through the Keynesian revolution and had obtained both public (political) and scientific recognition for its role in solving the ills of the 1920s and 1930s. Psychologists had been deeply involved in the American war effort, as studies such as *The American Soldier* (Stouffer *et al*, 1950) indicate, and they, plus associates in sociology, had begun to launch large programmes of survey research into human behaviour (notably the studies of communications and influence organized by Lazarsfeld, Berelson, and Gaudet 1944). All of this work had the following characteristics:

1. It was nomothetic rather than idiographic, focusing on the general trends and patterns and interpreting specifics within an explicit theoretical matrix.

2. It used numerical methods to analyse its data and so was scientifically 'respectable'.
3. It apparently had predictive power and so could be used in the development of public policy.

Much of the early impetus for change within human geography was American in origin; some of it was transferred to Britain very early, but in large part fell on deaf ears (Crowe, 1938). There was a long tradition of applied work in Britain, however, exemplified by the first land-use survey of the 1930s and Stamp's later involvement in the growth of town and country planning which started during the war and was put into effect under the 1945 Labour government. After 1945, several significant changes in emphasis began to typify research and teaching within human geography. These changes were commonly derived from external stimuli; they were derivative rather than indigenous innovations (Harvey, 1969) and became the foci of conflict and debate within the discipline. Ways in which these changes were introduced and the general timing of events will be discussed below, but it is convenient to identify, in a preliminary way, what these changes were.

The change in emphasis from idiographic to nomothetic forms of study was one such shift. Human geography prior to the early 1950s had been preoccupied with the pursuit of the unique; exceptionalism was a keynote of regional geography. On the one hand, a preoccupation with the unique was by no means restricted to human geography and Harvey (1969), for example, has discussed its presence in the historical discipline; on the other, there are geographers (James, 1972) who would question the extent to which it dominated pre-contemporary geographical thought. Similarly, Chorley and Haggett (1967) noted Aristotle's distinction between idiographic and nomothetic, and Sauer (1925) pointed out that although geography was devoted to descriptions of unique places as such geographers had for a long time been seeking to formulate illuminating generalizations about the earth and man's place on it. James (1972) argued that both Hettner and Hartshorne had been incorrectly quoted as saying that geography was essentially idiographic and was not concerned with general concepts. Although the distinction may have been recognized, it is clear that human geography in practice was centrally concerned with exceptionalism and stood in some contrast with the search for general laws in several branches of physical geography. From the isolated examples, such as von Thunen, Christaller, Weber, and Losch, a much more general shift towards a nomothetic discipline, in which the search for laws and models was a central concern, was one highly significant change in the contemporary period and one which, in Taylor's (1976) account, struck traditional geography at its very core.

A second significant change in the contemporary period has been towards the general adoption of numerical forms of analysis, of quantitative methodologies, and of statistical techniques. This change has again been questioned in terms of its novelty; James (1972) and others have argued that mathematics in particular aspects of geographical study have a long pedigree. Only very recently, however, has what has variously been termed the 'quantitative revolution' (Burton, 1963) and the 'statistical and models revolution' (Wilson, 1972) taken place. As Gregory (1976) has outlined, it was already being contended in the early 1960s that the 'revolution' was over, as the new practice of using statistical techniques and quantitative methodologies was already established. Taylor (1976) sees quantification as adding the degree of difficulty to a broader process of change in human geography which allowed a reordering of paradigms and priorities within the discipline. Over a decade of increased quantification has now produced a generation of more numerate geographers for whom the development of more scientific methodologies is an easier task.

A third change discernible in contemporary geography, that from normative to behavioural modes of study, was in part a reaction against some of the early excesses of quantification and models based upon the assumption of economic man. As quantification in human geography was paralleled in other social science disciplines, notably economics, psychology, and some forms of political science, so the behavioural emphasis could be related to the shift towards phenomenology over a range of subjects. In essence, phenomenology, as developed in psychology (Lee, 1976) and other social sciences, emphasizes the individual, the subjective, and the concept of imagery; within human geography the emergence of a behavioural emphasis implied a move against the use of aggregate statistics, against the assumptions of economic or optimizing man, and towards both study of the individual as the initial data unit and analysis of the perceived experiences and images upon which behaviour was based. As introduced into human geography, this approach has brought a focus of atten-ion upon the behavioural environment (Kirk, 1963), upon spatial imagery (Gould and White, 1974), and upon the whole question of the decision-making process (Brown and Moore, 1970).

As a further main thrust of change in the contemporary period, and one which is not yet fully articulated, there has been since the late 1960s a general reaction against positivism as a conceptual position and the examination of alternative philosophical stances within human geography. Haggett (1975) summarized positivism as a philosophical position which holds that our sensory experiences are the exclusive source of valid information about the world. Three main strands of the positivist viewpoint are the idea of consensus in society, determinism of personal or environmental forces, and scientific method. These were strands which had strong appeal to a 'new' geography of the 1950s and 1960s, which was being carried along on the wave of quantification and a belief in the value of model building and a more scientific methodology. Reactions against positivism have been several and have had the effect of modifying its more extreme expressions; Haggett (1975) now suggests that most geographers would adopt compromise positions—a diagnosis which is probably correct. As most practising geographers of the 1950s and 1960s had a largely pragmatic approach which included little awareness that they were working within a positivist mould, however, carefully considered philosophical positions, compromise or otherwise, may still be comparatively rare.

Phenomenology and the behavioural emphasis have provided one reaction against positivism; others have included the call for a conflict rather than a consensus view of society (Eyles, 1974), a move which for some has found the work of Dahrendorf (1959) as a point of reference but which owes its major stimulus to the century-old writings of Karl Marx, whose influence has permeated geography much later than other disciplines. Part of the debate on changes in philosophical position within human geography (Harvey, 1969) has been clouded by the diversity of terminology. Whereas Eyles (1974), for example, centres upon criticisms of functionalism, which he identifies (Eyles, 1974, p. 34) as 'essentially a positivistic method of explanation ... (which) ... tries to exclude subjectively formulated models of action', Chisholm (1975) concentrates upon differences between positive and normative theory. That this kind of debate and, in particular, a closer questioning of the tenability of positivist theories is not peculiar to human geography is clear from the strongly similar debates which are occurring in other social science disciplines (see, for example, Taylor, Walton, and Young's (1973) account of the 'new' criminology).

Finally, a change which has become more clearly articulated in human geography has been the specific 'politicization' of some research. This has been reflected in a more diffuse sense of the need to make research more relevant to the contemporary needs of society and in the increasing reference to a Marxist philosophical base. It can be argued that applied research has a long-established tradition in human geography and that earlier events of the contemporary period had merely distracted geographers from that role. During the last decade, however, there has been a much more persistent questioning of the ways in which geographical research should be made relevant and for whom it should be relevant. Should geographers be content to concentrate their efforts on the spatial outcomes of social problems or should they more profitably examine the societal structures and allocative systems which produce the problems in the first instance? Is ameliorative or diagnostic research merely counter-revolutionary (Harvey, 1973)? Will nothing less than a revolutionary commitment suffice? Harvey's plea for the acceptance of a Marxist method of dialectic has found growing support among many geographers, but there is a problem of personal belief which most (e.g. Chisholm, 1975; Morrill, 1974) have found it impossible to accept in its entirety.

Having so far identified the major paradigms which have influenced the geographical discipline as a whole and also the more significant changes or innovative trends which have appeared in human geography since the Second World War, it remains to examine the ways in which urban geography has developed against this background of tradition and change.

The origins of urban geography

Several reviews of the early development of urban geography (Berry and Horton, 1970; Carter, 1972) have identified the very early examples of town studies and the ways in which the subject has changed over time. These initial works were strongly descriptive and amounted to little more than observations on the general characteristics of urban places. For Carter (1972) it was the replacement of description by interpretation of location which laid the foundations for urban geography to develop as a special study. From the pioneering works of Hassert (1907) and Blanchard (1911), a form of urban geographical study which centred around the analysis of site and situation became established. Although this basic format was soon subject to advance and modification, it provided a schema for elementary town study by geographers which was to persist over several decades of the twentieth century. The environmentalist paradigm, in particular the need to relate the artifacts of human occupance to the physical geographical base, was strongly mirrored in this type of study. An overreliance on the site-situation approach was already being criticized in the 1920s, and Aurousseau (1924) and Crowe (1938) used town studies as examples of geographers concentrating upon the inanimate objects of landscape rather than upon people and movement. In many ways, however, site-situation studies were the precursors of the urban morphological mode of analysis and perhaps the only truly indigenous line of evolution within urban geography. As the morphologists looked in increasing detail at the built fabric of towns and the way in which it had evolved (Conzen, 1960; Smailes, 1955), they were building a form of urban geography which continued without major conceptual change until the early 1960s when it was still centrally concerned with the inanimate qualities of the city and its setting. Changes there had been, such as attempts by Smailes (1955) to emphasize geographical rather than historical forms of analysis in the study of townscape and the moves towards generality (Conzen, 1960, 1962), but the urban morphological trend up to this time remained descriptive and essentially idiographic.

Urban morphological study, developed within the discipline, reflected the practised methodologies of the subject as a whole. Other major influences upon urban geography before the contemporary period were derived from external rather than from internal sources; their effects are therefore symbolic of change and adaptation over the broader field of knowledge, but through either ignorance or arrogance on the part of geographers they had little real influence on the geographical study of urban environments. Early theorists on city location (Cooley, 1894; Weber, 1899) considered routeways to be the key, and cities were located at the breaks in transportation systems. Economic theories, as developed by Hurd (1903), also allowed the evolution of geographical studies which were not environmentally based but rather looked to the economics of location and incorporated considerations of costs, land values, and rents and of concepts such as accessibility and nodality.

A second stimulus, by no means unrelated to the work of Hurd (1903) and the land economists, came from the Chicago school of urban ecology (Park, 1925) which introduced new concepts of order and generality to the study of cities. Of equal importance, these 'ecologists' brought people themselves to the forefront of attention rather than allowing the focus to remain upon the environmental stage, natural or man-made, upon which human behaviour was enacted.

If economics gave the idea of studying the functions and activities of urban places a powerful thrust and provided much of the rationale for Christaller's (1933) early work and the subsequent high level of interest in central place theory, so social ecology provided the social dimension to urban geographical study and took the subject away from its rather sterile preoccupation with bricks and mortar.

Unfortunately, neither of these two main derivative sources had anything like immediate effect; the barriers to the diffusion of new ideas into urban geographical research and practice proved extremely absorbent indeed. Despite a seminal paper by Harris and Ullman (1945), which made clear the stimuli to geographical study that were available from economics and sociology but whose publication during a major war undoubtedly delayed its impact, it was really only from the 1950s that their general applications and possibilities became fully realized. Then, whereas the economics source was to strengthen and change drastically the geographical study of the town as a point or location, so the social ecology source was to have considerable repercussions upon the analysis of the town as an area. Reviews of the state of urban geography in the 1950s, such as that by Mayer (1954) and a collection of readings (Mayer and Kohn, 1959), illustrated some diversity of types of study and an awareness of new foci, such as central place theory and urban models, but still reflected the emphases of the pre-1950s; over the decades which followed the pace of change was to be much greater, and it is to the characterization of the process of change and its significant innovations that we can now turn.

SPATIAL ANALYSIS AND URBAN GEOGRAPHY IN THE CONTEMPORARY PERIOD

A number of scholars had key roles in relaying both developments in other disciplines and general shifts of emphasis in the body of knowledge as a whole into human geography. In one sense these individuals were responsible for change though the nature of their contribution has been questioned. Both James (1972) and Taylor (1976) have discussed the question of whether these people were innovators rather than individuals who reidentified some element which had always been present in human geography and gave it a new kind of prominence. Notable among the innovators were two American (Fred K. Schaefer and Bill Garrison) and one Swedish (Torsten Hagerstrand) geographers.

Schaefer's (1953) contribution was a single essay in which he attacked the areal differentiation philosophy, particularly its uniqueness or idiographic aspects, propounded by Hartshorne (1939, 1959). As an alternative he proposed the need for geographers to develop morphological laws of patterns, both of single phenomena and of several related phenomena, from which process laws might be developed in combination with the work of other social scientists. Hartshorne's (1955, p. 242) closely argued reply to the Schaefer article accused him of defective scholarship and of an almost complete misrepresentation of both the German sources used and of *The Nature of Geography* itself. Despite this severe criticism, which could not be answered because of Schaefer's untimely death in 1953, the germs of the ideas launched by Schaefer were acknowledged by the new theoreticians of the early 1960s as fundamental influences upon their way of thinking (Bunge, 1962), and, either contemporaneously or subsequently, Schaefer's colleagues at Iowa (McCarty, Hook, and Knos, 1956) were adapting statistical methods to forms of geographical analysis and had moved some way to the establishment of laws and generalizations. It is surprising in many ways that the devastating indictment of Schaefer's paper (Hartshorne, 1955) was not influential upon those who took up the ideas in the 1953 article, but undoubtedly Schaefer's plea for a move away from exceptionalism was one of the most influential single events of the 1950s.

Hagerstrand's work at Lund was conducted very much in isolation, not being translated from his native Swedish until well into the period of change (Pred, 1967; Wagner and Mikesell, 1962), but the influence of his development of statistical nomothetic approaches was felt in America because of his visit in the early 1950s to the University of Washington at Seattle where Garrison was involved with a group of researchers, many of whom became household names in urban geography (such as Berry, Dacey, Marble, Morrill, and Nystuen). The interests of this group were very much in spatial laws of two main kinds. The first were concerned with the patterns of points on the earth's surface, of which the main examples were clearly urban places; the second were of flows of goods and people, based upon a view of humans as exceptionally rational beings who reacted to the various costs of moving from one place to another by keeping them at a minimum. Their main stimuli were clearly from economics, both those provided by Christaller's central place theory and those from regional scientists/economists such as Isard, Losch, Dunn, Greenhut, and Ponsard (see Berry, 1959; Garrison, 1959, 1960). Their work was strongly mathematical, focusing, for example, upon operational models developed in linear programming, though they also adopted statistical procedures to present their morphological and associational laws and to test their notions about the economic rationality of men (Garrison, 1956; Garrison and Marble, 1967).

Theory and quantification

The impact of this small band of influential scholars was both rapid and enormous, and was made effective by their energetic research and by a capacity to write and publish their new insights into the development and application of human geography. Within a relatively few years, training in statistics—though not in mathematics—was considered a *sine qua non* for postgraduate and undergraduate students in most North American universities; by an interesting process of diffusion and some independent development of statistical usage (see Gregory, 1976), similar ideas had been developed in Britain, notably by Dick Chorley, Stan Gregory, and Peter Haggett. Studies in urban geography proved especially amenable to the impact of this move towards increased quantification, and the role of Brian Berry, who promoted the analysis of settlement patterns and sought spatial order in the size and location of towns and cities, villages and hamlets, neighbourhood and regional centres, was considerable. Urban geography had some additional advantage in that the rediscovery of central place theory, a process helped by Baskin's (1966) translation of Christaller, provided a comprehensive spatial model which, both as a whole and in its many individual facets, provided a rich testing ground for many elements of an emerging quantitative methodology: Dacey's (1962) reexamination of Brush's (1953) earlier empirical analysis of central places in south-west Wisconsin, using nearest-neighbour analysis, and Berry and Garrison's (1958a) calculation of threshold populations were two of the best-known early studies. Central place theory, with its emphasis upon both point patterns and the flows of goods and consumers, provided the initial main testing ground for quantification in urban geography.

The winds of change spread innovative techniques into other aspects of urban geography. Regression models provided a set of hypothesis-testing procedures; potential theories were framed and reframed, and by 1963 Burton was able to argue that the 'quantitative revolution' was already over in the sense that the necessity for the use of statistical methods was established and the *avant-garde* practitioners of such methods had become accepted members of the professional establishment. This view may have been premature but has certainly been validated by time, and Gregory much later was able to argue (Gregory, 1976, p. 394): 'My contention is that the move to quantification not only encourages the development and generation of theoretical constructs, but also provides a useful tool for the furthering of our now traditional enquiries'.

Within urban geography, the new methods were put to a variety of uses, such as the classification of settlements (Smith, 1965), the examination of the rank-size rule for the populations of urban places (Berry and Garrison, 1958b), and the analysis of urban population densities (Berry, Simmons, and Tennant 1963). A major innovation of the early 1960s was associated with a new interest in the social ecology of Park and Burgess and with the more widespread realization that *people* lived in cities and that there was spatial order in residential patterns. There had clearly been an awareness of these facts for some time (Burgess, 1925; Harris and Ullman, 1945; Hoyt, 1939) which gave to studies of the internal structure of the city useful models in the form of simple spatial generalizations which a generation of urban geographers were to test, examine, and debate. From the enormously influential empirical work of the Chicago school came other concepts, notably those of the natural area (Zorbaugh, 1929) and of the invasion-succession growth processes (Burgess, 1925), which were to provide stimuli for closely allied lines of research. Not only were there, at one level of spatial resolution, operational models of the city which could be tested but there was also at another level the idea that the city was a mosaic and the problem was one of the identification of the bases of residential differentiation of the parts of the mosaic and their characterization.

As the study of the social geography of the city developed (Jones, 1960), geographers were to become centrally concerned with people as social beings, and another major impetus in this direction was received from outside the discipline. Shevky and Bell (1955) formalized their theory and typology of social area analysis and focused attention upon the population census and its small area statistics as a primary data source. Such a data set provided a natural stimulus for the application of a quantitative methodology to what was, in part at least, the traditional geographical problem of regionalization and for which the possibility of more sophisticated statistical procedures had already been demonstrated outside geography by Tryon (1955) and by Schmid and his collaborators (Johnston, 1976). The school of factorial ecology within urban geography (Berry, 1971) developed in relation to the census data set and the study of residential differentiation (Herbert, 1972; Johnston, 1971). Census data were ransacked to provide indices of differences between the various parts of urban areas; the availability of computers (used by geographers as high-speed calculating machines) allowed mass manipulation of these data sets and, very rapidly, the study of intraurban residential patterns ousted central place investigations from their primacy within the interests of urban geographers.

Throughout the 1960s the methodology of those investigations was both extended and sharpened. The aim was to be scientific—as physics and chemistry are—and to provide quantifiable theories and laws; models became more sophisticated, their language became more symbolic, and mathematics rather than the now-accepted statistics became the expressed desiderata (Wilson, 1972). Some doubts on this trend were gaining strength as many of the quantitative methods failed to 'deliver the goods' in terms of new insights and certainly in terms of practicalities. Mathematical statisticians were convinced by the ways in which geographers had acquired sound knowledge of statistical theories but were less sure that they were being used to best effect. Whether the problem or the kind of result justified the sophisticated level of methodology and whether the assumptions and necessary conditions for statistical analysis were being met in the geographical data matrix—these are issues and questions which have prompted an ongoing debate on the role of quantification in human geography.

The thrust towards quantifiable laws and theories was well exemplified in Harvey's (1969) treatise on *Explanation in Geography*. These theories had a basis, often perhaps only implicit, in mechanistic assumptions of human decision-making; the concept of economic or perfectly rational man who made decisions on the basis of complete knowledge and omniscience and who was translated by geographers into spatial man (Nystuen, 1963), whose choice of locations was based upon the minimization of movement costs. Later, there were models adopted from Parsonian sociology, which accepted a view of society as composed of individuals allocated to particular places within the economic and social order from which, by dint of personal effort, they might escape to a higher level. The members of these various groups then compete for territory, with the resulting spatial order representing a consensus acceptance of a certain pattern. These derivative sources, and the ways in which they were translated into geographical models and theories, ensured an essentially positivist and functional suite of postures. As quantification itself and the question of scientific bases for the discipline were the natural handmaidens of these philosophies, urban geography by the later 1960s had assumed in its overall practice what was essentially a conservative, stereotyped, and rather abstracted character.

FIRST MURMURINGS: THE BEHAVIOURAL ALTERNATIVE

Concern with this nomothetic, rationalistic methodology developed in the United States in the mid-1960s. Within human geography, it was initially expressed in statements by scholars such as Lowenthal (1961) and Tuan (1968), who shared a humanistic concern for the study of landscapes, and it had strong precedents and parallels in the social sciences at large with the advancement of phenomenology as an alternative to the implicit positivism of the quantitative theorists. In psychology, the work of Lewin (1938) is often taken as the initiation of a phenomenal approach; in sociology, phenomenology spawned a diverse literature and a related set of stances. In a phenomenological perspective, the existence of an objective reality is denied and each individual is recognized as having a lived world of experience within which decisions are made and which are reflected in, for example, man's models of nature and his tastes in landscape (Lowenthal and Prince, 1964). As geographers have emphasized the phenomenological perspective, different cultural groups have been socialized to appreciate different aspects and components of the natural world, in whose image they create their own worlds, and the study of human behaviour in physical space can be pursued only through knowledge of these perceptions, just as the study of behaviour in social space can only be comprehended in the light of people's ideas about society (Powell, 1971). Thus there is no need for geographers to erect models of reality against which human behaviour can be compared; all humans already have these models, and it is for geographers to discover what they are and how they are used (Guelke, 1974).

This focus on how individuals make decisions was brought into the mainstream of human geography by Pred, Wolpert, and others. These workers questioned whether the economic and sociological models, which had so far dominated the shift to a nomothetic philosophy, were allowing any development of geographical understanding, since the deviations between the patterns of the models and those on the earth's surface were too great to be accounted for by irrationality of behaviour or by stochastic variations from the general law. Wolpert (1964), in his classic study of the productivity of Swedish farms, showed that farmers are imperfect decision-makers in terms of normative economic models, and Pred (1967, 1968) attempted to develop a more general model of behaviour and location based on people's information and their ability to use it. Others, such as Webber (1972), worked on models of how people might react in situations of uncertainty, seeing humans as gamblers in games against their physical, social, and economic environments.

The 'behavioural approach' was introduced to urban geography through studies of movement patterns. Consumer behaviour in the use of service centres provided one natural focus at it allowed a new kind of examination of some of the main tenets of central place theory. The intraurban residential mobility process provided a second major strand, allowing a new dimension to be added to the proliferation of studies on factorial ecology and residential differentiation. Rees's (1970, p. 307) comment on Burgess, 'But he missed the point of his own model of the city. The movement of people from one residence to another *as the city grows* is the very mechanism by which zones and natural areas (disorganized or organized) are created', could also have been applied to many of the factorial ecology studies of the 1960s, whose emphasis was upon pattern; the processes which led to the mosaic were scarcely considered by geographers.

Early attempts at describing movement patterns in the migration field were in terms of distance-decay laws (Morrill and Pitts, 1967), and these were followed by models of how decisions are made in terms of both whether and where to move. Major features of this were the search through space for information, and Brown and Moore's (1970) model of the residential decision-making process was one of the best-known efforts of its kind. In their schema, as in others, a flow diagram of the step-by-step process of decision-making created a framework within which individual acts could be structured; both the process as a whole and its individual parts could be closely identified. Such models used derived behavioural concepts such as place utility, stress, activity space, and awareness space. The last two of these became incorporated into a whole field of 'mental map' studies, following Gould's (1965) seminal statement in which investigations were made of the quality and quantity of information that people had of various places.

Unlike the pioneer works of Lowenthal and Tuan, the urban studies which adopted the behavioural approach neither focused on the activities of particular individuals nor adopted the more discursive, literary style which was typical of geographical phenomenology. The concerns of urban geography—where people shop, work, live, and move to, etc.—involved millions of decisions, many of them made daily, which even when sampled required the quantitative arsenal of the earlier methodology in order to find the spatial order, the morphological laws, and the laws of association. Thus Gould's mental map studies are based on components and regression analyses and on an inferred spatial order—such as in distance-decay patterns—from their coefficients (Gould, 1975; Gould and White, 1974), and major programmatic statements still clearly adopted most of the earlier methodology.

FURTHER MURMURINGS: POLITICAL ECONOMY

By the early 1970s, both the quantitative–theoretical and the behavioural approaches were coming under attack—on new grounds. This development, termed 'radical' and 'structural' by some (Robson, 1976), with origins in the civil rights and anti-Vietnam movements in the United States in the late 1960s, is based upon the following critique:

1. The quantitative–theoretical methodology is grounded in a model of society in which the prices of goods and services are determined in open competition between buyers and sellers, with both sides having equal weight and no individual being powerful enough to influence the price. This may be true of some products—notably those produced by farmers (Warntz, 1959) and particularly peasant farmers (Gould and Sparks, 1969)—but the major trend in society in recent years has been the development of monopoly capitalism, in which the seller is in a much stronger position than the purchaser in the determination of prices, as clearly illustrated in the case of urban land values (Harvey, 1973).
2. Functionalist sociology, with its emphasis on consensus arrangements among social groups, is similarly unreal. Capitalist society comprises socioeconomic groups between which the operative processes are conflict and not merely competition, dissensus as opposed to consensus. The principal commodity over which the conflict rages is power, most of which is held in the hands of a small capitalist class who are able to manipulate the rest (Miliband, 1969). Geographical patterns can thus only be interpreted through this conflict between unequal groups in terms of their control over resources.
3. The quantitative methodology is able at best only to describe patterns, and its predictive powers for planning and policy purposes produce solutions which will continue the current situation; it has followed essentially an 'extrapolative ethic' (Berry, 1973). In this sense, the subject is in the hands of a power elite—those with greatest weight in the conflict—since its descriptions are unable to isolate the causes of what it studies (its focus is on laws of correspondence and not on laws of cause and effect) and its prescriptions can only carry this current inequality of power forward. Given that most of the social and economic problems of the world are fundamentally a consequence of inequalities in power at all spatial scales (Coates, Johnston, and Knox, 1977), then their solution will only come about through recognition of this fact, followed by action to remove the inequities and not merely to patch up the associated ills (Bunge and Bordessa, 1975).
4. The behavioural approach is a reductionist one, which sees the individual as an independent decision-maker and not one whose actions are very much constrained by the institutional structure of his society, be it capitalist or socialist, primitive or advanced. Behaviouralism in its extreme form would take us back to the idiographic, exceptionalist stances which have proved so inhibiting to theory formation in human geography in the past.

The thrust of this critique is often clearly political. Much of its base is in the writings of Karl Marx, achieving a major influence on English-speaking geography for the first time—though the influence of Marx upon geographical writing in some other countries has a longer pedigree (James, 1972). *Antipode*, which is the major journal for American and other English-speaking geographers of this persuasion, is dominated by a Marxian view of class conflict. Within urban geography, the main direction of work based upon this thesis is in the study of housing markets and residential patterns, providing critiques of ways in which urban geographers have analysed both pattern and process (Gray, 1975). Some of the work has taken the form of empirically-based indictments of the mechanisms of the property market (Ambrose and Colenutt, 1975); other items either provide evidence of behaviour by individuals—such as building society managers (Boddy, 1976) and real estate agents (Palm, 1976)—operating within the constraints of the capitalist system, or are more general critiques of urban 'theory' within the context of the political economy of monopoly capitalism.

In the empirical critiques, the determinants of house prices are seen not merely in the differential rents which result from variations in accessibility but also in the monopoly and class-monopoly (absolute) rents which can be demanded because of the fixed supply of land, a constraint often exaggerated by the activities of governments, planning agencies, financial institutions, and others (Harvey, 1974) in the face of an always-growing demand for better housing, fuelled by the need of capitalism to maintain high levels of consumption (Harvey, 1975). The residential differentiation within urban areas is thus interpreted as a result of decisions by those with power in the property market; the housing conditions of various social and economic groups are a consequence of these decisions; and the intraurban segregation of households reflects not the choices of individuals but the constraints within which they must work (Gray, 1975), which is not to deny the possibility, at least for some groups, of considerable choice within the general constraints. Recent work on local authority tenants in British urban areas, for example, suggests that within the public sector some choice mechanism does operate through the media of waiting lists and transfers (Bird, 1976; Herbert, 1976). The general criticism that much previous work on residential processes was too preoccupied with choice and spatial outcomes and gave insufficient scrutiny to the allocative systems which are the antecedents of both patterns and processes is valid, though an awareness of these other factors is not new.

Although some general statements, and in particular the more wide-ranging, such as Harvey's essays (1973, 1975, 1976), do attempt to interpret urban patterns and processes within the general model of monopoly capitalism, most of the empirical studies in this mould are in many senses very similar to those associated with the behavioural approach. Whether the subject is the role of building societies (Boddy, 1976), public housing managers (Gray, 1975), or estate agents (Palm, 1976), the focus is really on the perceived world of the decision-maker, with only infrequent reference to how that world is constrained by the encompassing socioeconomic system. Study of the 'managers' or 'gatekeepers' of the system adds an important new dimension to urban geography and one which is being pursued in other disciplines also (Pahl, 1975), and it is these from which geographers have derived most of their stimuli. However, the more awesome task of looking at the system itself, at societal structure and its beliefs, values, and political philosophies, has found little practical expression to date in geographical research and writing, though David Harvey has made a significant contribution to an emerging debate.

EVOLUTION OR REVOLUTION? THE SOCIOLOGY OF URBAN GEOGRAPHY

It would be quite wrong to imply that little has really changed with regard to empirical urban geography. Compared to 1950, or even 1960, very considerable changes have affected the practice of the subdiscipline and have changed its character almost completely. Where practices and types of study problem reminiscent of the previous time period survive, they have been modified almost beyond recognition; even more 'traditional' approaches such as urban morphology have moved in directions which meet the criticisms of the early 1960s and provide them with a more rational place in an evolving discipline. Urban geographers are more sophisticated in the quantitative methodologies which they employ; a basic statistical competence is almost universal, but at the same time a healthy, informed, and mature scepticism of the proper role of quantification is now evident. Harvey concluded his text on *Explanation in Geography* with the dictum 'By our theories you shall know us' (Harvey, 1969, p. 486) and indeed urban geographers have moved some way in that direction, though the record of indigenous theory formation is still not remarkable. (Perhaps one reason for the absence of indigenous theory is its impossibility. As Harvey (1973) and others now argue, disciplinary boundaries within the social sciences are largely obfuscatory. Society must be studied as a whole, and its use of space, which is the main focus of much geographical endeavour, cannot be studied independently or be the source of independent theory.)

On a broader front, urban geographers have also become more aware of the existence of alternative methodologies and philosophies and have shown a willingness to delve into the literature of the evolution of thought in the social sciences. New concepts rarely have an internal relevance only, and the waves of innovations which have repercussions throughout the literature are now more easily identified and incorporated into urban geography. It is unlikely that time lags of the scale which preceded the arrival of innovations from the earlier part of this century will be replicated. There is also a greater acceptance of the fact that an investigation of the human condition cannot be ideologically neutral; geographers may agree completely on basic facts and even diagnoses, but the prescriptions for change may spring from a fundamental belief system and still produce alternative, if not opposed, strategies. To this end, there is among geographers a debate over whether these changes involve a series of revolutions in method, approach, and philosophy, or whether—as some would argue (Chisholm, 1975)—they are merely variations on the same theme and represent a steady evolutionary course. To investigate this particular aspect of the debate requires cognizance of literature concerned with the sociology of science (Mulkay, 1975).

The general view of science is of objective searching for comprehension—of a pursuit for truth which surpasses all understanding. Scientists are open-minded, objective individuals who accept the given rules of scientific method and discourse and who proceed to push back the frontiers of knowledge on the basis of their own ideas and those published by others. Success as a scientist reflects differing abilities to shift the frontiers: the competition is between equals in all except ability.

This model of science—whether applied to geography or any other discipline—suffers from two defects. The first concerns its views of scientists, and in particular of their attitudes and aspirations. Rather than being conventional conformists rising through a career structure simply by dint of hard work—as a functionalist view of society would suggest—they are individuals with personalities and aspirations, at least some of them desiring power within an academic community where this commodity is far from equitably distributed. As in the study of society at large, so in academic society the norm of consensus must be replaced by that of conflict. In this conflict, their research and publication forms a major avenue for the prosecution of their aspirations, not *in* the conventional mould but, very frequently, as critics *of it*, proposing alternative methodologies and procedures, subject matter, and philosophies.

Academic career structures are hierarchical and pyramidal, so that the larger a discipline becomes, the greater the competition for a relatively small number of powerful positions. This has been so with geography, and other social sciences, in recent years. Academic departments in universities and other higher education institutions have expanded rapidly and the new generation of geographers of the 1960s needed to find intellectual niches—which were novel—within which they could advance their career prospects relative to those who conformed to the accepted rules and procedures and slowly won promotion for themselves.

The nature of the career structure in academic life to some extent generates new approaches to traditional subject matter, as ways in which aspirants for power can obtain recognition as being 'out of the ordinary'; thus Harvey (1973) saw the quantitative revolution as in part a shabby contest for power. As already suggested, the rate of change is related to the size of the discipline. It is also a function of external catalysts. Similar changes are likely to be occurring in other disciplines and, with the greater interdisciplinary contact of recent years, these changes are likely to feed off each other and to generate even more in an exponential manner. Society, too, is changing at an increasing rate, as Toffler (1970) has pointed out, and its demands have also had their influences upon the academic disciplines, with geographers, for example, jumping onto such bandwagons as the environmentalist and ecocatastrophe movements and the greater variety of approaches to physical planning, finding these both politically valuable topics for concern as well as springboards for career development.

The classical model of science is a conservative one, since its set of rules and accepted procedures limits experimentation and the pursuit of alternatives. Its second failing, therefore, is that it often does not recognize its inability to solve certain problems thrown up by its results, since these demand a novel approach unconstrained by the accepted canons of scientific methods. Eventually, because of this failure, the discipline becomes more remote from the reality it is trying to portray. Change is brought about by recognition of the need for a revolution in method, by the adoption of a new paradigm of how work should proceed (Kuhn, 1962). According to this view of scientific disciplines, periods of what are termed 'normal science', in which the conservative model holds sway and researchers concentrate on adding further knowledge to the accepted model, retesting, verifying, and extending its laws, are punctuated by revolutions or paradigmatic shocks, when the accepted model is overthrown because of its inability to answer the current questions.

This second view of how science proceeds, which is clearly an extension of the first, also fails to give a complete picture, again because it ignores certain aspects of human frailty. The first of these concerns the inability of many, especially established, scientists to accept or perhaps even to understand the nature of the revolution that has overtaken them. While often paying lip-service to it, they will attack it (Taylor, 1976) and continue to work in the conventional model of the time when they became accepted members of the academic community. Their criticism cannot be pushed too far, however, because of another frailty. Within the academic community, as elsewhere, leading figures build up their 'empires', their departments and 'spheres of influence' and, like all bureaucrats, a basic set of aspirations is focused on the growth of these departments and the status and power that they bring, both within and outside the particular scientific community. Revolutions threaten this power structure and must therefore be countered, not by frontal attack, which carries with it the danger of embarrassing humiliation if not defeat, but by political manoeuvring, the most common form of which involves cooption of revolutionaries into the power structure—once their following is clear—which both reduces the threat to the establishment and strengthens the overall power of the empires. Burton (1963) and Taylor (1976) have both discussed the progress of the quantitative revolutionaries in this context. Burton asserted that even by the early 1960s they were part of the establishment, and Taylor examined the conditions under which they were accepted and the ways in which 'traditionalists' both reacted and safeguarded their positions. Where the revolutionaries have political connotations, however, it is not yet clear how adequate this model will be; Peet (1975) complains of the failure of radical geographers to obtain tenured positions in departments of geography at American universities, citing himself and Harvey as the only individuals who had been able to maintain their academic professional status. In a discussion which followed this assertion, Harries (1975) replied that this was a function of the employer—Peet and Harvey both work for private universities!

Incorporation of criticisms of the Kuhnian revolutionary paradigm produces a third view of scientific progress—the branching model. According to this, methods of normal science will occasionally throw up alternative approaches which seek a reorientation of disciplines towards new philosophies, methodologies, subject matters, or applications. The individuals who lead these will set up branches of the discipline, which develop their own normal science, but usually will not break away from the discipline, since this is to injure the larger political world of academia. In time, particularly if conflict over personal power and status within the discipline is intense, this new branch will in itself raise problems, the solution of which requires a further branch. Eventually, as generations of scientists die, branches may wither with them, perhaps to be revitalized by later generations.

These various perspectives on science have all been applied to human geography in recent years. Freeman (1961), for example, has suggested that there is 'nothing new under the sun'; and Taylor (1976, pp. 138–139) noted similar reactions from Henderson (1968) and Edwards (1974) to the progress of the quantification and modelling debate. Chisholm (1975) has argued that revolutions are misnomers for the ways in which changes have occurred; the basic theme has been one of consistency—evolution rather than revolution—with differences which are largely of emphasis and in the ways in which problems are solved. Chorley and Haggett (1965, 1967), Harvey (1973), Burton (1963), and many others have, on the other hand, labelled the changes as 'revolutions', despite the fact that they do not replace but rather augment and modify more traditional orders which often remain in attenuated form. (The augmentation is not the desire of the 'revolutionaries', of course, who want complete change but who are thwarted by the innate conservatism of the establishment.) There needs to be a great deal wrong with existing paradigms and orders to justify revolutions; faults may be recognized and agreed but they need not, for all, be grounds sufficient for the overthrow of the existing system.

Although this discussion of the changing approaches, varying emphases upon existing paradigms, and levels of acceptance of innovation and reformulation has been phrased in very general terms as applying to geography as a whole, it is clear that it applies centrally to urban geography which, perhaps because of its numerical importance among practitioners in recent years, has been somewhat in the vanguard of the changes. In providing a more particular interpretation of this part of the discipline, we would choose to do so within the framework of the branching model. Major changes have occurred and there have been 'revolutions' in method and philosophy. But these have not replaced traditional methods and approaches; they have been added to them. None is completely acceptable or accepted, even after twenty years or more (Taylor, 1976). Indeed, methodological, philosophical, and ideological debates continue to be intense.

Evidence in support of the branching model comes from the fact that few of the 'revolutionaries' have deserted geography and set up alternative disciplines; the only possible exception to this is regional science, which was a breakaway from economics that attracted some geographers to its departments but many aspects of it were incorporated into geographical syllabi. And, of course, individuals have left urban geography either to join some esoteric, usually interdisciplinary research centre, or to go into applied branches of the discipline, notably those involved in the planning profession. A few, such as Colin Bell, Ray Pahl, and Duncan Timms, have become leaders in the associated field of urban sociology. But the main feature of the new developments is that they have remained within geography and their major journals are accepted as geographical. Thus, the quantitative branch spawned *Geographical Analysis* and led contemporaneously to a revision of *Economic Geography*, both of which have strong pro-urban biases. The integration of mathematical modelling and statistical analysis with planning procedures led to the inception of *Environment and Planning* and *Regional Studies*, as well as a range of journals in regional science. The strength of this branch within urban geography remains great, producing a massive volume of work which provides quantitative descriptions of spatial patterns and changes, of spatial associations and the correspondences between a wide range of phenomena, and of probable future patterns within the constraints of the capitalist status quo.

Although a behavioural revolution is perceived by some to have occurred in the late 1960s (Cox and Golledge, 1969), the influence of this branch has yet to be fully developed. Its emphasis upon decision-making strengthened the focus upon process rather than pattern which was already beginning to appear in the mid-1960s, and its return to the individual, as the initial building-block for providing data, both improved the quality of information available and increased its range considerably. For specific themes, the constraints imposed by census data could be circumvented by *ad hoc* social surveys and, with these, urban geographers were able to demonstrate the unreality of economic man as the working basis for models. The imperfections of decision-making have been demonstrated in a range of studies, from analyses of firms seeking locations to those of households searching for new homes.

One of the problems with the behavioural perspective has been its reductionism. Having returned to the individual as the unit, how then does the geographer return to his appropriate level of generalization? The aggregate is the appropriate scale, generalizations are the aims; behavioural input allows these generalizations to be reached from a better qualitative base—the aggregate is both better compounded and understood. Over a wide range of social sciences, the problem of reconciling macro- and microscale approaches, aggregate and individual data is now recognized (Dogan and Rokkan, 1969), and urban geographers, as others, have the task of approaching this problem. One possibility, already exploited by urban geographers, is that of using aggregate statistics as a framework from which to develop behavioural approaches (Herbert, 1976; Herbert and Evans, 1974; Walker, 1975). Behavioural perspectives may naturally belong to a scale below that traditionally used by urban geographers, but it has already been demonstrated that they may hold the key to some of the central issues in urban research. The real nature of the decision-making process, the form of satisficer man, the relationship between objective and subjective space (Herbert and Raine, 1976)—these are all research themes of unfulfilled potential in urban geography. The main journal in this area (*Environment and Behavior*) is peripheral to the concerns of many urban geographers, but the central journals of the profession often contain important papers on this theme and the branch is established and has a significant perspective to offer.

Whereas the behavioural perspective has been fairly widely spread over human geographical research as a whole, the structural/radical changes of the

1970s have made their impact more particularly in urban geography and the principal journal of this branch (*Antipode*) contains a considerable volume of urban material. (The other area of major impact is the study of economic development, again based on Marx and on later workers such as Franck; see Brookfield, 1975.) That this has occurred is in some ways not surprising, for the focus of the current approach is the inequality of life-chances imposed by the operation of the capitalist system, and most of the problems which this involves are concentrated into the major cities of highly urbanized societies. In other ways, however, the focus on the city may be exaggerated in this initial stage and will become less specific over time. If attempts to identify problem areas in empirical terms and to prescribe ameliorative action at the scale of urban locality are to be labelled 'status quo' or even 'counter-revolutionary' (Harvey, 1973), then the focus of attention for the structural/radical school must eventually be the larger scale of society, its value systems, and arrangement of power and resources. A feature of this branch is that it is much more interdisciplinary in nature than previous ones, with many of its members seeing disciplinary boundaries as counterproductive hindrances to the advancement of research. In this sense, it may be that a true revolution will occur, with the development of a new discipline parallel to, if not overriding, geography being a possibility, but the current retrenchment throughout the academic world may severely hinder the possibility of such separation.

THE APPLICATION OF GEOGRAPHY IN THE URBAN ENVIRONMENT

The growth of industrial capitalism was characterized by, and advanced because of, the widespread cooption of academic-intellectual effort into the economic system. Not surprisingly, it was the physical scientists who were initially involved in the movement away from the 'ivory tower', for it was they, particularly in the applied science offshoots, who provided many of the technological and technical breakthroughs necessary for the increases in the surplus value of labour which fuelled the growth of capital. Major contributions also came with the development of the techniques of global warfare in the twentieth century and the growth in size and influence of the military–industrial complex, with which many scientists are deeply involved.

The important public role of physical scientists was observed by those who wished to emulate them in terms of methodology, and making a contribution to public policy became a part of the scientific ethos to which, increasingly, social as well as physical scientists were attached. As we have already noted, it was economists and social psychologists who first achieved a recognition of relevance—as disciplinary groups, rather than as isolated individuals—to be followed by sociologists and social administrators. Emulation of this apparent eminence thus became a desideratum of human geographers, too, and 'policy implications' increasingly formed the basis of the conclusions of positivist research reports.

As already stressed, there are those historians of geography who stress long-term continuity in the aims, objectives, and approaches in geographical work, and such writers would claim, justifiably, that human geographers have for long been instrumental in aiding public policy formulation. Thus the exploration paradigm provided basic facts, not only to fill 'capes and bays' school texts but also to form the basis for colonial enterprise as Western capitalist economies extended their interests to the less-developed world; Chisholm's series of *Commercial Geographies* are clear examples of such applied geography. The environmentalist paradigm also provided a basis for public policy debate and was, for example, the reason for Griffith Taylor's move from Australia to North America following the political attack on his determinist interpretation of Australian outback development.

It was the regionalism paradigm, however, which provided the first major area within which human geographers could practise their expertise in the service of governments. This avenue was opened by the development, after the Second World War, of physical planning programmes—which were initiated for a variety of reasons, such as the oversight of urban reconstruction, the limitation of urban sprawl into good agricultural land, and the laying out of an ordered, segregated pattern of land uses which improved the quality of life for all inhabitants, especially those of large cities. The land-use survey methods devised by geographers, notably Stamp and Platt, in the 1930s were ideally suited to the perceived tasks of planning, which involved the mapping of existing land uses, the evaluation of land capability, and the design of zoning schemes which separated 'non-conforming' land uses. This type of physical planning, aimed at creating a better environment which, it was believed, would in turn create a better society, had great demands for personnel in the heady days of the immediate post-war years, and many human geographers found important careers in this expanding profession.

In the 1950s and 1960s, planning became increasingly concerned with movement patterns, a concern made necessary by the rapid growth of vehicle ownership and of traffic congestion within towns. This new emphasis on flows, and their relationships with land-use arrangements and urban structure, occurred contemporaneously with the growth of spatial analysis in human geography, with its twin focus on spatial patterns and interactions. Again, therefore, it seemed that urban geographers could play an important role in the development of transport and traffic policies and considerable effort was poured into the development of models of urban systems (both interurban and intraurban) which linked movement and land use and allowed prediction of the impact of changes in the latter on the former. Notable among these efforts, which involved a greater sophistication of mathematical modelling than had previously been general in geographical work and which involved close collaboration between geographers, economists, regional scientists, and practising planners, was the work of two British teams, one at the Centre for Environmental Studies at London, led by Wilson, and the other at the University of Reading, where the main collaborators were Batty, Cripps, and Foot; for both, the work of Lowry was a major stimulus.

Work on these large urban models continues and is developing with respect to two important changes in the wider social environment. The first of these is concerned with the growing ecological consciousness of society, with which geographers have long been concerned—most notably in recent years with the work of Gilbert White and his colleagues. The ecological consequences of different urban plans—on air pollution, fuel use, etc.—have been recognized and analysed (e.g. Berry *et al.*, 1973). Second, modellers have reacted to the growing literature on social justice and have translated this into territorial justice with an emphasis on system design which aims to optimize equity—in the location of facilities such as those for health care—rather than overall efficiency.

In all of this applied work, geographers have worked closely with government—often *for* government through funded research or in direct employment—at a national, regional, and local level. Their aim has therefore been, at least implicitly, to help maintain the position of those governments by improving, within the goals which those governments set, the operation of the current socioeconomic system, in its spatial context. Such research and practice is seen by critics of the current socioeconomic system as status quo or counter-revolutionary—as the shoring up of a capitalist structure which they wish to replace. Discussion of relevant research is prefaced, therefore, by the question 'relevant to whom?'. The current radical arguments are that within a capitalist system governments must be organized as guardians of, and encouragements for, the capitalist ethos. Whatever the alternative that they espouse, such critics of applied geography in the positivist mould claim that any public policies brought into being as a consequence of geographical research and advocacy are likely, in the long run if not the short, to increase the inequalities between the capitalist and working classes.

In the current debate, therefore, applied geography usually has either a humanitarian (Bunge) or a socialist (Harvey) connotation, with a clear emphasis on the need to restructure society. As is becoming increasingly apparent, such restructuring is not feasible through spatial planning alone. Some spatial engineering can marginally improve the life-chances of the relatively deprived, but alone it is insufficient to produce a new, equitable, just society. Hence planning other than that organized either for immediate amelioration of problems or to meet justifiably extrapolated trends (Berry, 1973) is not acceptable to those with a revolutionary ideology. For them, geography cannot exist in isolation (even in any sense separate) from the totality of social science. Not only is social science not just the sum of its disciplinary parts; those parts have no valid separate existence. Acceptance of this view sees geography *per se* having no role whatsoever in planning, which is not to say that a geographical view is irrelevant within a totality.

CONTINUING URBAN GEOGRAPHY AND THE PRESENT SERIES

We have presented urban geography here as a stereotype of human geography as a whole, as a field characterized by absorbing debate and by a number of strong research traditions. The three branches of geography are all represented in urban studies. Quantitative empirical research in the positivist mould of the natural sciences undoubtedly remains the dominant branch, but its position is under attack from radical geographers of the structuralist branch, who would have major revisions if not revolutions in geographic thought. The behavioural branch remains, alive and viable if of lesser importance, and there are still those who argue for the more traditional values of the normal science of the 1940s and 1950s. This characterization of the branching nature of the discipline, and its links back with the changes which have come into vogue since the Second World War, is fairly unambiguous. There is also the 'tree' itself, however, or the core which unifies the branches and gives them some communality, to be identified. A first point has already been implicitly made. Urban geography is a subset of human geography, which is itself a subset of the discipline of geography.

For geography as a discipline, the two major concerns of practitioners are what Haggett (1975) has termed the 'ecological system' that links man with his environment and the 'spatial system' which links one region with another in a complex interchange of flows. The former concern inherits the main environmentalism paradigm of the modern period, the latter the spatial analysis paradigm of the contemporary period. That these are initial but not sufficient commentary on geography as a discipline is evidenced by the changes and innovative paradigms which have influenced human geography. At the point where human and physical geography diverge, the study of environment assumes contrasted forms, spatial analysis provides similar methodologies, and in both branches *particular* concepts and features appear. Human geography has been characterized by the contents already outlined; urban geography within this broader field focuses upon the city as a territorial social system and upon the attendant processes of urbanization which produce it both in individual settings and in regional systems. Whereas the unity of urban geography and the extent to which branches devolve into separatism are open to question, so the wider unities of human geography and the discipline as a whole are similarly under scrutiny. So far, although examples of division into semiautonomous units within universities or regroupings under interdisciplinary headings exist, the major trend for continuity, unity, and integration appears politically more expedient and academically more acceptable to the large majority of geographers.

The aim of this series of volumes is to chart the continuing progress of these, and any other as yet unborn, branches of urban geographical study, and to present the debate among proponents of the various branches which will doubtless continue. Organization of the series into a focus upon geographical approaches to the urban environment recognizes the contemporary cohesion of a set of perspectives which adds up to an urban geography. There is no intention to replace or even to compete with those academic journals in which particular pieces of research and discussion of philosophical and methodological issues have always been reported. Our brief will be a wider one in the sense of presenting fuller accounts than those traditionally published in the journals. Some of these will reflect the type of research currently being undertaken in the various branches of urban geography by presenting overviews of large programmes of research, with summaries of their findings. Others will review particular types of research, highlighting their strong and weak points, their value in applied work, and the possible ways in which they might develop. Philosophical and methodological debates will not be ignored, since it is in these that true progress is often made. For the former, the philosophical issues, it is of primary importance to scrutinize in a scholarly way the conceptual stances implicit in various branches, their relationships one with the other, their contribution to the discipline as a whole, and the directions in which evolution must occur. For the latter, the growth of methodologies and associated techniques has been a strength of urban geography over the past two decades. The greatest need now may be for a selective reappraisal of the tools we possess, for a rigorous examination of the assumptions made and practices adopted, and for a need to disseminate new knowledge in a comprehensive and, particularly, in a comprehensible way.

REFERENCES

Ackerman, E. A. (1945). Geographic training, wartime research and immediate professional objectives. *Annals, Association of American Geography*, **35**, 121–143.

Ackerman, E. A. (1958). *Geography as a Fundamental Research Discipline*. Research Paper No. 53, Department of Geography, University of Chicago, Chicago.

Ambrose, P., and Colenutt, R. J. (1975). *The Property Machine*, Penguin, Harmondsworth.

Aurousseau, M. (1924). Recent contributions to urban geography: a review. *Geographical Review*, **14**, 444.

Baskin, C. W. (1966). *Central Places in Southern Germany*, (translation of Christaller). Prentice-Hall, Englewood Cliffs, New Jersey.

Berry, B. J. L. (1959). Recent studies concerning the role of transportation in the space economy. *Annals, Association of American Geographers*, **49**, 328–342.

Berry, B. J. L. (Ed.) (1971). Comparative factorial ecology. *Economic Geography* (supplement), **47**.

Berry, B. J. L. (1973). *The Human Consequences of Urbanization*, Macmillan, London.

Berry, B. J. L., and Garrison, W. L. (1958a). The functional bases of the central place hierarchy. *Economic Geography*, **34**, 145–154.

Berry, B. J. L., and Garrison, W. L. (1958b). Alternate explanations of urban rank-size relationships. *Annals, Association of American Geographers*, **48**, 83–91.

Berry, B. J. L., and Horton, F. E. (Eds.) (1970). *Geographic Perspectives on Urban Systems*, Prentice-Hall, Englewood Cliffs, New Jersey.

Berry, B. J. L., Simmons, J. W., and Tennant, R. J. (1963). Urban population density: structure and change. *Geographical Review*, **53**, 389–405.

Berry, B. J. L., *et al.* (1973). *Land Use, Urban Form and Environmental Quality*. Research Paper No. 155, Department of Geography, University of Chicago, Chicago.

Bird, H. (1976). Residential mobility and preference patterns in the public sector of the housing market. *Transactions, Institute of British Geographers*, NS **1**, 20–33.

Blanchard, R. (1911). *Grenoble: Etude de Geographie Urbaine*, Paris.

Boddy, M. (1976). The structure of mortgage finance: building societies and the British social formation. *Transactions, Institute of British Geographers*, NS **1**, 58–71.

Brookfield, H. C. (1975). *Interdependent Development*, Methuen, London.

Brown, L. A., and Moore, E. G. (1970). The intra-urban migration process: a perspective. *Geografiska Annaler*, Series B, **52**, 1–13.

Brush, J. E. (1953). The hierarchy of central places in south-western Wisconsin. *Geographical Review*, **43**, 380–402.
Bunge, W. (1962). *Theoretical Geography*. Lund Studies in Geography, Series C, No. 1, C. W. K. Gleerup, Lund.
Bunge, W. (1973). The geography of human survival. *Annals, Association of American Geographers*, **63**, 275–295.
Bunge, W., and Bordessa, R. (1975). *The Canadian Alternative: Survival, Expeditions and Urban Change*. Geographical Monograph No. 2, York University, Toronto.
Burgess, E. W. (1925). The growth of the city. In R. E. Park, E. W. Burgess, and R. D. McKenzie (Eds.), *The City*, University of Chicago Press, Chicago.
Burton, I. (1963). The quantitative revolution and theoretical geography. *Canadian Geographer*, **7**, 151–162.
Carter, H. (1972). *The Study of Urban Geography*, Edward Arnold, London.
Chisholm, M. (1975). *Human Geography: Evolution or Revolution*, Penguin, Harmondsworth.
Christaller, W. (1933). *Central Places in Southern Germany*, Gustav Fischer, Jena.
Coates, B. E., Johnston, R. J., and Knox, P. L. (1977). *Geography and Inequality*, Oxford University Press, Oxford.
Chorley, R. J., and Haggett, P. (1965). *Frontiers in Geographical Teaching*, Methuen, London.
Chorley, R. J., and Haggett, P. (1967). *Models in Geography*, Methuen, London.
Cooley, C. H. (1894). The theory of transportation. *Publications of the American Economic Association*, **9**, 5–7.
Conzen, M. R. G. (1960). *Alnwick, Northumberland: A Study in Town Plan Analysis*, Institute of British Geographers Monograph, London.
Conzen, M. R. G. (1962). The plan analysis of an English city centre. In K. Norborg (Ed.), *Proceedings of the I. G. U. Symposium in Urban Geography*, C. W. K. Gleerup, Lund.
Cox, K., and Golledge, R. (1969). *Behavioral Problems in Geography: A Symposium*. Northwestern Studies in Geography No. 17, Northwestern University, Evanston.
Crowe, P. R. (1938). On progress in geography. *Scottish Geographical Magazine*, **54**, 1–19.
Dacey, M. F. (1962). Analysis of central place and point patterns by a nearest neighbour method. In K. Norborg (Ed.), *Proceedings of the I.G.U. Symposium in Urban Geography*, C. W. K. Gleerup, Lund.
Davies, W. K. D. (1972). *The Conceptual Revolution in Geography*, University of London Press, London.
Dahrendorf, R. (1959). *Class and Class Conflict in Industrial Society*, Routledge, Kegan and Paul, London.
Dickinson, R. E. (1929). The markets and market area of Bury St. Edmunds. *Sociological Review*, **22**, 292–308.
Dickinson, R. E. (1933). The distribution and functions of smaller urban settlements of East Anglia. *Geography*, **18**, 19–31.
Dickinson, R. E. (1945). The morphology of the medieval German town. *Geographical Review*, **35**, 74–97.
Dogan, M., and Rokkan, S. (Eds.) (1969). *Quantitative Ecological Analysis in the Social Sciences*, The M.I.T. Press, Cambridge, Massachusetts.
Edwards, K. C. (1974). Sixty years after Herbertson: the advance of geography as a spatial science. *Geography*, **59**, 1–9.
Eyles, J. (1974). Social theory and social geography. *Progress in Geography*, **6**, 27–87.
Freeman, T. W. (1961). *A Hundred Years of Geography*, Duckworth, London.
Garrison, W. L. (1956). Applicability of statistical inference to geographical research. *Geographical Review*, **46**, 427–429.
Garrison, W. L. (1959, 1960). The spatial structure of the economy, I, II and III. *Annals, Association of American Geographers*, **49**, 232–239 and 471–482; **50**, 357–373.

Garrison, W. L., and Marble, D. F. (1967). *Quantitative Geography*, Parts I and II. Northwestern University Studies in Geography, Nos. 13 and 14, Evanston.
Gould, P. R. (1965). *On Mental Maps*. Discussion Paper No. 9, Michigan Inter-University Community of Mathematical Geographers.
Gould, P. R. (1975). Acquiring spatial information. *Economic Geography*, **51**, 87–99.
Gould, P. R., and Sparks, J. W. (1969). The geographical context of human diets in southern Guatemala. *Geographical Review*, **59**, 58–82.
Gould, P. R., and White, R. (1974). *Mental Maps*, Penguin, Harmondsworth.
Gray, F. (1975). Non-explanation in urban geography. *Area*, **7**, 228–235.
Gregory, S. (1976). On geographical myths and statistical fables. *Transactions, Institute of British Geographers*, NS **1**, 385–400.
Guelke, L. (1974). An idealist alternative in human geography. *Annals, Association of American Geographers*, **64**, 193–202.
Haggett, P. (1975). *Geography: A Modern Synthesis*, Harper and Row, New York.
Harries, K. (1975). The geography of crime: a political rejoinder. *Professional Geographer*, **27**, 280–282.
Harris, C. D., and Ullman, E. L. (1945). The nature of cities. *Annals, American Academy of Political and Social Science*, **242**, 7–17.
Hartshorne, R. (1939). *The Nature of Geography*, Association of American Geographers, Lancaster, Pennsylvania.
Hartshorne, R. (1955). Exceptionalism in geography re-examined. *Annals, Association of American Geographers*, **45**, 205–244.
Hartshorne, R. (1959). *Perspective on the Nature of Geography*, Rand-McNally, Chicago.
Harvey, D. (1969). *Explanation in Geography*, Edward Arnold, London.
Harvey, D. (1973). *Social Justice and the City*, Edward Arnold, London.
Harvey, D. (1974). Class-monopoly rent, finance capital and the urban revolution. *Regional Studies*, **8**, 239–255.
Harvey, D. (1975). The political economy of urbanization in advanced capitalist societies. In H. M. Rose and G. Gappert (Eds.), *The Social Economy of Cities*, Sage Publications, Beverly Hills. pp. 119–163.
Harvey, D. (1976). Class structure in a capitalist society and the theory of residential differentiation. In R. Peel, M. Chisholm, and P. Haggett (Eds.), *Processes in Physical and Human Geography: Bristol Essays*, Heineman, London. pp. 354–372.
Hassert, K. (1907). *Die Stadte Geographisch Betrachtet*, Leipzig.
Henderson, H. C. K. (1968). Geography's balance sheet. *Transactions, Institute of British Geographers*, **45**, 1–10.
Herbert, D. T. (1972). *Urban Geography: A Social Perspective*, David and Charles, Newton Abbot.
Herbert, D. T. (1976). The study of delinquency areas: a geographical approach. *Transactions, Institute of British Geographers*, NS **1**, 472–492.
Herbert, D. T., and Evans, D. J. (1974). Urban sub-areas as sampling frameworks for social survey. *Town Planning Review*, **45**, 171–188.
Herbert, D. T., and Raine, J. W. (1976). Defining communities within urban areas. *Town Planning Review*, **47**, 325–338.
Hoyt, H. (1939). *The Structure and Growth of Residential Neighborhoods in American Cities*. Federal Housing Administration, Washington.
Hurd, R. (1903). Principles of city land values. *New York Record and Guide*, **1903**, 19–21.
James, P. (1972). *All Possible Worlds: A History of Geographical Ideas*, The Odyssey Press, New York.
Johnston, R. J. (1969). Urban geography in New Zealand. *New Zealand Geographer*, **25**, 121–135.
Johnston, R. J. (1971). *Urban Residential Patterns*, Bell, London.
Johnston, R. J. (1976). Residential area characteristics: research methods for identifying

urban sub-areas—social area analysis and factorial ecology. In D. T. Herbert and R. J. Johnston (Eds.), *Social Areas in Cities, I. Spatial Processes and Form*, Wiley, London. pp. 193–236.

Jones, E. (1960). *A Social Geography of Belfast*, Oxford University Press, Oxford.

Kirk, W. (1963). Problems of geography, *Geography*, **48**, 357–371.

Kuhn, T. S. (1962). *The Structure of Scientific Revolutions*, University of Chicago Press, Chicago.

Lazarsfeld, P. F., Berelson, B., and Gaudet, H. (1944). *The People's Choice*, Columbia University Press, New York.

Lee, T. R. (1976). Cities in the mind. In D. T. Herbert and R. J. Johnston (Eds.), *Spatial Perspectives on Problems and Policies*, Wiley, London. pp. 159–188.

Lewin, K. (1938). *The Conceptual Representation and Measurement of Psychological Forces*, Duke University Press, Durham, N. Carolina.

Lowenthal, D. (1961). Geography, experience and imagination: towards a geographical epistemology. *Annals, Association of American Geographers*, **51**, 241–260.

Lowenthal, D., and Prince, H. C. (1964). The English landscape. *Geographical Review*, **54**, 309–346.

McCarty, H. H., Hook, J. C., and Knos, D. C. (1956). *The Measurement of Association in Industrial Geography*, Department of Geography, University of Iowa.

Mackinder, H. (1919). *Democratic Ideals and Reality*, Henry Holt, New York.

Mayer, H. (1954). Urban geography. In P. James and C. F. Jones (Eds.), *American Geography: Inventory and Prospectus*, Syracuse, New York.

Mayer, H. M., and Kohn, C. F. (Eds.) (1959). *Readings in Urban Geography*, University of Chicago Press, Chicago.

Miliband, R. (1969). *The State in Capitalist Society*, Weidenfeld and Nicholson, London.

Morrill, R. L. (1974). Review of Social Justice and the City. *Annals, Association of American Geographers*, **64**, 475–477.

Morrill, R. L., and Pitts, F. (1967). Marriage, migration, and the mean information field. *Annals, Association of American Geographers*, **57**, 401–422.

Mulkay, M. J. (1975). Three models of scientific development. *Sociological Review*, **23**, 509–526.

Nystuen, J. D. (1963). Identification of some fundamental spatial concepts. *Papers of the Michigan Academy of Science, Arts and Letters*, **48**, 373–384.

Pahl, R. E. (1975). *Whose City?*, Penguin, Harmondsworth.

Palm, R. (1976). Real estate agents and geographical information. *Geographical Review*, **66**, 266–280.

Park, R. E. (1925). Suggestions for the investigation of human behavior in an urban environment. In R. E. Park, E. W. Burgess, and R. D. McKenzie (Eds.), *The City*, University of Chicago Press, Chicago.

Peet, R. (1975). The geography of crime, a political critique. *Professional Geographer*, **27**, 277–280.

Powell, J. M. (1971). Utopia, millenium and the co-operative ideal: a behavioural matrix in the settlement process. *Australian Geographer*, **11**, 606–618.

Pred, A. (1967). *Behavior and Location I.* Lund Studies in Geography, Series B, No. 27, C. W. K. Gleerup, Lund.

Pred, A. (1968). *Behavior and Location II.* Lund Studies in Geography, Series B, No. 28, C. W. K. Gleerup, Lund.

Rees, P. H. (1970). Concepts of social space. In B. J. L. Berry and F. E. Horton (Eds.), *Geographic Perspective on Urban Systems*, Prentice-Hall, Englewood Cliffs, New Jersey.

Robson, B. T. (1976). Editorial introduction. *Transactions, Institute of British Geographers*, NS **1**, 1.

Sauer, C. O. (1925). The morphology of landscape. *University of California Publications in Geography*, **2**, 19–35.

Schaefer, F. K. (1953). Exceptionalism in geography: a methodological examination. *Annals, Association of American Geographers*, **43**, 226–249.

Shevky, E. and Bell, W. (1955). *Social Area Analysis*. Stanford University Press, Stanford.

Smailes, A. E. (1946). The urban mesh of England and Wales. *Transactions and Papers, Institute of British Geographers*, **11**, 85–101.

Smailes, A. E. (1955). Some reflections on the geographical description and analysis of townscapes. *Transactions, Institute of British Geographers*, **21**, 99–115.

Smith, R. H. T. (1965). Method and purpose in functional town classification. *Annals, Association of American Geographers*, **55**, 539–548.

Stoddart, D. R. (1966). Darwin's impact on geography. *Annals, Association of American Geographers*, **56**, 683–698.

Stouffer, S. A. *et al.* (1950). *Measurement and Prediction, Studies in Social Psychology in World War II*, Princeton University Press, Princeton.

Taylor, I., Walton, P., and Young, J. (1973). *The New Criminology*, Routledge, Kegan and Paul, London.

Taylor, P. J. (1976). An interpretation of the quantification debate in British geography. *Transactions, Institute of British Geographers*, NS **1**, 129–142.

Toffler, A. (1970). *Future Shock*, Random House, New York.

Tryon, R. C. (1955). *Identification of Social Areas by Cluster Analysis*, University of California Press, Berkeley.

Tuan, Y. F. (1968). Discrepancies between environmental attitudes and behaviour, examples from Europe and China. *Canadian Geographer*, **12**, 176–191.

Wagner, P. L., and Mikesell, M. W. (1962). *Readings in Cultural Geography*, University of Chicago Press, Chicago.

Walker, R. L. (1975). Urban sub-areas as sampling frameworks, a further development. *Town Planning Review*, **46**, 201–212.

Warntz, W. (1959). *Towards a Geography of Price*, University of Pennsylvania Press, Philadelphia.

Webber, M. J. (1972). *The Impact of Uncertainty on Location*, A. N. U. Press, Canberra.

Weber, A. F. (1899). *The Growth of Cities in the Nineteenth Century: A Study in Statistics*, The MacMillan Company, New York.

Wilson, A. G. (1972). Theoretical geography: some speculations. *Transactions, Institute of British Geographers*, **57**, 31–44.

Wolpert, J. (1964). The decision to migrate in a spatial context. *Annals, Association of American Geographers*, **54**, 537–548.

Wrigley, E. A. (1965). Changes in the philosophy of geography. In R. J. Chorley and P. Haggett (eds.) *Frontiers in Geographical teaching*, Methuen, London, 3–20.

Zorbaugh, H. W. (1929). *The Gold Coast and the Slum*, University of Chicago Press, Chicago.

Chapter 2

Geography and Logical Positivism

Leonard Guelke

Although geographers are not particularly inclined towards philosophy, the evolution of their discipline has been greatly affected directly and indirectly by philosophical ideas. The influence of philosophy, or more precisely the philosophy of logical positivism, has been particularly important in shaping the character of modern geography. In the 1950s and 1960s, many geographers in emphasizing the importance of laws, theories, and prediction in empirical research implicitly adopted a logical positivist view of science and scientific explanation. The connection between geography and logical positivism was made explicit by Harvey (1969), who presented a thorough logical positivist analysis of geographic explanation. In this essay an attempt is made to assess critically the general consequences of the widespread adoption of logical positivist ideas in geography. The analysis is not primarily concerned with identifying the basic sources from which geographers acquired their philosophical ideas. Rather, the emphasis will be on an examination of the extent to which the philosophical and methodological writings of geographers as well as research procedures in the discipline have been affected by logical positivism.

Before investigating the nature of logical positivist influences in geography it will be useful to examine the broader issue of the relationship between philosophy in general and geography. Many geographers are skeptical of the value of philosophical and methodological discussion because such discussion so often appears to be devoid of empirical or procedural relevance. Such skeptics have reasonable grounds for their opinions because geographers writing about philosophical and methodological issues have often become enmeshed in issues of pure philosophy which have no implications for empirical research. In other words, geographers with an inclination for philosophy have not always shown enough discernment in their choice of philosophical issues.

An example of a purely philosophical issue, which was vigorously debated in the geographic literature in the early 1950s, is the question of free will versus determinism (Clark, 1950; Jones, 1956; Martin, 1951; Montefiore and Williams, 1955). The advocate of free will would argue that we are presented with real choices from among which to select. Our selections could be influenced by various factors such as our constitutions and past experience, but would not be determined by them. The determinist, on the other hand, would argue that our actions are an inevitable outcome of our heredity and past experience. This issue is considered irrelevant for geographers, because our work would not be affected by the adoption of either one of these views. Although a geographer might be convinced that an event of human origin was the inevitable outcome of a specific set of conditions, he could never collect enough replicable data to prove that the same conditions would always give rise to the same outcome. And even if this 'impossible' feat was achieved, a philosopher might still argue that the possibility of other outcomes was not precluded by the fact that several individuals freely chose the same course of action under specific conditions. In other words, the question of free will versus determinism is not a matter that can be settled by empirical research and should be left to philosophers (Hartshorne, 1959, p. 156; Harvey, 1969, p.7).

If geographers have often become embroiled in pure philosophical issues they have often neglected philosophical questions with major consequences for empirical research. The arguments over environmental determinism, for example, could usefully have focused on questions relating to the verification of scientific laws and theories rather than on philosophical questions of determinism, possibilism, and probabilism. As most geographers have a primary interest in empirical research I think it is important that only issues with some bearing on the status and procedures of our empirical work should be discussed. In this essay I will, accordingly, concentrate on those philosophical issues of logical positivism which I consider of importance for evaluating the status of our knowledge and for assessing the validity of the procedures that we use in pursuit of such knowledge.

A philosophy of geography if it is to be valuable to geographers must elucidate problems that arise in the course of geographical research. Geographers, in seeking to answer questions about their discipline, have given the philosophy of geography a dual character. On the one hand, it has included issues of demarcation and subject matter. What precisely are geographers concerned to study? How can one differentiate geography from geology, botany, etc.? These issues were thoroughly discussed by Hartshorne (1939) and others, but do not command much attention today. Yet the way in which one defines the subject matter of geography has important implications for the other basic issue of the philosophy of geography. That issue concerns explanation in geography. How do geographers explain the phenomena within their domain? Are there special problems of explanation in geography? How do geographers support their explanations? These questions have much in common with those asked in other disciplines, although there will be some issues of special concern to geographers. In this essay I will concentrate on the question of explanation in geography, but will include references to its subject matter, where this issue is of importance for understanding geographic approaches to explanation.

In examining the ways in which geographers have discussed problems of explanation in their discipline it is useful to make a distinction between philosophical and methodological issues. I consider philosophy to provide the basic underpinnings of actual research procedures or methodology. For example, a strict behaviourist might seek to explain the behaviour of subjects in terms of a stimulus–response theory or input–output model. An idealist, on the other hand, with a commitment to understanding, might devise ways of inferring the thought assumed to lie behind an action. A variety of methodologies consistent with the basic premises of these two philosophies could be devised. In other words, a philosophy of explanation is considered the foundation of a specific methodology, although the distinction might become a little blurred at times. The idea that methodology can be separated from philosophy is rejected (Harvey, 1969, pp. 7–8). Although some philosophical issues are of no consequence to geographers, it does not follow that those philosophical issues which do have some relevance in research are identical with methodology.

LOGICAL POSITIVISM

The early logical positivist or logical empiricist movement was closely associated with the University of Vienna (Kraft, 1953). This university had already achieved high standing as a centre of empiricist philosophy when Moritz Schlick was appointed to the chair of inductive sciences in 1922. Schlick gathered around him an impressive group of scientists, mathematicians, and philosophers. The group included Neurath, Carnap, Feigl, Waissmann, Zilsel, Kraft, Kaufmann, and Hahn. Although never a member of this group, which became known as the Vienna Circle, Wittgenstein exercised an important influence on the group through his (1922) book *Tractatus Logico-Philosophicus* and in discussions with some of its members. In 1930, *Erkenntis*, a periodical devoted to the ideas of the Vienna Circle, came out under the editorship of Carnap and Reichenbach, and in 1934 a series with the title *Einheitswissenschaft* was commenced under Neurath's editorship. These publications, together with numerous books, were important vehicles for disseminating the ideas of the logical positivists. In addition, the growing interest in logical positivism was reflected in a series of international conferences devoted to important themes of the movement. Among conference themes were causality, with an emphasis on physics and biology (Copenhagen, in 1936), an international encyclopaedia of unified science (Paris, in 1937), and the language of science (Cambridge, England, in 1938). The Second World War put an end to these conferences, but not before the logical positivists had become an important new movement on the philosophical scene.

As the logical positivist movement gained recognition in philosophical circles, the importance of the Vienna Circle itself declined, barely surviving the 1930s. In 1936 Schlick was murdered by a disappointed student. Other early members of the Vienna Circle moved away. Feigl and Carnap went to the United States, where they took positions at the University of Minnesota and the University of Chicago respectively. Waissmann and Neurath went to England. Logical positivism, however, took on new life as philosophers not closely associated with the Vienna Circle joined the movement. Among the leading logical positivists in the United States (in addition to Feigl and Carnap) were Morris, Bridgman,

Nagel, Reichenbach, Von Mises, Hempel, and Bergmann. In England the movement was represented by Ayer, Stebbing, and, in most of its essentials, Popper. The above list of names is by no means exhaustive and I have concentrated on those philosophers who have at one time or another been quoted by geographers.

The logical positivist movement must be seen in the context of developments in philosophy and science as a whole if it is to be properly understood. One of the most basic and oldest problems of Western philosophy is concerned with defining the relationship between mind, on the one hand, and the external world, on the other. At one extreme of this issue have been those philosophers who have maintained that only the mind is 'real'. The external world is seen as a creation of mind in a greater or lesser degree. At the other end of the mind–body controversy have been philosophers who have denied that the mind is anything more than a manifestation of physical and chemical forces. For these philosophers the only real world is the material world of atoms, molecules, magnetic fields, and the like. As one nineteenth century materialist philosopher expressed it, 'the brain secretes thought, just as the liver excretes bile' (Passmore, 1968, p. 36). Lying between these two extreme positions are many intermediate ones, but the philosophers who emphasize the paramount position of mind can be broadly considered to be 'idealists', while those emphasizing the external or material world can be classified as 'realists' or 'materialists'.

After Kant, idealism dominated Western and particularly German philosophy. The widespread acceptance of idealist ideas had some important methodological implications for physical and social science. For idealists, the special nature of human behaviour necessitated a distinctive mode of understanding. The idealist philosophers Dilthey and Rickert, whose writings were influential in the late nineteenth and early twentieth centuries, drew a basic distinction between nomothetic and idiographic sciences (Nash, 1969, pp. 5–6). The latter group of sciences, which included history and sociology, used the method of understanding (or *Verstehen*) to explain human activities. History and sociology were seen as autonomous disciplines (*Geisteswissenschaften*), with distinctive procedures of their own, quite different to those employed by the physical sciences. The outstanding representative of idealism in the English-speaking world was Collingwood. For Collingwood, human beings shared with other phenomena material attributes (the outside of events), but they also had insides (minds), the contents of which had to be uncovered if a human action was to be properly understood (Collingwood, 1946, pp. 213–214).

The logical positivist movement was in many respects a reaction against idealist philosophy. The early members of the Vienna Circle were mostly physical scientists and mathematicians with strong interests in philosophy. The scientific background of the group made its members extremely suspicious of the more traditional philosophy, and there was much to be suspicious about. Philosophers were inclined to use terms which were never defined and to make statements about the human condition without hard evidence or in a way which made them virtually impossible to verify. The philosopher Hegel was, perhaps, typical of this kind of philosopher, and his work, which included absurd comments on physical science, was thoroughly despised by the rigorous, empirically minded members of the Vienna Circle.

A major objective of the logical positivists was to establish empirical knowledge on secure logical and observational foundations (Ashby, 1964; Von Mises, 1968). The proper role of philosophy was seen to lie in the logical analysis of statements with a view to clarifying their meaning. The logical positivists accordingly placed a good deal of emphasis on the use and meaning of language. They were particularly concerned to ground all empirical statements on observation or experience. This empirical orientation was given formal expression in the 'principle of verifiability' (Hempel, 1959). On this principle all statements which purported to say something about the real world had to be open to verification (in principle). In other words, for all empirical claims there were appropriate observations to be made against which such claims could be checked. Any empirical statement not open to verification (in principle) was labelled 'meaningless' (Carnap, 1959).

The logical positivists recognized two kinds of meaningful statements: tautological and empirical ones (Ashby, 1964, pp. 502–504). The statements of mathematics and logic were considered tautologies, not in a trivial sense but in the sense that they contained no information not implied in the basic axioms. The task of mathematics was to elucidate relationships among functions which might not be immediately obvious. The theorems of Euclid, for example, are all derived from a few basic axioms, and the purpose of the theorems is basically one of bringing out the implications of these axioms. The other kind of meaningful statement included all factual knowledge of the universe, which conformed to the principle of verification. This was the domain of the empirical sciences.

The strong emphasis on observation and verification as the foundations of scientific knowledge led the logical positivists to advocate a unified conception of science (Von Mises, 1968, pp. 205–230). All worthwhile knowledge about the world had to be testable (often implying measurable) and intersubjective or objective. The idealist conception of an autonomous human and historical field was rejected. The method of *Verstehen* was seen as inherently subjective, because there were no acceptable procedures for testing the truth of the conclusions arrived at by this method. However, the logical positivists did not reject empathetic understanding as a technique of scientific investigation, but insisted that the worthwhile results could be formulated in a manner which conformed to scientific criteria of verification. These criteria, it was argued, were equally applicable to all branches of empirical knowledge from history to physics, although it was recognized that more precision was possible in some sciences than in others. The unity of science was a fundamental tenet of logical positivist philosophy.

The idea of the unity of science was pushed furthest by Neurath and Carnap. Passmore (1968, p. 376) has described the basic position of Neurath:

At his [Neurath's] hands, logical positivism allies itself with behaviourism;

all statements about 'experiences', he argues, can be expressed in 'the language of physics', i.e. by reference to processes in space and time. This is the essence of Neurath's 'physicalism', which is closely related to his 'thesis of the unity of science'. Since all empirical statements, according to Neurath, can be expressed in the language of physics—what cannot be thus expressed is either tautologous or nonsensical—there are no 'spiritual sciences', to be contrasted with 'natural sciences'; all sciences are equally 'natural' and for this reason form a unity.

The logical positivists' goals of objectivity and testability were incorporated in their basic model of scientific explanation. This model, known as deductive-nomological explanation, comprised a deductive argument of the form:

$$\left.\begin{array}{l} C_1, C_2, \ldots, C_k \\ \\ \underline{L_1, L_2, \ldots, L_k} \end{array}\right\} \text{Explanans}$$

$$E \qquad \text{Explanandum}$$

Here, the sentences $C_1, C_2, \ldots, C_k$ describe the initial or determining conditions; $L_1, L_2, \ldots, L_r$ are general laws. The explanandum E, that is the event to be explained, is deduced from the initial conditions and laws set out in the explanans (Hempel, 1965, pp. 336–338). An important corollary of deductive-nomological explanation is that there is no logical distinction between the explanation and prediction of a given event. An explanation refers to an event in the past, a prediction to an event in the future. The model, because of its predictive character, enabled logical positivists to reject intuition as a basis of explanation. For example, astrology is rejected not because it is preposterous but because it fails empirical tests, and Einstein is accepted in spite of propositions that contradict common sense because of successful predictions.

The application of the model was easier in some areas of empirical research than in others. In physics and chemistry, for example, replicable experimental procedures open to general inspection allowed new results to be checked and rechecked. The result was an extremely precise body of well-confirmed deterministic and probabilistic laws. In astronomy the application of physical laws permitted precise predictions. In many areas complexity made the application of the deductive-nomological model extremely difficult; some concessions were made in application but not in principle. Where precise knowledge was lacking, as in history, a probabilistic formulation of the model was advocated. The deductive-nomological model was set up in such a way that only general statements open to objective confirmation were capable of satisfying the basic requirements of the model.

The question of how scientists arrived at their laws was secondary to the question of whether the proposed laws allowed accurate predictions to be made. Logical positivists did not make a fundamental distinction between deductive and inductive laws, although it was considered desirable to give laws theoretical support. Laws which were embedded in theories were sometimes referred to as theoretical laws or simply theories. A theoretical statement of this kind performed the same function as a law in deductive-nomological explanation. However, if theories were to have scientific status and explanatory power within the context of deductive-nomological explanation, they had to be open to objective, empirical verification. Unfalsifiable theories failed to meet the minimum requirements of scientific acceptability. In the social sciences theories have often been formulated as *a priori* models. Such models have the same structure as theories but rest on assumptions of 'ideal' conditions. This type of model and the empirical statements derived from them cannot be given a role in explanation until verified by empirical tests.

Although the logical positivists frequently disagreed among themselves, they shared a common approach to philosophy and science. As geographers we need not concern ourselves with many of the philosophical issues which engaged the attention of logical positivists, such as Carnap's work on language and the issues of 'emergence' and 'physicalism'. The basic commitment of the logical positivists to the unity of science, to empiricism, to deductive-nomological explanation, to objectivity, and to empirical verification was an important element of logical positivism—widely shared by the proponents of this philosophy—and had important implications for empirical research in general and geography in particular. In evaluating the logical positivist philosophy of explanation it is important to see it in terms of its fundamental objectives. These objectives were a body of empirical knowledge that was clearly formulated, grounded in experience and observation, and was open to objective verification. The element of personal judgement (intuition) was to be eliminated in this quest for secure knowledge. The logical positivists were not against imaginative intuition in the formulation of an explanation, but insisted that all candidate explanations should be testable within the framework of deductive-nomological explanation.

LOGICAL POSITIVISM AND GEOGRAPHY

The widespread adoption in geography of the fundamental tenets of logical positivism is generally associated with the quantitative revolution and theoretical geography. Yet logical positivist ideas were already implicitly accepted by many geographers prior to their widespread adoption in the 1960s. The emergence of the new geography was less of a radical new departure than it was a logical extension of ideas which were already generally accepted by many geographers. The question of why geographers adopted a new emphasis in their discipline when they did, rather than a decade earlier or later, must be left for historical research. Another important question which also awaits historical research is the channels through which geographers were made aware of logical positivist ideas. Until Harvey, geographers read little philosophy and presumably acquired their philosophical ideas indirectly either from general philosophical texts or from the people in other disciplines.

The seminal work on the philosophy and methodology of modern geography in the English-speaking world is Hartshorne's *The Nature of Geography* (1939). In writing this, Hartshorne was greatly influenced by German geographers, particularly Hettner, and gave little attention to other schools of geography. On publication, *The Nature of Geography* became the standard reference on philosophical and methodological questions and remained so for almost two decades thereafter. Although Hartshorne is frequently identified with the 'exceptionalist' view of the discipline, which holds that geography has distinctive problems and methods of its own quite different from those of other disciplines, his position was more complex than is implied by this designation. In fact, Hartshorne (1939) was a firm supporter of the scientific approach in geography and his views incorporate a number of logical positivist ideas. Hartshorne insisted on the unity of physical and human geography and implicitly accepted the basic deductive-nomological model of explanation. He was of the opinion that observation and classification were necessary first steps in the formulation of geographic laws and theories. All these ideas accorded well with the basic positions of logical positivism.

Hartshorne, however, was not a thoroughgoing logical positivist because he made concessions to the practice of geography not in accord with logical positivist ideas. In making these concessions Hartshorne was influenced by writings of idealists such as Dilthey and Rickert. Logical positivists were not averse to taking account of difficulties within different empirical sciences, but they would not have made the kind of accommodation Hartshorne made between the ideal of science and the reality of geographic research. Hartshorne accepted the idea that uniqueness was a special problem of geography (and a a few other disciplines) and took over the nomothetic/idiographic classification of sciences from idealist philosophers. This kind of distinction was completely alien to logical positivists, who insisted that science was indivisible. Neither was this position in accord with Hartshorne's own view that geographers needed laws in their explanations. The use of the nomothetic/idiographic distinction appears to have been an attempt to explain the paucity of laws in both human and physical geography. Yet precisely because Hartshorne accepted the deductive-nomological model of explanation his position on uniqueness was a major barrier in the way of scientific explanations.

In practice, studies done within the Hartshornian framework were often overly descriptive. The importance he placed on classification would have been less of a burden to geographers had he at the same time insisted on the search for causal laws and generalizations. But at this point Hartshorne's view that geographers were unlikely to discover laws but should in any case do the best they could was, in the absence of an alternative, an invitation to description. The tendency to description was reinforced by Hartshorne's advocacy of map-overlay techniques in regional geography. This encouraged a correlative view of the discipline and discouraged those geographers who accepted his ideas from putting their work in a wider spatial or temporal context (Guelke, 1977).

The Nature of Geography was open to criticism from the first person who was not prepared to accept Hartshorne's modifications of the scientific method.

In fairness to Hartshorne, it should be pointed out that he was, in writing *The Nature of Geography*, concerned to discourage the kind of theoretical geography then being produced by environmental determinists and probably gave more emphasis to empirical work than he would have in the absence of environmental ideas. There were, however, few geographers who had either the inclination or background to challenge Hartshorne's views in *The Nature of Geography* and thirteen years passed before Schaefer's important paper, 'Exceptionalism in Geography: A Methodological Examination', was published (1953). In this paper Schaefer adopted an explicit and uncompromising logical positivist position. Schaefer, unlike Hartshorne, was acquainted with logical positivist ideas at first hand, and after his untimely death the logical positivist philosopher Bergmann, a colleague of Schaefer's at Iowa, saw the proofs of his paper to press. Schaefer's paper is seen by many as a forceful attack on Hartshorne, as indeed it was, but the two men were closer together on philosophical issues than might at first be imagined. Schaefer, like Hartshorne, accepted the deductive-nomological model of explanation, the unity of science, and most elements of logical positivism, although he has little to say on issues relating to verification. Where he disagreed with Hartshorne was on the problem of uniqueness, which he maintained was not a barrier to nomothetic explanation. Yet Schaefer was evidently convinced enough by Hartshorne's arguments in *The Nature of Geography* to feel that uniqueness (complexity) did, perhaps, provide a barrier to the discovery of laws, and redefined geography as 'spatial analysis'.

Schaefer's redefinition of geography was not, of course, part of logical positivism, but it was directly derived from his interpretation of the logical positivist thesis on explanation. The emphasis on space was clearly designed to make it possible for geographers to discover laws by avoiding the quagmire that was regional geography. Yet the notion of geography as spatial analysis is not without problems. What exactly did he mean by space? The study of distributions on the earth's surface would probably be fairly generally accepted as a definition of space in a geographic context. But is it really possible that scholars could be interested in distributions as such without specifying what they are? Would anyone, to use a temporal equivalent, say they were interested in the time interval between events without specifying the nature of the events? And even if one specified that one was interested in the time interval between wars would this kind of interest really be the basis for an independent discipline? The time intervals between wars might be an interesting element in the study of war, but scarcely a study in its own right. Yet Schaefer was apparently arguing that the study of spatial relationships (and Schaefer excluded time, as Hartshorne did, from geography) could be an independent law-seeking science.

The new emphasis on space in geography, although a by-product of Schaefer's concern with scientific explanation, was not a logically necessary move. Logical positivists had always argued that uniqueness was not a property peculiar to any one discipline. In fact, everything, in a certain sense, they argued, was unique understood in terms of general laws and theories. In other words, geographers were not prevented from giving deductive-nomological explanations because their subject matter involved unique regions or areas. This was Hartshorne's error and to some extent Schaefer's as well. However, the subject matter of geography was such that the laws likely to be needed by geographers would come from other disciplines. In other words, geography would have had to be conceived as a law-consuming science rather than a law-generating one. This would have placed geography in a similar position to history, which had attracted the attention of such logical positivists as Hempel (1965, pp. 231–243). Yet, surprisingly, the idea of geography as essentially a law-consuming science was not advocated by either Schaefer or Hartshorne, although both of them recognized that geographers would use laws from other disciplines. Geographers were given a basic choice of describing the unique or seeking spatial laws (Hartshorne, 1959, p 146).

Schaefer had outlined the fundamentals of a logical positivist geography, but the 'new' geography that emerged in the late 1950s and the 1960s was selective in the emphasis it gave to the ideas of Schaefer. Schaefer's concept of geography as spatial analysis received general support, but the emphasis of much of the early work in the new geography was statistical rather than deductive nomological. The spatial viewpoint was accepted because it allowed for statistical analysis. Burton (1963), who came closer than Schaefer to identifying the essential concerns of the new geography, is not too concerned with philosophical issues of deductive-nomological explanation. He justified the need for statistical analyses on the grounds that: (a) they were more rigorous and (b) they prevented self-deception (Burton, 1963, p. 157). The first statement means little unless the context is specified. The second statement is certainly questionable. Although Burton obviously had in mind the self-deception of visual correlation, the use of statistical correlation has probably created more self-deception than any other method of analysis used in geography. In correlation analysis, imposed order was mistaken for empirical order, statistical correlation for deductive-nomological explanation, and trend forecasting for scientific prediction (Guelke, 1971). The use of the word 'explain' in a statistical sense is most misleading, because in such a sense it carries no connotation of cause. Yet in everyday language it often has such causal implications. In consequence, and in spite of disclaimers, geographers have seen statistical analysis as an end in itself, when such 'analysis' is basically a mathematical description. Although Burton regarded the adoption of quantitative methods as a move towards a scientific geography, he is vague about precisely what is meant by this term.

It would be wrong to suggest that the new geography was nothing more than statistical analysis, although such analysis was a major, if not the predominant, ingredient out of much of the early work. In addition, there was theoretical geography, which came a lot closer to meeting the requirements of logical positivism. For Burton, the evolution of theoretical geography was a reaction against concern with the unique (Burton, 1963, p. 156). Here again the idea of space as a central theme served the needs of the new geography, because it provided a basis for seeking generalizations. The pattern of towns on the landscape, for example, could be analysed from a spatial point of view in a way which avoided emphasis on its unique elements.

However, the real forces behind the rapid growth in the quantitative and theoretical movements in geography were pragmatic rather than intellectual. The idea of universities as 'ivory towers' was giving way to more mundane concerns. Universities were expected to produce problem-solvers or social-technologists to run increasingly complex economies, and geographers were not slow in adopting new positions appropriate to the new conditions. Statistics and models were ideal tools for monitoring and planning in complex industrial societies. The work of the new geographers, however, often lacked a truly intellectual dimension. Many geographers were asking: 'Are our methods rigorous?', 'What are the planning implications of this model?', and not 'How much insight does this study give us?', 'Is my understanding of this phenomenon enhanced?', 'Does this study contribute to geography?'. The last-mentioned question was considered of little consequence. Yet it should have been asked, because one of the weaknesses of the new geography was a lack of coherence.

An attempt to provide the new geography with more substantial philosophical foundations was made by Harvey in his book *Explanation in Geography* (1969). Harvey read widely in the philosophy of science literature and his book presented a thoroughgoing logical positivist interpretation of the status and prospects of geographic research. Although Harvey suggested that his book was basically concerned with methodology, it was in fact much concerned with philosophical and logical questions of explanation. Harvey based much of his analysis of explanation on philosophers such as Carnap, Hempel, and Nagel, and many other logical positivists were cited. In writing *Explanation in Geography* Harvey had an advantage over most earlier writers on methodology because of his strong philosophical background. This advantage was not put to good account. When he wrote *Explanation in Geography* Harvey was convinced of the correctness of the basic positions of the logical positivists and much of the effort in his book is devoted to showing how geography might be accommodated within the bounds of this philosophy.

Harvey accepted the basic deductive-nomological form of explanation from the logical positivist philosophers. However, when it came to assessing the application of the model in geography he was quite vague. In reply to his own question of whether laws are employed in geography, Harvey (1969, p. 107) wrote: 'Given the very imprecise criteria available for distinguishing scientific laws from other kinds of statements, such a question may appear rather senseless'. In spite of this, Harvey stated that such an investigation was important, but '... the attempt will perforce prove rather inconclusive'. The casual way in which Harvey approached the most crucial of all questions affecting the possibility of scientific explanation in geography, and indeed the viability of the deductive-nomological approach itself, is quite amazing. He failed to make clear that, without reasonably well-confirmed laws, the deductive-nomological model cannot perform its intended function, namely of providing a scheme for rigorously objective explanations. As soon as one begins to compromise on the kinds of statement one is prepared to admit as laws, the objective foundation of this model is destroyed. There is little point in geographers making their explanations conform to a model if they cannot supply the essential ingredients for its successful application. Where reasonably well-confirmed laws are not available, one might produce explanations with a scientific form, but one cannot give them real scientific content.

In *Explanation in Geography* Harvey followed the basic logical positivist positions on explanation, theories, the unity of science, languages, mathematics, and many other issues. In his discussions of philosophical questions he provided geographers with some useful background. However, he was often annoyingly vague about the status of the quotations he cited. Frequently one has no idea whether he supported the ideas quoted or not—a style of writing which is all too common in contemporary geography and has little to recommend it. If Harvey set out philosophical positions reasonably clearly, he was less precise on the geographic applications of the positions he supported. For example, when the practice of geography failed to measure up to the criteria of scientific enquiry, he attributed the shortcomings of geography to the 'stage' of its development (Harvey, 1969, p. 76; see also Chorely and Haggett, 1967, p. 33). Such an explanation implies that all disciplines will, of necessity, follow the path taken by chemistry and biology, and is firmly premised on the logical positivist interpretation of scientific activity. It is important that geographers should know about the formal requirements of theory, but this knowledge will not be of much value unless it is applied to the actual theories of geography. Why bother with learning the formal requirements of verification if one has no intention of ever using them?

Although Harvey performed a valuable service for geographers by introducing them to the important literature of the philosophy of science, he was not successful in creating a viable bridge between what geographers did and what philosophers of science had to say about explanation. The crux of logical positivism was its concern with verification. The emphasis on testability of all empirical propositions was designed to eliminate subjectivity from scientific activity and to ensure a value-free body of scientific knowledge. The fact that much of the theory of social science is not value-free was not a shortcoming of logical positivism, but a failure of those who adopted a scientific or positivist approach to apply criteria of scientific enquiry to their theoretical propositions. Harvey failed to bring out this essential weakness of much social science, however, and missed an opportunity of rejecting geographic theory on logical positivist principles. Instead, Harvey rejected logical positivism in favour of Marxism, and in his book *Social Justice and the City* (1973) he presented some arguments to justify his change of position, which are quite revealing of his understanding of logical positivism and merit a brief review.

In *Social Justice and the City* Harvey apparently rejected the idea of objective science. He argued that even natural science should be interpreted in relation to its materialistic basis and observed (Harvey, 1973, p. 121): 'Material activity involves the manipulation of nature in the interests of man, and scientific understanding cannot be interpreted independently of that general thrust'. In the West, Harvey (1973, p. 122) maintained, one would expect natural science 'to reflect a drive for manipulation and control over those aspects of nature that are relevant to the middle class'. In consequence, Harvey (1973, p. 127) concluded that 'those revolutions of thought which are accomplished in the natural sciences pose no threat to the existing order since they are constructed with the requirements of that existing order broadly in mind'. While recognizing there is some truth in the foregoing argument, particularly in relation to applied science or technology, the general thrust of Harvey's argument is an incredible interpretation of the history of scientific thought.

The foundation of modern man's control over nature was achieved by people who were dedicated to understanding nature not in class terms but as a quest for knowledge, often for its own sake. Did Galileo have 'the requirements of the existing order broadly in mind' when he argued for the Copernican theory? Were Pasteur. Darwin, and Einstein accepted because they 'posed no threat to the existing order' or because their theories were capable of explaining facts that had previously been difficult to account for? The goal of pure science has been to understand nature is an end in itself. This understanding often has practical implications, but these implications are not always appreciated at the time a theory is formulated. Logical positivists insisted that scientific theories, however preposterous, be subject one and all to the same rules of empirical verification. Under rigorous testing the phoney or untrue ideas would be eliminated and a body of well-confirmed theoretical knowledge would emerge. The search for verifiable knowledge is an intellectual goal that, I feel, must remain the foundation of any serious quest for true understanding.

The problem of knowledge in the social sciences poses difficulties which are not so easily disposed of. Social and economic theories are often tied to assumptions which favour one or other group in society. Different interest groups, not surprisingly, have adopted theories of society which are likely to advance their particular cause most effectively. However, this type of self-interested theory has nothing to do with science, because the adherents of such theory do not feel bound to change their views in the face of empirical evidence. Such theories are best conceived as ideologies or untestable theories and as such must be considered to be essentially political weapons in the hands of those who adopt them. The idea that this kind of theory can be classified as counter-revolutionary or revolutionary (from whichever vantage point one takes) establishes a political criterion for theory acceptance. However, one need not follow Harvey to this point. One only has to insist that all social science theories must be capable of being tested and refuted. This criterion will effectively eliminate theories which are incapable of explaining empirical facts and, when properly applied, will be blind to whether a theory is revolutionary or counter-revolutionary, however one cares to define these terms. In the final analysis Harvey's idea that a political criterion of acceptability be applied to geographic theory is a dangerous one, not because it poses a threat to the existing order but because, if accepted, it would sound the death knell of free enquiry.

It might be objected that if logical positivist principles were to be consistently applied to all social science theory few, if any, theories would be left. I see no cause for alarm here. If our theories cannot explain facts as they are, the state of our general knowledge is revealed to be meagre. I would rather admit that our theories are inadequate than be placed in a position of having to choose between Adam Smith, Keynes, or Marx, particularly as I consider there exists a viable, non-theoretical approach to the study of human behaviour which avoids the need for this kind of ideological commitment.

From Hartshorne to Harvey geographical writing on philosophy and methodology has to a greater or lesser degree shown the influence of logical positivist ideas. The idea that geographers should produce explanations that conform to a scientific model of some kind has been a common theme among authors who differ on other issues. This scientific commitment, I believe, has been a mistake, because it has encouraged geographers to change their style of enquiry to conform with whatever happens to be the latest interpretation of the scientific method. In seeking methodological purity, geographers have lost sight of the fact that methodology is but a means to an end. It is not a formula that can guarantee worthwhile or significant work.

URBAN GEOGRAPHY

The following review of recent work in urban geography is not concerned with assessing its empirical value but with analysing its philosophical foundations. Although I conclude that empirical work in urban geography falls short of meeting minimum requirements of logical positivism, this does not imply that it is of little value. Science is concerned with a certain kind of knowledge, but not all knowledge has to be scientific (in the logical positivist sense) to be useful. Much urban geography is of value to planners and governments, who are less concerned about science than with usable research results. For example, trend forecasts have little in common with scientific predictions, but such forecasts can be extremely useful in many situations. The purpose of a philosophical analysis of empirical work is seen to be concerned with the status of our knowledge and with the validity of the approaches by which it is acquired.

Few areas of geography were more affected by logical positivist ideas than urban geography. Although a few geographers had concerned themselves with cities before 1950, urban geography was not considered a major field of specialization and it did not become so until the late 1950s and the 1960s. The lack of a strong urban studies' tradition in geography probably hastened the adoption of new approaches in urban geography. Basic concepts derived from logical positivism gained wide acceptance; urban geographers accepted the idea of geography as spatial analysis, the central importance of theory in empirical work, and the necessity of rigorous methodology (quantitative methods). Urban geography was, in other words, to be approached from a nomothetic rather than an idiographic point of view. Most urban geographers rejected the idea that human settlement was not amenable to scientific analysis and implicitly accepted the logical positivist position on the unity of science.

The essence of the new urban geography was clearly brought out in the work on central place theory. It would be difficult to underestimate the importance of central place theory in the evolution of modern urban geography. The basic theory has stimulated more interest and generated more empirical studies than any other theory in geography. The theoretical models of Christaller and Losch were tailored perfectly to the needs of an emerging nomothetic emphasis in urban geography. On the basis of a model like Christaller's, it was possible for geographers to treat a large variety of urban places from a general point of view. Yet, although urban geography apparently conformed to the procedures employed in physical sciences, it fell short of meeting basic requirements of scientific acceptability. The basic formulation of central place theory was hypothetical in character, and under the criteria of logical positivism could not be accorded scientific or explanatory status until verified with empirical evidence. Although geographers were well aware of the simplifying assumptions of Christaller, and, indeed, many studies were produced to show that the real world was more complex than the one postulated by Christaller or Losch, these models acquired a kind of extraempirical status. They suggested research questions but were not affected by the answers.

The widespread and enduring appeal of a model such as Christaller's (either in its original or modified forms) is not explained in terms of its empirical validity or its success in explaining real-world situations. Rather, the success of a model of the Christaller variety is clearly based on its appeal to our rational natures. Such models deal with simple worlds in which people are perfectly rational. It is not difficult for us to accept the idea that a farmer will grow the most profitable crop or that consumers will minimize distance in relation to specific purchases. In a model formulation such notions appear self-evident; however, they rest on intuitive principles, not empirical ones. Unlike Newton's laws of motion or other physical theories, Christaller lacks any empirical confirmation. The deductive form of models such as this, however, tends to hide its weak foundations.

The appeal to intuition makes it possible for one to reject Christaller on the basis of scientific criteria. If people really behave as postulated by a model the onus is on its author to produce empirical evidence to support his claim. The basic logical positivist criterion of objective empirical confirmation is violated where this cannot be done. The conclusive empirical evidence in support of Christaller has yet to be produced. The explanatory power of this model (unlike physical theories based on well-confirmed empirical laws) is really based on the ability of those who use it to see rational connections between the thought and action of the hypothetical inhabitants of this invented world. In the absence of empirical support, models are best conceived as examples of hypothetical idealist geography without empirical status.

In practice, however, such models have been considered the foundations of theoretical geography and have been endowed with empirical status. The confusion over the status of models has been so general that studies which found that the real world was rather different from the one postulated by a model have often been considered significant empirical contributions to urban geography. For example, the trivial findings of Murdie (1965), who discovered that Old Order Mennonites had different shopping habits from other Canadians, could only be considered of value by those who actually believed central place theory had some empirical status. The way people shop is, of course, affected by cultural factors—who (in the absence of Christaller) could ever have believed otherwise? It might be objected that even obvious facts need confirmation and that Murdie has provided us with interesting details about variations in shopping habits. However, Murdie and others have failed to accept the logical implications of their own work. When a physical scientist discovers that a theory fails to conform to reality he either modifies his old one or formulates a new one. He is not content, as many geographers have been, to suggest that there exists a factor which should be taken into account without specifying how the theory or model in question should be modified. In the absence of a detailed statement of how empirical findings like Murdie's are to be related to central place theory, the effort involved in getting precise data is wasted.

The logical character of *a priori*, hypothetical models has been badly misconstrued by many urban geographers, who imagined it was possible to test them in empirical situations (Carter, 1975, p.117). A host of studies along the lines of Murdie's appeared in the literature, which conclusively demonstrated the shortcomings of the Christaller and the Losch models. Yet despite the accumulation of data refuting central place theory, beginning geographers were frequently introduced to central place studies through Christaller's original model. The remarkable adherence to models without empirical status is explained only if one takes account of the theoretical bias of the new geography. This theoretical and anti-idiographic attitude prevented urban geographers from drawing the obvious conclusion from empirical evidence, namely that urban systems were extremely complex and often were not amenable to general treatment. Modifications to a model which made it more realistic in one area would likely make it less realistic somewhere else. Instead, a fiction was maintained that empirical work was somehow contributing to the development of general urban theory, rather than accepting the idea that central place systems were, after all, unique in the sense that specific elements could not be explained in general terms. Central place studies have now hit an impasse, which is unlikely to be resolved until urban geographers reassess their empirical work outside a nomothetic framework.

The point is not that it is impossible to make general statements about urban systems but that such statements are usually of limited value in understanding real-world situations. Harvey (1969, p. 102), in discussing laws in geography, produces the following example: 'Towns of similar size are usually found at similar distances apart'. This type of general statement, even if true, seems to me to be rather trivial. It would be more valuable if it could be quantified, but this is obviously impossible. Other generalizations of urban geography relating to distance decay, to hierarchies, and to the size of trade areas are all useful aids in demonstrating general tendencies, but are of limited value in actual case studies unless the concepts are extracted from the theories in which they are embedded. The attempt to apply central place theory to empirical situations, on the assumption that the theory (at least in its ideal-type formulations) is true, repeats the error geomorphologists made in applying the Davisian cycle of erosion to landform analysis. *A priori* theories or models can be valuable as aids to understanding, but become barriers to research when accorded empirical status.

Other areas of urban geography followed a similar approach to the one adopted in central place studies, but tended to be more empirical and statistical. Although theories or models of urban structure and development were available few of them were as plausible as the central place models of Christaller or Losch, and they consequently played a more limited role in generating research. A fairly representative group of urban studies outside central place topics were the ones on residential location (e.g. Murdie, 1969; Rees, 1970). In such studies large numbers of variables were processed statistically and measures of associations among them derived. Although attempts were often made to relate results to general models, the status of these studies owed little to such models. That status was descriptive rather than explanatory. The measures of statistical association failed to provide insight into the phenomena so painstakingly described or to provide much understanding of the nature of urban society. These criticisms also apply to the work on urban classification, which was similarly lacking in explanatory content (e.g. Smith, 1965).

Attempts to develop more realistic models of urban phenomena, under the heading of 'behavioural geography', were made by several geographers concerned about the simplistic *a priori* behavioural postulates of urban theory. The emphasis of much behavioural research was on the actual activity of consumers and others as this activity was affected by individual perceptions of available choices. Behavioural geographers drew upon the techniques and methods of psychology in seeking to measure individual preferences. Having established such preferences, attempts were made to incorporate them within a more realistic urban geography.

Behavioural geography was entirely consistent with the basic aims of nomothetic spatial geography. Behavioural geographers were prompted to investigate actual preferences in specific situations, not with a view to testing existing *a priori* models and theories but with a view to giving them stronger empirical foundations (Rushton, 1969). These goals were quite similar to those of other geographers who sought, for example, to work out the implications that uneven population distributions might have on the pattern of towns in central place theory. In a review of behavioural geography, Golledge, Brown, and Williamson (1972, p. 77) specifically linked the objectives of this movement to the scientific goals of formulating laws and theories.

Although behavioural geographers were moving in a direction which promised a more realistic empirical approach, the movement was handicapped by its close links with spatial theory in geography. In urban geography, for example, central place theory suggested many of the questions that should be investigated, and great emphasis was devoted to travel patterns and space preferences. The opportunity to provide geographers with a deeper understanding of causal relationships in the urban geographical situations that were investigated was missed. Nevertheless, the behavioural approach has obvious possibilities if behavioural geographers can divorce themselves from theoretical spatial geography and examine urban questions in a broader context.

This very brief review of the kind of work being done by urban geographers will have served its purpose if it has established that a gulf existed between the professed ideal of a scientific geography and the reality of actual achievement. The new urban geographers were unable to develop theory of a general kind which was capable of empirical verification; neither were laws of human spatial behaviour discovered. Yet in spite of these shortcomings, most urban geographers kept their commitment to the scientific approach—and paid a high price for it. The nomothetic approach (or rather its interpretation in geography) proved inadequate in the face of the diversity of the real world. There were many generalizations that could be made, but after the obvious limitations of distance on human activity had been described a good many questions remained. Urban geographers became trapped in a similar way to the determinists. The latter, having assumed that the environment was of critical importance in the explanation of human activity, not unnaturally sought environmental explanations of human geographical phenomena. The former have done much the same thing with space, but there are obvious limits to spatial explanations of spatial phenomena.

The real tragedy of the nomothetic approach has been to divert the geographers' attention from specific aspects of urban systems in different parts of the world, or to encourage them to look upon such aspects as unwanted 'noise'. An analogy with history will help clarify this point. There are several generalizations about man's quest for power and status. The historian does not see his task in studying the past as requiring him to produce more evidence in support of these generalizations. Rather, he takes them for granted and shows how such tendencies have influenced historical developments in unique historical contexts. I think urban geographers would do well to emulate the historians in this area by taking it for granted that space (or distance) is a factor in urban development and attempting to show how, in combination with many other things, this factor might have contributed to the evolution of a specific urban pattern. There is a wide variety of factors in need of analysis which has often been avoided by those with a philosophical commitment to spatial generalizations.

Every city or urban system is the end-product of historical evolution, which has been affected by changing political, social, and economic, as well as geographical, forces. Political decisions such as zoning, for example, have affected individual cities in very different ways. I consider that new geographers must lose their aversion to uniqueness, recognize the limitations of spatial factors as explanatory variables, and concentrate on causal factors rather than descriptive ones if progress is to be made in urban geography, conceived as an intellectual field. This will not necessarily involve a rejection of a scientific approach, which is not averse to the study of the unique, but this approach will have to be reformulated to take account of some of the special problems of disciplines like geography. Generalizations can, of course, be valuable, but nothing but misunderstanding is likely to be achieved by the insistence that all explanations be forced into the procrustean bed of simplistic theories and models.

ALTERNATIVES TO LOGICAL POSITIVISM

The dissatisfaction of many geographers at the level of understanding achieved in the application of statistical techniques and *a priori* models to geographic phenomena has led them to explore alternatives to positivism. Among these alternatives are Marxism, phenomenology, and idealism. In assessing these alternatives I will keep in mind the criteria which the logical positivists set up for evaluating scientific explanations. The strong commitment logical positivists had to establishing empirical knowledge on secure foundations makes their objections to certain kinds of explanation of great interest.

The Marxist analysis of phenomena of urban geography has much to offer (Harvey, 1973). The analysis of capitalist economic order is certainly more likely to yield interesting results than a preoccupation with spatial variables. The assumption that capitalism is impressed on the landscape carries the search for causal explanation several steps forward. Although Marxist ideas can be stimulating, Marxism is a theoretical system and its empirical content must ultimately rest on the success of its theories in explaining and predicting actual events. In other words, the logical positivist tenet that any theory must be testable and refutable if it is to be given empirical status is seen to be applicable to all general theories, including astrology and Marxism. It is at this point that Marxism poses several problems. Marxists are not prepared to accept empirical evidence not in accord with the basic propositions of the system they have adopted. Any theory can be protected from negative evidence: such evidence can be reclassified, explained away with an *ad hoc* hypothesis, or simply dismissed. However, when theory becomes unrefutable—whether it be environmental, spatial, or Marxist—it loses its empirical foundation and explanatory power. Such theories have no place in objective, intellectual enquiries and ultimately constitute barriers to understanding. It is understandable that Marxist geographers reacted against the 'status quo' economic bias of spatial analysis, but the Marxists will have to give more attention to the foundations of their own work if bias is really to be eliminated from geography. The goal of objective analysis might be difficult or even impossible to attain in practice, but it would seem to be a necessary one for any discipline seeking to provide non-ideological understanding of the real world.

The phenomenological movement in geography can also be seen as a reaction against spatial analysis. The phenomenologists object to the level of abstraction of models and theories. An underlying idea in phenomenology is to analyse human behaviour in terms of actual experience. Our experience of the world is a rich experience, a compound of the emotions, the intellect, and the senses. A phenomenological description seeks to capture this experience in all its facets. The scientist, by abstracting an element here and an element there, destroys the coherence and the meaning of these elements as they are actually experienced. The phenomenologist seeks, in the words of a recent advocate of this position, 'to grasp the dynamism of the life world' (Buttimer, 1976, pp. 277–292). In this undertaking a key concept is that of 'layers of meaning'. The idea is that we endow the world with meanings and it is the task of the researcher to uncover the meanings given to various elements in the landscape. These meanings might include economic, social, personal, and symbolic ones, and a single object might encompass several layers of meaning. An old church, for example, might be of importance to the inhabitants of an urban area on a social, personal, and symbolic level, but for an economic planner it might simply be seen as an obstacle in the way of an expressway development.

The phenomenologists are as much concerned with the description of experience as they are with explanation as such. The basic problem of the approach is that it lacks criteria of verification. If a geographer comes across a fountain while walking through a city and writes a poem about the meaning of this experience, it presumably qualifies as phenomenological geography. A geographer could interview migrant workers and give us a picture of the migrant experience—of the loneliness of the first weeks away from home, of the hard work, of the joy of a letter from home, of the sense of relief at the end of the contract, of the anticipation of returning home. All this, however, would not really answer the question of 'why' the migrants left home in the first place. I do not doubt that emotions are an important part of life but only doubt whether phenomenological analysis can help us answer questions about man's use of the earth. Unless phenomenologists provide some objective criteria for measuring meaning, phenomenological geography becomes indistinguishable from landscape painting or poetry. It has power to touch our emotions but it does not give us the tools to understand or explain human behaviour in an intersubjective or objective way.

An important alternative philosophy to positivism, which enjoys considerable support among historians but is not at present widely accepted by geographers, is idealism. The idealist philosophy draws a fundamental distinction between the explanation of human activity and other phenomena. The explanation of a human action involves uncovering and understanding the thought behind it (Collingwood, 1956, p. 203). Such understanding, which is sometimes referred to as *Verstehen*, is not the kind of understanding associated with emotional identification or empathy. Rather, an idealist analysis will focus on the beliefs and ideas behind individual and group actions, although due allowance will be made for the emotional and physical conditions of those being investigated (Guelke, 1974, pp. 194–195). The idealist shares the phenomenologist's concern with understanding the different meanings people attach to their surroundings, but at an intellectual rather than an emotional level.

In the area of environmental perception there is some common ground between idealism and behaviourism. The idealist, however, is primarily concerned with establishing a link between thought and action rather than the analysis of images and their origins. Moreover, the idealist, unlike the behaviourist, seeks to explain actions in terms of reasons, not laws or theories.

The idealist approach has been criticized on the grounds that thought is private and that the verification of idealist interpretations is impossible. The logical positivists were undoubtedly justified in criticizing much idealist work which was not open to verification of any kind. However, there are procedures, which resemble those of a court of law rather than a laboratory, for testing the worth of an idealist explanation (Guelke, 1974, pp. 200–201). A well-verified idealist explanation will be one in which a pattern of behaviour can be shown to be consistent with certain underlying ideas. Where data are presented which are not in accordance with a proposed explanation a new hypothesis will be needed, unless it can be shown that the conflicting evidence can be accounted for in some convincing way. However, even where strict procedures are adopted for testing idealist explanations one cannot guarantee mistake-free interpretations. The complex nature of human societies and lack of pertinent data makes it inevitable that many idealist interpretations will be of a tentative character.

Although a number of geographers recognize the potential value of idealism in a discipline like history, they remain unconvinced that this philosophy could be successfully applied in economic or urban geography. The crux of objections to idealism appears to be related to the fact that geographers are more involved with societies en masse than are traditional historians, and the idealist approach is only considered appropriate to understanding the actions of specific individuals. This objection, however, is not a valid one. The assumption that thought lies behind human action is not related to the numbers involved or the social positions of the people in question. If thousands of people drive motor cars to their places of work the idealist assumes that each of these journeys is a considered action involving thought. In such situations the investigator will not be able to look at each case individually, but he will seek to isolate the general factors involved in typical circumstances. In seeking to isolate major factors in such decisions the idealist might well make use of statistical procedures. However, the value of statistical analysis will largely depend on its successful integration in the general interpretation or explanatory thesis being developed. In other words, a thesis or interpretation is needed before raw data or statistical associations become evidence

The example presented in the previous paragraph is not to be considered a new approach. Many geographers have used this kind of analysis for years. The point I am trying to make is that from a philosophical point of view any analysis that rests on the ability of a researcher to understand the action of those being investigated in terms of thought is basically an idealist approach. This approach is clearly differentiated from one in which an investigator seeks to impose order on the data he collects and to understand relationships in terms of laws and theories. The power of an explanation involving the law of gravity, for example, derives from the law itself—it is a well-verified, testable empirical fact that bodies (of a certain size) are attracted to each other in relation to their masses and the distance separating them.

Although superficially people might appear to be attracted, for example, to the CBD (central business district) as one body is attracted to another, no general statements about the movement of people have been formulated which can meet minimum requirements of lawfulness. In the absence of such laws our understanding of why people are attracted to the CBD is dependent on our appreciating that in the context of modern economies it makes good sense for many individuals to transact their business in a central location. Whether geographers recognize it or not they are constantly rethinking the thoughts of those being investigated, and their best explanations are those relating thought and action in real-world situations. Not all work in geography will be concerned with explanation; many studies aim to establish facts rather than explain them. Such studies are obviously an important contribution to the discipline, because we cannot explain the real world until we know what is in need of explanation. However, the ultimate goal of geography is not seen as accurate description but as the explanation of the phenomena of the earth's surface. It is in this task that idealism is advocated as a responsible and viable alternative to the law-seeking theoretical approach of logical positivism.

Idealism is seen as an appropriate philosophy for a fundamental understanding of human behaviour similar to the kind of fundamental understanding theoretical knowledge gives us of the physical world. Although the idealist approach is essentially academic in the sense that an idealist is concerned not with manipulation but with understanding, the results of the kind of fundamental understanding provided by idealist analysis are, just as fundamental physical research, of potential practical value. Planning is obviously premised on an understanding of situations as they exist. The scholar makes a valid contribution to society by providing (as far as this is possible) an unbiased account of a society. It must be left to the planners, politicians, and other activists to use the knowledge academics provide them. An accurate perspective on the world and its problems is unlikely to emerge from scholars who are engaged in political action themselves, whether or not such action is in the interests of weak or powerful interest groups.

There might be some logical positivists who would describe any explanation which attempted to provide an accurate account of what happened as an 'explanation sketch'. In other words, explanation of human actions in terms of ideas is open to a logical positivist interpretation, and an important debate in the philosophy of history has centered on this question (Dray, 1966; Hook, 1963; Nash, 1969). The logical positivist attempt to bring history within the scientific fold has met with considerable opposition from historians and philosophers of history. I am of the opinion that the idealist interpretation of thought-dependent explanations is most convincing, but would be glad to leave the debate about the precise logical character of explanation to philosophers. It seems to me that geographers will achieve all that can be expected of them if their explanations are based upon a careful analysis of available data, are interpretative in the sense that the causes behind phenomena are investigated, are open to criticism, modification, and, perhaps, rejection, and are not unduly influenced by preconceived theories or dogmatic beliefs. In short, if geographers can create a critical, intellectual field with an emphasis on sound scholarship, the question of the precise logical form of explanation will take care of itself. Too often geographers have made a fetish of methodology and emphasized a particular form of enquiry—all of which means little if the studies conforming to a contemporary fad are devoid of ideas or insight, or lack empirical support.

CONCLUSION

The basic objectives of the logical positivist movement remain of importance to science, including geography. The logical positivists sought to establish knowledge of the world on secure logical and empirical foundations. To this end they gave considerable attention to the problem of meaning in language. They held that many problems of traditional philosophy were the result of philosophers failing to appreciate the structure of language and its implications. Other problems arose when philosophers failed to define their terms in ways which could be verified. The logical positivists were particularly opposed to metaphysical doctrines which they saw as being without empirical support. All knowledge (with the exception of identities) must be grounded in experience and must be capable of verification. This objective is certainly worthy of support from all geographers who wish to see communicable research results open to empirical verification and critical analysis.

The logical positivists presented a philosophy of explanation based on their fundamental objectives. This philosophy made no distinction between kinds of empirical phenomena and argued that there were no fundamental differences between the physical and social sciences. This was the doctrine of the unity of science and it constituted a basic tenet of the logical positivist movement. For the logical positivists scientific explanation was assessed in terms of the deductive-nomological model. A scientific explanation, whether it dealt with atoms or people, was one which conformed to the deductive-nomological model. On this model, prediction and explanation were logically identical. The model provided a rigorously objective means of testing candidate laws or hypotheses before endowing them with empirical status. It also enabled scientists to eliminate such pseudo-theories as astrology on empirical grounds. Deductive-nomological explanation, however, can only be successful where reasonably well-confirmed laws are available.

The deductive-nomological model has undoubtedly worked well in the physical sciences where experimental procedures are well developed. Its application in social science and history has created several difficulties. On the logical positivist view, one either has deductive-nomological explanation or one does not have an explanation at all, and considerable attention has been given to making the model workable in social science and history. Yet the deductive-nomological model cannot be modified in any basic way without weakening the very reason for its existence, namely, as a means of providing objective explanations of empirical phenomena. If empirical criteria for acceptance of a theory or law are relaxed, one might allow certain intuitively reasonable theories or laws to be included in an explanation. The danger, however, is that by weakening empirical criteria of acceptance one allows the entry of intuitively unreasonable propositions and pseudo-scientific theories (i.e. one has no logical grounds to exclude them). If one excludes these propositions on intuitive grounds, the very reason for the existence of the deductive-nomological model is threatened, because it was formulated with the intention of eliminating subjective judgement in the acceptance or rejection of empirical propositions.

Several geographers who accepted the basic deductive-nomological model have considered problems of its application in geography. Hartshorne, in discussing the scientific character of geography, argued that the complexity of the earth's surface made it difficult for geographers to discover laws. On pragmatic rather than logical grounds, he considered it unlikely that many laws would be discovered in geography. Schaefer rightly maintained that laws were the essence of science and concluded that geographers should seek to discover spatial laws. This conclusion does not follow, but it provided a powerful incentive for geographers to abandon the study of the unique in exchange for more tractable spatial problems. Schaefer, in calling for laws, never defined exactly what he meant, and gave little attention to their empirical verification. Harvey gave a more detailed account of explanation in terms of logical positivist principles, but he, too, remained vague about verification criteria of laws and theories.

The modern geographers who have attempted to fit geography within deductive-nomological explanation have often done so by sacrificing key concepts of the model itself. This allows explanation to have the form of the deductive-nomological model but not the substance. If deductive-nomological explanations or general explanations of concrete phenomena are to have any explanatory power, it seems reasonable to insist that such explanations rest on laws or theories meeting the minimum criteria of verification. In other words, laws and theories must be testable and refutable if they are to be accorded empirical status and explanatory power. If such laws are unavailable then deductive-nomological explanation is not possible. The logical positivists were in fundamental agreement that unverifiable theoretical constructs had no place in science.

If deductive-nomological explanations are problematical in human geography, it remains to suggest an alternative. I think the majority of geographers would agree that geography must remain a science in the broad sense that it should be founded on observation and that explanation should be open to critical analysis. It should always be possible to object to an explanation if the meaning of its terms is not clear. Where geographers seek to explain phenomena in terms of causes—be they theories, laws, or tentative hypotheses—all other geographers have a right to demand that the evidence on which an explanation rests be open to general scrutiny. I would think that geographers could all support a geography dedicated to clarity, consistency, and critical analysis of all explanations.

On the basis of the criteria set out in the previous paragraph, we can eliminate some approaches to geography. Marxism is rejected not because it is not suggestive, not because it contains no insight, but because it is an untestable theory. It is speculative rather than critical in approach. Or, briefly, the Marxists accept certain propositions as a basis for analysis. The task of empirical research is to show how events conform to these propositions rather than to devise ways of testing them. At the same time we can eliminate all general theories in geography which are not formulated in a way in which they are testable or refutable. Phenomenology can also be dismissed as being too subjective as the foundation of a scientific-type discipline. The phenomenologists might, for example, provide evocative descriptions of the lives of Appalachian mountain folk, but in geography we must seek verifiable, communicable knowledge rather than evocative descriptions of doubtful empirical status.

In a recent paper King (1976, p. 308) suggested that

> The emphasis in economic and urban geography should be shifted from the formal analysis of sterile propositions relating to abstract competitive settings to less formal, but still rigorous, analysis of real world situations in which values, conflict, power, the public sector, and the individual are given greater prominence.

How such a programme might be achieved within a positivist framework is by no means clear, but the idealist approach seems perfectly suited to the emphasis advocated by King. The idealist is concerned with real-world situations (or unique ones as they might have been described before the quantitative revolution) because this approach is premised on understanding concrete situations without laws or theories. Moreover, values, conflict, and power are unlikely to be understood without an investigation of the ideas guiding the actions of those under study. Such ideas will only be properly understood if placed within the context of a society or culture. In other words, actions cannot be understood in terms of reasons unless the social, economic, political, and geographical factors likely to influence individual and group decisions are reasonably well known. Idealism I believe permits, in principle, investigations of real-world situations unbiased by formal theory, but an individual researcher, of course, is unlikely to be free from all biases; the ultimate quality of our explanations in geography will rest upon the critical assessment they receive from the profession as a whole.

REFERENCES

Ashby, R. W. (1964). Logical positivism. In D. J. O'Connor (Ed.), *A Critical History of Western Philosophy*, The Free Press, New York.

Burton, I. (1963). The quantitative revolution and theoretical geography. *The Canadian Geographer*, **7**, 151–162.
Buttimer, A. (1976). Grasping the dynamism of life world. *Annals, Association of American Geographers*, **66**, 277–292.
Carnap, R. (1959). The elimination of metaphysics through the logical analysis of language. In A. J. Ayer (Ed.), *Logical Positivism*, The Free Press, Glencoe, Illinois.
Carter, H. (1975). *The Study of Urban Geography*, 2nd ed. Edward Arnold, London.
Chorley, R., and Haggett, P. (1967). Models, paradigms and the new geography. In R. Chorley and P. Haggett (Eds.), *Models in Geography*, Methuen and Co. London. pp. 19–41.
Clark, K. G. T. (1950). Certain underpinnings of our arguments in human geography. *Transactions, Institute of British Geographers*, **16**, 15–22.
Collingwood, R. G. (1946, 1956). *The Idea of History*, Oxford University Press, New York.
Dray, W. (Ed.) (1966). *Philosophical Analysis and History*, Harper and Row, New York.
Golledge, R. G., Brown, L. A., and Williamson, F. (1972). Behavioural approaches in geography: an overview. *The Australian Geographer*, **12**, 59–79.
Gould, P. (1969). *Spatial Diffusion*, Commission on College Geography. Resource Paper No. 4, Association of American Geographers, Washington, D. C.
Guelke, L. (1971). Problems of scientific explanation in geography. *The Canadian Geographer*, **15**, 38–53.
Guelke, L. (1974). An idealist alternative in human geography. *Annals, Association of American Geographers*, **64**, 193–202.
Guelke, L. (1977). Regional geography. *Professional Geographer*, **29**, 1–7.
Hartshorne, R. (1939). *The Nature of Geography*, Association of American Geographers, Lancaster, Pennsylvania.
Hartshorne, R. (1959). *Perspective on the Nature of Geography*, Rand-McNally and Company, for the Association of American Geographers, Chicago.
Harvey, D. (1969). *Explanation in Geography*, Edward Arnold, London.
Harvey, D. (1973). *Social Justice and the City*, Edward Arnold, London.
Hempel, C. G. (1959). The empiricist criterion of meaning. In A. J. Ayer (Ed.), *Logical Positivism*, The Free Press, Glencoe, Illinois.
Hempel, C. G. (1965). *Aspects of Scientific Explanation*, The Free Press, New York.
Hook, S. (Ed.) (1963). *Philosophy and History*, New York University Press, New York.
Jones, E. (1956). Cause and effect in human geography. *Annals, Association of American Geographers*, **46**, 369–377.
King, L. J. (1976). Alternatives to a positive economic geography. *Annals, Association of American Geographers*, **66**, 293–308.
Kraft, V. (1953). *The Vienna Circle: The Origin of Neo-positivism*, Philosophical Library, New York.
Martin, A. F. (1951). The necessity for determinism. *Transactions, Institute of British Geographers*, **17**, 1–12.
Montefiore, A. C., and Williams, W. M. (1955). Determinism and possibilism. *Geographical Studies*, **2**, 1–11.
Murdie, R. A. (1965). Cultural differences in consumer travel. *Economic Geography*, **41**, 211–233.
Murdie, R. A. (1969). *Factorial Ecology of Metropolitan Toronto*. Research Paper No. 116, Department of Geography, University of Chicago, Chicago.
Nash, D. H. (Ed.) (1969). *Ideas of History 2: The Critical Philosophy of History*, E. P. Dutton and Company, New York.
Passmore, J. (1968). *A Hundred Years of Philosophy*, 2nd ed. Penguin Books, Harmondsworth.
Rees, P. H. (1970). Concepts of social space: toward an urban social geography. In B. J. L. Berry and F. E. Horton (Eds.), *Geographic Perspectives on Urban Systems*, Prentice-Hall, Englewood Cliffs, New Jersey. pp. 306–94.

Rushton, G. (1969). Analysis of spatial behavior by revealed space preference. *Annals, Association of American Geographers*, **59**, 391–400.
Schaefer, F. K. (1953). Exceptionalism in geography: a methodological examination. *Annals, Association of American Geographers*, **43**, 226–249.
Smith, R. H. T. (1965). The functions of Australian towns. *Tijdschrift voor Economische en Sociale Geografie*, **56**, 81.
Von Mises, R. (1968). *Positivism: A Study in Human Understanding*, Dover Publications, New York.
Wittenstein, L. (1922). *Tractatus Logico-Philosophicus*, translated by C. K. Ogden. Kegan Paul, London.

Chapter 3

Urban Models in the Planning Process

Michael Batty

INTRODUCTION

It is now over twenty years since Voorhees (1955) presented his famous paper outlining a general theory of traffic movement, thus initiating a period of intense activity in the development of systematic methods of land-use and transportation planning. Voorhees' work was and still remains a landmark in the field, for not only did it represent the fact that traffic could be modelled quantitatively—a fact which had been known then for some years (Lighthill and Whitham, 1955)—but it also served to demonstrate and disseminate the idea that theories and models of traffic flow could be used to inform planners about traffic problems and possible solutions to such problems. Since the late 1930s, traffic congestion had become a significant problem in North American cities, inhibiting movement in the central city and leading to a flight of economic activity to the less-congested suburbs, and by the early 1950s the problem had become serious enough to justify a systematic attack by traffic engineers. The first large-scale transportation studies fostered the development of operational models based on theories of traffic flow, these models being used to gain a deeper understanding of the complexity of movement in cities and, perhaps more significantly, to provide an 'artificial laboratory' in which the traffic engineer could 'experiment' with possible solutions to the transport problem. And these artificial laboratories were only made possible by the enormous advances in computer technology which have continued apace in the post-war years.

The relationship between traffic and land use, which now seems so obvious, was also an area for some debate during the 1950s. Problems of traffic, traditionally the prerogative of engineers, were immediate and pressing, and it is not surprising that the first transportation studies treated land use as a peripheral concern. But the publication of Mitchell and Rapkin's (1954) book *Urban Traffic: A Function of Land Use* did much to convince engineers of the importance of land use as the generator of traffic, and by the late 1950s transport planners began to consider explicitly the configuration and structure of land use. The traffic models and transport planning process developed during these years naturally led to the idea that land use might also be modelled using appropriate theoretical structures, and in 1959 the first land-use models were attempted by Hansen (1959) in Washington and by Harris (1960) in Penn-Jersey. Thus, within the space of a decade, urban planners like transport planners had the rudiments of an artificial laboratory in which to generate and test land-use plans. A concern for solving transport and land-use problems, together with the new computer technology, did not alone present the possibility for developing operational models: the appropriate theory also had to exist. In the field of transportation, elementary theories of traffic generation, distribution, and assignment based on a mixture of common sense and analogy with physical theory provided the basis for modelling; combined with available micro- and macroeconomic theories of location such as central place theory, regional economic (Keynesian) theory, and so on, these ideas constituted a minimal base on which to develop land-use models. In these early years, the motivation for modelling largely came from planners and engineers, and although theorists responded by producing refined and often new, more relevant theory, the dominant thrust for the development of urban models came from and continues to come from practitioners.

It would be wrong to give the impression that urban theorists were unaware of or disinterested in the practical usefulness of their research, although a cursory review of the field might lead to the idea that theory and practice are less integrated than is scientifically acceptable. But there are good reasons for this, and these relate to the intrinsic and perennial difficulties faced by social scientists in applying the formal canons of scientific inquiry. This problem of testing a theory against reality will be broached again and again in this paper in an effort to highlight the philosophical difficulties faced in applying theory to urban planning. In the post-war years, however, social science theory in general and urban theory in particular have been intensely developed, and the ethos which surrounded social science has been so important to the development of urban models that a brief review of the critical issues is essential. Many will be familiar with the fact that post-war social science has been dominated by the quest for rigour and systematic exposition, and although the roots of this quest can be traced back indefinitely, it was in the 1920s and 1930s that the real momentum for these developments were established. Shackle (1967) refers to this time as 'the years of high theory' when the formal systems which characterize modern economics were laid down by Keynes, Hicks, Kaldor, and Samuelson, among others. In psychology, in sociology, in political science, too, as well as in the more hybrid field of locational economics, the foundations were being laid for modern theory. And all of these theories were characterized by the common assumption that progress and understanding could only come through rigorous exposition, which inevitably implied the use of axiomatic mathematical analysis. By 1950, an enormous momentum had been built up, and for the first time new developments in mathematics, such as game theory and certain aspects of topology, were also being fostered by the social as well as the physical sciences.

Paralleling these developments, there were forces at work to unify science itself. Of particular significance to social science was the development of the general systems theory (Bertalanffy, 1970) which sought to interpret and advance the diverse branches of science as special or specific forms of a general systems model. Such a model was phrased in terms of system structure and behaviour, of a hierarchy of subsystems and components, of a control function, and of system states such as equilibrium. This model has found immediate use in social science as witnessed by the flurry of books which have appeared entitled 'A Systems Approach to ... '. In the fields of location theory and land-use–transportation planning, developments have occurred which can be seen as part of this wider context. Location theory has not resisted the steady march of mathematical economics, nor the quantitative revolution of the geographical sciences; in planning, too, explicitly systematic processes of decision and action have been developed. Indeed, the change from the architectural focus of the subject to a fully fledged social science has been accomplished in less than a decade (McLoughlin, 1969) and it is instructive to note that these developments have occurred in the later rather than earlier post-war period. The implication of this discussion is that this period of systematic social science is being drawn to a natural end due to certain difficulties which have been encountered and in no way resolved. In another sense, the optimism of the earlier period has given way to a more pessimistic view of what can be accomplished rigorously, and in the future a more considered and tentative view is likely to dominate the development of social science. It is not appropriate to develop this point here, but later in this paper the difficulties which beset systematic social science in general will be illustrated by urban modelling in particular, for this field provides an admirable case study.

This, then, is the context for a discussion of urban models in the planning process. This paper attempts to examine, in as comprehensive a way as possible, the use of urban models—i.e. mathematical models of cities and regions designed for solution on a digital computer—which inform the planner about urban location problems and their solution. From one point of view, the subject area is quite restrictive for the models which will be outlined relate mainly to the spatial configuration of the urban system and say little about the aspatial or non-spatial processes which inevitably structure the space. In a similar way, the use of the models is restricted to an explicitly spatial or physical planning process, a process which is based on the type of broad-brush strategy planning characteristic of British physical planning in the last decade. The urban models which are described have been developed primarily in response to this type of planning process (Batty, 1972), and related models such as those dealing with non-spatial problems of resource allocation in local government, with corporate or social planning, for example, will not be developed here. Yet the restrictive nature of the discussion still permits some generalization, for the problems faced in developing urban models are similar to the problems faced in developing other models, and this enables some conclusions to be drawn about the general issues in developing models for social problem solving.

As a prelude to describing the use of specific models in a specific planning situation, it is important to establish in some detail what the model-building process is attempting to do, what the planning process is attempting to do, and how these two processes relate to one another. It is possible to develop a perspective on urban modelling by tracing the relationship between certain theories and models, but although such relationships will be alluded to throughout the paper, a more relevant focus here is on the *processes* of modelling and planning. Already, the strong practical–procedural motivation for land-use and transportation models has been mentioned, and many of the critical issues involved in using models in the planning process relate to methodology rather than substantive theory. Hence the emphasis adopted here. The model-building process, which is an integral part of what is loosely called 'the scientific method', is first discussed and the relationship between theory and model is stressed. A classification of models is produced which helps to introduce the terminology and techniques defining the field. The planning process as it has developed in Britain during the last decade is then introduced; the important distinctions between technical and political aspects, between positive and normative orientations, and between passive and active systems are mentioned. The way in which the model-building process fits into the planning process and vice versa is then illustrated, and this provides a structure on which to develop more substantive discussion.

Clearly it is impossible in a review such as this to deal with all types of urban model, but there is a class of urban models which demonstrates a large number of the characteristics of all urban models, and such models will be described here. Linear and non-linear techniques, partial and general systems, aspatial forecasting and spatial allocation procedures, positive and normative (optimization) orientations—these are some of the notions which will be introduced, and an attempt will be made to hammer together the rudiments of an operational urban model using these ideas. To provide a real demonstration of urban models in the planning process, it is necessary to have a real example, and the rest of this review will deal with the application of this operational model to the process of New Town planning, using Peterborough as an example. The process of building the model of Peterborough will then be described: the design of the spatial system, the algorithms required, the data base, and the statistical estimation of the model will be detailed. At this point, the model will be used in the planning process in two ways: to test the proposed New Town plan for Peterborough which is at present being implemented and to show how the model can inform the planner about alternative New Town plans. Some exceedingly thorny issues are raised in such an exercise which involve the juxtaposition of positive and normative thinking, and it is hoped to demonstrate how such a practical process focuses on some of the most difficult questions of social science philosophy.

Another challenge will be taken up in this paper, and that involves a non-algebraic exposition of these ideas. For those who are accustomed to using formal mathematical language, it is often difficult to present these ideas any differently. But as planners in particular and social scientists in general are not steeped in mathematics, some translation is required in the interests of communication. Fortunately, most of the ideas of social science, even the most esoteric theorems of general equilibrium analysis and welfare economics, can be and should be explained simply and intuitively, and it is quite possible and most desirable to explain urban models in this way. And after all, the central purpose of this paper is to explain how models can be used in planning, rather than to develop model-building skills which can be acquired elsewhere (Batty, 1976; Wilson, 1974). To avoid any possible ambiguity, however, a technical appendix will contain a formal statement of the model developed and used in Peterborough, for this will enable more technically minded readers to explore these models further.

THE MODEL-BUILDING PROCESS

Models, theories, and the scientific method

The term 'model', in its current usage, involves a well-defined process on which to develop a theoretical understanding of some real phenomena, and the notions of theory and model must be regarded as complementary and interdependent. In short, the model-building process can be regarded as one in which theory is tested and refined, and it is thus an integral part of the scientific method. In essence, any theory involves an abstraction from the complexity of the reality and a good theory is some statement of order or pattern for what, at first sight, might appear to be chaos. But a good theory is not only this, for the statement must be generally recognized as useful in aiding understanding. In this sense, a good theory is one in which new perspectives or insights are generated by simplification. Usually, this simplification occurs in such a way that the *essential* order is extracted from the chaos, that the 'noise' which surrounds reality is filtered out in an efficient and parsimonious way. The process of theory formulation and testing is accomplished intuitively by setting hypotheses from which testable propositions can be deduced, or by inducing hypotheses from specific situations which also lead to propositions, testable on other situations. In all cases, theories are sets of testable propositions which are to be refuted or not by comparison with reality. There are different degrees of refutation but this process, which is loosely called the scientific method, is clearly cyclic, as is shown in Figure 3.1. Starting with hypotheses and tracing the cycle through experiment to a comparison against reality is commonly called 'deduction', in contrast to the process which begins with observation which is called 'induction'. In any real situation, there is much to-ing and fro-ing around this cycle, for nothing is purely inductive or deductive, yet Figure 3.1 captures the essential circularity of science and the scientific method.

The cyclical process is an intrinsically useful way of introducing the role of modelling in science, for the concept of a model hinges around the notion of a testable proposition. In science, testable propositions are usually developed in a direct sense in the laboratory, where the theory is used to predict the form of the

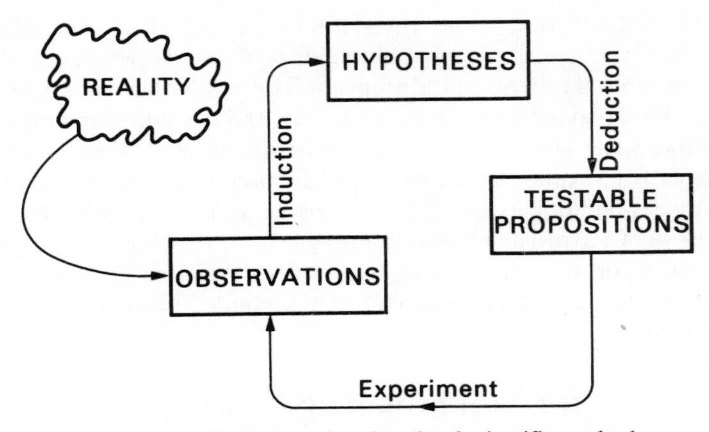

FIGURE 3.1. The conventional cycle of scientific method

real phenomena. The laboratory serves to compare controlled prediction with observations of the controlled but real phenomena. Although laboratory conditions do not exactly represent the phenomena in the real world, the link between laboratory and reality is determinate. That is, the results obtained are transferable from laboratory to reality because the real phenomena have been experimented with *directly*, even if under controlled conditions. In complete contrast, the social scientist can never test propositions directly on the phenomena of interest, for obvious reasons. Apart from the fact that real phenomena such as cities are impossible to control or observe in a laboratory sense, there are few societies which would tolerate such experimentation, for ethical reasons. Thus, in the social sciences and indeed in certain natural sciences, which deal with animate, sentient phenomena (medicine, for example), the idea of testing propositions directly is an anathema.

In these circumstances, experimentation must be *indirect*; propositions must be tested not on the actual phenomena but on an 'artificial' form of the phenomena, and thus the notion of a model of the phenomena appears. Indeed, a working definition of a model might be taken as a tool for testing theory in an artificial rather than natural environment, indirectly rather than directly on the real phenomena of interest. A model represents the juxtaposition of theory and laboratory, useful for indirect experimentation, and thus such a model must constitute the *modus operandi* of the social sciences. In this sense, a model is a translation of a theory into a form which is testable, and Harris's (1966a) definition which states that 'a model is an experimental design based on theory' appropriately sums up these points. From this discussion, it might be thought that models are the peculiar prerogative of the social and human sciences, but this is not the case; many types of physical phenomena, in fact most types, can be represented artificially using mathematical symbolism in computer environments. Thus models are useful in all fields. But in the social sciences they are essential, for scientific progress is impossible without them. Therefore

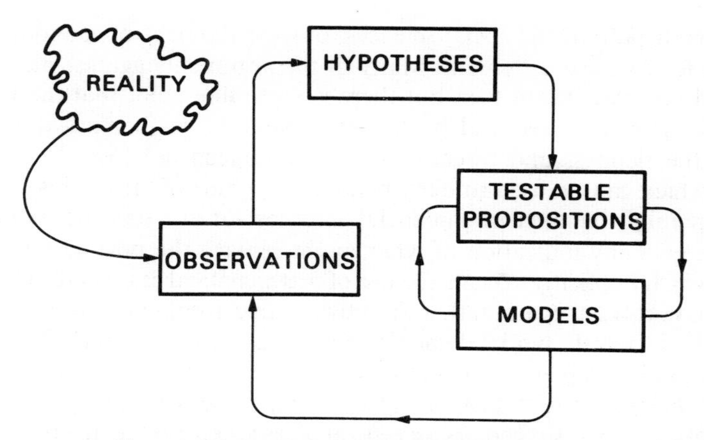

FIGURE 3.2. Models in the scientific method

the design of a model based on a theory constitutes an additional stage in the cycle of scientific method which involves the development of an artificial form of the phenomena under study. The diagram in Figure 3.1 can thus be modified to incorporate the idea of a model; this is accomplished in Figure 3.2.

In Figure 3.2, the steps between the various stages in the cycle involve thought processes which inevitably involve abstraction, simplification, and changes in the amount of information transmitted. There is an inevitable filtering process at work between these stages in which information is distorted and changed so that the succeeding stage is feasible. In Ashby's (1956) terms, each step represents a loss in the variety of the original reality, although if requisite variety is maintained, this loss is not critical. For the theory to be useful, requisite variety must be sought for only then will the theory have any explanatory power. Of particular concern here is the step between theory and model. It is most unlikely that models capable of being tested in the traditional scientific way can capture all the essential features of the theory to which they relate. Social science theories tend to be highly ambiguous, but for purposes of testing models must be completely unambiguous. Implicit in this discussion is the fact that operational models which generate artificial phenomena must be mathematical in form and probably computable. This is not always the case; for example, Ashby's (1952) model of an ultrastable system—his 'Homeostat'—was constructed out of a magnet, electrodes, wire, and water, and was used to demonstrate stability in the human nervous system. Ashby also demonstrated the same principle using a mathematical system, thus showing that different 'artificial' environments can be used to simulate the same phenomena. Nevertheless, the most general models to date have been mathematical, but this does not mean that models will always be cast in this mould. It was Bertrand Russell who said that we use mathematics to describe the world because we have not yet invented anything better.

In many fields, the use of mathematics is no longer an issue, but there is still enormous dispute in the social sciences, outside the field of economics, as to the need for axiomatic thought. Many of the arguments against mathematics are based on prejudice or fear, but there is a genuine point that the variety of social life is often so reduced by theory capable of mathematical expression that all the richness and essence of the phenomena are lost. And there are models which can be used to demonstrate this point of view. This is likely to be a perennial dilemma of the social sciences for the essentialist argument does not give any indication of what might replace the normal scientific approach which implicitly accepts the use of mathematical reasoning. This debate is long and protracted, and rather than spend time arguing the merits of mathematics, it is worth while demonstrating the need for both models and mathematics in the planning field by example.

In the 1930s, theories purporting to explain the size and distribution of cities containing market centres, or central places, were postulated by Christaller (1933) and Losch (1944). Central place theory, as it became known, was concerned with explaining the size of market centres and the spacing of such centres by reference to the competitive structure of the market for service goods. Christaller derived the original theory inductively on the basis of observations on the settlement pattern in southern Germany, whereas Losch worked deductively towards the same types of hypotheses in the tradition of classical economics. But in no sense were these theories testable in any direct way until a decade or so ago, when techniques of analysis had progressed sufficiently for the construction of an appropriate artificial environment. Developments of central place theory in the 1950s did involve some rudimentary testing of the theory, but this was accomplished on an almost superficial level using linear statistical models and graphical analysis. A good statement of these early tests of the theory is contained in the book by Berry (1967). Not until the development of mathematical models of retail behaviour in the early 1960s by Huff (1963), Lakshmanan and Hansen (1965), and McLoughlin, Nix, and Foot (1966) was full-scale testing even a possibility. Even then, these retail models were highly simplified representations of the early theory in which much information was lost, as reference to the recent survey by Davies (1976) shows. The early attempt by Reilly (1931) to develop a 'model' of the central place system cannot be considered an appropriate means for testing propositions about central place systems, for this 'model' involved comparing predicted and observed activity at retail centres, based on the definition of the shopping hinterland. And it has been known for some years that geographical space can be partitioned into zones or hinterlands which give exact, and hence trivial, predictions. As the hinterland is a derived, not observed, phenomenon, tests of models which use it as a basis for comparison cannot be considered as scientific.

There has never yet been a real test of the original central place theory of Christaller and Losch, for so much of the original theory is missing from the present-day retail models. Notions concerning hierarchy, product differentiation, demand and price, externalities, and so on have not yet been encompassed in a testable central place model, although there are signs that hierarchical and pricing strategies are now being incorporated into retail models (Guy, 1976; Wade, 1973; Wilson, 1975). With this rate of progress, the original theory will probably be tested within the next ten years, but it will take the design of more powerful mathematical models than are presently available to effect this. Little wonder that there is enormous dispute about the use of mathematics and the application of conventional scientific method if progress is so slow.

Models for prediction and prescription

A major goal of science is to devise theories which are powerful predictively, not only under the conditions which fostered their invention but under other conditions as well. Good theory therefore provides results which can be generalized to other situations—at other times, in other places. In what has been said already, it has been implied that the prime role of modelling is in explanation, in generalization, and in understanding the phenomena better, but this need not be entirely so. It is often argued in planning that the prime role of modelling is to provide a structure or a starting point for solving inherently difficult problems which have an undisciplined form. This argument does not assume that the model need be 'correct' in any testable sense for it to be useful. Thus, the model might help the analyst or planner to prescribe a better state of the world by imposing a discipline on the planning process where it is felt that such discipline is more important than correctness. In this sense, models might be used predictively to yield alternative solutions which are then compared in relative terms, thus suggesting that the absolute values produced by the model need not be 'correct' in terms of some reality. Despite this argument that models used prescriptively need not be predictively correct, most would agree that the first step in any planning process is to establish the predictive power of the model. Before prescriptive use, most planners would accept that useful models must be predictively 'correct' although the degree of correctness which would be taken as acceptable might be less than in the situation where the motivation for modelling was mainly for purposes of explanation. Therefore, the model-building process displayed in Figure 3.2 is still valid in terms of the planning process to be outlined here.

This question about the predictive or prescriptive role of the model also relates to the form of the model adopted and to the model-building process, and it must be explored from this viewpoint, as well as from the viewpoint of the planning process. Ideally, any model which is to be used for both predictive and prescriptive ends must be consistent in both contexts, and thus must be capable of addressing both sorts of issue. In practice, however, there is usually a strong distinction between predictive or 'positive' models, as they are called, and prescriptive or 'normative' models, due mainly to the way in which theory and technique have developed. Models have been developed for one purpose or the other, and there are few, if any, models which attempt to build in prediction and prescription as different ends of some logical continuum. This is largely because positive and normative structures have not been theoretically related in terms of changes in the social system. For example, it is difficult to see how a model could be built in which the superficially non-rational and actual behaviour of individuals, groups, and institutions could be related to the theories of rational, normative behaviour of those same entities. Consequently, because the process of change linking positive with normative has rarely been studied, different theories and indeed different techniques have come to characterize these two types of model, and these appear to be mutually exclusive of one another. An example suffices to illustrate the point: the locational behaviour of the household can be modelled using the economic theory of consumer choice based on utility maximization, and a variety of models starting with Alonso (1964) have sought to cast this type of spatial behaviour in such a mould. In essence, locational behaviour is seen as reflecting a rational process in which an individual chooses his allocation of scarce resources, one of which is housing, by maximizing his utility. The theory is intuitively appealing and elegantly conceived but has been rarely posed in a testable form. In contrast, other approaches to household location are explicitly positive: those based on statistical models, e.g. the Greensborough model of Chapin and Weiss (1962), seek to explain such behaviour by selecting variables which appear significant from the point of view of statistical theory. It is exceedingly difficult to see how both these models can be related, for they are founded on different techniques which cannot be collapsed into one another.

In the models to be outlined later in this paper, some predictive power is essential and thus the model-building process illustrated in Figure 3.2 will be used. At this stage, it is useful to elaborate the model-building process in a little more detail, for the actual process of comparing predictions with observations has yet to be described. To this end, it is necessary to provide some general definitions which relate to the structure of the model, for it is this structure which is manipulated during the model-building process. The components of any model, i.e. the observable elements of the theory on which the model is based, are described as 'variables' which are usually related in a formal sense by equations. In general, the set of variables can be partitioned into those whose values are known before the model is set up (the *input*, *independent*, or *exogenous* variables) and those whose values are predicted by the model (the *output*, *dependent*, or *endogenous* variables). It is assumed that the causal structure of the model is such that the input variables can be defined in an appropriate way. Often, the output variables are subdivided into intermediate and final variables, the intermediate variables being computed as a matter of course in the model but not holding the same predictive interest as the final output variables.

Associated with the model's variables and equations is another set of quantities which are called 'parameters'. These parameters are unknown in terms of their value, for their purpose is to give some measure of uniqueness to the model. Most theorists accept that no model can be general in every sense, for most mathematical systems are only general in a relative sense, e.g. up to a constant of proportionality. Parameters, sometimes called 'constants', are thus used to determine absolute values such as orders of magnitude, strengths of relationships, and rates of change. Clearly, these parameters have to be determined in every model application, and the process of estimating their value is called 'calibration'. The process is usually accomplished by trial and error or by numerical analysis using statistical measures which show how well the model fits the particular situation. Furthermore, there is a great deal of interest in the sensitivity of the model to changes in parameters, and much of the calibration process is regarded as one in which the 'robustness' of the model to withstand changes to the parameters is explored. In certain circumstances, the term 'calibration' is taken to include other aspects of the model-building process such as setting up the data system, designing computer algorithms, and so on, but here the term will be restricted to the parameter estimation process.

In no sense can the process of calibration be regarded as establishing the validity of the model's testable propositions, but there is enormous confusion about the role of calibration. Calibration is usually achieved by fixing the parameter values so that some measure of fit between the model's predictions and observations is optimized, although this is clearly a very different matter from establishing the validity of the model. However, because the process of examining the model's predictive power by comparing predictions with observations is superficially similar to the calibration process, some have confused calibration with validation (Sayer, 1975). It is possible to get a perfectly calibrated model in which predictions are identical to observations, and although calibration criteria which enable such mathematically trivial solutions to occur have occasionally been adopted, they are not generally used in urban modelling (Batty, 1976); criteria based on order-of-magnitude statistics, etc., are clearly more valid. Indeed, in a number of studies, although the model has been perfectly calibrated, the model's predictions have been poor, and this serves to show the essential difference between calibration and validation (Batty and March, 1976). In such a situation where the same set of observations is used for both calibration and validation, the only true test of the model is to use two different sets of observations, from different time periods for example. If calibration and validation criteria are the same, however, this will still not reveal the difference; what is logically essential in every model-building process is that, first, the criteria for calibration and validation must be different and, second, different sets of observations must be used for calibration and validation if this is possible (Lowry, 1965).

The process of testing a model's propositions cannot solely depend upon any single application, for only if sufficient examples are produced which demonstrate that the model's theory must be refuted will new theories and models be designed. Even in such a situation, the model may not be refuted because the model is intuitively acceptable in terms of the 'paradigm' which governs the subject area (Kuhn, 1962). In the opposite way, a model which cannot be refuted through application will not be accepted if it is counterintuitive. For example, the various activity-allocation models to be presented in

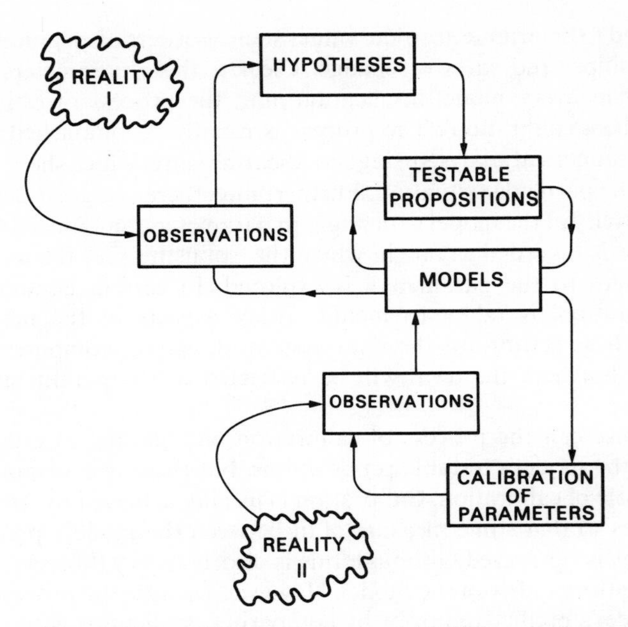

FIGURE 3.3. Calibration in the model-building process

this paper have performed well in terms of the match of predictions and observations, but are logically simplistic. Urban economic location models are logically complex and more intuitively acceptable, but the results of their testing have been disappointing. In such cases, neither model can be clearly rejected or accepted. To conclude this discussion, it is worth while extending the model-building process to include formally the calibration stage. This is demonstrated in Figure 3.3 where the difference between calibration and validation is clarified. Before this overall process is related to the planning process, further comment on the structure of models is necessary so that certain modelling terminology can be introduced.

Organizational principles for urban models

Hardly a paper is written reviewing urban models which does not contain some classification which is designed to clarify the wide array of available model types. This paper is no exception for dichotomous classification is an eminently useful way of quickly introducing the general reader to the theoretical and methodological issues in urban modelling. Urban modelling is potentially as large a field as urban theory, on the assumption that for every theory there is a model, and some means of grasping the essential arguments is necessary.

Rather than developing and classifying the various theories which underpin various urban models, a classification of models enables a general overview to be established, and in a later section this overview will be elaborated by reference to *particular* theories and models. The classification to be developed here has been used by others before, and it has been distilled from the reviews by Harris (1968), Lowry (1968), and Wilson (1968). A critical distinction can be made between substantive features or characteristics of a model, which mainly relate to theories, and methodological issues which relate to techniques. This distinction will be accepted here, and four substantive characteristics are first presented.

The positive–normative basis of any model has already been introduced, and this will be used time and again in the rest of this paper, but a particularly important characteristic is the degree of comprehensiveness of a model. One can distinguish between *partial* and *general* models, a partial model being one which is concerned with only one identifiable subsystem of the urban system and a general model being concerned with two or more subsystems. There has been a tendency in the development of urban models to seek more and more comprehensive forms, but it is now clear that there is no one-to-one correspondence between the degree of comprehensiveness and the degree of explanation. However, in the context of land-use planning, where there is particular concern about the interrelationships between land use, general models are likely to be more valued than partial. Yet many available models, e.g. shopping models, transport models, housing market models, and so on, are partial by their very nature, and thus there is continual tension between the quest for generality and what can actually be achieved. A second important distinction is with regard to the dynamic or temporal element. Models range from *static* through *quasi-dynamic* to *fully dynamic*, but in the development of the field most models have been conceived statically for a variety of reasons: time-series data have been difficult to obtain, urban theory has been static in that the spatial, not temporal, dimension has been the most important (Batty, 1970a), and dynamic effects have been difficult to hypothesize and almost impossible to observe. But herein lies another dilemma. Planning is concerned with change through time yet most operational models can only be used in a crude comparative static way.

The third and fourth characteristics relate to the level of aggregation of the model. First, models can be conceived at various levels of 'sectoral aggregation'; population can be disaggregated into various social, economic, age–sex groups, or cohorts, employment can be classified by occupations, industries, functional basis, and so on. This 'macro–micro' dimension relates to the classic aggregation problem in economics—relating the national economy to the various institutions, groups, and agents which make the economy work. Clearly, there are competing forces towards aggregation or disaggregation. Statistically, macromodels stand a better chance of validation, but in terms of explanation micromodels are preferable. From a data point of view, macromodels are more feasible, but the planning process may require models which are predictively useful at the microscale. The second type of aggregation is spatial, and spatially disaggregated models are necessarily useful to spatially disaggregate land-use planning. Yet there are many spatially aggregate models (population, employment forecasting models, etc.) which are used in planning, and this also exhibits a further tension between what is required and what is feasible. In terms of the models to be introduced here, these various dimensions provide an easy way to define the field. Most of the models relevant to the planning process, to be outlined in the following section, are positive in emphasis, both partial and general, static, macro from a sectoral viewpoint, and spatially disaggregate. In contrast, theoretical models such as those in urban economics tend to be normative, partial, static, micro, and spatially aggregate. A direct comparison of operational models, the subject of this discussion, with theoretical models can be seen by contrasting the models in the book by the author (Batty, 1976) with those in the book by Papageorgiou (1976).

From a technical perspective, there are three useful categories. By far the most important is the distinction between *linear* and *non-linear* forms of relationships, and this means of classification also has implications for theory. Because linear mathematics has been so thoroughly developed in comparison with non-linear, linear models are easier to build. But reality tends to be non-linear, and linear models can usually be seen as special cases of non-linear. In terms of models which use optimization, linear rather than non-linear are more feasible, but the inappropriateness of linear systems often means that such models are pervaded with difficulties concerning their representation of reality. In terms of optimization techniques which are essential to normative modelling, linear models are inappropriate and non-linear models are difficult to construct; thus there is a natural bias towards positive rather than normative modelling. In this paper, most of the models will be non-linear, and with this decision comes a much more hybrid approach to model development. Non-linear techniques are more appropriate to the kind of theory on which relevant urban models can be based, but there are fewer standard solution and estimation procedures available; consequently, trial-and-error procedures become the order of the day.

With regard to solution procedures, *direct* and *indirect* solution methods can be defined. Direct methods involve some immediate solution, often simultaneous, whereas indirect methods are sequential and embody trial-and-error, iterative, or recursive (cyclical) processes and simulation (solution in stages) techniques. Finally, the mathematical form which represents the model can be classified as *continuous* or *discrete*. The models developed here are necessarily discrete in that this is necessary for their operation, although they originally might be based on continuous functions. A good example of such a continuous model, operated in discrete terms, is the interaction model due to Angel and Hyman (1976) which is capable of analysis in continuous terms. However, most of the models presented here are not usually represented in continuous terms, for they are not as capable of extensive mathematical analysis as are urban economic models, for example. In this sense, such models are based more on operational than on theoretical considerations. A final point is worth stressing: the models to be outlined here have been designed primarily for use in the urban planning process, and although their theoretical basis is important, there is a continuing dilemma between what is feasible in practice and what is theoretically acceptable. In the following section, the requirements of urban models from the viewpoint of the planning process will be outlined and in later sections an attempt will be made to demonstrate the model-building and planning processes using actual models and a real example.

THE PLANNING PROCESS

Active and passive, normative and positive systems

There is an essential difference between the development of models for predictive or prescriptive use which lies at the heart of social science philosophy. Predictive modelling assumes that the system of interest is stable, constant, or *passive* whereas in prescriptive modelling the system of interest is clearly *active* or changing, in that prescriptions alter the form of the system itself. Notwithstanding Heisenberg's principle of uncertainty in modern physics, for this level of discussion physical systems can be regarded as passive whereas social systems are active. Thus, the task of making observations, predictions, or prescriptions on a social system alters the system itself and confounds the analysis. Therefore, any model-building process which treats the social system as passive cannot be completely acceptable. This, then, is the crux of the argument against the use of scientific method in social science, and it has enormous implications for the future development of these subject areas. Taken to an ultimate conclusion, all the canons of scientific inquiry can be turned upside down; e.g. if reality can never be regarded as constant, then there is never any way of validating a theory apart from discovering some universal theory, which is philosophically and logically impossible. At the same time, no social science theory can ever be proven right or wrong even in the most restrictive sense. There seems no way out for the use of the scientific method in social science, but if science is not to be used, this is a prescription for doing nothing, for there is nothing to replace it.

There are ways around this dilemma, however, which do not resolve the problem but do help the analyst to proceed. Usually, a degree of constancy or passiveness in the reality is assumed or the justification for modelling is taken to be the need for some discipline in social problem solving. This may seem a far cry from urban planning, but it is of fundamental importance. The question which is implicitly asked over and over again is: 'How is one able to use positive methods, validated on some passive reality, when one is concerned with normative problem solving on some active reality?' Put more directly in a planning context, the question concerns the reasons why planners use models of actual cities when they are concerned with designing better cities anyway. The answer relates to one of compromise: clearly, planning is partly a learning experience; the planner exists within some reality which is not completely changing and thus models of that reality enhance his understanding. The limits to which such models can and should be used in prescription is one of the central themes to be explored in this paper.

There is another dimension to this argument, and this relates once again to the extent to which the model takes on a positive or normative role. It is possible to build models of some reality which are general enough to encompass the planning function as some subsystem of the model. On the other hand, the model might be treated as some subsystem of a wider 'meta' system—the planning process. The extent to which the model will incorporate the planning function or the planning function will incorporate the model will vary from context to context, and will depend upon the degree of comprehensiveness of the model plus the extent to which positive and normative considerations can be related. There are models available which subsume the planning function directly; control engineering models, for example, embody the idea of control as a subsystem of a larger system, as do the centralized planning models of economics which are usually structured around some optimization procedure. In this context, however, the planning process and the model-building process are much more separate, although still interdependent. Positive models inform the normative process in such a way that models tend to be seen more as subsystems of the planning system. That is, land-use planning processes can exist quite separately from land-use models, and in the following section such planning processes and their relationship to urban models will be described.

The technical planning process

The process of physical planning which has developed in Britain over the last fifty years is a technical problem-solving function of government which, although largely independent of the political process, is complementary to it. The technical process is designed to inform: to provide advice to the political process where the actual decision making occurs. The process is also motivated by certain outside ideals adopted by the planners themselves, and thus the technical process is not purely advisory but has some informal executive power of its own. At the present time, this technical–political process is being very much tested due to the so-called 'failure' of government to 'deliver the goods' in the post-war years, and there are many suggestions for new planning processes in which technical and political considerations are more freely mixed (Friedmann, 1973; Michael, 1973; Schon, 1971). However, it is the technical process which is of importance here because it is this in which urban models have been developed.

The planning process attempts to devise more efficient, more socially just cities by rearranging their spatial form and by changing the rules which precondition the form—i.e. the space standards, the aesthetics, the pattern of movement, and so on. From very early times, planners attempting to do this have adopted a rational decision model which seeks to generate some best solution, solves the problems, and meets the ideals of the community at large. Until the early 1960s, the rational decision model was based on the simple notion that *one* best solution or master plan could be produced by a mainly intuitive process in which problems were first observed (survey), then understood (analysis), and finally solved (plan). This survey–analysis–plan problem-solving module was first formalized by the father of British town planning, Patrick Geddes (1915), some sixty years ago.

The developments in social science which fostered the field of urban modelling, described in the introduction, have also changed the form of the planning process in the last fifteen years. The systematic techniques of problem solving based on mathematical developments in optimization theory, game theory, and decision theory have all combined to provide a more explicitly rational model of plan making, in which mechanical procedures have been introduced to aid imagination and intuition. In particular, the techniques of operations research and cybernetic management (Beer, 1959) have been utilized. Perhaps the most important new concept in the planning process in recent years has been the notion of uncertainty. The idea that there may be many, not just *one*, solution to the planning problem has come from optimization theory in which the concept of a solution space is defined. Uncountable numbers of solutions appear to exist for almost trivial problems, and the combinatorial explosion which results from enumerating all possible solutions must be clearly managed by powerful techniques. In planning, the general idea that a series of alternative solutions might summarize in some way the form of the solution space has been introduced in the place of the single 'master plan'. Although certain gross assumptions have to be made about the boundedness and continuity of the solution space for the idea of alternatives to be tenable, these developments have required explicit techniques to *generate* and to *evaluate* large numbers of plans. Plan generation and plan evaluation have thus become the central stages of the rational planning process.

To generate and to evaluate alternative plans, some criterion of optimality, called an 'objective function', is necessary. Thus, early in the planning process a set of goals or objectives which the plan must meet must be prescribed. In turn, these goals depend upon problems to be solved and ideals to be met by the plan, and it is clear that the specification of sets of goals is a design or planning exercise in its own right: in fact, it is the idea that each stage of the planning process can be judged to be a planning process itself which gives the process its hierarchical character. The specification of goals, the generation of alternative plans to meet these goals, their evaluation, and the subsequent choice are stages of the process which are all informed and executed using models of a positive or normative nature. Models in this sense act as a buffer between the reality and the process for operating or changing the reality, and Figure 3.4 demonstrates this idea in relation to a conventional form of the physical planning process. Note that this process still embodies the original idea of survey–analysis–plan, although uncertainty about the plan is introduced through the notion of alternatives.

A major characteristic of the planning process is that the uncertainty is resolved by operating the process many times, i.e. by operating the process cyclically. Although the stages in Figure 3.4 appear to be related in a more-or-less

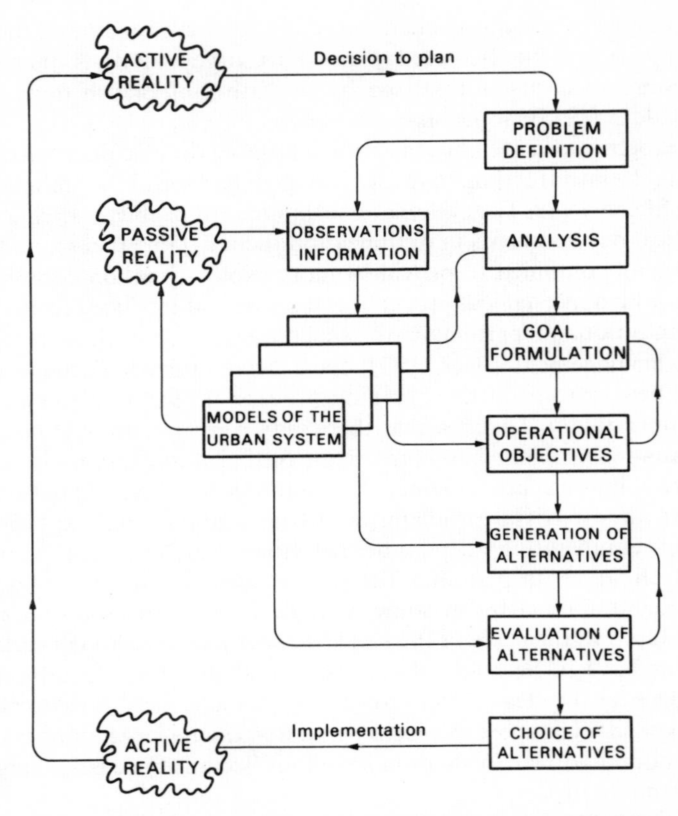

FIGURE 3.4. The planning process based on rational decision making

sequential fashion, there is likely to be much to-ing and fro-ing between the stages, and there is certainly no agreement as to the most appropriate starting point. Like the cyclical model-building process in which uncertainty about the most appropriate hypothesis is resolved through learning and experiment, the planning process is one of learning in a sequential fashion. For example, it may be that analysis of the existing system reveals a problem to be solved, and thus this involves a goal to be formulated, but, to study the problem in the first place, some goal as to what is required must be specified. Thought processes such as these cannot be organized simultaneously and therefore the planning process is inevitably cyclic rather than linear sequential (Boyce, Day, and McDonald, 1970).

An essential requirement for such cyclic processes is that they be convergent in some sense; i.e. that the number of alternative solutions to the problem be systematically narrowed by some error-correcting feedback. If the process is one of conscious learning, then this is likely to be so, but often the process has to be

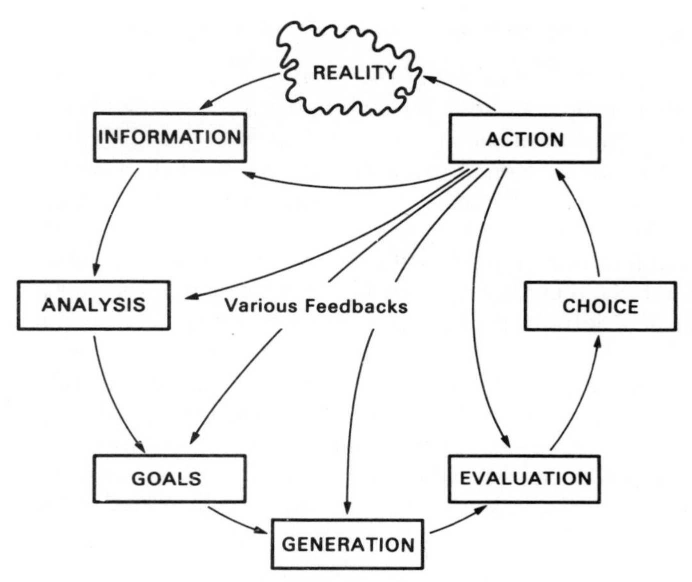

FIGURE 3.5. A fully cyclic planning process

terminated through constraints such as the time available. Chadwick's (1971) model of the process involves two stages, the first in which the solution space is fixed by alternative plans and the second in which a final plan is synthesized within the bounds set by the set of alternatives. Etzioni's (1968) model of planning as mixed scanning also develops a similar idea embodying high and lower level learning in which coarse bounds are set by scanning and then reworked in more detail. The most articulate cyclic process, however, is the strategic choice approach due to Friend and Jessop (1969), in which the notion of sequential learning is quite explicit. The process is illustrated in Figure 3.5 and in more recent expositions (Bather, Williams, and Sutton, 1976; Hickling, 1974) the cyclic nature of the process is assumed to operate indefinitely through real time, with little need for the process to converge in any defined sense.

These planning processes are idealized models which do not necessarily match the actual process, although the relative independence of technical and political planning processes has meant that many technical processes similar to those in Figures 3.4 and 3.5 have been implemented. The convergence of such processes has not been explored either, and in practice it is clear that the exigencies of time have been used to effect a measure of closure on the process. Although these processes are hybrid in that they have evolved from a mixture of practical common sense and theoretical reasoning, most of the operational urban models developed to date have been designed to inform and help the planner through different stages of such a process. The model-building process in Figure 3.3 fits into the process in Figures 3.4 and 3.5, and in the following section the links between these two processes will be explored in more detail.

Relationships between the model-building and planning processes

It is worth while summarizing the form of these two processes and their general relationships towards one another before any detailed discussion is attempted. From the previous description, it is assumed that models of the urban system are developed using an explicit cycle of scientific method in which the phenomena of interest are assumed passive or unchanging. Various models are developed which are judged useful to different stages of the planning process, and thus these models will reflect both positive and normative aspects of urban and planning theories. Furthermore, these models are also developed on the basis of intuitively acceptable theories whose form is not exclusively dominated by the need for social action; models based on theories which are accepted purely for their explanatory value are therefore useful to planning. Finally, the outputs from the planning process clearly affect the reality in an active sense, and thus the whole process must be reworked if a new plan is to be prepared. Models which were validated previously may therefore be no longer valid. These general relationships are illustrated in Figure 3.6.

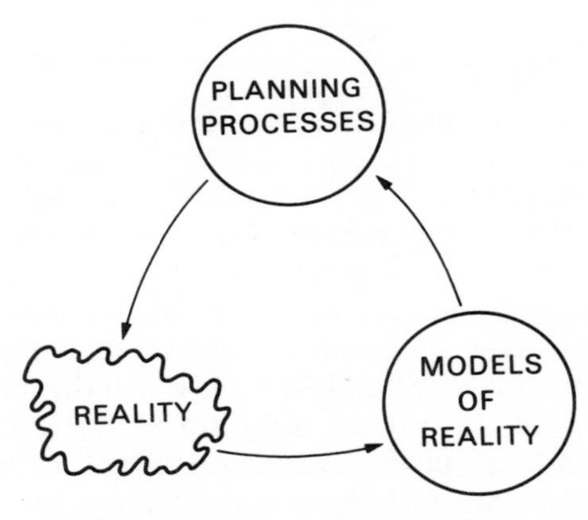

FIGURE 3.6. Assumed relationships between the model-building and planning processes

In the planning process outlined above, and illustrated in Figure 3.4, wherever the process draws upon information about the reality a model can be used to structure this activity. In fact, as was pointed out in an earlier section, any abstraction or indeed perception of the reality can be regarded as a model, although for these purposes the term 'model' will be restricted to the use of mathematical techniques at the various stages. There are two types of model, which merge into each other, that are useful in the process, and this distinction relates once again to positive and normative issues. Positive models of the urban system are clearly useful at various stages for increasing understanding about the planning problem (learning) or for elaborating upon normative plans in a positive way at the evaluation stage. Normative models, on the other hand, may be normative in terms of the urban system or normative in terms of the thought processes used to generate optimal plans. For example, linear programming models of the urban system such as the TOPAZ (technique for optimal placement of activities in zones) due to Brotchie and Sharp (1975), the South-east Wisconsin model (Schlager, 1965), and the extended Herbert—Stevens model (Wheaton, 1974), as well as the linear programming model presented in later sections of this paper, can be used to generate actual plans. The design models due to Alexander (1964) and Harris (1971) are normative in a different way, for these models are optimal with respect to the planning process rather than the urban system. In this paper, normative modelling will be restricted to the domain of the urban system.

As no one model is general enough to help the planner at every stage of the technical process, normally a variety of models are used of which one may be appropriate to one or several stages. Individually, each model may seem inconsistent with the others, but consistency is maintained through the discipline imposed by the planning process itself. A typical problem to which this type of modelling pertains can be described as follows: the problem is to prepare a land-use plan for a metropolitan area in which the main output is a pattern of land uses at some future date. There may be some aspatial aspects to the problem which relate to the processes which generate the spatial structure, but the dominant interest is in terms of location because it is felt that only spatial controls can be used to implement the plan. In such a case, it is very clear that models pertaining to each of the land uses in locational terms, or to any combination of these land uses, would be important. Moreover, different ways of modelling the same activity may be useful at different stages of the planning process, and to demonstrate these points models appropriate to each of these stages will be examined. Rather than illustrate these models in theoretical terms, it is worth while showing how actual models can be used at various stages of an actual planning process. In Figure 3.7, the process developed for the Nottinghamshire–Derbyshire subregional planning study is presented, and from this chart the various models used at different stages can be identified. Some elaboration of the types of model used in this study now follows, before the tenor of this paper changes towards an examination of the workings of urban models and their means of construction.

Early in the process in what is loosely referred to as the 'analysis stage', various partial and more general models were developed for the Nottinghamshire–Derbyshire study. For example, positive spatial models of the transport and retail systems, a more general spatial model linking these sectors to the residential sector (and similar to one of the models to be outlined later), and aspatial forecasting models of the employment and population sectors were developed. In each case, the model had to be calibrated in some sense to the subregion at a base date, although the means of calibration varied from simple direct calculation of rates in the case of the forecasting models to more complex, indirect numerical analysis for the spatial models. A further model based solely on normative considerations was also devised at an early stage to relate

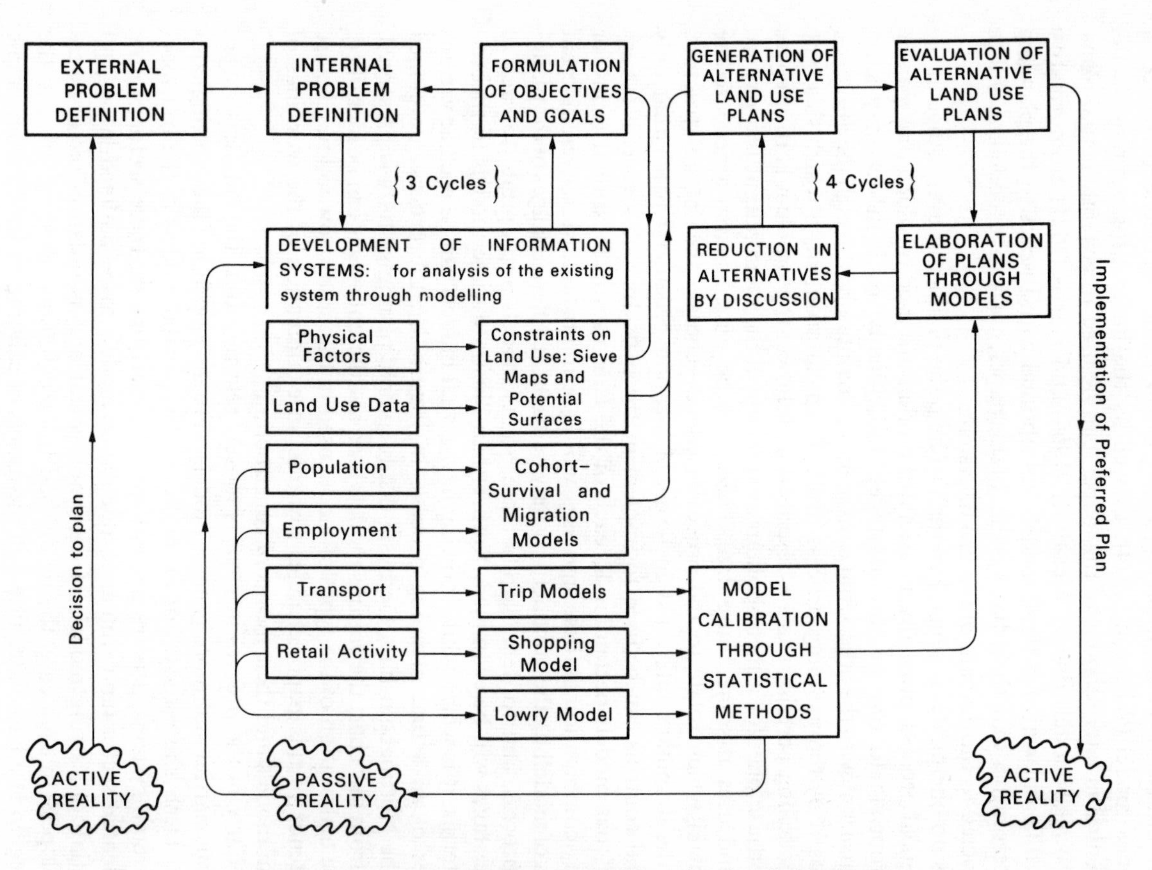

FIGURE 3.7. The Nottinghamshire–Derbyshire subregional planning process

land-use and physical constraint data to the generation process, but it was not necessary to calibrate this model.

These various models were all used to help generate and evaluate a series of alternative land-use plans which were progressively reduced to a single strategy in four cycles of generation and evaluation. The forecasting models were used to establish the orders of magnitude and land-use requirements of future population–employment levels, and variations in these predictions led to different sets of alternatives. In a spatial sense, the normative constraint model was used to bound the solution space by filtering or sieving out unsuitable land and searching for land of greatest potential. Finally, the spatial transport, shopping, and activity allocation models were used to fill in the detail of the alternative strategies in a positive sense, prior to evaluation. Thus these positive models were used as a brake or a check on the normative emphasis of the plan generation–evaluation phase. The actual generation of the strategies and their evaluation was achieved intuitively by the planners in brainstorming sessions, and in this case the results of modelling were only used to provide additional advice. One of the critiques of this type of process is that the use of such positive models tends to bias the plan towards a trend-based perpetuation of the existing reality. However, a careful analysis of these kinds of planning studies in Britain does not seem to support this view; in fact, it appears that there are several planning studies which have not used any type of positive modelling whereas there are none which have used only positive techniques. One final point is worthy of note, relating to the apparent duplication of models to treat the same phenomena. In such instances, this is usually acceptable due to the uncertainty surrounding the suitability of various techniques and the need to 'hedge one's bets'.

The context in terms of the rationale for model development within a technical plan-making process has now been established, and it is immediately clear that all possible types of model cannot be discussed in detail here. But it is possible to develop one particular general model of the urban system and to show how this can be used in the planning process, thus inferring and generalizing this experience to the use of other models. In the following sections, such a model will first be introduced not only in theoretical terms but also in terms suitable for the kind of planning problem described above. The actual design and construction of the model and its calibration will then be described, and finally its use will be illustrated in generating and evaluating alternative plans. In no sense will this discussion be totally comprehensive, but enough avenues should be opened to give readers an idea of the issues, the dilemmas, and the paradoxes which are involved in using urban models in the planning process.

THE STRUCTURE OF AN URBAN MODEL

Forecasting and location, generation and allocation

It is possible to classify the mechanisms used in urban models into those which are concerned with *generating* or deriving variables of interest from input variables, and those which are concerned with *allocating* output variables to different areas or zones of the spatial system. Although generation need not be mutually exclusive of allocation, most such mechanisms do tend to be conceived independently of each other; and in this discussion, mechanisms used for generation are referred to as 'forecasting models' whereas those used for allocation are 'location models'. For example, many regional economic models such as regional multipliers, input–output models, etc., are essentially concerned with generation, not spatial allocation. In the input–output model, intermediate production is derived from final demand; in the cohort–survival population model, new levels of population are generated autonomously by applying various rates of change to previous levels, and so on. In contrast, allocation models are essentially concerned with locating one set of activities, given information about the location of patterns of other activities and the factors which affect such location decisions. In a shopping model, for example, available expenditure from the population is allocated to retail centres where such money is expended in the form of retail sales. A special class of allocation models is concerned with spatial distribution rather than location; in the case of the transport model, the location of activity-producing or generating trips and activity-attracting trips is fixed, and the interest centres about the pattern of distribution which integrates the two sets of activities or trip ends. It is worth noting, however, that there are models which combine generation and allocation such as linear econometric models, e.g., the EMPIRIC model (Hill, 1965; Irwin and Brand, 1965), the various coefficients of which reflect both the generation (in terms of the magnitude of activity) and the predicted pattern of location of the dependent variable.

In the terminology of a previous section, forecasting and location models tend to be partial models from which more general models are constructed, and although a general model need not contain mechanisms for generation and allocation, it is likely that both these mechanisms will be required if the model is to be useful in the planning process. General models which involve the assembly of partial models can be loosely or strongly coupled. For example, it is possible to build an employment–population model in which employment and population are forecast separately, and then the imbalance between them corrected by a migration model. If this correction were a once-for-all affair, then the model would be loosely coupled, but its couplings could be strengthened by feedback of the effects of the imbalance and a reiteration of the whole sequence. In a spatial context, Lathrop and Hamburg's (1965) model for the Buffalo region involves the stringing together of a series of allocation models, one for each land use, in a loosely coupled scheme, whereas the model to be presented in this section will be more strongly coupled in that significant feedback between the activities will be incorporated.

A series of requirements for a general model can be defined which relate to the degree to which activities affect one another. Ideally, the model should be conceived in systems terms, each subsystem relating to some activity or land use which can be defined in a fairly unambiguous way. Industrial, retail or commercial, residential, and recreational land uses or activities are distinct functionally and physically, and these will constitute the model's subsystems or components. The relationships between these subsystems concern both generation and allocation, and if there exists a further set of relationships between generation and allocation, the model is strongly coupled. In terms of generation, it must be possible to derive the magnitudes of the various subsystem components from some exogenous input or from the other subsystems of the model. For example, final demand in the input–output model generates intermediate demands whose level is in turn affected by interrelationships between these intermediate activities. Turning to allocation, relationships between the spatial pattern of land uses are typically considered as spatial interaction, which may be explicitly physical in terms of traffic or may be functional in terms of linkages within the production or consumption process. For example, the main relationship between population in residential areas and employment in industrial areas is the journey to work, whereas the relationships within the employment or industrial sector are expressed as commodity flows, communication patterns, or spatial demands. In Figure 3.8, relationships between various subsystems or sectors are shown, together with the relationships and subsystems which form the model of this section. From Figure 3.8, it is clear

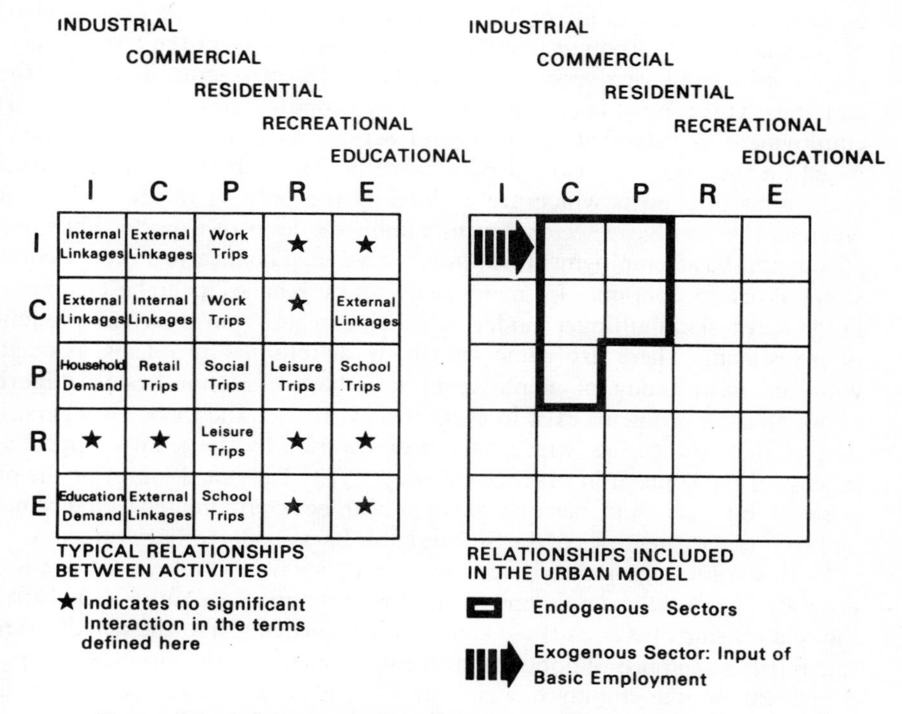

FIGURE 3.8. Relationships between activities in an urban system

that extensions to the model to be presented here are logically not difficult, and this is one of the major advantages of the framework presented below.

Finally, any model requires a 'motor' or input to drive the generation and allocation mechanisms. In the input–output model, final demand acts as the motor, although there are often other input variables involving strengths of relationship, etc., without which the motor cannot function. In general, the model's exogenous variables must be relatively independent of the model itself; i.e. the 'environment' of the system which is being modelled must be relatively independent of the system, otherwise the environment itself is also a source of interest. This relative independence is frequently difficult to establish in functional as well as spatial terms, and one of the most frequent criticisms of any model is directed to this point. In this sense, then, the fuel which energizes the motor is an input from the system's environment. In the following sections, first the generation of activities and then their allocation will be discussed in more detail; the general model will then be assembled by combining both these mechanisms.

The generation of activities: the economic base mechanism

The generation mechanism adopted here is an artificial procedure for deriving levels of population and service employment from given levels of industrial employment. The causality of the mechanism is unidirectional, from industrial employment, and although population is allowed to affect the level of service employment, and vice versa, industrial employment is not affected by these activities. This type of logic is referred to as 'economic base theory'. Industrial employment is classified as basic and service as non-basic; the theory is based on the notion that the driving force behind a spatial economic system is in terms of exports which are exclusively the product of the basic sector, whereas the non-basic sector depends upon the level of exports. Thus, basic affects non-basic employment but not vice versa. The idea has been a cornerstone of macroeconomics for many years, and it reaches its highest expression in the Keynesian multiplier models in which consumption is seen as a function of investment. There are some enormous definitional problems associated with the partitioning of employment into basic and non-basic categories, although such problems exist in every theory. In fact, the theory has persisted despite these difficulties, which have been dwarfed by the relative appeal and success of the concept in practice (Massey, 1973; Tiebout, 1962). For the purposes of this discussion, basic employment can be approximated as the primary and secondary categories of the SIC and non-basic as the tertiary category.

In this context, population and non-basic (service) employment are to be generated from basic employment, and for these purposes ratios summarizing the relationships between these activities are needed. First, the activity rate α is defined as the ratio of population to employment, i.e. the number of persons dependent on one employee, which may be taken as the average family size. Second, there is the population-serving ratio β which is the ratio of service jobs demanded by the population to population. And third, there is the employment-serving ratio λ which is the ratio of services required by the total employment sector to total employment. These constitute the linkages within the economic sector expressed in terms of employees demanded. The ratios or parameters can be easily calculated from known values at some base date, and thus the 'calibration' problem is trivial. Given the values of these parameters, it is now worth while sketching how population and non-basic employment can be generated from basic employment.

Imagine a hypothetical problem in which the basic sector contains one industry: a steelworks. Employment in the steelworks drives the economic motor of the system in the following way. From this basic employment, basic population (families associated with the steel workers) can be generated using the activity rate α. This increment of population demands to be serviced in terms of its consumption, as does the steelworks itself in terms of its production process, and by application of the ratio β to population and λ to basic employment these services are derived. These services have associated dependents in terms of population which are generated by applying the activity rate; in turn, this population and the services previously generated require further services to make consumption and production feasible, and these are generated by applying the two service ratios. This service employment generates a further increment of population which generates more services, and so on. Clearly the process of generation is iterative, but the real question is 'Does it ever stop?' or 'Will it ever converge?'. If the increments of population and services get smaller, then this will be so, and this depends upon the values of α, β, and λ. An example serves to demonstrate the point.

Let us assume some arbitrary data which imply ratios with realistic values. The basic sector contains 100 employees, services depending on population contain 100, services depending upon total employment contain 50, and the population sector contains 750 people. Total employment is the sum of basic and service, which is 250. The activity rate α is the ratio of population to total employment, $750/250 = 3$, which can be assumed to be the average family size in the system. The population-serving ratio β is the ratio of population-dependent services to population, $100/750 = 0.1333$, and the employment-serving ratio λ is the ratio of employment-dependent services to employment, $50/250 = 0.2$. Starting with the input of 100 basic employees, the following generation procedure is used:

START

1. Apply α to basic employment to get basic population: $100 \times 3.00 = 300$
2. Apply β to basic population to get population services: $300 \times 0.13 = 40$
3. Apply λ to basic employment to get employment services: $100 \times 0.20 = 20$

NEXT ITERATION

4. Calculate total increment of services from population and employment: $40 + 20 = 60$
5. Apply α to service increment to get population increment: $60 \times 3.00 = 180$
6. Apply β to population increment to get population services: $180 \times 0.1\dot{3} = 24$
7. Apply λ to previous service increment to get employment services: $60 \times 0.20 = 12$

GO BACK TO NEXT ITERATION above until convergence.

The procedure listed above is a good example of an 'algorithm'; its structure is displayed in the block diagram given in Figure 3.9 and the various increments of activities computed on successive 'iterations', or repeats of stages 4 to 7 above, are graphed in Figure 3.10. Note that Figure 3.9 is drawn to bring out the iterative and convergent nature of the process.

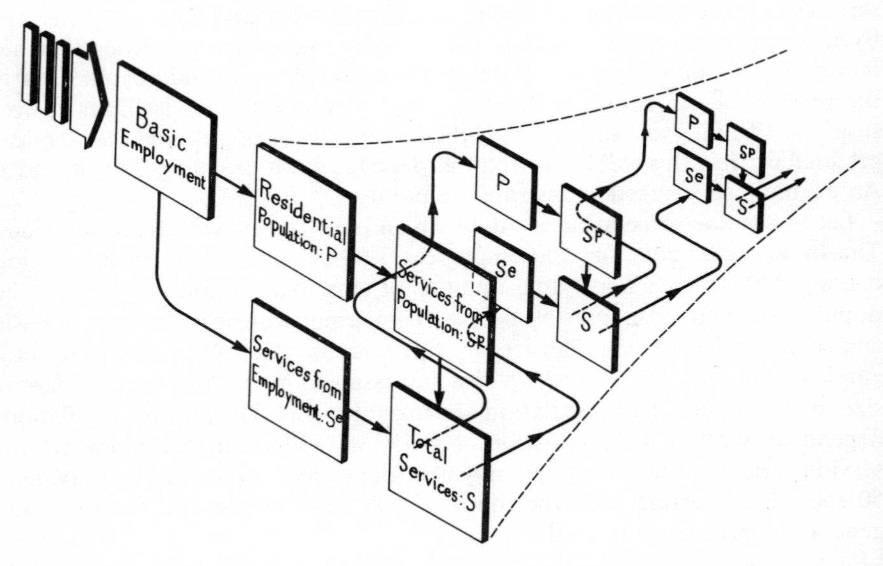

FIGURE 3.9. The generation of activities through the economic base mechanism

From Figure 3.10, it is quite clear that the increments of activity get smaller, given these reasonable values for α, β, and λ. As the number of iterations increases, the increments of activity become too small to worry about. For example, on the seventh iteration, the number of employment-dependent services drops below 1 person; on the ninth iteration, the number of population-dependent services drops below 1; on the tenth, the total increment in services

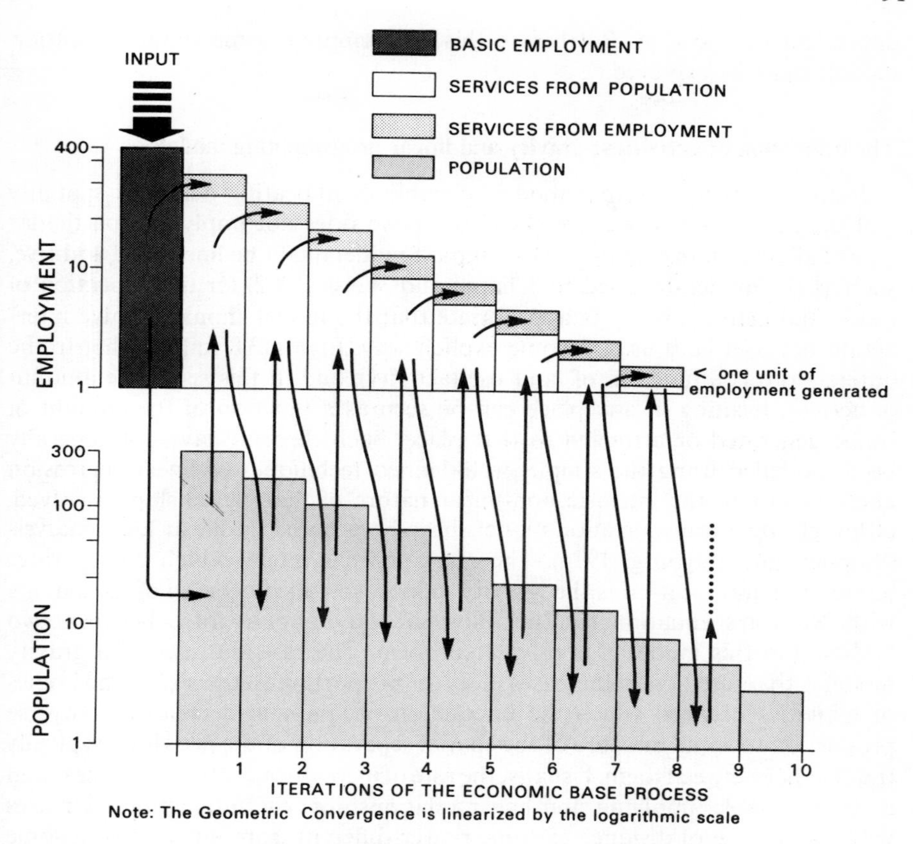

FIGURE 3.10. Convergence of the generation process

is below 1; and on the thirteenth, population drops below 1 person. In formulating a cut-off limit, any of these criteria would be acceptable, for by the seventh iteration, over 97 per cent. of all activity has been generated. Besides this absolute convergence, the cumulative totals of activities converge towards the known total values from which the ratios were originally computed. There is nothing magical in this process for it is mathematically simple and forms converging geometric series whose properties are familiar to students studying high school mathematics. It can easily be shown that the process must converge if service employment is positive and basic employment exists, for then α, β, and λ would be defined in such a way that the series would converge (Batty, 1976). It is easy to extend this type of generation procedure to encompass other activities, and it is obviously a convenient mechanism for forecasting dependent activities, given the system ratios α, β, and λ and basic employment. This type of algorithm immediately suggests the way in which location could be incorporated—by locating activities within the procedure after each increment of activity has been generated and thus making generation in some sense dependent on location. But before this is attempted, some suitable location models must be explored.

The allocation of activities; gravity and linear programming models

There are many different models capable of allocating activities spatially and the generation procedure sketched above does not imply any particular type of allocation mechanism. The simplest model might be linear and additive, such as the model designed by Chapin and Weiss (1962) for the allocation of residential activity, but it is appropriate that the model should involve interaction between land uses in some explicit way. Figure 3.8 implies that traffic (interaction) is a function of land use (activity), and in this sense the amount of activity locating in any place can be seen as a function of the amount of traffic generated or attracted to that place. Such theories have not generally been modelled using the simple, well-defined techniques of linear regression analysis, due to the intrinsic non-linear nature of the relationships involved, although some transportation models have been based on linear logit analysis (Stopher and Meyburg, 1975). The most popular model which incorporates interaction and location is the 'gravity model', so-called because of its analogy with Newton's equation for the universal gravitational force between two bodies, and this model is non-linear in form. The essential idea of a gravity model is that interaction increases in direct proportion to the size of the bodies or activities between which the interaction occurs, and decreases in inverse proportion to some measure of the spatial separation of the activities, typically the distance between them. Usually, the rate of increase or decrease in interaction is itself variable, implying non-linear relationships; e.g. interaction decreases with the inverse of distance to some power different from unity or with some function of distance such as the negative exponential. In three-dimensional physical systems such as a solar system, the exponent on distance is 2, as in Newton's original law, and in two-dimensional systems it is 1 (Coleman, 1964; Zipf, 1947); in social systems the value of this exponent has been estimated according to the specific situation using a process of calibration. Despite the simplicity of the idea, there is an enormous amount of empirical evidence which supports the notions embodied in the gravity model (Carrothers, 1956; Taylor, 1975), although its basis is essentially statistical rather than theoretical.

An important development in the use of gravity models in traffic and land-use planning concerns the formulation of models subject to different degrees of constraint. The original use of the gravity model to distribute trips on a transport network required that the trips generated and attracted by the model be subject to known constraints on the magnitude of the trip ends. Procedures such as those due to Fratar (1954) and Furness (1965) were evolved to ensure that such models were 'balanced' in this sense. In the development of gravity models for retail studies (Huff, 1963; Lakshmanan and Hansen, 1965), such models had to allocate given amounts of expenditure to shopping centres, and were thus subject to constraints on trip generation only. In contrast, some of the early gravity models developed by geographers (Taylor, 1975) were not subject to any constraints on the particular location of activities. The formalization of gravity models into a family whose members are subject to these varying degrees of constraint is due to Wilson (1974); in the context of urban modelling, the most useful models are those which are subject to constraint on one set of locations at one end of the trip but not the other. For example, models which predict the interaction between one set of activities and another, in which the distribution of one set of activities is known and it is required to find the location of the other, are the most useful in this context, and an example will help clarify this point.

Consider the simple three-zone spatial system in Figure 3.11. It is required to build a model which predicts the journey from work to home, which is subject to the constraint that the model predicts no more and no less than the known distribution of employment at the workplace. This known distribution is shown in Figure 3.11 (a), and the gravity model based on independent variables such as residential attractiveness and intervening distance is used to 'spread' this known activity from workplace zones to residential zones. In Figure 3.11 (b), the arrows indicate the interaction from work to home, and the model is so constructed to ensure that no more and no less than the activity shown in Figure 3.11 (a) leaves the workplace zones. Figure 3.11 (c) shows the amount of activity entering a residential zone, and by adding up the amount of activity

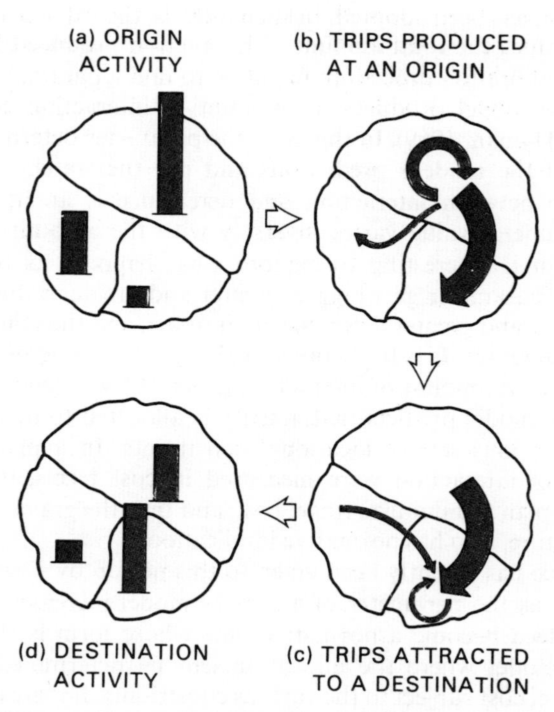

FIGURE 3.11. The essential idea of spatial allocation

entering this zone the amount 'locating' there is determined, as shown in Figure 3.11(d). This, then, is a location model, and if the model is also subject to constraints on residential location, such as capacity constraints or policy constraints due to planning control, etc., these can be incorporated in a variety of ways. The Furness procedure referred to above, or any of the redistribution procedures such as those due to Lowry (1964) or Crowther and Echenique (1972), can be used to meet these constraints on location. The notion of constraining gravity models in this way is also aided by visualizing the pattern of interaction as a matrix or table of accounts whose rows are origins and columns are destinations; constraints on origins and/or destinations can be met by various iterative procedures in which constants are introduced into the gravity model. For those readers who wish to explore these models further in terms of these simple visual explanations, the papers by the author (Batty, 1970b) and by Echenique (1971) and the books by Masser (1972), C. Lee (1973), and Reif (1973) concentrate on this mode of presentation.

The usual measures of attraction and deterrence to interaction in a gravity model relate to some index of intrinsic locational attraction which incorporates size and to some measure of spatial impedance, frequently distance, travel time, or generalized cost. The intrinsic non-linearity of these relationships is determined by parameters or constants which have to be determined during calibration, and in most applications to date only one parameter, on the deterrence function, has been adopted. In such models, the value of this parameter uniquely determines the total amount of interaction produced by the model, and a relevant calibration procedure might be to find a parameter value which ensures that the model produces an amount of interaction equal to some observed total (Hyman, 1969). In this way, the parameter determines the order of magnitude of the model's predictions and not the statistical fit. Because the relationship between interaction and deterrence is an inverse one, the size of the parameter value varies inversely with the amount of interaction generated, and it is interesting to explore what happens as this parameter changes. As the parameter gets bigger, greater and greater values of distance. say, create greater and greater deterrence to interact, and thus the total amount of interaction decreases. It is fairly obvious that, as the value of the parameter tends to infinity, the amount of interaction generated will tend to a minimum value, where the model predicts that activity is allocated to its nearest centre, subject to the various sets of locational constraints. In a planning context, if the amount of interaction were measured in cost terms, it might be an objective of the plan to minimize travel cost, and thus the gravity model, which is positive in nature, also has normative implications.

Some credence has recently been given to this notion by Evans (1973), who has shown that as the parameter of a gravity model increases to infinity the model does indeed become a normative one, whose form is that of a linear programming model where the allocation can be determined by explicitly minimizing travel cost subject to the various constraints. If there are no destination constraints, then the linear programming form of the model can be solved

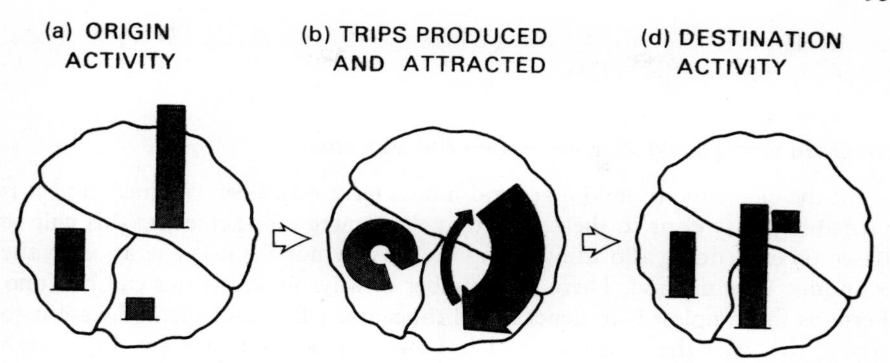

FIGURE 3.12. Allocation to the nearest centre by linear programming

directly by allocation to the nearest centre, and if there are ties, then multiple solutions exist. This is shown for the three-zone example in Figure 3.12. If there are constraints on the destination locations, the model can be solved in various ways, but each is more complicated: by running the gravity model with a large value parameter, by using Dantzig's simplex method of linear programming, or by formulating the model as a strict linear programming transportation problem and solving by Hitchock's method—any of these will suffice. As noted in a previous section, there are many problems of using linear programming, and one of the most important relates to the sparseness of the interaction matrix. This is clearly seen in Figure 3.12(b) where the pattern of interaction is much sparser than in Figure 3.11(b), and thus is probably more unrealistic.

From theoretical and practical viewpoints, this relationship between gravity and linear programming models is extremely important. Evans' (1973) recent paper demonstrates that many such models may be cast in a maximizing framework, thus extending the work of those who have sought to derive gravity models from extremal principles (Beckmann, 1974; Charnes, Raike, and Bettinger, 1972; Wilson, 1967). From a practical viewpoint, these results are especially significant; in an earlier section, it was argued that few, if any, models exist with both positive and normative aspects, thus making it difficult to trace explicit relationships between the positive and normative aspects of the planning process. But Evans' (1973) results show that this is now possible, and in the later application sections of this paper both positive and normative (linear programming) versions of the gravity model will be developed. This will enable the planner to ask such questions as 'How close are the positive and normative patterns of location generated by the gravity model?', 'How artificial is the notion of designing a city in which interaction is at a minimum?', and so on. Finally, this relationship opens the way to more realistic extensions of the gravity model in which an objective function of a non-linear kind incorporating factors other than interaction cost is used. In this way, these models connect up to other normative models based on linear and non-linear programming such as the Herbert–Stevens models (Wheaton, 1974) and the TOPAZ model (Brotchie and Sharpe, 1975).

An urban model integrating generation and allocation

All the elements to build a general model have now been outlined, and it is probably pretty clear to the reader that the strategy for achieving this will be based on embedding allocation, using the gravity model, into generation by the economic base method. There is a number of ways in which this can be done. Perhaps the simplest is to generate all the activity first and then allocate it to zones; this was the structure which Lowry (1964) used for his Pittsburgh model. However, it ignores any feedback between generation and allocation, and thus Garin's (1966) method in which increments of activity are generated and immediately allocated in sequential linear fashion is preferable, and has been more widely used. A third method, which aids calibration, involves generating the increment but allocating the sum of increments so far, and this is the method used by Baxter and Williams (1975). In the model to be applied here, Garin's method will be used, for this has the advantage that generation and allocation are consistently related in a quasi-dynamic manner.

The generation and allocation processes are stitched together in the following way. From the given distribution of basic employment, the residential locations of these workers are predicted using a residential location model based on gravity principles. Then the population associated with these workers is derived by summing the number of work–home trips arriving in each zone and scaling these using the activity rate. The services demanded by the population for consumption and those required in the production process are generated from the population and basic employment respectively, and these are then allocated to service centres using gravity models–one to allocate service demand generated in the residential areas to service centres and one to allocate service demand in employment centres to those same service centres. These service employees live in residential areas and are allocated to such areas using the same gravity model used previously to allocate basic employees to residential areas. In turn, the population associated with these services and the services themselves require more services, and thus the procedure of generation and allocation is repeated until a convergence limit of the kind described previously is met and the process is terminated. The formal characteristics of this process are examined in the Appendix to this chapter, but for these purposes it is sufficient to note that the model is well behaved and mathematically tractable. A diagrammatic explanation of the process is presented in Figure 3.13, which represents a synthesis of the generation process shown in Figure 3.9 and the allocation process of Figure 3.11. In Figure 3.13, allocation is presented using a gravity-type model, but equally well a linear programming or logit-type model could be used to effect the allocation. The reader should be able to trace the generation procedure and the allocation through the diagram and should be able to prove that the process converges. The data for this example are the same as those used for

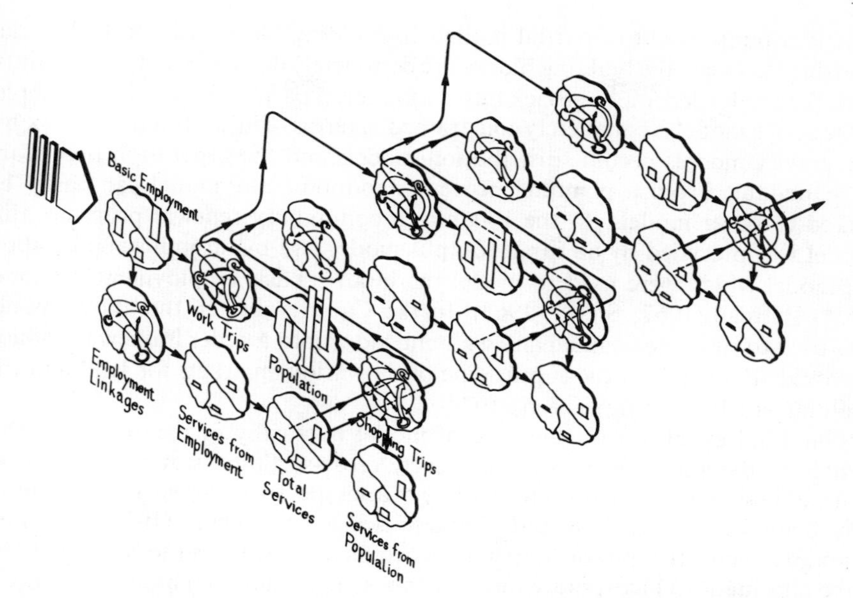

FIGURE 3.13. The generation and allocation of activity in sequential form

Figure 3.10. Constraints on location will be explored in the next section.

The model presented above is probably the most widely used of all urban models for it has a tremendously strong structure which can be easily aggregated or disaggregated, constrained or unconstrained, dependent upon the circumstances. Indeed, the simplest versions can be built extremely quickly and the data requirements are modest. The original model structure is credited to Lowry (1964), with modifications by Garin (1966) and Harris (1966b), although it is true to say that this genus of model was reflected in other North American work of the early 1960s (Goldner and Graybeal, 1965; Lathrop and Hamburg, 1965). The model has been extensively developed in Britain (Batty, 1972, 1976) at Cambridge, Reading, and the Centre for Environmental Studies, but there have been many applications elsewhere, notably in Latin America (Echenique, 1975), in Holland (Paelinck, 1975), and in Canada (Hutchinson, 1975). The model is highly suited to the type of broad-brush land-use planning which is the subject of this paper, but many of the applications to date have reached this stage of use in neither forecasting nor predicting the effects of alternative plans.

The general framework of this model can be extended in many ways. Disaggregation is an obvious and clear elaboration, but the generation structure can be extended to embrace other land uses or activities. Indeed, the structure of the model is similar to that of an input–output model, and although the above presentation focuses on two dependent and one independent sector there is no problem in extending the framework to embrace several dependent sectors (Wilson, 1974). Only data availability has restricted the development of such a model so far. One of the most appealing features of the model is the fact that it is built up out of partial models in building-block fashion. If the relationships between the building blocks are completely determined by constraints, then the model decomposes back into a number of partial models. For example, if the above model is completely constrained in terms of its destination locations, the gravity models become distribution models and the generation procedure is redundant. From a planning process standpoint, the model can easily be linked to other models. In the Pittsburgh community renewal program, this model was preceded by an input–output model and by an industrial location submodel which were used to model the input—basic employment (Crecine, 1964; Putman, 1967; Steger, 1965). In the Caracas model, the above model was used to simulate demand and was embedded into a wider framework which involved simulation of the supply side of the various markets for land and the building stock (Echenique *et al.*, 1974).

One final extension to this type of model is worthy of mention, and this relates to dynamics. The model is clearly cross-sectional static, comparative static at best, but there has been a variety of attempts to make the model temporally dynamic. The earliest and simplest is due to Crecine (1964), but later attempts due to the author (Batty, 1976), to Sayer (1975), and to Wilson (1974) have all sought to incorporate mechanisms which relate to making the process of generation dynamic. Only the models due to Crecine and the author have been made operational, and although these models are less easy to make dynamic than to extend in other ways such as disaggregation, data availability tends to be the inhibiting factor on this kind of development. In the next section, questions such as those concerning data will be broached directly when the actual process of building the model for a real problem will be presented, using the town of Peterborough as an example. The issues to be raised below are quite different in nature from those already considered, but they are an essential part of using models in the planning process.

THE DESIGN AND CONSTRUCTION OF AN URBAN MODEL

Algorithms and programs

There are four main stages involved in the model design process based on the specification of the model's algorithm and computer program, the data base for the model, the design of the spatial system of zones, and the process of calibration. Although these are interdependent, the clearest way to begin is by describing the algorithms used in the model, for these are least related to the specific characteristics of the study area. Only a brief description of the model design process can be given here, but interested readers who desire a longer, more through treatment are referred to the book by the author (Batty, 1976). The essential structure of the model's algorithm and computer program which is based on this follows the description of the sequential iterative process of generation and allocation described above. It is possible to formulate the same model in simultaneous terms using matrix equations and to program the model accordingly, but this has not been done here. There are many advantages to simultaneous solution but the main disadvantage is that it does not allow the model-builder to examine the model's convergence, and this was desirable here for other purposes (Batty, 1977).

A number of additional routines have been incorporated into the algorithm, and these must be described. A convergence limit requiring five overall model iterations was specified, and then the final totals were generated by making an approximation to all the increments after the fifth iteration in the manner developed by Cripps and Foot (1969). But perhaps the largest addition to the structure outlined previously involved the use of locational constraints. In this model, constraints on the maximum amounts of residential population and total service employment were used; the mechanisms which were designed to ensure that these constraints were met were based on redistributing any excess created by constraint violation, on any iteration, to zones whose constraints had not been violated. Zones which had reached their limit were not then considered for allocation on further iterations. The model is complicated by the need to maintain consistency between the generation of population and service employment, which requires some backtracking between constraint mechanisms in the following way. In a typical iteration, the previous increment of service employment is used to generate and allocate the next increment of population. If this population violates the maximum population constraint in any zone, the excess (the actual population less the constraint limit) is allocated back to its origin (employment) zone and reconverted into employment which is reallocated on the next iteration. The population which has been allocated on this iteration and the previous increment of service employment, less the excess, are now used to generate the new increment of service employment. If this employment violates any of its constraints, the excess is allocated back to its population or employment centre in proportion to its initial allocation. It is then reconverted into its original activity, but at this point excess population from the excess service employment must be allocated further back to the original employment centre. This, in turn, reduces the increment of service employment used to start the whole process in the first place, and it means that employment-dependent services must be reduced accordingly.

The constraints procedure destroys the strict form of the economic base procedure, for excess activity calculated from the constraint violations is allocated on a later iteration. Because the procedure is artificial it can be used to special advantage in the linear programming (LP) model. On any one iteration of the LP version of this model only enough activity is allocated from each zone to meet the constraint limits. The constraints are never violated and thus the LP model can be solved immediately by inspection, without any iteration. In fact, the model works in the same way described above except that excess activity is not allocated back to its origin zones proportionately, but according to a ranking of the time–distance values. This written explanation of the model's algorithm is difficult, and it can be supplemented by reference to the Appendix, where the model's formal structure is set out. In this sense, it provides a good demonstration that although an intuitive grasp of mathematical modelling can be gained without mathematics, mathematics is almost always required to explain the operational details of a model.

The computer program for the model is divided into three main sections—

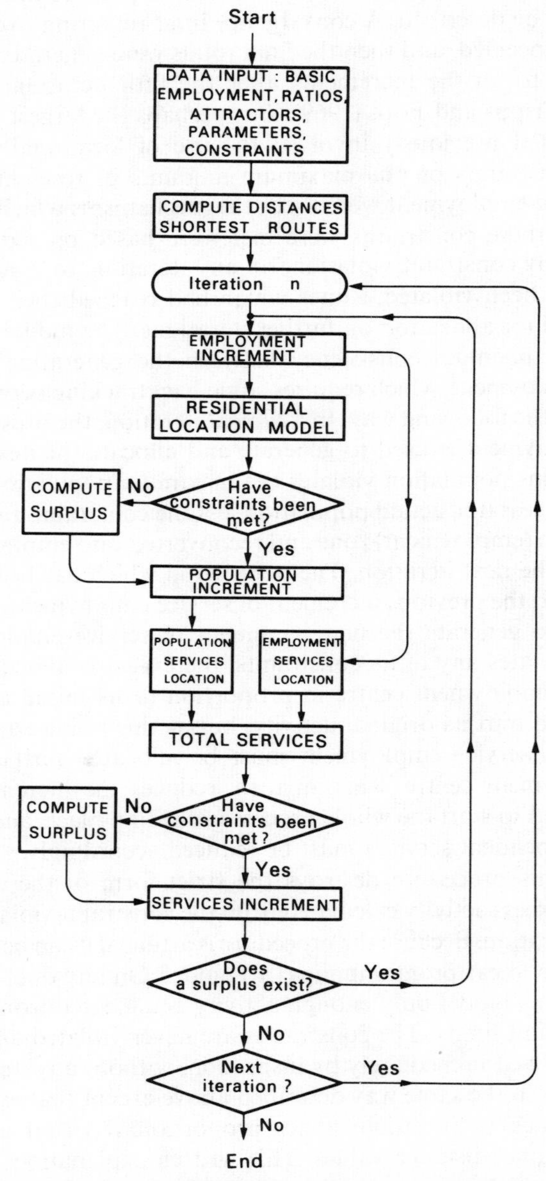

FIGURE 3.14. General structure of the Peterborough model

dealing with data management, generation and allocation, and statistical testing. The initial section concerned with data management involves computing the various system ratios α, β, and λ, reading in exogenous employment and locational attraction data, and assembling the time-distance matrix using a shortest-routes program. The generation–allocation procedure is based on two sub-programs—one for the initial generation and allocation, and the other for regeneration and reallocation due to the constraints procedures. Finally, two subroutines dealing with statistical tests are incorporated: first, there is a program concerned with calculating the amount of travel and the mean travel or trip lengths which are used in calibration; and, second, there is a program which computes various goodness-of-fit statistics, such as mean square errors, correlations, etc., used in assessing the model's overall performance. The various subroutines are linked together by the flow chart presented in Figure 3.14.

The data base and spatial system design

The town of Peterborough was chosen to demonstrate urban models in the planning process for two reasons: first, because a reasonably good data base was available —e.g. an input–output model had already been constructed for the town by Morrison (1972) and shopping models had been built by Wade (1973)—and, second, because the town was the subject of a plan for expansion with New Town status. These conditions combined to provide a useful demonstration project for urban modelling. Although an extremely good employment base for the town was immediately available from the data published in the book by Smith and Morrison (1974), these data were aspatial in character, pertaining to the whole town. The basic–non-basic split was effected spatially using a variety of surveys—the 1971 enumeration district data of the population census, traffic surveys, the Peterborough master plan report, Kelly's Directory, and so on—and the final synthesized data set was based on 55 internal zones, defined according to criteria described below. Population was available from the 1971 Census and split of service employment into employment-dependent and population-dependent services was based on the division into the commercial and retail sectors of the SIC; this was obtained from Smith and Morrison (1974). In this sense, the allocation of employment-dependent services was based on a service demand gravity model while the allocation of population-dependent services was based on a retail gravity model. Although this was a somewhat arbitrary partition of service employment, it sufficed for this demonstration project.

The time-distance matrix was based on 'over the road' measures of travel time, weighted according to an inverse relationship between speed and population density and measured over a skeletal link network between zone centroids. A crude work-trip matrix was available from the workplace tables of the 1971 Population Census and was supplemented by information from a cordon traffic survey. This enabled the computation of mean work-trip lengths: the mean retail trip length was taken as 15 per cent. below and the mean service demand trip length as 5 per cent. below this value. The measures of locational attraction were based on observed population and service employments for the residential and service location models respectively, and despite the tautological nature of this specification, which is argued out elsewhere (Batty, 1976), these measures of attraction fulfil the requirements posed by the need to ensure correct dimensionality (Broadbent, 1970; Haynes, 1975).

Two main issues had to be resolved by the design of the spatial (zoning) system for the model. An internal zoning system for the town itself had to meet criteria such as zone homogeneity, geometric regularity, and nodal positioning, and there had to be a sufficient number of zones to ensure that the interaction generated by the model was large enough to be detected across zone boundaries (Broadbent, 1969). Taking account of the availability of data in spatial units such as wards, parishes, and enumeration districts, 55 internal zones were eventually defined; these are shown in Figure 3.15. Some of these zones contained no activity but were included because plans for expansion of the existing town involved those areas. The second equally important question involved the relationship between the town of Peterborough and areas outside the town—between the 'system' and its 'environment'. Of obvious importance is the idea that the system boundary should be so drawn as to minimize the degree of interaction with the external environment, but it is often difficult to define a global minimum either because of the original zoning system used in observing and collecting the raw data or because of limits on the size of the problem.

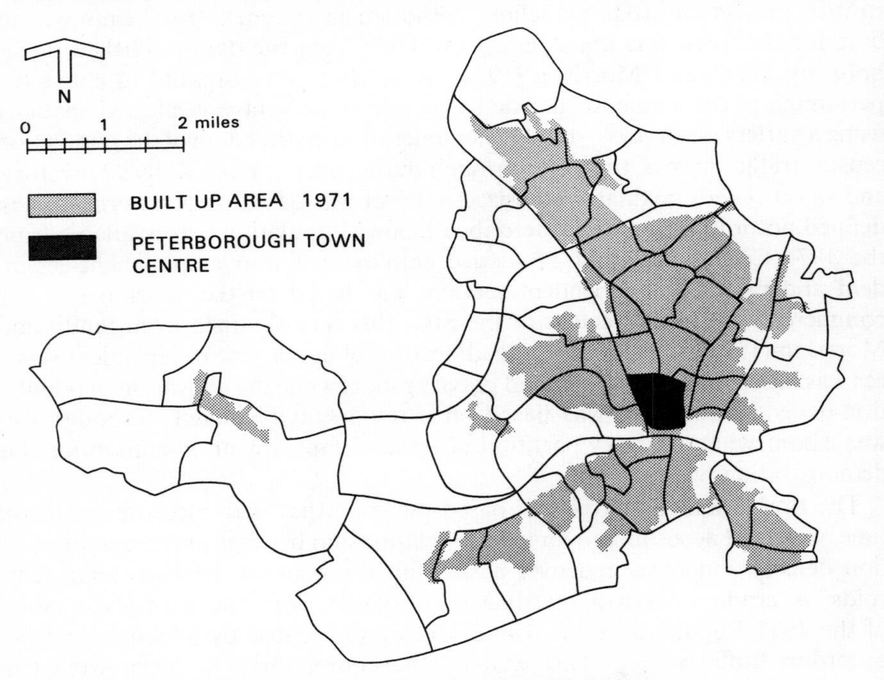

FIGURE 3.15. The internal zoning system

Therefore, it is necessary to include some representation of the system's environment in the form of 'dummy' or external zones, usually conceived at a higher level of aggregation than the internal zones. Methods are available to design models in which the relationships between the system and its environment are simulated in a coarse or inelegant way, thus enabling the degree of dependence between the system and its environment to be represented in a passive sense (Batty, 1976; Wilson, 1974).

In this model, the constraints procedures outlined above were used to model this relationship. As the interaction between the system and its environment was known in terms of the work trips, it was necessary to use these interactions to synthesize an artificial distribution of population, service, and basic employment in the external zones consistent with the generation ratios α, β, and λ defined for the internal zoning system. The constraints procedure was then used to ensure that this artificial distribution of activity was simulated on the first iteration of the overall model, by specifying very large locational attractions for the external zones. Thus the dependence between the system and its environment was established on the first iteration of the model and could be ignored on subsequent iterations. The method follows the one designed for the Area 8 pilot model (Batty *et al.*, 1974) and is formally presented in the Appendix. A visual explanation of this logic is given in Figure 3.16. The spatial system based on the 'dummy' external zones, and including the internal zones, is presented in Figure 3.17. The degree of closure between internal and external zones is quite low: some 28 per cent. of the total work-trip activity within the internal zones resides in the external zones, and in terms of this total activity 11 per cent. resides in the system and works in the external zones. An inner ring of dummy

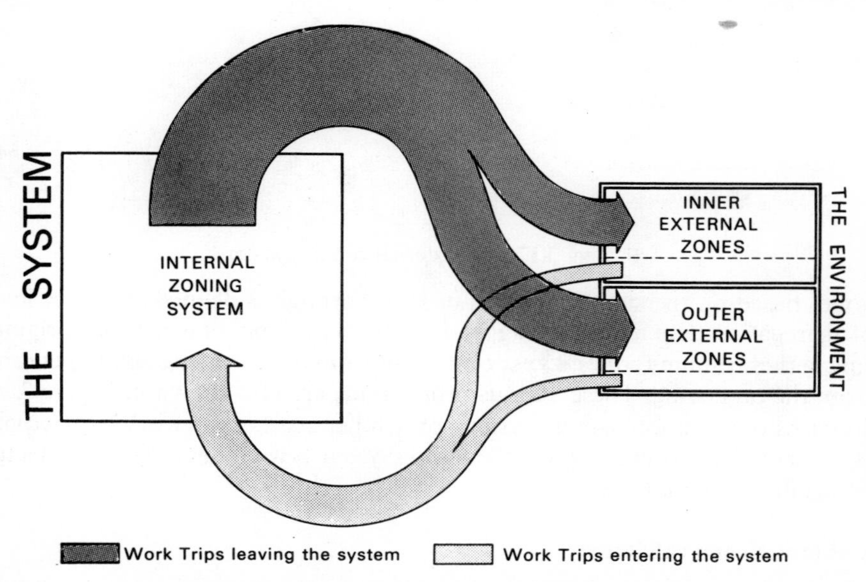

FIGURE 3.16. The relationship between the spatial system and its environment

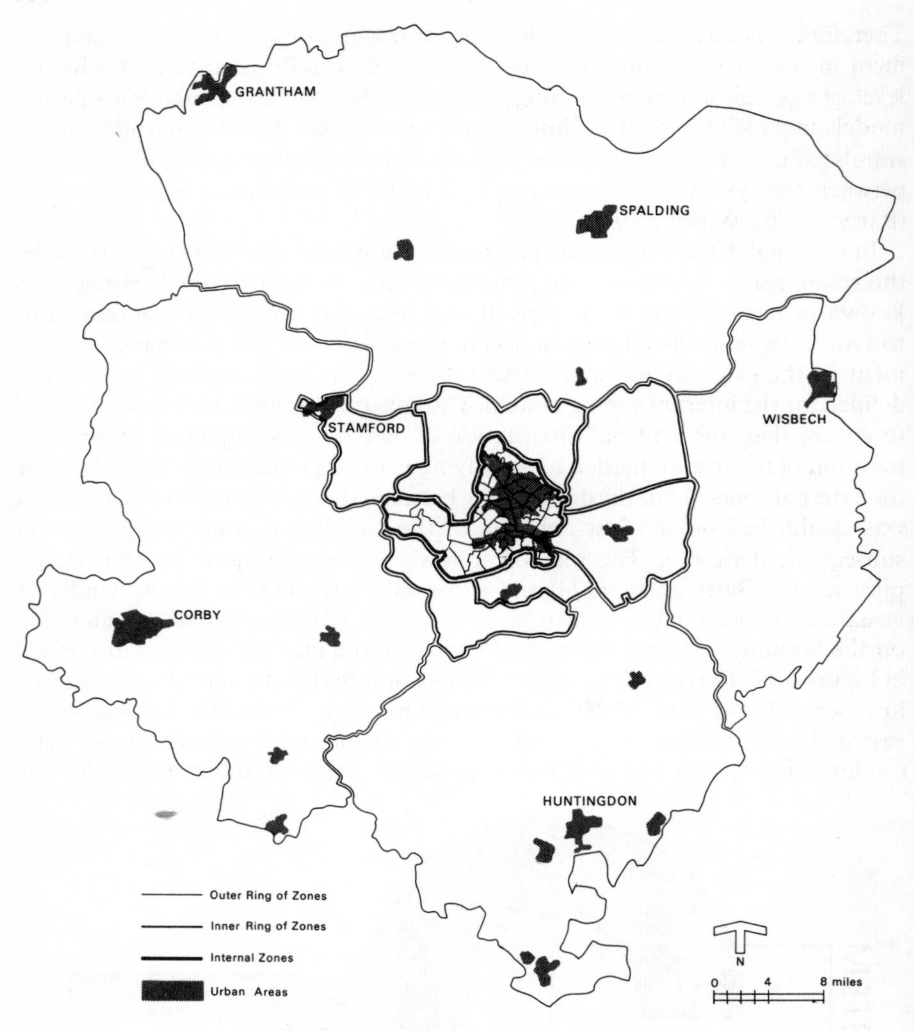

FIGURE 3.17. The external zoning system

zones based on the suburban areas of Peterborough is defined at a finer level of aggregation than an outer ring, and of the 28 per cent. of work trips originating in these dummy zones, 13 per cent. come from the inner ring and 15 per cent. from the outer ring. These various proportions are also shown in Figure 3.16. In terms of the whole zoning system, only 8 per cent. of the work-trip activity is intrazonal, thus implying that the zoning system is well conceived as a detector of significant spatial interaction.

Calibration and validation

Within the cycle of scientific method illustrated previously in Figure 3.3 an essential distinction is made between calibration and validation. Calibration is concerned not with optimizing the model's performance but with determining parameter values which fix the order of magnitude of the model's predictions; i.e. establishing the amount of travel generated by the model, the various activity levels, and so on. In contrast, validation is the process of evaluating the performance of the model by comparing the model's predictions against observations, and although some calibration procedures have been based on fixing parameter values through optimizing performance, these two stages should not be confused. In this model, the various activity ratios α, β, and λ can be estimated directly from data, but the process of determining the parameter values μ_1, μ_2, and μ_3, which relate to the residential, employment-dependent service demand, and population-dependent retail models respectively, is more complex. These three parameters are constants which control the influence of time-distance in the location models; in fact, they are parameters of the negative exponential functions used to represent the effect of time-distance. As each of these location models is interrelated through the generation process, these parameters depend on one another and must therefore be estimated simultaneously.

There are two principles of model calibration which are of prime importance in estimating parameter values; these have been explored in some depth during the last decade. For every parameter there must be a statistic reflecting the model's properties, which varies as the parameter value varies. If the parameters are interrelated, then these statistics must be interrelated, and the calibration problem can be viewed as one in which values of the parameters must be found which optimize the set of statistics in some way. Abstracting this idea, it can be shown that the calibration problem can be formulated as a problem of solving n equations (relating to the statistics) in n unknowns (the parameters); these equations will usually be non-linear and interdependent, and thus some non-linear simultaneous equation-solving technique is necessary. A variety of schemes has been tried for models such as these, ranging from simple trial-and-error 'grid' search to Newton–Raphson gradient search-type methods, involving linearization of the equation system and iterative solution (Batty, 1976). The second principle involves the types of statistic which most suitably reflect the model's requirements for calibration. This problem has also received considerable attention recently, and it is now clear that the best statistics relating to the 'friction of distance' parameters of an interaction model deal with the amount of distance travelled. In particular, Hyman (1969) has demonstrated that the mean trip length is a suitable statistic, although this fact is also implicit in the statistical derivations of interaction models pioneered by Wilson (1967). In many earlier models of this genre, statistics based on the actual performance of the model were used, but such statistics are often subject to logically and mathematically trivial optimum values, as well as confusing calibration with validation, and have now largely been abandoned.

In the Peterborough model, it was assumed that the three parameters were relatively independent of one another, a fact common to several previous urban models (Batty, 1976), and the order of magnitude of each parameter was determined by a simple grid search around the values fixed by first-approximation formulae (see Masser and Brown, 1976). These values were then used together in the model, and some variation around these values led to a set of final values which reflected the observed amount of travel in the system; i.e. the parameter values were fixed to make the model predict trip lengths equal to the observed trip lengths. In fact, the initial approximations gave poor values because the external zone constraint procedure, in which constraints on external trip making were satisfied on the first iterations of the model, distorted the parameter values quite significantly; two of the parameter values finally obtained have a different sign from that hypothesized, but this is completely accounted for by the nature of the algorithm used. Readers who wish to explore this question further are referred first to the Appendix and then to any other development of an urban model (e.g. Crowther and Echenique, 1972) for comparative purposes. A considerable amount of 'eyeballing' was therefore necessary during the calibration process, but the final trip lengths generated by the model are within 4 per cent. of the observed values. This is sufficiently close for this application, and these values are shown in Table 3.1.

Using these parameter values, the performance of the model can be assessed by examining the predictions of activity—population and service employment—against the observed activity at the 1971 base date. A direct comparison of the predicted and observed trip distributions is not possible because of data deficiencies, but the various statistics showing the goodness of fit of activities reveal a reasonable performance. Table 3.2 records these statistics, and it is immediately clear that the location of service employment is quite good in comparison with population, which is only just acceptable, given the fact that some 8 out of the 55 zones had reached their population constraint. Figure 3.18 shows the spatial distribution of these activities and also the interaction patterns associated with these distributions. Note that in the case of the service demand pattern, interaction is represented by flows of service employees and is based on an aggregation of the employment and service dependent patterns. These patterns are also aggregated to show gross interaction, i.e. interaction in both directions. The location of activity in the external zones has not been shown because this is completely constrained to reflect known distributions.

TABLE 3.1. Parameter values from the calibration process

Submodel	Parameter value	Predicted trip length	Observed trip length
Residential location (μ_1)	– 0.0130	79.0901	80.0000
Employment service location (μ_2)	0.0165	75.6817	76.0000
Population service location (μ_3)	– 0.0003	70.4132	68.0000

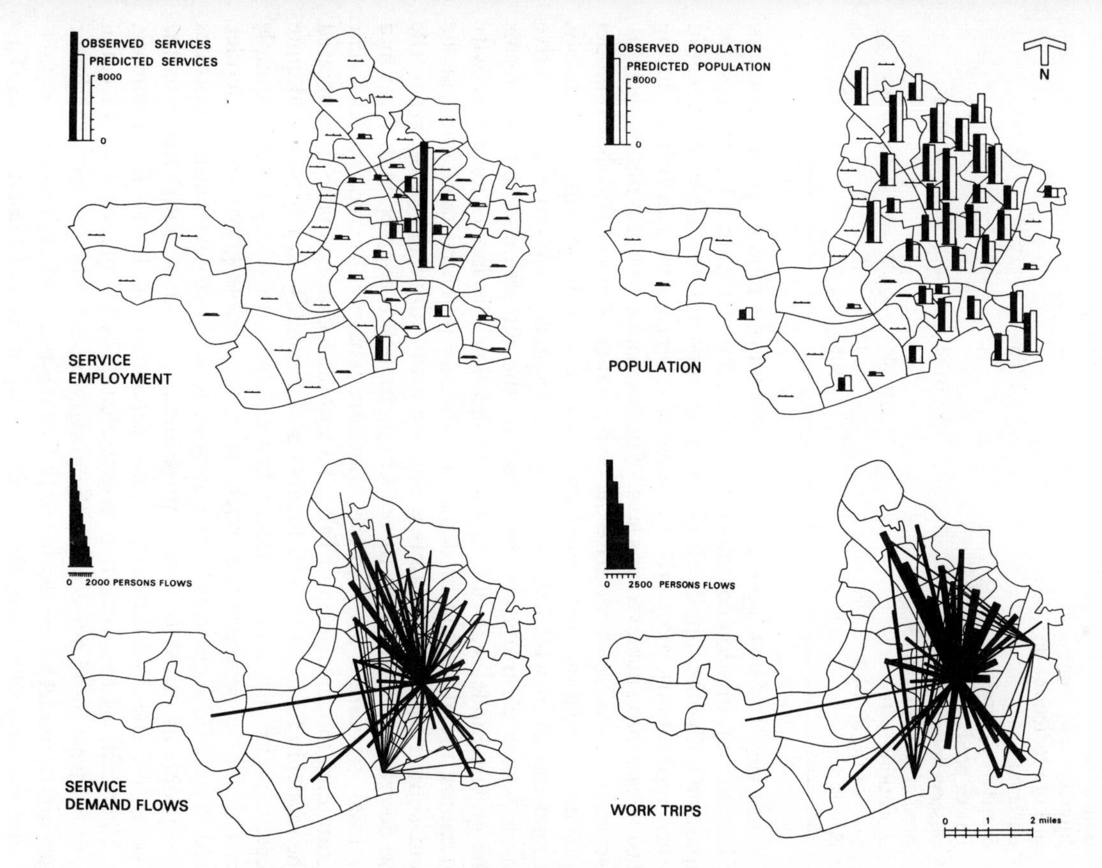

FIGURE 3.18. Spatial predictions from the gravity-based model

TABLE 3.2. Performance of the gravity-based activity allocation model

Calibration statistic	Total service employment	Population
Coefficient of determination, R^2	0.9981	0.9063
Intercept *a* of regression line of predictions on observations	– 1.1786	110.5789
Slope *b* of regression line of predictions on observations	1.0144	0.9415
Sum of the squared deviations	29 394	10 987 788
Sum of the absolute deviations	305	15 082

It is not easy to know how good or how bad this model's performance is, based on the information contained in Table 3.2 and Figure 3.18, unless some comparison with other applications and other models is available. With regard to other applications, most urban models of this genre built in Britain during the last decade have achieved this level of performance, so this is not too helpful. However, it is possible to compare the performance of this gravity-based model with a linear programming equivalent, using the ideas described previously. A second model in which activities were allocated to optimize an objective function whose elements corresponded to the attraction–deterrence terms of the gravity model was run. In this application, the model locates activity to maximize the attraction or deterrence for any potential interaction in the system, subject to the constraints which are artificially fixed according to the above description. Each of the three location models is adapted in this way and the formal structure is given in the Appendix. The performance of this linear programming model is given in Table 3.3 and the locational patterns generated by the model in Figure 3.19. The model's performance is clearly poor and quite unacceptable for use in any planning context, but it provides a stark example against which to compare the much more reasonable gravity-based model. Indeed, Figure 3.19 presents a very strange looking city which demonstrates all the problems posed by linear programming models; with regard to the sparseness of the interaction patterns generated by linear programming, only 2 per cent. of the work-trip matrix contains trips greater than or equal to 1, in contrast to 45 per cent. in the gravity model. Furthermore, the linear programming model has generated only 26 zones out of 55 with positive population, and the constraints have been met exactly in each of these 26 zones. This is a feature of the solution method, but it illustrates the difficulties of working with a seemingly reasonable model. It also illustrates the problems of operational modelling which are of such importance in developing models in a planning context. But comparisons of one model against another, as in this case, are an

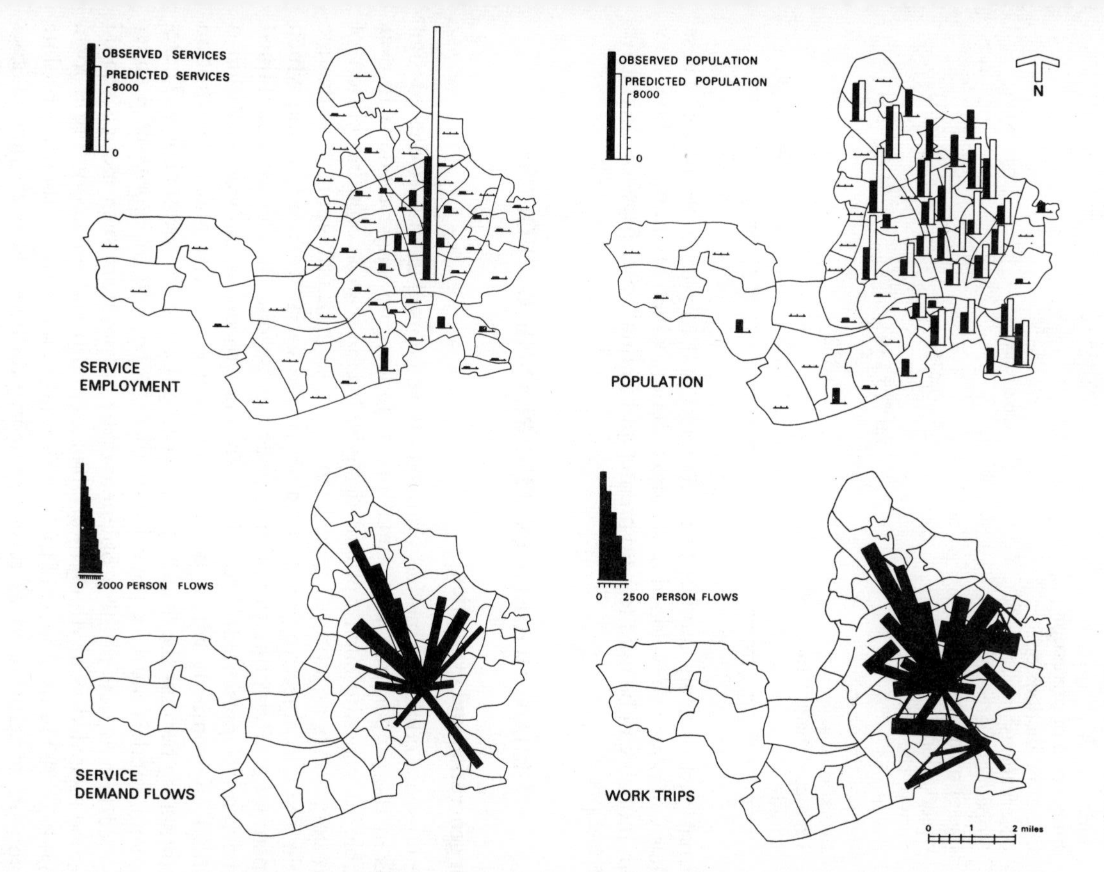

FIGURE 3.19. Spatial predictions from the linear programming model

TABLE 3.3 Performance of the linear programming activity allocation model

Calibration statistic	Total service employment	Population
Coefficient of determination, R^2	0.9335	0.6203
Intercept a of regression line of predictions on observations	262.6296	681.9638
Slope b of regression line of predictions on observations	0.4756	0.6203
Sum of the squared deviations	160 715 186	64 440 554
Sum of the absolute deviations	26 352	36 035
Predicted mean trip length	57.1635	44.2844

essential part of using models to understand and to plan cities better. These models will now be developed in the next section, which attempts to show how urban models can be used to help predict and evaluate the effects of alternative land-use plans.

URBAN MODELS IN THE PLANNING PROCESS

Plan generation and evaluation

In no sense could the models outlined above be used as fully fledged design tools in the preparation of optimal plans. Indeed, no single model will ever be able to generate such optimal designs, because an acceptable notion of what constitutes an optimal plan is too diverse and ambiguous to subsume within a single objective function. In short, the social welfare function which the planner is attempting to optimize goes way beyond the elements contained in the models presented here. The planning process is embedded within a political environment which is sufficient in itself to complicate the notion of optimality beyond the limits of the existing theories of social choice. Therefore, such models must be regarded as tools to be used to *inform* the planner about certain aspects of the problem and the output from such models should never be regarded as anything more than a conditional prediction of the form 'What if ... ?'. The usefulness of these tools is in a relative rather than an absolute fashion, in structuring ideas rather than in producing answers, and it goes without saying that their acceptance must be largely a personal matter. Thus, these models cannot provide a complete organizational structure for the planning process for they tend to be used at various stages, the stages being structured according to principles based on rational decision making within a political environment. The structure shown in Figure 3.7 for the Nottinghamshire–Derbyshire subregional planning process admirably demonstrates this point.

Although urban models are used in planning to help in understanding the problems of the system of interest—by organizing the data-collection process and focusing on pertinent theoretical issues—the models presented here can never be valued solely for this use; if the prime goal is one of understanding, there are much more theoretically acceptable models available (Papageorgiou, 1976). The value of the models developed here is in their ability to help in unravelling the heart of the planning process: the problem of plan-generation and plan-evaluation. The process of generating plans, be it a single master plan or a series of alternative plans, and their consequent evaluation is an iterative one, in which the plan or set of plans is successively refined in an effort to converge on an optimal solution.Clearly the invention of planning solutions must begin using some purely intuitive notions, and thus the use of an urban model would be to generate and/or evaluate certain consequences of the plan. For example, a series of alternative solutions might be devised in terms of the location of basic employment and transportation, and an activity allocation model might be used to generate consistent locations of population and service employment. In this sense, the model would be used to 'put flesh on the skeleton', and then the consequences of the model's predictions could be evaluated in terms of some preconceived notions about the form of the plan. Used in a cyclical fashion, such a model can help in reducing the solution space within which possible plans exist by enabling the planner continually to test his intuition against some well-defined base—the model. Within this overall process, some partial optimization might take place. Of the two models discussed above, the linear programming version was able to generate location patterns which optimized some criterion relating to benefit (attraction) or cost (deterrence), and thus the use of such a model would involve explicit optimization.

However, the purpose of the model is to provide a structure on which to base a much wider process of intuitive optimization through which the planner proceeds. For example, in the Nottinghamshire–Derbyshire study the process of generation and evaluation went through three stages: thirteen alternatives were first reduced to six, then six to three, and finally the preferred alternative was chosen. At each stage, the set of alternatives was refined on the basis of an intuitive evaluation supported by conditional predictions from a variety of models: constraints mapping techniques, transport, shopping, activity-allocation, and population models, and so on. In this paper, the activity-allocation model is to be used in two ways: to test the impact of the proposed Peterborough New Town and to compare this proposal with nine other alternatives which reflect development in very different locations. No iterative process of generation evaluation will be implied, but a series of spatial indicators based on accessibility computed for each alternative will serve as a basis for comparison.

Alternative New Towns for Peterborough

The original design for the New Town by the planning consultants (Hancock and Hawkes, 1967) reflects a number of criteria used to bound the physical solution space within which the proposal was made. In particular, the north-west quadrat of land around the existing town of Peterborough was excluded from any development due to its scenic and other natural qualities. Thus the zoning system shown in Figure 3.15, for which data were available for these models, reflects the shape of the New Town, which involves an expansion of Peterborough to the west. Therefore, a number of possible alternatives, e.g. expansion to the north-west, could not be tested, and in this sense the set of nine alternatives to be developed below is slightly biased by the zoning system which reflects the actual proposal. The scale of expansion in the New Town is quite large: in 1971 the population was 87,500, and the New Town is likely to involve an additional 60,000 persons or more by 1981. Although this increase will partly be due to natural growth, some 10,000 additional jobs in the basic sector will be required to reach this target (assuming that the 1971 multiplier remains stable). The New Town plan involves a large-scale expansion to the west of the existing town towards the A1 national traffic route, and the form of the New Town is based on a fairly dispersed pattern of jobs and services, with two district centres located to the west and two to the north of the existing town. The New Town plan is shown in Figure 3.20. Sufficient data on new transport

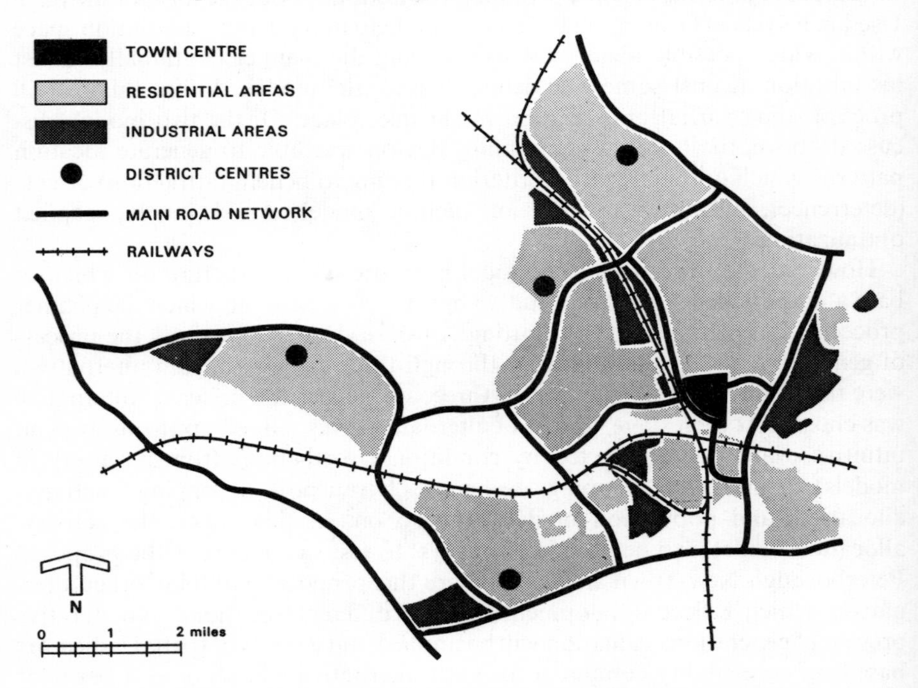

FIGURE 3.20. The proposed Peterborough New Town

routes and basic jobs are available to test the impact of this New Town on the existing town in the manner previously reported by the author (Batty, 1969) for Central Lancashire New Town and by Cripps and Foot (1969) for Milton Keynes.

To demonstrate the use of the model, nine 'alternative' New Town plans have been defined, in such a way that these reflect a wide range of spatial configurations. With 55 zones, the number of possible alternatives in terms of location is astronomical, but many of these zones must be ruled out on *a priori* grounds. There are many physical difficulties due to topography, natural phenomena worthy of preservation, mineral workings, land liable to flooding, capacity constraints on development, and so on, which reduce the set of feasible alternatives; these constraints are shown in Figure 3.21. There appear to be nine distinct centres which could form the basis for some set of spatially distinct alternatives, and simply taking different combinations of these locations one is able to generate some $\Sigma_{k=1}^{9} \binom{9}{k} = 3\,282$ alternatives. Varying the amount of development in each of these alternatives and differentially ordering the land uses would give rise to another astronomical set of alternatives. However, the point has been made that the number of alternatives is potentially explosive, and some way must be found to control this explosion. The original set of nine alternatives, which are shown schematically in Figure 3.21, are to be tested using the model, but there is no proof that the optimal alternative will be one of

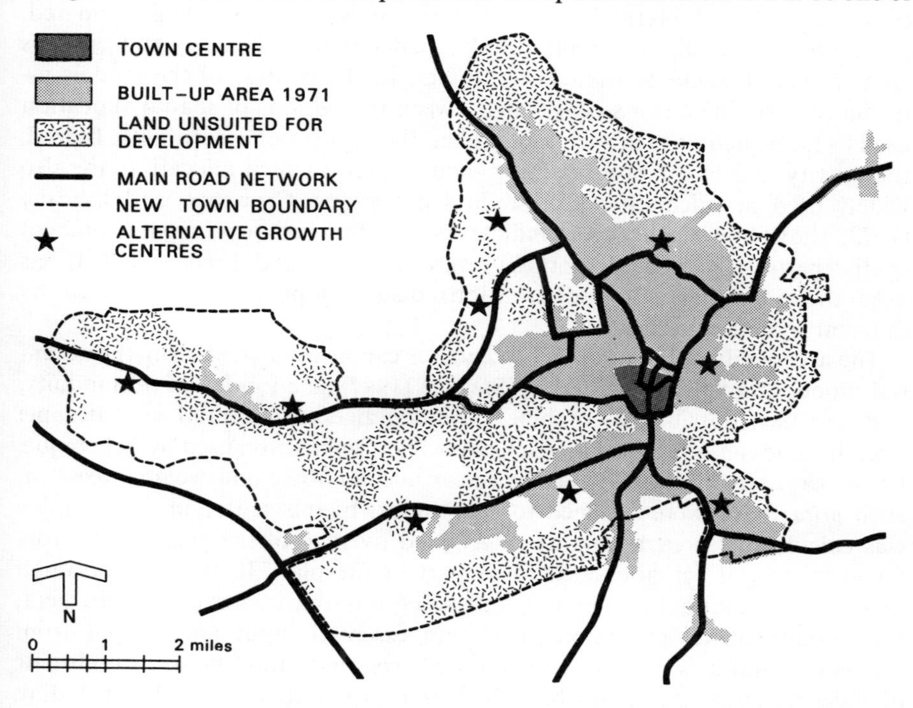

FIGURE 3.21 Alternative centres for the development of Peterborough

these nine plans and not one of the other 3 273; this neatly points out the fact that in practice there is no feasible model which will generate an optimal solution. It is something which limits the scope of formal optimization models in planning, but it helps to put some perspective on the intrinsic difficulties facing the urban planner, in particular, and the social scientist, in general. In the next section, the activity-allocation model based on gravity submodels will be used to test the impact of the actual New Town and the nine alternatives on each other and on the existing town. To this end, a set of indicators based on measures of accessibility will be introduced.

Spatial indicators in the evaluation of alternatives

In using any model to generate or elaborate a set of alternatives some means of comparing the alternatives is necessary. In many situations, comparison has been based on purely intuitive assessments in which differences in location are evaluated against some conceptual ideas about the efficiency of various locational patterns. But in a few instances, planners have attempted explicitly to calculate indices of spatial efficiency in terms of accessibility. For example, given a set of alternative plans whose differentiating feature is spatial, it is possible to measure the accessibility or 'degree of propinquity' of one land use or activity to another. In general, the greater the accessibility, the greater the opportunity of interaction with respect to the activities being compared, and higher values of accessibility imply greater spatial efficiency and perhaps greater spatial economy than lower values. In the context of the models introduced here, there is a strong link between the notions of spatial allocation used to locate activities in such models and the concept of accessibility. Indeed, the gravity and linear programming models used in such allocation are also widely used in calculating accessibility. Echenique, Crowther, and Lindsay (1972) show how such access indicators can be used to compare different spatial patterns generated by these types of model, and Breheny (1974) has used these indicators to judge various distributional effects produced by different spatial patterns.

The accessibility of one activity to another can be calculated using the potential model originally suggested by Stewart (1947) as an index of propinquity, and it is then possible to combine various indices of potential so that some overall value can be derived for each plan. The combination used by Echenique, Crowther, and Lindsay (1972) was linear and additive, and weights fixed on an *a priori* basis were assigned to each index. In this sense, an access index was calculated for each plan as a weighted average of the access indicators for each pair of activities located as part of the plan. In the Peterborough model, the locational patterns of four activities—basic, service employment, total employment, and population—are essential input and output from the model, and it is possible to compute access indicators between each pair of these patterns, including the access of any pattern to itself. By including only non-directional relations, ten indicators can be calculated; these are

TABLE 3.4. Spatial indicators based on accessibility

Accessibility indicator			Relative percentage weights, W_{kl}
k	l		
1 Basic employment	to 1 Basic employment	U_{11}	5
	to 2 Service employment	U_{12}	10
	to 3 Total employment	U_{13}	10
	to 4 Population	U_{14}	20
2 Service employment	to 2 Service employment	U_{22}	5
	to 3 Total employment	U_{23}	5
	to 4 Population	U_{24}	20
3 Total employment	to 3 Total employment	U_{33}	5
	to 4 Population	U_{34}	10
4 Population	to 4 Population	U_{44}	10

Weighted average accessibility:

$$U = \sum_{k=1}^{4} \left(\sum_{l=k}^{4} U_{kl} W_{kl} \right)$$

shown in Table 3.4. The formal basis for these indicators is discussed in the Appendix, which shows how these access factors relate to the structure of the model used to generate the locational patterns. The normalization of these indicators and the construction of the weighted average is also discussed in the Appendix. The weight of each index in the average is shown in Table 3.4, and these weights have been specified intuitively in terms of the author's preconception of the importance of these relationships in urban systems.

The average access indicator can be used as a kind of *post hoc* objective function in evaluating the efficiency of different spatial plans, and it is also possible to calculate the efficiency of the existing town and use this as a baseline for comparison. Each of the nine alternatives described previously, plus the actual New Town, has been elaborated using the gravity- and linear programming-based activity-allocation models, and average access indicators calculated from the predicted patterns. Input data in the form of gross changes in basic employment and the transport network to 1981 were used to generate these patterns. The use of the model in this comparative static way assumes that the predictions show some long-term equilibrium, which is associated with the 1981 pattern but perhaps take much longer to occur. Only the results of the gravity model runs are presented here because the linear programming models generate such 'unreasonable' patterns, as noted previously. However, these linear programming predictions are generally useful in the planning process as a further benchmark against which to compare the gravity model predictions. The access indicators computed for each plan are graphed in Figure 3.22; the non-weighted indicators and weighted indicators generate profiles for each plan which, when compared to the profile for the existing town, give

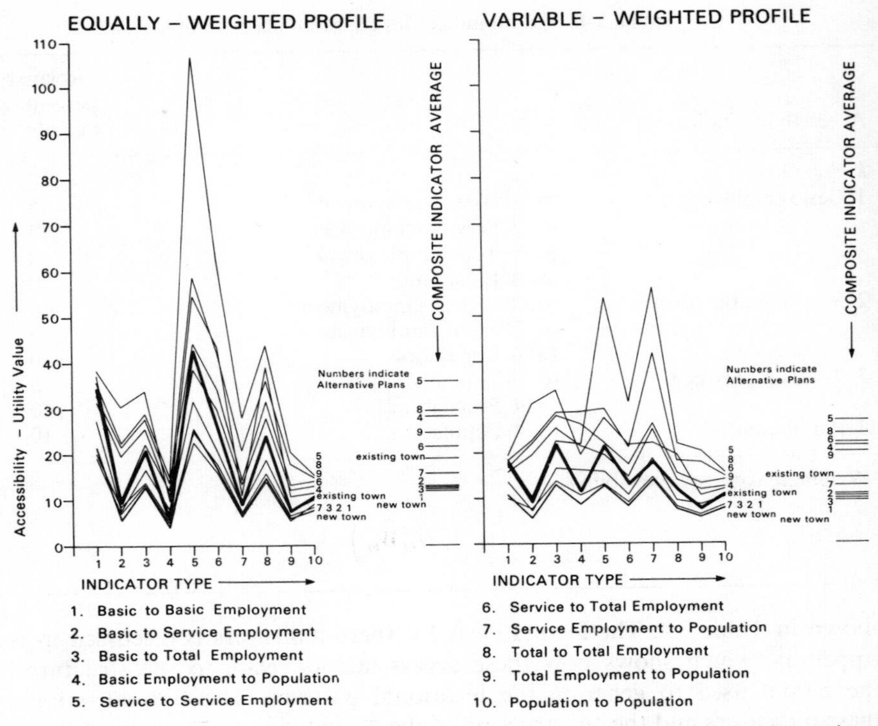

FIGURE 3.22. Access profiles for the existing town, the New Town, and the alternatives

some indication of the relative changes due to different locational configurations.

From the average access indicators, which are computed as sums of the values making up the weighted profiles in Figure 3.22, it is clear that the New Town and the three alternatives which are based on similar development to the west of the existing town are less efficient than the existing town. This appears to be due to the spatial remoteness of these western developments relative to existing development, and in terms of the service and residential trip lengths there is an inverse relationship with average access. This implies that the lower the average access, the greater the length of trip to shop and work. It could be argued that the New Town and alternatives based on western development do not capture any of the existing economies of scale in Peterborough, in contrast to the alternatives based on development around the existing town: to the immediate west, in Bretton to the north-west, in the east, and in the south. From the analysis, two alternatives stand out as considerably more efficient than the others. In the south, in Bretton, and in the eastern developments, the improvements in access in terms of the existing town are large, but average trip lengths remain the same as those at present. In short, it is likely that the network structure of the existing town is such that development in these areas is in the most accessible places anyway. Moreover, in terms of the profile for these two alternatives, the relative locations of basic employment to services and population appear more efficient than the existing town, as can be seen from the changes in profile in Figure 3.22. In both these alternatives, there is also a considerable increase in the accessibility of services to all other activities. However, it is in the alternative based on development to the immediate west of the existing town that the greatest changes in relative access are apparent. In this case, it appears that the pattern of basic employment is highly efficient, probably due to increasing concentrations of such employment in that area.

In summary, it is clear that alternatives which are more spatially integrated with the structure of the existing town are more spatially efficient: average access indicators are higher, trip lengths are the same or slightly lower, and there are no major shifts in existing activity caused by these new developments. In contrast, the developments to the west generate opposite kinds of effect. Because of the more dispersed overall pattern, trip lengths are much higher and access indicators lower; there is also some loss of activity, especially services from the existing town, which might be interpreted as outmigration to the new centres in the west. Whether or not the actual proposal for the New Town is acceptable depends upon the importance placed on the existing town. All that can be said from this analysis is that considerable variations in spatial accessibility and, in this interpretation, efficiency are caused by different town forms. The final choice depends on a host of other issues besides, but it is clear that an analysis of town form in this way helps to focus on this issue. When the New Town plan was proposed in 1967, this type of methodology was not available. Had it been, then it is possible that a different form would have been chosen.

To give substance to this point and by way of conclusion to the use of this type of model in the planning process, it is worth while exploring the actual impact of the proposed New Town in more detail. In Figure 3.23, the actual changes in services and population due to the New Town are shown; of these changes, most are due to the increase in basic jobs in or around those locations, but some change is due to the shift in existing activities. For example, nearly 1 000 service jobs are lost from the town centre to other locations and there is a general increase in services in the smaller centres, thus implying a much more decentralized pattern. This appears to be a general effect of the New Town plan which also increases the service-trip length by 36 per cent. and the work-trip by 28 per cent. Furthermore, the new service centres do not build up to the level anticipated and there is a proliferation of much smaller centres. Whether or not these are desirable trends is not a question which can be answered here, but the fact that such trends can be predicted from these kinds of urban model should be sufficient to open up such questions for further discussion. And to this end, such models have a useful role to play in the planning process.

CONCLUSIONS

To leave the reader with the impression that this idea of urban models in the planning process is widely accepted would be quite false. There is enormous dissent about the development of such models in particular, which mirrors

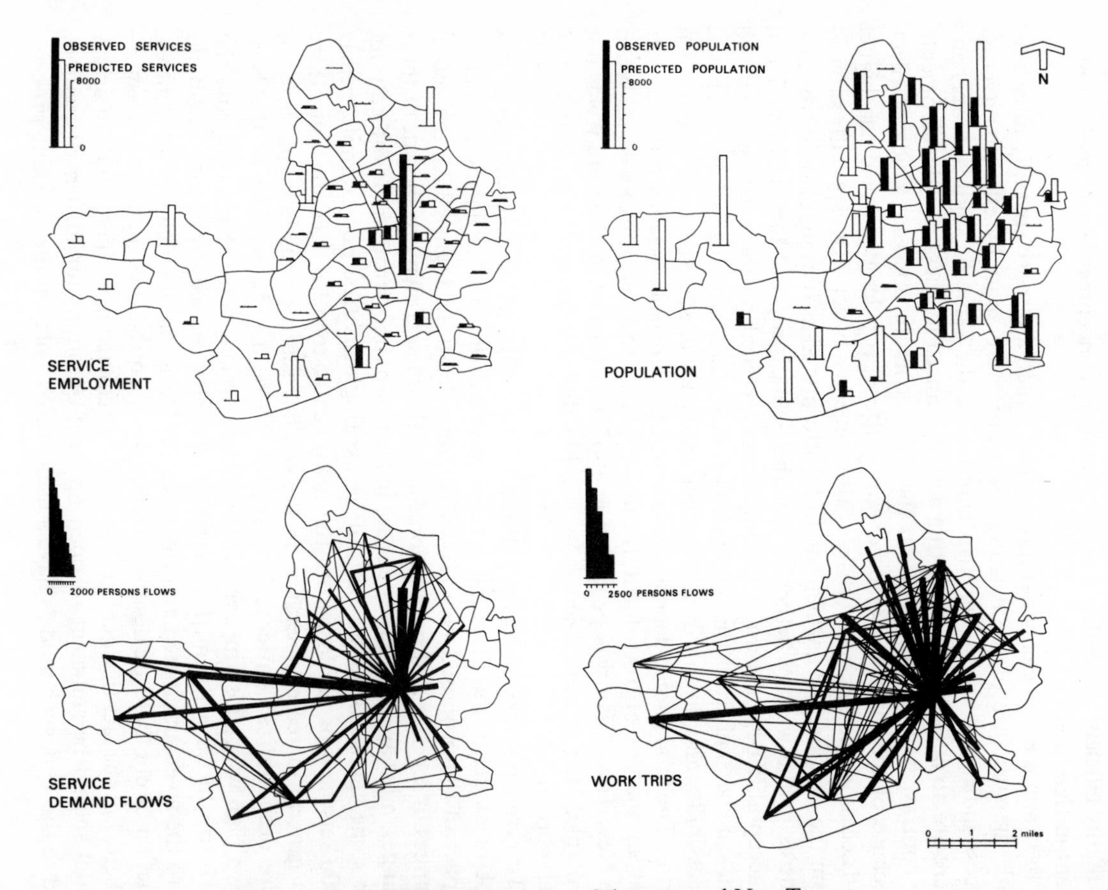

FIGURE 3.23. The spatial impact of the proposed New Town

a more general debate about the use of science in social science and about the appropriateness of scientific analogy. As a means of making the planning process more systematic, the techniques of urban modelling have been essential, and they represent the means through which planning has been transformed from a subject dealing with a relatively simple and certain concept of cities as three-dimensional artifacts to a subject based on treating the city as a complex social and economic phenomenon. Many would agree with this assertion, but some would argue that this has been their sole purpose and that, having accomplished the transformation, it is time for the development of a new, more relevant philosophy of planning in which such models would play no part. There are many variations on this view, but three main objections to the kinds of urban model presented here are worthy of mention.

The first main objection is essentially methodological, and it has already been implied earlier in this paper in the discussion of the model-building and planning process. The problem of prediction in social science is fundamental, for accurate prediction in some senses implies determinate behaviour, which in turn implies a lack of control over the future. This notion, which is clearly incorrect in social systems, is compounded by the fact that observation and then prediction may affect the very observations on which the predictions are made. This seeming impossibility in unravelling cause and effect leads to an awareness that scientific method is limited in dealing with social phenomena. Of course, this dilemma is of much wider concern that urban modelling, but modelling points up the problem in no uncertain terms. The implication of this argument is that the use of models requires an act of faith which can never be substantiated in the way modelling in the physical sciences can, for if the predictions of an urban model were to be correct this would in no way validate the model, just as their incorrectness would not invalidate the model either.

One would not expect the predictions of urban models to be correct, for their prime role is one of simplification, thus leading to a better understanding of the system of interest. The second objection is related to the relevance of the simplification. Some argue that, although the idea of simplification is a worthy one, the state of the art is such that useful simplification is not possible due to lack of relevant theory, the high cost of achieving such simplification, and so on. D. B. Lee (1973), Hoos (1972), and Brewer (1973) have argued this point quite cogently in the context of the North American modelling experience in the 1960s; their essential thesis is that urban models are simply not worth the time and effort involved. The insights to be gained from such model building are small in comparison to the effort expended and the models themselves are like huge dinosaurs—enormous structures containing minute brains. However, this view is based largely on the abuse rather than use of models in planning, and a careful analysis of other experiences, e.g. in Britain (Batty, 1975), does not reveal the same picture. It seems that where such models have been abused there has been a mismatch between the capability of the model and what it has been required to do. Such models can be used intelligently if the conditions under which they are applied match the potential which they have.

The third and final objection relates to antiscientific attitudes which sometimes masquerade under the banner of ideology. Antiscientific attitudes are bred through ignorance, fear, and a desire to preserve the status quo. There is little doubt that many who are reacting against the use of models in planning lack a sympathy for the scientific method and often articulate this lack of sympathy in the form of an ideology hostile to science. Contained within some ideologies, however, is a genuine belief that the ways of science will be unable to help in understanding or mitigating the human condition and that a method in which the essential quality of social phenomena can only be judged through experience is required. A scientific approach has to take the world as given before it begins to work, and this position is so much against the grain of ideologies which seek to change the world.

Despite these powerful forces of objection, urban modelling is able to help planners to structure their ideas and, at least by negation, to show them how to proceed. But there are limits to such rationality, and perhaps a more fruitful research frontier now involves exploring these limits. To say that planning requires an appropriate philosophy of social action sounds somewhat trite, but at least there is now a conscious desire among planners and researchers to become involved in these questions. The limits to such rationality can be explored in many ways, but the models presented in this paper are likely to be important in finding these limits. The dilemmas raised in developing and using urban models are probably of a perennial nature, and, although these problems might never be resolved, they will only become better understood when more experience is gained of their application in the planning process.

TECHNICAL APPENDIX: THE FORMAL STRUCTURE OF THE PETERBOROUGH MODEL

As it is possible to develop the structure of the model without specifying the actual forms used to allocate urban activity, the general linear structure of the model will first be described, followed by a discussion of the relevant gravity and linear programming location models. This then serves as a basis on which to introduce the method used to incorporate external zones into the model's equation structure. Finally, the accessibility indicators computed from the model's predictions and used in comparing alternative plans are presented.

The equation system and solution procedure

The system is based on the iterative sequence of generation and allocation of population from employment and further employment from the population, as described at length in the main text. The system ratios α, β, and λ (the activity, population-dependent serving and employment-dependent serving ratios respectively) control the speed of convergence of the process and ensure that the iterative sequence is geometrically convergent. This will not be demonstrated here for it is explored in detail elsewhere (Batty, 1976; Wilson, 1974). Variables are given a zonal notation through subscripts $i,j,k = 1,2,\ldots,N$ where, in general, i and k refer to 'origin' zones where employment is located and j to 'destination' zones where population resides; in any one iteration, the model begins by generating population in j from employment in i and then generates further employment in i from population in j and from previous employment in k. The input data which drive the economic base mechanism is basic employment $\{B_i\}$ and the allocation matrices linking origins and destinations are specified *a priori*: $p_{ij}(\mu_1)$ is the probability of working in i and living in j, $e_{ki}(\mu_2)$ the probability of working in k and generating services in i, and $s_{ij}(\mu_3)$ the probability of living in j and generating services in i. The parameters μ_1, μ_2, and μ_3 define the functions which form the allocation matrices; these are detailed below.

A typical iteration is notated by the index m; the input to the process is $E_i(m)$, employment in i on iteration m where for $m = 1, E_i(1) = B_i$, and for $m > 1, E_i(m) = S_i(m-1) + \rho_i E_i(m-1)$. $S_i(m-1)$ is the service employment generated on the previous iteration in i and ρ_i is the proportion of input employment on the previous iteration which was not allocated due to constraint violations. Note that $0 \leqslant \rho_i < 1$. First, population $P_j(m)$ is generated by

$$P_j(m) = \alpha \sum_i T_{ij}(m) = \alpha \sum_i E_i(m) p_{ij}(\mu_1) \tag{3.1}$$

where $T_{ij}(m)$ is the number of workers employed in i and living in j, referred to as work trips. The probability matrix $p_{ij}(\mu_1)$ is normalized to sum to unity over the j destination set; that is,

$$\sum_j p_{ij}(\mu_1) = 1 \rightarrow \sum_j T_{ij}(m) = E_i(m)$$

This normalization ensures that the work trips generated sum to some known constraint on origins, and in the spatial interaction literature the model on the extreme right-hand side of equation (3.1) is known as 'singly-constrained' or 'origin-constrained'.

Having generated the increment of population, it is necessary to check whether or not the constraints on population represented by $\{p_j^{\max}\}$ have been violated. If

$$\sum_{z=1}^{m} P_j(z) > P_j^{\max} \tag{3.2}$$

the following constraint mechanism is used. For any zone j in which the constraint has been violated, the surplus $\Delta P_j(m)$ is computed from

$$\Delta P_j(m) = \sum_{z=1}^{m} P_j(z) - p_j^{\max} \tag{3.3}$$

and proportionately redistributed back to its origin by

$$\Delta E_i^P(m) = \sum_j \frac{\Delta P_j(m)}{P_j(m)} T_{ij}(m) \tag{3.4}$$

$\Delta E_i^P(m)$ is the surplus input employment which is reallocated on the next iteration $m+1$. $T_{ij}(m)$ must also be adjusted:

$$T_{ij}(m) = T_{ij}(m)\left[1 - \frac{\Delta P_j(m)}{P_j(m)}\right] \quad (3.5)$$

and then the population increment is set as

$$P_j(m) = P_j^{\max} - \sum_{z=1}^{m-1} P_j(z) \quad (3.6)$$

The constrained zone j is no longer considered in later allocations, and this is effected by setting $p_{ij}(\mu_1), \forall_i$ for constrained j, to zero, and renormalizing.

The next step is to generate service employment. First employment-dependent services $S_i^e(m)$ are generated and allocated by

$$S_i^e(m) = \lambda \sum_k E_{ki}(m) = \lambda \sum_k E_k(m) e_{ki}(\mu_2) \quad (3.7)$$

$E_{ki}(m)$ is the demand for services in i from the employment generated at the previous iteration in i, and equation (3.7) is normalized so that

$$\sum_i e_{ki}(\mu_2) = 1 \rightarrow \sum_i E_{ki}(m) = E_k(m)$$

Population-dependent services $S_i^P(m)$ also need to be generated from the increment of population, and this is done by

$$S_i^P = \beta \sum_j S_{ij}(m) = \beta \sum_j P_j(m) s_{ij}(\mu_3) \quad (3.8)$$

where $S_{ij}(m)$ is the number of services demanded in i by persons living in j. Equation (3.8) is normalized by a destination constraint

$$\sum_i s_{ij}(\mu_3) = 1 \rightarrow \sum_i s_{ij}(m) = P_j(m)$$

The increment of total service employment $S_i(m)$ is calculated from

$$S_i(m) = S_i^e(m) + S_i^P(m) \quad (3.9)$$

and if

$$\sum_{z=1}^{m} S_i(m) > S_i^{\max} \quad (3.10)$$

where $S_i^{\max}$ is the capacity constraint on service employment, constraint mechanisms similar to that in equations (3.2) to (3.6) are invoked.

The surplus $\Delta S_i(m)$ is computed from

$$\Delta S_i(m) = \sum_{z=1}^{m} S_i(m) - S_i^{\max} \quad (3.11)$$

and this surplus is redistributed back to the employment and population activity from which it was generated in proportion to the associated service demand flows. For employment-dependent services, the surplus employment $\Delta E_k^e(m)$ to be reallocated on the next iteration is given by

$$\Delta E_k^e(m) = \sum_i \frac{\Delta S_i(m)}{S_i(m)} E_{ki}(m) \tag{3.12}$$

and service demand flows $E_{ki}(m)$ are adjusted by

$$E_{ki}(m) = E_{ki}(m)\left[1 - \frac{\Delta S_i(m)}{S_i(m)}\right] \tag{3.13}$$

$S_i^e(m)$ could also be adjusted, but this is not necessary because, as will be demonstrated below, another cycle of the same iteration will be required to generate consistent distributions which do not infringe the constraints. For population-dependent services, these have to be reallocated back to the population which generated the services and this surplus population $\Delta P_j^S(m)$ back to the employment from which in turn the population was generated. Then

$$\Delta P_j^S(m) = \sum_i \frac{\Delta S_i(m)}{S_i(m)} S_{ij}(m) \tag{3.14}$$

and

$$S_{ij}(m) = S_{ij}(m)\left[1 - \frac{\Delta S_i(m)}{S_i(m)}\right] \tag{3.15}$$

$S_i^P(m)$ can be adjusted if required and $\Delta P_j^S(m)$ must then be reallocated to derive surplus employment $\Delta E_i^S(m)$. This is done by

$$\Delta E_i^S(m) = \sum_j \frac{\Delta P_j^S(m)}{P_j(m)} T_{ij}(m) \tag{3.16}$$

and $T_{ij}(m)$ is once again readjusted by

$$T_{ij}(m) = T_{ij}(m)\left[1 - \frac{\Delta P_j^S(m)}{P_j(m)}\right] \tag{3.17}$$

$P_j(m)$ can also be adjusted if required.

At this stage, a series of surplus employments $\Delta E_i^P(m)$, $\Delta E_i^S(m)$, and $\Delta E_i^e(m)$ has been calculated, but the distributions of population and service increments only take account of the surplus $\Delta E_i^P(m)$. Therefore, the system of equations must be solved again, but this time starting with a new value for the input employment $E_i(m)$ called $E_i(m')$ calculated from

$$E_i(m') = E_i(m)(1 - \rho_i) \tag{3.18}$$

where

$$\rho_i = \frac{\Delta E_i^P(m) + \Delta E_i^S(m) + \Delta E_i^e(m)}{\Delta E_i(m)} \tag{3.19}$$

Clearly ρ_i is the proportion of activity to be redistributed on a later iteration.

It can easily be proved that none of the constraints will be violated if equations (3.2), (3.7), (3.8), and (3.9) are solved starting with $E_i(m')$, but it is likely that no one constraint will actually be met either. In such a problem, one constraint or set of constraints, i.e. on population or services, is likely to dominate the solution, and if some equilibrium in which the dominant constraints are actually met is required, then equations (3.1) to (3.19) must be solved iteratively without using equations (3.2) and (3.10) on the second and subsequent iterations. A similar type of constrained equilibrium is a feature of the Cambridge stocks–activities model (Batty, 1976). However, it is unlikely that such iteration is worth while because the generation procedure is fairly artificial in any case and it is quicker to generate and allocate new activity, as well as reallocating old activity, than to spend time only reallocating the old activity.

For the next iteration $m+1$, the matrices $e_{ki}(\mu_2)$ and $s_{ij}(\mu_3)$ must be renormalized to take account of the fact that certain zones i may have reached their constraint, and this is done by setting the locational attractions of these zones to zero. The new input employment for iteration $m+1$ is calculated from

$$E_i(m+1) = \rho_i E_i(m) + S_i(m) \tag{3.20}$$

and $E_i(m+1)$ is substituted into equation (3.1). Equations (3.1) to (3.20) are repeated until some convergence limit is attained, and the process of generation and allocation resulting from the initial input of basic employment is deemed to have worked itself out.

The allocation procedures: gravity and linear programming models

The three allocation matrices were based on singly-constrained gravity models composed of two terms: a simple measure of locational attraction and a negative exponential function of spatial deterrence based on travel time. These matrices are stated as follows:

$$p_{ij}(\mu_1) = \frac{R_j \exp(-\mu_1 d_{ij})}{\sum_j R_j \exp(-\mu_1 d_{ij})} \tag{3.21}$$

where R_j is the attraction of zone j to employment at i, measured by the population residing at j in the base year 1971, and μ_1 is a parameter of the negative exponential distribution of travel time d_{ij}. The demand for services by employment is based on a similar function

$$e_{ki}(\mu_2) = \frac{H_i \exp(-\mu_2 d_{ki})}{\sum_i H_i \exp(-\mu_2 d_{ki})} \tag{3.22}$$

where H_i is the attraction of zone i measured by total employment at the base date and μ_2 is a parameter of the negative exponential. Lastly, population-dependent demand is calculated from

$$s_{ij}(\mu_3) = \frac{F_i \exp(-\mu_3 d_{ij})}{\sum_i F_i \exp(-\mu_3 d_{ij})} \tag{3.23}$$

F_i is the total service employment in i at the base date and μ_3 is a parameter. It is possible to combine equations (3.22) and (3.23) in the main model and thus reduce the calibration problem from a three- to two-parameter estimation. In the Peterborough model both the three- and two-parameter models were tried, and in the research into urban model calibration which accompanied this application the two-parameter version was used (Batty, 1977).

It is now quite well known that as the parameters μ_1, μ_2 and μ_3 tend to infinity, then the models in equations (3.21) to (3.23) tend to linear programming models in which total distance or travel time incurred is minimized (Evans, 1973). In terms of, say, the residential location probability $p_{ij}(\mu_1)$, and assuming no ties, this means that

$$p_{ij}(\infty) = \begin{cases} 1, \text{ if } p_{ij}(\infty) = \min\limits_j [p_{ij}(\infty)] \\ 0, \text{ otherwise} \end{cases}$$

If there are ties for the minimum value, then this indicates the existence of multiple solutions. However, as these models have no destination constraints in the form given above, they are trivial LP models which can be solved by inspection. For the above models, travel time was not minimized; instead, the function of attraction–deterrence as calibrated by the gravity model application was maximized. For the residential location model, the problem was set up as follows: choose $T_{ij}(m)$ on iteration m so that composite attraction–deterrence is maximized, that is,

$$\max \sum_i \sum_j T_{ij} R_j \exp(-\mu_1 d_{ij}) \tag{3.24}$$

subject to the origin constraints

$$\sum_j T_{ij}(m) = E_i(m), \forall_i \tag{3.25}$$

and the destination constraints

$$\alpha \sum_i \sum_{z=1}^{m} T_{ij}(z) \leqslant P_j^{\max}, \forall_j \tag{3.26}$$

In fact, equation (3.26) can be rewritten as

$$\alpha \sum_i T_{ij}(m) \leqslant P_j^{\max} - \sum_i \sum_{z=1}^{m-1} T_{ij}(m), \forall_j \tag{3.27}$$

which indicates that the LP problem is different at every iteration of the general model.

The LP model in equations (3.24), (3.25), and (3.27) can be solved as a transportation problem using Vogel's approximation method for a good starting solution and Hitchcock's algorithm from then on. However, such a sequence of LP problems is particularly time-consuming in computer terms for large problems such as these. For example, the Peterborough problem has 65 zones and involves the active consideration of 4 225 variables; the choice of variables is subject to 65 origin, 65 destination, and one dummy constraint, which reduces to 130 constraints in total. This is an enormous problem computationally and thus an approximation method has been devised. It is possible simply to use Vogel's rule which gives quite good approximations to the optimum, but here the structure of the generation process, within which the LP is embedded, can also be used to aid solution. Rather than using any iterative LP code to meet the constraints, the idea is that the constraints are chosen on any general model iteration m so as to make the LP problem relatively trivial to solve. Because the constraints are a function of the iterative generation process, and as this process is somewhat arbitrary, it is possible to redesign the process so that only enough activity is ever allocated on any iteration just to meet, but not violate, the constraints. In fact, this is the process used to incorporate constraints in the framework outlined above in equations (3.1) to (3.20). However, proportionate reallocation of surplus activity is not appropriate and therefore the procedure is modified as follows.

For the residential location model, first $T_{ij}(m)$ is chosen by inspection, assuming *no* destination constraints are operable. Then

$$T_{ij}(m) = \begin{cases} E_i(m), \text{ for } \max\limits_j [R_j \exp(-\mu_1 d_{ij})] \\ 0, \text{ otherwise} \end{cases} \tag{3.28}$$

The population increment is calculated as usual:

$$P_j(m) = \alpha \sum_i T_{ij}(m) \tag{3.29}$$

and if

$$P_j(m) > P_j^{\max} - \sum_{z=1}^{m-1} P_j(z) \tag{3.30}$$

the surplus $\Delta P_j(m)$ computed as in equation (3.3) is reallocated; in short, only sufficient activity $(1-\rho_i)E_i(m)$ to meet the dominant constraint is allocated on this iteration and $\rho_i E_i(m)$ is allocated on a later iteration. When the dominant destination constraint is defined, that destination is never again considered for allocation, and thus the dimensionality of the problem is successively reduced through the iterations. Thus, no LP-type iterations are required. However, the surplus cannot be reallocated back to the origin proportionately to $T_{ij}(m)$, for this would be blatantly suboptimal. For any zone j, the elements $R_j \exp(-\mu_1 d_{ij})$ must be ranked from worst to best, and the reallocation is achieved sequentially from worst-to-best ij pairs until the constraint is met exactly.

Then, for any zone j with a surplus $\Delta P_j(m)$, the following algorithm is used which considers each $T_{ij}(m)$ in the order produced by the above ranking from worst to best. The origin surplus $\Delta E_i^P(m)$ is set equal to before the algorithm begins and X_i indicates the amount of activity to be reallocated back to the origin i for a given destination j. That is,

$$X_i = \begin{cases} T_{ij}(m), & \text{if } T_{ij}(m) \leqslant \Delta P_j(m) \\ \Delta P_j(m), & \text{if } T_{ij}(m) > \Delta P_j(m) \end{cases} \tag{3.31}$$

$$\Delta E_i(m) = \Delta E_i(m) + X_i \tag{3.32}$$

$$\Delta P_j(m) = \Delta P_j(m) - X_i \tag{3.33}$$

The trip $T_{ij}(m)$ is now adjusted as follows:

$$T_{ij}(m) = \begin{cases} 0, & \text{if } \Delta P_j(m) > 0 \\ T_{ij}(m) - X_i, & \text{if } \Delta P_j(m) = 0 \end{cases} \tag{3.34}$$

If the first condition in equation (3.34) holds, equations (3.31) to (3.33) are repeated until the second condition in equation (3.34) is reached. When this is so, the reallocation has been accomplished according to the ranking of zones from worst-to-best attraction–deterrence values.

This type of linear programming solution leads to an optimum configuration of trips, different from that which would be generated if the constraints had to be met exactly on each iteration. But as the iterative process is arbitrary, the procedure outlined above is quite acceptable and certainly advantageous from the point of view of feasibility and cost of operation. Analogous procedures have been used to generate employment and population-dependent services which involve location based on the maximization of attraction–deterrence values. In these cases, the reallocation is effected using the worst–best ranking algorithm presented above, by finding the locations in which the constraints are dominant and by excluding those locations from further consideration in subsequent iterations. In terms of the general equation system given in the previous section, equations (3.1), (3.7), and (3.8) are specified using iteration calculated in a way similar to equation (3.28), and the surplus redistributing algorithms given in equations (3.2) to (3.6), (310) to (3.13), and (3.14) to (3.17) are formulated using the worst–best ranking algorithm in equations (3.31) to (3.34).

The external zone problem

There are many ways in which the environment of a spatial system can be considered in a model of that system. The general idea is to establish explicitly the amount of energy interchange between the system and its environment, so that the relative dependence or independence of the system is incorporated into the model; in spatial systems flows of people, information, goods, etc., into and out of the system constitute this interchange which is economic in character, and these flows structure the spatial competitiveness of the system in terms of other systems contained in the environment. In this model, it was decided to take account of these flows by formulating the model to reproduce them exactly, and to this end artificial but consistent data were produced for the external zones. This method parallels the method used for the Area 8 sub-regional model (Batty *et al.*, 1974). First note that i, j refer to origin and destination zones in the internal system I, and k, l to origin and destination zones in the external system Z. The ratios α, β, and λ are computed from totals in I, and if these are used to generate activity in Z then prespecified activity in Z must be consistent with the generation process. Service trip patterns are not known, for all that are available are the flows T_{il} and T_{kj}. As the interest is only on the flows between internal and external systems, flows of the form T_{kl} are never computed, or are computed assuming infinite deterrence between k and l which is the same thing. The volume of work trips destined for any external zone l and the associated population P_l can be calculated from

$$P_l = \alpha \sum_i T_{il} \tag{3.35}$$

and total employment in $k(E_k)$ from

$$E_k = \sum_j T_{kj} \tag{3.36}$$

Note that other trips destined for l or originating in k are assumed to be zero, because there is no interest in them. Employment E_k must be decomposed into B_k, S_k^e, and S_k^p to maintain consistency with the internal zone ratios β and λ,

$$S_k^e = \lambda E_k \tag{3.37}$$

and

$$S_k^p = \beta P_l \qquad (l = k) \tag{3.38}$$

Basic employment B_k is then calculated from

$$B_k = E_k - S_k^e - S_k^p \tag{3.39}$$

B_k may be negative to satisfy equation (3.39), but this poses no problems at the calibration stage.

Because no interaction is allowed within the external zones, to satisfy constraints on services and population in equations (3.35), (3.37), and (3.38), all interaction must be between the internal and external systems. Thus the gross dependence of the system on its environment could be established if these constraints were met. To achieve this, it is possible simply to fill up the external zones in the first few iterations of the general model and then, once the constraints have been met, to disregard them in future iterations. In practice, this is done by specifying extremely large attraction values on the external locations and operating the model in the normal way. But there are problems with this scheme; although it enables the dependence to be established, it is difficult to use predictively and, because of the artificiality of the external zone data, it tends to complicate trip-length estimation. For example, in situations where the environment contains large cities with very different ratios, the service-trip lengths can be severely biased. Other methods which do not have these problems but are much more demanding in terms of computer time are also possible (Masser and Brown, 1976).

Spatial indicators based on accessibility

Given m activity patterns which form the inputs or outputs from any urban model, there is a total of m^2 relationships between each of these patterns, taken two at a time. In fact, it is possible to disregard $(m^2 - m)/2$ of these patterns because they have already been accounted for due to the symmetrical nature of the calculation. Therefore, for m patterns, there are $(m^2 + m)/2$ relationships, which might be accessibilities of one activity to another in the case of a spatial system. For example, in the Peterborough model, four activities—basic, service, and total employment and population—are defined and ten accessibility measures can be computed for these four patterns: basic to basic, to service, to total employment, and to population; service to service, to total employment, and to population; total to total employment and to population; and population to population. The accessibility measures between these activities are calculated in the conventional way, using the potential measure first suggested by Stewart (1947), but, because there is need for comparison between different alternative plans, it is necessary to remove size effects so that the comparison is in relative location terms. Then, for any activity k existing in zone i, called X_{ik}, a new variable x_{ik} is defined to the following normalization:

$$x_{ik} = \frac{X_{ik}}{\sum_i X_{ik}} \qquad (k = 1, 2, \ldots, m) \tag{3.40}$$

The accessibility U_{kl} between any activity k and l is then calculated from

$$U_{kl} = G\left[\sum_i x_{ik} \sum_j x_{jl} d_{ij}^{-2}\right] \qquad (k = 1, 2, \ldots, m;\ l = k, k+1, \ldots, m) \tag{3.41}$$

An inverse square function of distance has been assumed in this accessibility measure and a constant of proportionality ensures that the index is scaled to workable values. In this study, $G = 10^5$.

For each alternative plan, an overall index of accessibility U has been calculated by forming a linear combination of the measures U_{kl} and reflecting their relative importance using a set of weights w_k fixed *a priori*. This index is thus calculated as

$$U = \sum_{k=1}^{m} \left(\sum_{l=k}^{m} U_{kl} w_{kl} \right) \tag{3.42}$$

The function in equation (3.42) is linear and additive and is subject to all the criticisms and difficulties involved in the construction of simple additive utility functions. This is not the place to develop this critique; suffice it to say that equation (3.42) is useful as a means of demonstrating the idea of spatial indicators.

ACKNOWLEDGEMENTS

The author would like to thank Ian Gilliver for his help in formulating the initial version of the Peterborough model and in preparing the data base necessary for the model's operation; and Sheila Dance who made such a magnificent job of drafting the diagrams.

REFERENCES

Alexander, C. (1964). *Notes on the Synthesis of Form*, Harvard University Press, Cambridge, Massachusetts.

Alonso, W. (1964). *Location and Land Use*, Harvard University Press, Cambridge, Massachusetts.

Angel, S., and Hyman, G. (1976). *Urban Fields*, Pion Press, London.

Ashby, W. R. (1952). *Design for a Brain*, Chapman and Hall, London.

Ashby, W. R. (1956). *An Introduction to Cybernetics*, Chapman and Hall, London.

Bather, N., Williams, C., and Sutton, A. (1976). *Strategic Choice in Practice*. Geographical Papers No. 50, Department of Geography, University of Reading, Reading, Berkshire.

Batty, M. (1969). The impact of a New Town. *Journal of the Town Planning Institute*, **55**, 428–435.

Batty, M. (1970a). *Spatial Theory and Information Systems*. Urban Systems Research Unit Working Paper No. 3, Department of Geography, University of Reading, Reading, Berkshire.

Batty, M. (1970b). *Introductory Model-Building Problems for Urban and Regional Planning*. Urban Systems Research Unit Working Note No. 8, Department of Geography, University of Reading, Reading, Berkshire.

Batty, M. (1972). Recent developments in land use modelling: a review of British research. *Urban Studies*, **9**, 151–177.

Batty, M. (1975). In defence of urban modelling. *Journal of the Royal Town Planning Institute*, **61**, 184–187.

Batty, M. (1976). *Urban Modelling: Algorithms, Calibrations, Predictions*, Cambridge University Press, Cambridge.

Batty, M. (1977). *Pseudo-Dynamic Urban Models*. Unpublished paper, Department of Geography, University of Reading, Reading, Berkshire.

Batty, M., Bourke, R., Cormode, P., and Anderson-Nicholls, M. (1974). Experiments in urban modelling for county structure planning: The Area 8 pilot model. *Environment and Planning A*, **6**, 455–478.

Batty, M., and March, L. (1976). *Dynamic Urban Models Based on Information-Minimising*. Geographical Papers No. 48, Department of Geography, University of Reading, Reading, Berkshire.

Baxter, R. S., and Williams, I. N. (1975). An automatically calibrated urban model. *Environment and Planning A*, **7**, 3–20.

Beckmann, M. J. (1974). Entropy gravity and utility in transportation modelling. In G. Menges (Ed.), *Information, Inference and Decision*, D. Reidel Publishing, Dordrecht, Holland.

Beer, S. (1959). *Cybernetics and Management*, English Universities Press, London.

Berry, B. J. L. (1967). *Geography of Market Centers and Retail Distribution*, Prentice-Hall, Englewood Cliffs, New Jersey.

Bertalanffy, L. von (1970). *General System Theory*, Allen Lane, The Penguin Press, Harmondsworth.

Boyce, D. E., Day, N. D., and McDonald, C. (1970). *Metropolitan Plan-Making*, Regional Science Research Institute, Philadelphia, Pennsylvania.

Breheny, M. J. (1974). Towards measures of spatial opportunity. *Progress in Planning*, **2**, 85–142.

Brewer, G. D. (1973). *Politicians, Bureaucrats and the Consultant: A Critique of Urban Problem-Solving*, Basic Books, New York.

Broadbent, T. A. (1969). *Zone Size and Spatial Interaction in Operational Models*. CES-WN-106, Centre for Environmental Studies, London.

Broadbent, T. A. (1970). Notes on the design of operational models. *Environment and Planning*, **2**, 469–476.

Brotchie, J. F., and Sharpe, R. (1975). A general land use allocation model: application to Australian cities. In R. Baxter, M. Echenique, and J. Owers (Eds.), *Urban Development Models*, The Construction Press, Lancaster.

Carrothers, G. A. P. (1956). An historical review of the gravity and potential concepts of human interaction. *Journal of the American Institute of Planners*, **22**, 94–102.

Chadwick, G. F. (1971). *A Systems View of Planning*, Pergamon Press, Oxford.

Chapin, F. S., and Weiss, S. F. (1962). *Factors Influencing Land Development*, Institute for Research in Social Science, University of North Carolina, Chapel Hill, North Carolina.

Charnes, A., Raike, W. M., and Bettinger, C. O. (1972). An extremal and information-theoretic characterization of some interzonal transfer models. *Socio-Economic Planning Sciences*, **6**, 531–537.

Christaller, W. (1933, translated 1966). *Central Places in Southern Germany*, Prentice-Hall, Englewood Cliffs, New Jersey.

Coleman, J. S. (1964). *Introduction to Mathematical Sociology*, The Free Press of Glencoe, New York.

Crecine, J. P. (1964). *TOMM: Time Oriented Metropolitan Model*. C. R. P. Technical Bulletin No. 6, Department of City Planning, Pittsburgh, Pennsylvania.

Cripps, E. L., and Foot, D. H. S. (1969). A land use model for subregional planning. *Regional Studies*, **3**, 243–268.

Crowther, D., and Echenique, M. (1972). Development of a model of urban spatial structures. In L. Martin and L. March (Eds.), *Urban Space and Structures*, Cambridge University Press, Cambridge.

Davies, R. L. (1976). *Marketing Geography*, Retailing and Planning Associates, Corbridge, Northumberland.

Echenique, M. (1971). A model of the urban spatial structure. *Architectural Design*, **41**, 277–280.

Echenique, M. (Ed.) (1975). *Modelos Matematicos de la Estructure Espacial Urbana: Aplicaciones en America Latina*, SIAP, Buenos Aires.

Echenique, M., Crowther, D., and Lindsay, W. (1972). A structural comparison of three generations of New Towns. In L. Martin and L. March (Eds.), *Urban Space and Structures*, Cambridge University Press, Cambridge.

Echenique, M., Feo, A., Herrera, R., and Riquezes, J. (1974). A disaggregated model of urban spatial structure: theoretical framework. *Environment and Planning A*, **6**, 33–63.

Etzioni, A. (1968). *The Active Society*, The Free Press of Glencoe, New York.

Evans, S. (1973). A relationship between the gravity model for trip distribution and the transportation problem in linear programming. *Transportation Research*, **7**, 39–62.

Fratar, T. J. (1954). Vehicular trip generation by successive approximation. *Traffic Quarterly*, **8**, 53–65.

Friedmann, J. (1973). *Retracking America: A Theory of Transactive Planning*, Anchor Press-Doubleday, New York.

Friend, J. K., and Jessop, W. N. (1969). *Local Government and Strategic Choice*, Tavistock Publications, London.

Furness, K. P. (1965). Time function iteration. *Traffic Engineering and Control*, **7**, 458–460.

Garin, R. A. (1966). A matrix formulation of the Lowry model for intra-metropolitan activity location. *Journal of the American Institute of Planners*, **32**, 361–364.

Geddes, P. (1915). *Cities in Evolution*, Williams and Norgate, London. (Republished 1949).

Goldner, W., and Graybeal, R. S. (1965). *The Bay Area Simulation Study: A Pilot Model of Santa Clara County and Some Applications*, Center for Real Estate and Urban Economics, University of California, Berkeley, California.

Guy, C. (1976). *The Location of Shops in the Reading Area*. Geographical Papers No. 46, Department of Geography, University of Reading, Reading, Berkshire.

Hancock, T., and Hawkes, J. (1967). *Greater Peterborough: Draft Basic Plan*, Hancock and Hawkes Architect-Planners, London.

Hansen, W. G. (1959). How accessibility shapes land use. *Journal of the American Institute of Planners*, **25**, 73–76.

Harris, B. (1960). *Linear Programming and the Projection of Land Uses*. Penn-Jersey Paper No. 20, Penn-Jersey Transportation Study, Philadelphia, Pennsylvania.

Harris, B. (1966a). The uses of theory in the simulation of urban phenomena. *Journal of the American Institute of Planners*, **32**, 258–273.

Harris, B. (1966b). *Note on Aspects of Equilibrium in Urban Growth Models*, Department of City and Regional Planning, University of Pennsylvania, Philadelphia, Pennsylvania.

Harris, B. (1968). Quantitative models of urban development: their role in metropolitan policy-making. In H. S. Perloff and L. Wingo (Eds.), *Issues in Urban Economics*, The Johns Hopkins Press, Baltimore, Maryland.

Harris, B. (1971). Planning as a branch and bound process. *Papers of the Regional Science Association*, **26**, 53–63.

Haynes, R. M. (1975). Dimensional analysis: some applications in human geography. *Geographical Analysis*, **7**, 51–67.

Hickling, A. (1974). *Managing Decisions: The Strategic Choice Approach*, Mantec Publications, Rugby, Northamptonshire.

Hill, D. M. (1965). A growth allocation model for the Boston region. *Journal of the American Institute of Planners*, **31**, 111–120.

Hoos, I. R. (1972). *Systems Analysis in Public Policy*, University of California Press, Berkeley, California.

Huff, D. L. (1963). A probabilistic analysis of shopping center trade areas. *Land Economics*, **39**, 81–90.

Hutchinson, B. G. (1975). Tools for urban land use-transport strategy planning. *Canadian Journal of Civil Engineering*, **2**, 85–97.

Hyman, G. M. (1969). The calibration of trip distribution models. *Environment and Planning*, **1**, 105–112.

Irwin, N. A., and Brand, D. (1965). Planning and forecasting metropolitan development. *Traffic Quarterly*, **19**, 520–540.

Kuhn, T. S. (1962). *The Structure of Scientific Revolutions*, University of Chicago Press, Chicago.

Lakshmanan, T. R., and Hansen, W. G. (1965). A retail market potential model. *Journal of the American Institute of Planners*, **31**, 134–143.

Lathrop, G. T., and Hamburg, J. R. (1965). An opportunity accessibility model for allocating regional growth. *Journal of the American Institute of Planners*, **31**, 95–108.

Lee, C. (1973). *Models in Planning*, Pergamon Press, Oxford.

Lee, D. B. (1973). Requiem for large scale models. *Journal of the American Institute of Planners*, **39**, 163–178.

Lighthill, M. J., and Whitham, G. G. (1955). On kinematic waves II: a theory of traffic flow on long crowded roads. *Proceedings of the Royal Society, Series A*, **229**, 317–345.

Losch, A. (1944, translated 1954). *The Economics of Location*, Yale University Press, New Haven, Connecticut.

Lowry, I. S. (1964). *A Model of Metropolis*, RM-4035-RC. The RAND Corporation, Santa Monica, California.

Lowry, I. S. (1965). A short course in model design. *Journal of the American Institute of Planners*, **31**, 158–166.

Lowry, I. S. (1968). Seven models of urban development. In G. Hemmens (Ed.), *Urban Development Models*. Special Report No. 97, Highway Research Board, Washington, D.C.

McLoughlin, J. B. (1969). *Urban and Regional Planning: A Systems Approach*, Faber and Faber, London.

McLoughlin, J. B., Nix, C. K., and Foot, D. H. S. (1966). *Regional Shopping Centres: A Planning Report on North West England*: Part 2: *A Retail Shopping Model*, Department of Town and Country Planning, University of Manchester, Manchester.

Masser, I. (1972). *Analytical Models for Urban and Regional Planning*, David and Charles, Newton Abbott.

Masser, I., and Brown, P. (1976). *Spatial Representation and Spatial Interaction*, WP-8. Instituut voor Planologie, Rijksuniversiteit Utrecht, Utrecht, Holland.

Massey, D. B. (1973). The basic:service categorisation in planning. *Regional Studies*, **7**, 1–15.

Michael, D. N. (1973). *On Learning to Plan—and Planning to Learn*, Jossey-Bass Publishers, San Francisco, California.

Mitchell, R. B., and Rapkin, C. (1954). *Urban Traffic: A Function of Land Use*, Columbia University Press, New York.

Morrison, W. I. (1972). *Urban Interindustry Analysis: An Input–Output Study of the Peterborough Economy*. Unpublished Ph.D. dissertation, University College, London.

Papageorgiou, G. J. (Ed.) (1976). *Mathematical Land Use Theory*, D. C. Heath, Lexington, Massachusetts.

Paelinck, J. H. P. (1975). Testing accessibility. In R. Baxter, M. Echenique, and J. Owers (Eds.), *Urban Development Models*, The Construction Press Lancaster.

Putman, S. H. (1967). Intra-urban industrial location model design and implementation. *Papers of the Regional Science Association*, **19**, 199–214.

Reif, B. (1973). *Models in Urban and Regional Planning*, Intext Publishers, London.

Reilly, W. J. (1931). *The Law of Retail Gravitation*, Reilly, New York.

Sayer, R. A. (1975). *Dynamic Spatial Models of Urban and Regional Systems*. Unpublished D.Phil. thesis, University of Sussex, Falmer, Sussex.

Schlager, K. J. (1965). A land-use plan design model. *Journal of the American Institute of Planners*, **31**, 103–111.

Schon, D. (1971). *Beyond the Stable State*, Maurice Temple Smith, London.

Shackle, G. L. S. (1967). *The Years of High Theory*, Cambridge University Press, Cambridge.

Smith, P., and Morrison, W. I. (1974). *Simulating the Urban Economy*, Pion Press, London.

Steger, W. (1965). A review of analytical techniques for the community renewal program. *Journal of the American Institute of Planners*, **31**, 166–172.

Stewart, J. Q. (1947). Empirical rules concerning the distribution and equilibrium of population, *Geographical Review*, **38**, 461–485.

Stopher, P. R., and Meyburg, A. H. (1975). *Urban Transportation Modeling and Planning*, D. C. Heath, Lexington, Massachusetts.

Taylor, P. J. (1975). *Distance Decay in Spatial Interactions*. CATMOG No. 1, Geo-Abstracts, Norwich.

Thorburn, A. (Ed.) (1969). *The Nottinghamshire–Derbyshire Subregional Study*, The Nottinghamshire–Derbyshire Subregional Planning Unit, Alfreton, Derbyshire.

Tiebout, C. M. (1962). *The Community Economic Base Study*. Supplementary Paper No. 16, Committee for Economic Development, New York.

Voorhees, A. M. (1955). A general theory of traffic movement. *Proceedings of the Institute of Traffic Engineering*, **1**, 46–56.

Wade, B. (1973). *Greater Peterborough Shopping Study: Technical Report*, Planning Research Applications Group, Reading, Berkshire.

Wheaton, W. C. (1974). Linear programming and locational equilibrium: the Herbert–Stevens model revisited. *Journal of Urban Economics*, **1**, 278–288.

Wilson, A. G. (1967). A statistical theory of spatial distribution models. *Transportation Research*, **1**, 253–269.

Wilson, A. G. (1968). Models in urban planning: a synoptic review of recent literature. *Urban Studies*, **5**, 249–276.

Wilson, A. G. (1974). *Urban and Regional Models in Geography and Planning*, John Wiley, London.

Wilson, A. G. (1975). Retailers' profit and consumers' welfare in a spatial interaction shopping model. In I. Masser (Ed.), *Theory and Practice in Regional Science*, Pion Press, London.

Zipf, G. K. (1947). *Human Behavior and the Principle of Least Effort*, Addison-Wesley, Reading, Massachusetts.

Chapter 4

Patterns of Migration: A Macroanalytic Case Study

William A. V. Clark and Karen L. Avery

INTRODUCTION

As population numbers increase, so too do issues of population policy. On the one hand, there are demographic, non-spatial issues of fertility and birth rates and of population increase in general; on the other hand, there are specifically spatial questions which are related to the location and relocation of people. It is this latter group of questions, a small but important subset of all those problems related to population policy in general, which constitutes the province of migration studies. The ramifications of the processes of human relocation are extensive, complex, and still only partially understood. Indeed, the patterns and causes of population movements have only recently been subject to extensive investigation.

It is the attempt to extend the body of knowledge on migration and particularly the patterns of migration within cities with which this essay is concerned. The first half of the paper is directed towards a broad review of geographical and sociological attempts to describe large-scale migration matrices. The review is necessarily selective and emphasizes those approaches to intraurban migration which have both analysed spatial patterns and also dealt with large interaction matrices. Following a discussion of micro- and macroanalyses of intraurban migration, aspects of distance decay, directionality, and Markov analyses of large matrices are examined. The second half of the paper is an empirical analysis of migration in Amsterdam. A relatively short section is devoted to the description of the data and data base. There is a brief comment on the basic population flows to set the scene for the introduction of entropy measures and their application to population flows over time. The body of the research is contained in a review of Wilson's development of the entropy model, the application of the model to migration flows in Amsterdam, and the evaluation of the entropy maximizing model as a predictive device. The implications of this investigation of large-scale migration matrices are reviewed in the concluding section.

MICRO- AND MACROANALYSES OF INTRAURBAN MIGRATION

For some time the study of intraurban migration was distinguished from migrations at a national or international scale on the basis of perceived differences in their respective causes. While economic forces were used as explanations of state-to-state or region-to-region moves, a different set of forces was employed to explain relocation within cities. A more recent emphasis on constructing models which stress the individual decision-making processes involved in household relocation within either city or region has tended to blur these earlier distinctions. Nonetheless, there are still some important differences between the research foci of demographers, economists, and geographers interested in intraurban migration and those interested in interregional population shifts. Work on the latter still emphasizes the economic aspects of household relocation whether it is via a human capital approach or through the simpler analysis of job opportunities and wage differentials. On the other hand, those more interested in the intraurban relocations of households have emphasized the changing requirements of families as they go through their life-cycles from young adulthood to old age.

Research on intraurban migration has undergone significant changes since Simmons' (1968) review. The studies which he reviewed are, for the most part, descriptive accounts of the intraurban migration process. It is from these studies conducted at different urban scales and in different parts of the world that there emerged the generalizations of short distance, within-neighbourhood movements, largely related to the changing needs of the family life-cycle. More recently, research has been directed to the analysis of actual decision making involved in residential mobility and the processes through which individual households approach and solve the problem of relocation. Studies by geographers, demographers, and sociologists have taken different approaches to the general problem of explaining individual behaviour, although it is this latter problem which has been the principal guiding force in all the investigations.

As migration research has dealt more specifically with the notions of who moves and where they move, the conceptual bases of intraurban migration studies have tended to separate into two broadly defined categories. The older of these focuses primarily on the analysis of the origin and destination sets and the aggregate interaction and migration flow patterns between them. The more recent approach, which appears to have been developed as a response to certain perceived inadequacies of the more macroanalytic studies, has been directed toward the behaviour of the individual migrant. For example, while early macroanalyses of intraurban migration focused on the aggregate flows between origins and destinations (Albig, 1933; Caplow, 1949; Green, 1934) and central city–suburban differentials (Schnore, 1957, 1963; Taueber and Taueber, 1964), more recently macroanalyses have included studies of directional bias (Adams, 1969) and the investigations of the structure of migration matrices (Ginsberg, 1972a, 1972b, 1973; McGinnis, 1968). The microanalytic approaches initially focused on the reasons for movement (Rossi, 1955) and have recently expanded to include work on stress and mobility (Brown and Moore, 1970; Clark and Cadwallader, 1973; Wolpert, 1965), the search behaviour of individual households (Barrett, 1973), the relationship between commuting and residential relocation (Lansing, 1966; Lansing *et al.*, 1964), and housing satisfaction as a predictor of mobility (Butler *et al.*, 1969).

The two approaches are not mutually exclusive; they often have similar objectives and investigate closely allied aspects of migration. The behavioural approach addresses the potential migrant's decision to change his residence, the behaviour of the migrant as he searches for a new residence, and the manner in which the selection of destination site is made. The potential migrant is viewed as continually engaging in a reevaluation of how well his current residence satisfies his needs and aspirations, which are modified by changes in his own characteristics and those of his surroundings. The decision to move is one possible response to the individual's dissatisfaction with his residence. The migrant's search for new housing is controlled by the actual spatial structure of the available housing stock and by the migrant's perception of that stock. Alternative destinations within the migrant's search space are evaluated in terms of their potential ability to satisfy his needs and aspirations. Most research of this type tends to foeus on specific aspects of migrant behaviour, such as the conditions of stress prompting the decision to move, the criteria which the migrant uses in evaluating the current and alternative residences, spatial biases of the migrant's search space, the role of differential access to various sources of information in shaping the search space, and the influence of the spatial structure of the housing market.

In contrast to the microanalytic concern with individual migrant behaviour, the macroanalytic approach places greater emphasis on the interactions among areas and the expression of this interaction in the form of migration. Thus there is a concentration on the analysis of the aggregate migration flow patterns and the ecological characteristics of origin and destination areas. Macroanalysis attempts to define the ecological factors associated with spatial variations of out- and in-migration patterns and to identify spatial regularities in migration streams. The latter of these two objectives is predicated on the assumption that spatial biases in aggregate flow patterns reflect the structure of origins and destinations and the spatial differentiation of the characteristics of potential migrants. Macroanalytic studies of intraurban migration tend to concentrate on the interrelationships of such factors as the socioeconomic and demographic characteristics of out- and in-migrants and of sending and receiving areas; the spatial structure of origins and destinations; and the distance, directional, and sectoral biases of migration streams. Relationships of this nature have been modelled in a static framework more often than have the microanalytic studies.

Despite the differences between the micro- and macroanalytic approaches to intraurban migration, there is a considerable amount of overlap in their respective goals, foci, and methodologies. Both are ultimately concerned with achieving a greater comprehension of the complex factors which affect the intraurban migration process and with identifying regularities in migration patterns, for the purpose of acquiring better explanatory, descriptive, and predictive capabilities with regard to migration. Both approaches encompass the analysis of the characteristics of migrants, origins, and destinations, though with somewhat differing immediate objectives. At times, the methods of analysis are identical, as in the techniques used to measure the geometry of search spaces and migration fields.

The behavioural and macroanalytic studies are complementary rather than competitive approaches and yield insights into each other as well as into migration as a whole. For instance, knowing why an individual decides to move and how he seeks and evaluates new residence sites can lead to an understanding of why some districts are areas of net out-migration while others are areas of net in-migration. Being able to identify the spatial biases of aggregate flow patterns and the characteristics of origin and destination areas can aid in the prediction of an individual's out- and in-migration patterns.

The choice of approach is likely to be determined by the analyst's theoretical predilections and by the level of aggregation of suitable data. Each orientation is favoured by conceptual considerations and methodological advantages. To the behaviouralist, the analysis of the individual migrant's decision-making and search processes is basic to an understanding of aggregate patterns of movement. The microanalyst often argues that the use of aggregate data obscures individual-level relationships. The macroanalyst is less concerned with the individual decision-making and search procedures *per se* than with the collective outcomes of individual decisions to migrate which, when aggregated, express one aspect of the human interaction among places. Using aggregate data reduces the complexity of individual patterns and facilitates the perception of general migration characteristics. There is also a sound conceptual argument favouring the macroanalysts' use of aggregate data. Relationships operating at a macrolevel of analysis cannot necessarily be inferred from microlevel data. From a pragmatic point of view, information on individual migrants is often more difficult to obtain. In sum, the primary difference between the behavioural and macroanalytic approaches to intraurban migration studies is in their respective theoretical orientations. Each mode of analysis can provide information relevant to the other and each can yield insights into migration which may not be gained from the other. Thus macro- and microanalysis are both supplementary and complementary approaches to migration studies.

There is an additional subdivision of both behavioural and macroanalytic approaches which is particularly important for geographic studies of intraurban migration. Although any subdivision of the research on intraurban migration is useful only for pedagogic reasons, a spatial and non-spatial breakdown of research within macroanalytic and behavioural methodologies emphasizes the individual contributions to be made by demographers, sociologists, and geographers. Although each of these disciplines has made contributions in both spatial and non-spatial areas, the emphasis on a spatial–non-spatial breakdown eliminates the likelihood that research on decision making for individual relocation will be confused with the spatial outcome of that decision making. Thus, the work of Ginsberg (1972a), Spilerman (1973), and McFarland (1970) has gone some way to bringing greater understanding of the forces involved in intraurban migration, while Barrett (1973) has considered the impact on space of the space-searching procedures undertaken by the potential migrant. The macroanalytic non-spatial studies have dealt with the stationarity of large-scale migration matrices (Ginsberg, 1972a, 1972b; Rogers, 1968) and the structural characteristics of origin and destination matrices (Berry and Schwind, 1969). The macrospatial analyses have been either descriptive (Caplow, 1949) or only implicitly spatial, such as those studies by Stouffer (1940), Morrill (1963), and Moore (1966), in which some distance function was used as a surrogate for spatial interaction. The principal aim in raising this question of spatial and non-spatial elements in intraurban migration is to emphasize the relative contributions of geographic investigations. The more detailed review discussion which follows will indicate the relative contributions of the spatial and non-spatial studies within a micro–macroanalytic framework.

THE DEVELOPMENT OF A MACROANALYTIC INTRAURBAN MIGRATION LITERATURE

The literature which deals with intraurban migration is extensive, and whereas it was once largely descriptive it is now more analytical. There have been substantial advances in modelling intraurban migration, but the division between the modelling and explanation of individual behaviour and explanations of aggregate population flows has been deepened. Neither approach has yet come close to predicting population movements, and it is likely to be a long time before satisfactory individual behavioural models are developed. Furthermore, detailed studies of the interaction between urban structure and intraurban migration are limited. The difficulties of merging individual data on relocation and aggregate data on the structural characteristics of the city suggest that a renewed emphasis on macroanalyses of intraurban migration may be a profitable approach to linking spatial behaviour and spatial structure and a useful first step in the rational formulation of comprehensive urban policy which focuses on the continuing redistribution of population within and between cities.

Although the focus of this essay will be on macroanalytic studies of intraurban migration, it is worth reiterating the basic propositions which seem to be accepted as general statements about intraurban migration. Four generalizations had already emerged by the early 1960s:

1. Migrants are more likely to move shorter distances than longer distances and this probability has been approximated with a variety of distance decay functions.
2. Migrants within cities are motivated primarily by reasons associated with changes in the family life-cycle.

3. Migrants throughout the 1940s and 1950s moved outward from the centre of the city towards the urban periphery.
4. Renters were more likely to move than owners, and those who moved more often made up a significant proportion of all movers.

Since that time there has been an explosion of research on intraurban migration, particularly on demographic and non-spatial aspects of population relocation.

There are several extensive reviews of the intraurban migration literature which emphasize the microanalytic aspects of population relocation. Simmons (1968) thoroughly reviews the demographic, sociological, and geographical literature focusing on the three questions of who moves, why they move, and where they move. Moore (1972), on the other hand, is more concerned with reviewing and further developing analytic approaches to urban migration. His review includes a discussion of both micro- and macroanalytic approaches to modelling the intraurban migration process. However, the most extensive recent review is contained in the monograph by Speare, Goldstein, and Frey (1974). Although the study is directly concerned with reporting on a detailed questionnaire of movers within Rhode Island, there are descriptions of the characteristics of migrants and the attempts to model the process whereby migrants relocate within the city. There are several hundred articles and books which deal with intraurban migration, and many of these studies are listed in Shaw (1975). There is a much less complete coverage of macroanalyses of intraurban migration. Because the work reported in this study is that framework, some attempt is made to provide a review and structural typology of the macroanalytic studies.

Distance decay functions and gravity formulations

A fundamental part of the question of where people move is the determination of how far they are likely to move. Mathematical statements of the probability of movement between two points separated by a distance D have been made and tested for a variety of different types of movement. The underlying assumption of these distance decay functions is that people tend to move shorter distances rather than longer distances. The basic form of the function is

$$p(D) = c\, e^{-bDa} \tag{4.1}$$

where $p(D)$ is the probability of movement between individual unit areas at distance D apart, and c, b, and a are constants. The most commonly used form is the Pareto, where

$$p(D) = c\,D^{-b} \tag{4.2}$$

Morrill (1963) cites a number of objections to the use of the Pareto function in migration studies, including the fact that for short distances it usually overestimates the amount of movement. Morrill and Pitts (1967) have concluded that the Pareto function may be best suited for temporary, non-costly moves.

Moore (1966) notes that the Pareto function seems to give better fits to observed moves as the size of the migration field increases. Lognormal and exponential forms of the distance decay function have also been used in migration analyses, most notably in Kulldorf's (1955) study of migration from the rural community of Asby in Sweden. The equations are

$$p(D) = ce^{-b(\log D)^2} \tag{4.3}$$

$$p(D) = ce^{-bD} \tag{4.4}$$

Moore (1966), among others, has outlined several objections to using such pure distance functions in intraurban migration studies. First, the functions assume that the base population is distributed symmetrically. As this is seldom the case in urban areas, it happens that the opportunity to move a given distance is not a monotonically decreasing function. Second, it is difficult to adapt the functions to accommodate populations which are not homogeneous in their socioeconomic or ethnic character and hence have varying distributions of migration opportunities.

The application of distance decay functions has not been limited to modelling the distribution of movement lengths. Moore (1971) has shown that variations of the basic distance decay function given in equation (4.1) can be effectively used to model the distribution of population turnover rates in a mononuclear city for short-run predictions. Population turnover measures the proportion of the population for which moves out of dwellings in the study area are exactly balanced by moves into the same area, and is given as

$$\begin{aligned} T_t &= \frac{E_t + M_t}{P_t} \qquad \text{if } I_t \geqslant E_t \\ &= \frac{I_t + M_t}{P_t} \qquad \text{if } E_t > I_t \end{aligned} \tag{4.5}$$

where E_t is the number of out-migrants during the time interval t, I_t is the number of in-migrants, M_t is the number of movers within the area, and P_t is the average population of the area.

The fact that the pure distance decay functions have not been completely successful in explaining the spatial aspects of intraurban migration has not diminished the importance of the role of distance in migration models. The frictional effect of distance as a barrier to movement enters explicitly into the classic macroanalytic gravity model of interaction formulated by Stewart (1947) and Zipf (1949). In its simplest form, the gravity model relates the volume of interaction (I) between two places i and j directly to the populations (P) of i and j and indirectly to the distance (D) separating i and j. The general form is

$$I_{ij} = \frac{f(P_i P_j)}{f(D_{ij})}.$$

Population in this model serves as a surrogate for physical mass and, of course, many other surrogates for both mass (e.g. job opportunities, dwelling vacancies) and distance (e.g. temporal or monetary travel cost) are possible and have been extensively tested. The gravity model seems useful for interurban migration modelling, but its utility for the intraurban case is hindered by the extreme paucity of reliable data collected at an areal scale sufficiently fine to reflect meaningful spatial differentials in the variables used to predict interaction.

These criticisms can be applied equally well to a second classic model of migration, the intervening opportunities model formulated by Stouffer (1940). The amount of migration from one place to another is expressed as a function of the attractive force of the destination and an inverse function of the attractive force of all other possible destinations nearer to the origin, which serves essentially as a surrogate for the friction of distance. But again the model has limited applicability in the intraurban case.

Whether distance operates in its own right or as a proxy for some other fundamental explanatory variable, distance as an impediment to migration has received much attention. It is well recognized that a large number of moves within the city take place over short distances (e.g. Caplow, 1949; Clark, 1970; Johnston, 1969a, 1969b; Rossi, 1955). However, the precise reasons for the dominance of short-distance moves are unclear. Simmons (1968) suggests that the decision to seek a nearby location may be a conscious effort to maintain spatial familiarity and social and institutional links or that it may be the result of imperfect knowledge of the city-wide housing vacancy set.

Directionality

Whereas distance bias may be relatively simply defined in terms of movement lengths, directional bias is rather more complex and is apt to be confused with sectoral bias. Brown and Holmes (1971, pp. 311–312) distinguish between directional bias which is 'defined in terms of another location (e.g. the central business district) within the movement field that is relevant to the movement decision ... ' and sectoral bias which is 'the degree to which a single movement is more likely to end in a place that is along a single axis through the origin'.

It has been frequently observed that there is a general tendency for migration to push outward from the central city towards the periphery (Caplow, 1949; Schnore, 1957). The explanation for this bias is not fully understood, but appears to be related to at least two concepts of urban residential growth processes. The first is derived from Burgess' (1925) theory that residential expansion results from pressure by newcomers to the city on available low-status rental housing in the central city. As density in this area increases, the recent in-migrants begin to filter into the better, surrounding neighbourhoods, thus initiating a process of invasion and succession whereby the residents of each successively higher status residential zone are forced to move further out from the centre in order to counter the lowering of the neighbourhood status.

A second explanation is based on Hoyt's (1939) theory of sectoral urban growth, which assumes that the causative mechanism is the obsolescence of the housing of higher income groups. New housing construction for these groups tends to take place at the city periphery, and the older housing left vacant is subsequently occupied by the next-highest status group, whose own housing has become obsolescent. Thus housing filters down to the lowest income residents and enables them to expand their neighbourhoods outwards from the city centre. The result of this filtering process is essentially the same as that of invasion and succession, the difference between the two being that filtering is not initiated by external pressures exerted by new immigrants.

A third possible reason for this particular bias in migration patterns is not derived from a theory of urban growth but rather from a consideration of how the various stages in a family's life-cycle produce changing housing needs, the satisfaction of which is constrained by the spatial structure of the housing market (Rossi, 1955). It is suggested that migration towards the suburbs is a characteristic of young, growing families motivated by an attempt to satisfy increased space requirements. These three mechanisms—invasion and succession, filtering, and change in life-cycle—are all grounded in the concept that sooner or later some subgroup of the urban population experiences a change in housing requirements or aspirations, that the adjustment to this change can be best made by moving to a new residence, and that the spatial structure of the urban housing market is such that a suitable residence is more likely to be found at a site further removed from the city centre. Extensive testing supports the validity of all three hypotheses (Adams, 1969; Johnston, 1969a, 1969b; Moore, 1969), although at the present time it is only possible to state that the outward directional bias is the result of a complex interrelationship of a variety of processes (Johnston, 1969a).

As a further explanation, it has been proposed that the typical urban resident has a mental map of the city which is wedge-shaped and pointed at the central business district (Adams, 1969). The mental map assumes this shape because most of the resident's daily and weekly travel patterns are radial with respect to the downtown area. Adding to this notion the assumption that many cities have a Burgess-type structure of concentric residential zones, Adams (1969, p. 312) proposes that a typical mover would be expected to move 'either outward toward the suburbs or in toward the central business district but not sideways'. Tests of the hypothesis by Adams and others (Brown and Holmes, 1971) have produced somewhat conflicting results.

Generalizations about distance, directional, and sectoral biases become more difficult when either two or all three are viewed simultaneously and when various population subgroups are analysed comparatively. Adams (1969) has suggested that in Minneapolis longer movements exhibit greater directional bias than do shorter movements, but this hypothesis is not supported by evidence on migration within Christchurch (Clark, 1971). Brown and Holmes (1971) imply that inner-city residents of Cedar Rapids tend to move to sites near their initial residences, with no marked directional or sectoral bias, while residents nearer the periphery are more likely to make longer, directionally-biased moves. This is partially confirmed by a study of relocations in Christchurch, where inner-city movements are essentially random while movements originating in the periphery tend to be biased towards the central business district (Clark, 1971). Johnston (1969b) notes, in contrast to part of Brown and Holmes' observation, that although short-distance movements are dominant in the inner area of Melbourne, there is a substantial amount of long-distance movement from the inner city to the outer suburbs. It is possible that some of these discrepancies may be due to the wide variation in techniques used to measure migration biases. Brown and Holmes (1971) attribute at least part of their contradiction of Adams' assessment of the importance of sectoral bias to the fact that the two studies used different modes of analysis.

Distance bias is often expressed in terms of a frequency distribution of the number of moves of varying lengths, but the measurement of directional bias, either alone or in conjunction with distance bias, has most often relied on the use of a vector representation of movement. The length of the vector indicates the movement length, the direction of the vector indicates the direction of the movement with respect to some reference point, and the width of the vector is sometimes varied according to the flow magnitude.

Price (1948) used vectors plotted on a circle and having a common origin to represent distance, direction, and magnitude of migration flows among the nine census divisions of the United States. The technique is graphically effective for a small number of origin–destination pairs, but is limited in utility as it requires the intuitive identification of migration trends. A more sophisticated variation on this type of vector representation is evident in the analysis of interstate migration streams by Tarver and Skees (1967). In this case, each state's vector summarizes the magnitude, weighted average distance, and weighted average direction of flows to or from all other states. As with the Price method, the identification of general trends is subject to the analyst's perceptual biases.

In similar fashion to the method of using frequency counts to discern distance bias, it is also possible to analyse directional bias in migration fields in terms of the number of moves from a common origin to equal-sized sectors measured in degrees. Clark (1971) has shown that a frequency count of this nature can be compared with hypothetical distributions by means of Kolmogorov–Smirnov statistics to test the correspondence between observed and model-generated angles of movement. This sort of test avoids the subjective interpretive element of the Price and the Tarver and Skees analyses, but, as Brown and Holmes (1971) point out, the choice of sector width is arbitrary and different widths may produce different results.

Wolpert (1967) demonstrates the calculation of the median and modal centres of flow in in- and out-migration fields. The median centre is basically a point of minimum aggregate travel while the modal centre is the point of origin or destination for the largest number of migrants. The median centre is judged to be the more useful measure as it preserves both the distance and directional properties of the migration fields. These measures of central tendency unfortunately yield no information on the dispersion of movement angles, and thus seem to be of limited utility in measuring directional bias.

Analyses of migration matrices

When we consider studies of origin–destination migration matrices it is helpful to distinguish between those studies which can be described as analyses of the matrices of flows and those studies which are in fact concerned with the behaviour of individuals which make up the aggregate origin and destination movements. Although the latter studies are often considered to be behavioural investigations, they are concerned with the structure of aggregates of individuals and thus are properly considered in this review.

Studies of any type which attempt to show the links between urban structure and intraurban migration are limited. Some studies have shown that families move within similar socioeconomic areas of the city (Goldstein and Mayer, 1961; Whitelaw and Robinson, 1972), although there is some dissent on this point (Brown and Longbrake, 1969, 1970). But given the overwhelmingly short distance of most moves this result is not surprising. More recently, attempts to link flows of population and the underlying urban structure have turned to behavioural investigations of the decision to move, and to a large extent these behavioural microanalytic studies are outside the scope of the present review.

Analyses of intraurban migration matrices *per se* are rare. One of the most comprehensive is contained in a detailed work on Toronto by Simmons (1974). A major part of the study is directed to analysing the flows between origins and destinations. Simmons employs the measures of distance and directionality similar to those we have already discussed, and two approaches which are focused on the migration interaction matrices as a whole. One approach involves the use of factor analysis to generate a set of migration fields or substructures within the flow matrix; a second aspect of the analysis uses some simple regression gravity models to predict flows between origins and destinations. Moore (1966) also uses a simple regression model to predict intraurban migration flows between a set of defined districts in which the intensity of flow is dependent on accessibility, vacancies, and the population of the sending district, and is able to account for about 70 per cent. of the variation in flows between subareas in Brisbane, Australia.

Although Simmons (1974) makes extensive use of cartographic analysis of population flows, two recent reports have suggested an alternative and perhaps more analytic cartographic presentation. Tobler (1975) uses a field of vectors to describe the pattern of flows which is implicit in a geographical interaction table. Most of the examples which he presents are for nations or regions, but the technique is obviously adaptable to cities as well. Some other spatial analyses of regional flows are presented in MacKinnon and Skarke (1975). The biproportional input–output analysis is potentially adaptable to the intraurban case.

By far the most pervasive approach to analysing the matrix of population flows within cities is contained in the work by those demographers, geographers, and sociologists who have attempted to use Markov models to understand and predict the interactions which are the result of the intraurban migration as a simple Markov process. Both Rogers (1968) in the interregional and Simmons

(1974) in the intraurban case treat migration as a first-order stochastic process, but Simmons concludes that the models applied are much too simple. There is substantial evidence that the intraurban migration process cannot be modelled as a simple Markov process. The major problem is that the probability of leaving a state *i* at time *t* is not independent of the past migration history of an individual, whereas a simple Markov process requires that the move from one state to another is dependent only on the state occupied immediately previous to the move. In addition, the observed transition probabilities do not remain constant over time and the population is not homogeneous. A great deal of research by urban sociologists and demographers has been devoted to designing solutions to the problems caused by applying Markov processes to intraurban migration. The most comprehensive attempt to model the migration process in a Markovian framework is that by McGinnis and his associates at Cornell (McGinnis, 1968; Myers, McGinnis, and Masnick, 1967). A constrained Markov model is used to incorporate the axiom of cumulative inertia that the probability of moving decreases over time. Although there are some doubts about the validity of that proposition, the original statements led to extensive research on the nature of homogeneity in intraurban migration matrices and the degree to which cumulative inertia is a function of individual behaviour or a function of the aggregate structure of intraurban migration matrices. McFarland (1970) has argued for the effects of inhomogeneity in migration matrices while Henry, McGinnis, and Tegtmeyer (1971) and Spilerman (1972, 1973) have suggested a variety of models to account for the variation in results found in analyses of cumulative inertia. More recently, Ginsberg (1971, 1972a, 1972b) has not only reviewed many of these investigations but has also introduced the semi-Markov process as an alternative to the first-order stochastic process. A comprehensive review of these technical studies can be found in Clark and Huff (1977).

The empirical research has not really kept pace with the theoretical developments. Studies by Morrison (1967), Land (1969), Speare (1970), and Speare, Goldstein, and Frey (1974) have provided some evidence that there is a duration-of-stay effect, although the form of the function is likely to be more complicated than the simple form reported in Morrison (1967) and Land (1969). Clark and Huff (1977) recently reported on more extensive testing of the concept of cumulative inertia and concluded that 'for the present the relationship between the prior residence history of an individual and his decision to move must be left as an open question'.

In summary we can say that while geographers have developed generalizations on the distances of moves, their directionality, and the nature of flows between areas of the city, the contributions of sociologists and demographers have been focused on the nature of predictions which can be derived from the analysis of aggregates of individual residential histories, particularly through the concepts of cumulative inertia and homogeneity. Economists have developed an interest in the intraurban migration process, mainly through a concern with the way in which the housing market creates and controls opportunities for relocation within the city. Although these studies (see Quigley, 1976, for example) do deal with large matrices, most of the models are focused on the behaviour of the individuals which have been aggregated into these matrices. In the framework we have generated in this study they are microanalytic investigations.

POPULATION MOVEMENTS IN AMSTERDAM

The data and statistical divisions of the Amsterdam Municipality

The empirical analysis conducted in this study is focused on the movements of the people between small areas of Amsterdam during the time period 1960–1970 (Figures 4.1 and 4.2). The basic data set consists of the aggregated moves of all individuals within and between these small areas. It was collected annually as part of the record-keeping function of the Bureau of Statistics of the Amsterdam Municipality. The areal units (buurtcombinatie or subdistricts) for which the data are aggregated are roughly comparable in character and purpose to the census tract divisions of the Census of Population in the United States. They have populations which range in size from 5 000 to 20 000 persons with an average size of about 8 000. There were 80 buurtcombinatie in 1960 and 89 subdistricts in 1970. Data were not collected for subdistricts 77 and 78 in the

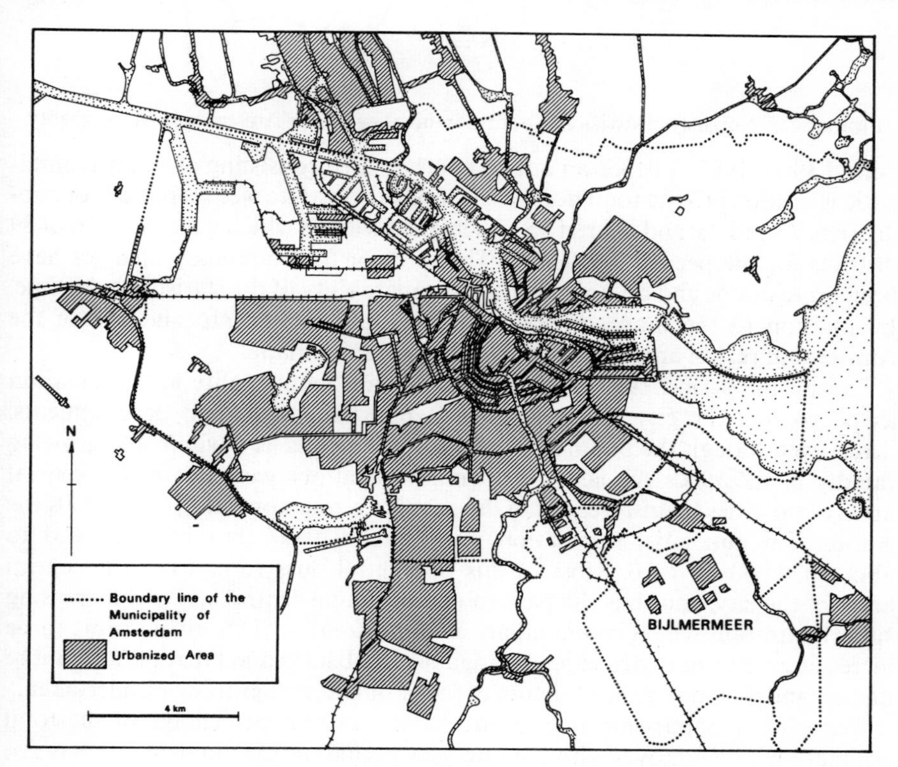

FIGURE 4.1. The Amsterdam region

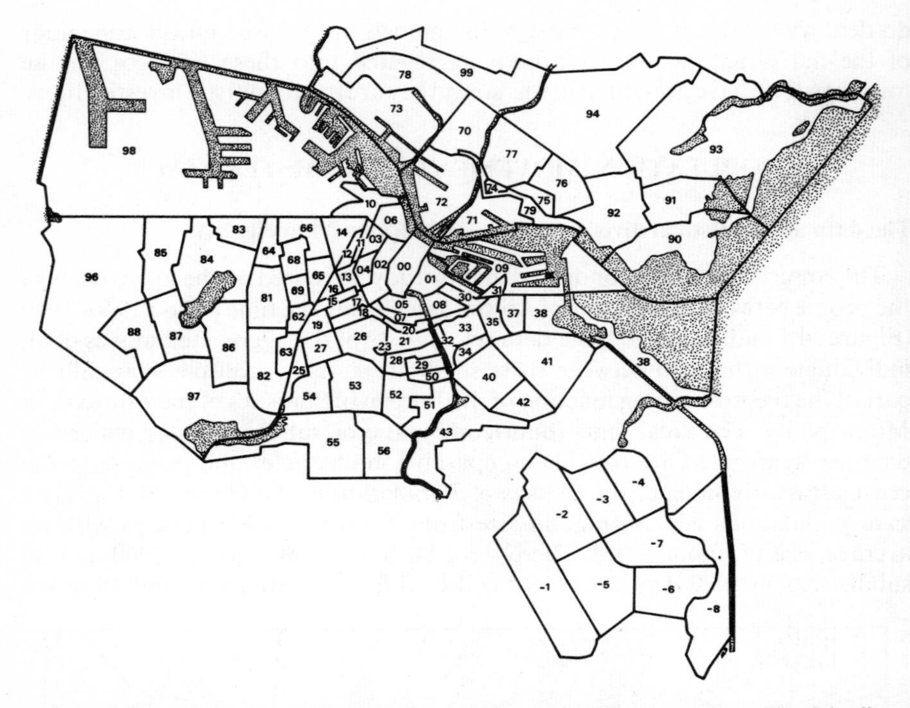

FIGURE 4.2. Subdistrict divisions (buurtcombinatie) of the Amsterdam Municipality

period 1960–1965. In 1966 an outer suburban area consisting of 8 buurtcombinatie was added to the total number of subdistricts, data were reported for subdistricts 77 and 78, and district 95 was merged with 98 which gave the total of 89 districts for the period 1966–1970. The three or four boundary changes have been quite minor and do not affect the comparability of the statistics over time. In addition to the moves between districts, the moves into and out of the Amsterdam region are recorded for each buurtcombinatie.

During the period 1960–1970 the Amsterdam municipality lost population as people left the city for surrounding suburban towns and developments. Thus, even though the population of the Netherlands as a whole was growing rapidly in the 1960s the fastest growing populations were not in the central areas of the cities themselves but in the suburban zones outside. In the 1960s the Amsterdam municipal population was about 870 000 but had declined to about 830 000 by 1970. Most of this population loss came from the central areas of the city, and thus the pattern of a declining central city and increasing suburbanization which is a familiar temporal trend in U.S. cities seems to be increasingly true in Dutch cities. It is against this background that the attempt to understand and model the structure of the population migration is undertaken.

The rate of population migration (defined as that percentage of the total population which moves within a one-year period) in the municipality has not varied a great deal over the ten-year period (Table 4.1). Detailed summary data

TABLE 4.1. Migration rates

Year	Total moves as a percentage of total population Men	Women
1960	15.6	14.2
1961	15.2	14.1
1962	13.8	12.2
1963	12.5	11.0
1964	12.8	11.4
1965	13.7	11.8
1966	14.6	12.7
1967	15.2	13.1
1968	16.0	13.9
1969	14.5	12.8
1970	16.5	14.9

TABLE 4.2. Migration and population totals

Year	Total in-migration	Total out-migration	Total internal migration	Total population (January)
1960	27 328	36 783	91 943	869 602
1961	27 877	35 262	88 891	866 342
1962	28 214	33 369	78 527	865 703
1963	26 756	31 220	69 947	866 830
1964	25 497	34 090	70 224	868 445
1965	28 427	36 910	72 825	866 290
1966	30 468	37 330	80 148	867 566
1967	27 236	39 372	81 652	861 612
1968	29 538	43 843	83 959	857 635
1969	30 256	46 752	84 741	845 821
1970	32 080	43 914	84 618	831 463

for aggregate migration for the whole city are illustrated in Table 4.2. We can note, first, that total out-migration has exceeded in-migration in every year in the study period (in several cases the out-migration was more than 10 000 persons greater than in-migration) and, second, that migration within the region has remained relatively constant, varying between 70 000 and 90 000 persons each year.

These figures for the city as a whole obscure the detailed variation which emerges when we consider the migration rates for in- , out- , and internal migration for each of the 80 or 89 small subdistricts. These detailed data are presented only for 1960 and 1970, as the initial and end points of the period under analysis (Tables 4.3 and 4.4). In both 1960 and 1970 the wide variation in mobility rates by subdistrict is most striking. For example, in 1970 within the central area of the city the rate of migration varies from 19.3 for buurtcombinatie 03 to 33.6 for the neighbouring district. This variability exists for migration into, out of, and

TABLE 4.3. Rates of in-, out-, and internal migration by subdistrict for 1960

Sub-district	Moves within Sub-district/ Total Moves	Moves within Amsterdam/ Total Moves	Moves out of Amsterdam/ Total Moves	Moves within Amsterdam/ Total Population	Moves out of Amsterdam/ Total Population	Total Moves/ Total Population
00	.1410	.7510	.2490	.1727	.0573	.2300
01	.1449	.7672	.2365	.1623	.0500	.2114
02	.0772	.7291	.2709	.1664	.0618	.2282
03	.2166	.8857	.1143	.1417	.0183	.1600
04	.1172	.8216	.1784	.1603	.0348	.1951
05	.0784	.7148	.2858	.1814	.0725	.2537
06	.1360	.8374	.1626	.1625	.0316	.1940
07	.0810	.7620	.2380	.1438	.0450	.1887
08	.0730	.8116	.2323	.1614	.0462	.1988
09	.1760	.6001	.3998	.1545	.1029	.2574
10	.2431	.8611	.1382	.1165	.0187	.1353
11	.1015	.8217	.1783	.1202	.0260	.1462
12	.1215	.7703	.2297	.1024	.0305	.1329
13	.0662	.7117	.2882	.1153	.0467	.1620
14	.1789	.8489	.1511	.1167	.0208	.1374
15	.1381	.8234	.1765	.1324	.0284	.1608
16	.1176	.8172	.1828	.1141	.0255	.1397
17	.0815	.7035	.2965	.1636	.0689	.2325
18	.0293	.6417	.3571	.2169	.1207	.3380
19	.0967	.7394	.5600	.1064	.0806	.1439
20	.0388	.7352	.2647	.2484	.0894	.3378
21	.1423	.7872	.2128	.1368	.0369	.1738
23	.0489	.7095	.2905	.0921	.0377	.1299
25	.1204	.6941	.3058	.1019	.0449	.1468
26	.1074	.5785	.4215	.1237	.0901	.2139
27	.0505	.6162	.3838	.1182	.0736	.1918
28	.1177	.7532	.2466	.1198	.0392	.1591
29	.1136	.7432	.2568	.0912	.0315	.1228
30	.0686	.6777	.3222	.1321	.0628	.1949
31	.1967	.8626	.1373	.1526	.0243	.1769
32	.0620	.7211	.2788	.1185	.0458	.1644
33	.1321	.7500	.2500	.1154	.0384	.1539
34	.1294	.7462	.2537	.1034	.0351	.1386
35	.1553	.7953	.2041	.1216	.0312	.1529
37	.1444	.7771	.2229	.0922	.0264	.1186
38	.1514	.7832	.2168	.0880	.0244	.1123
40	.1183	.6532	.3431	.0785	.0410	.1195
41	.1183	.5631	.4435	.0759	.0598	.1349
42	.1612	.6799	.3202	.0573	.0269	.0842

43	0	.7981	.2018	.1526	.0385	.1912
50	.0808	.7263	.2697	.1185	.0440	.1632
51	.1088	.6535	.3389	.0836	.0433	.1279
52	.1001	.5863	.4160	.0956	.0678	.1631
53	.1462	.4877	.5122	.0940	.0987	.1928
54	.1108	.6536	.3536	.0456	.0456	.1291
55	.0652	.4384	.5615	.0716	.0917	.1634
56	0	.4545	.5454	.0227	.0272	.0500
62	.0703	.6107	.3832	.0571	.0358	.0935
63	.1078	.6228	.3771	.1055	.0639	.1694
64	.0655	.5955	.3991	.0728	.0488	.1223
65	.0928	.6899	.3101	.0900	.0405	.1305
66	.1218	.7316	.2684	.0802	.0294	.1096
68	.1201	.7661	.2338	.0876	.0268	.1144
69	.1437	.8200	.1800	.1006	.0221	.1227
70	.1000	.6136	.3863	.0891	.0561	.1452
71	.1991	.7213	.2786	.0876	.0338	.1215
72	.1885	.7669	.2330	.0855	.0259	.1115
73	.2677	.7843	.2229	.1200	.0341	.1530
74	.1157	.7933	.2121	.0775	.0207	.0976
75	.1700	.7020	.3254	.0590	.0273	.0841
76	.0851	.5744	.4255	.0833	.0617	.1450
79	.2727	.6666	.3030	.0862	.0392	.1294
81	.1341	.5295	.4704	.0503	.0447	.0950
82	.0543	.7751	.2248	.1043	.0302	.1346
83	.0788	.5791	.4125	.0667	.0475	.1151
84	.0792	.6069	.3923	.0686	.0443	.1130
85	.0621	.9700	.4798	.1157	.0572	.1192
86	.0944	.4484	.5632	.0453	.0570	.1012
87	.0788	.4982	.5125	.0249	.0262	.0512
88	0	.6000	.4000	.0300	.0200	.0500
90	.1111	.3703	.6296	.0157	.0268	.0426
91	.2500	.8409	.1590	.0898	.0169	.1067
92	.3253	.7831	.2168	.1065	.0295	.1360
93	.2273	.4090	.5909	.0220	.0318	.0539
94	.0400	.3200	.6800	.0174	.0371	.0545
95	.1508	.7709	.1899	.1092	.0269	.1417
96	.2628	.5961	.2820	.0451	.0213	.0756
97	.1250	.7421	.2578	.0719	.0250	.0969
98	.0462	.8013	.1986	.2460	.0609	.3070
99	.0217	.8391	.1565	.2919	.0544	.3479

TABLE 4.4. Rates of in-, out-, and internal migration by subdistrict for 1970

Sub-district	Moves within Sub-district/ Total Moves	Moves within Amsterdam/ Total Moves	Moves out of Amsterdam/ Total Moves	Moves within Amsterdam/ Total Population	Moves out of Amsterdam/ Total Population	Total Moves/ Total Population
00	.1052	.7094	.2905	.1944	.0796	.2741
01	.1012	.7020	.2980	.1490	.0632	.2123
02	.0560	.6892	.3108	.1690	.0762	.2453
03	.1196	.8080	.1920	.1472	.0350	.1821
04	.0914	.8006	.1993	.1668	.0415	.2083
05	.0422	.6998	.3002	.1786	.0766	.2552
06	.0561	.8424	.1576	.2645	.0495	.3140
07	.0859	.7203	.2797	.1741	.0676	.2417
08	.0558	.7345	.2655	.1638	.0592	.2230
09	.0394	.4022	.5979	.1675	.2491	.4116
10	.1388	.8076	.1924	.1391	.0331	.1722
11	.0807	.7546	.2454	.1114	.0362	.1476
12	.1038	.7073	.2927	.1184	.0490	.1673
13	.0595	.6521	.3479	.1182	.0630	.1812
14	.1197	.8030	.1970	.1416	.0347	.1763
15	.0715	.7748	.2252	.1572	.0457	.2028
16	.0905	.7635	.2364	.1369	.0424	.1793
17	.0540	.6745	.3255	.1595	.0770	.2364
18	.0414	.6704	.3296	.1533	.0754	.2287
19	.0768	.6381	.3619	.1154	.0655	.1809
20	.0199	.6816	.3184	.1536	.0717	.2253
21	.1108	.7343	.2657	.1553	.0562	.2115
23	.0652	.6629	.3371	.1093	.0556	.1649
25	.0632	.6892	.3108	.1045	.0471	.1516
26	.0890	.6265	.3735	.1359	.0810	.2169
27	.0485	.5973	.4027	.1185	.0799	.1985
28	.0917	.7174	.2826	.1306	.0515	.1821
29	.0586	.6860	.3140	.0960	.0440	.1400
30	.0523	.6805	.3195	.1530	.0719	.2249
31	.0724	.7914	.2086	.1778	.0469	.2247
32	.0484	.7160	.2840	.1456	.0578	.2034
33	.0793	.7240	.2760	.1456	.0555	.2011
34	.0933	.7379	.2621	.1208	.0429	.1637
35	.0966	.7640	.2360	.1523	.0470	.1994
37	.1018	.7257	.2743	.1031	.0390	.1420
38	.0976	.7459	.2598	.0888	.0309	.1191
40	.0735	.5872	.4127	.0697	.0490	.1187
41	.1052	.5673	.4326	.0790	.0602	.1393
42	.0622	.5408	.4591	.0572	.0486	.1058
43	0	.6231	.3769	.1514	.0916	.2430
50	.0734	.6450	.3550	.1109	.0610	.1719
51	.0708	.6161	.3839	.8450	.0526	.1372

53	.1085	.5757	.4243	.1109	.0817	.1926
54	.0639	.6322	.3678	.0809	.0471	.1280
55	.0952	.4111	.5888	.0583	.0836	.1419
56	.0540	.3780	.6210	.0516	.0847	.1363
62	.0594	.6343	.3657	.0819	.0472	.1291
63	.0484	.6239	.3761	.0746	.0450	.1196
64	.0568	.6031	.3969	.0705	.0464	.1169
65	.0762	.6445	.3555	.0906	.0500	.1406
66	.0883	.6368	.3631	.0714	.0407	.1121
68	.1014	.6738	.3262	.0745	.0360	.1105
69	.0718	.6927	.3073	.0824	.0366	.1190
70	.0365	.4650	.5350	.0463	.0532	.0995
71	.1228	.6922	.3078	.0978	.0435	.1412
72	.1409	.6887	.3112	.0830	.0375	.1204
73	.0869	.5372	.4628	.0538	.0464	.1002
74	.0712	.7282	.2718	.0760	.0284	.1044
75	.0742	.5522	.4478	.0449	.0364	.0813
76	.0722	.4600	.5400	.0557	.0654	.1210
77	.1123	.4397	.5603	.0489	.0623	.1112
78	.0886	.5189	.4810	.0498	.0461	.0959
79	.1200	.5833	.4167	.0950	.0679	.1630
81	.0529	.5070	.4930	.0503	.0490	.0993
82	.0430	.5458	.4542	.0593	.0493	.1086
83	.0520	.5849	.4151	.0594	.0422	.1016
84	.0877	.6251	.3748	.0746	.0447	.1193
85	.1596	.5962	.4038	.0667	.0452	.1118
86	.0900	.4771	.5229	.0550	.0602	.1152
87	.0595	.4652	.5348	.0563	.0648	.1211
88	.0864	.4731	.5269	.0443	.0494	.0937
90	.2826	.5217	.4783	.0423	.0388	.0811
91	.2083	.6667	.3333	.0360	.0180	.0540
92	.0755	.5283	.4717	.0456	.0407	.0863
93	.1250	.5938	.4062	.0419	.0287	.0706
94	.1702	.4468	.5532	.0417	.0516	.0932
96	.1773	.6591	.3409	.0758	.0392	.1150
97	.0680	.4563	.5437	.0353	.0421	.0774
98	.0205	.5000	.5000	.0697	.0697	.1394
99	.0339	.5085	.4915	.0617	.0597	.1214
–1	.1286	.4857	.5143	.1518	.1607	.3125
–2	.1061	.4804	.5196	.1318	.1425	.2743
–3	.1130	.5188	.4811	.1339	.1242	.2580
–4	.1125	.7000	.3000	.7417	.3179	1.0000
–5	0	.5625	.4375	.4500	.3500	.8000
–6	0	0	1.000	0	.0924	.0924
–7	0	.2907	.7093	.1269	.3096	.4365
–8	.1318	.2248	.7752	.0195	.0672	.0866

within the city. It is also obvious that the rates of mobility are somewhat higher overall for central districts than for the districts towards the edge of the municipality. It is the attempt to capture this variability and to present the changes over time which has stimulated the present concern with both descriptive and predictive entropy measures of intraurban migration. Discussions such as that immediately above do not adequately summarize the complexity of mobility rates and processes in a city.

Description of flows

The complexity of the process of migration is emphasized in an even more dramatic fashion if the analysis is extended to the population flows among the areas. Figures 4.3 and 4.4 indicate the origins and destinations of flows exceeding 90 persons for 1960 and 1970. In 1960 the flows are directionally biased towards the western part of the city. In addition to the major flows into region 87 and to a lesser extent into region 86, we can note the large number of districts for which intradistrict movement dominates and the large number of moves which involve contiguous buurtcombinatie. The flows to region 87 come from several different parts of the city, including districts 26, 28, 34, and 52 in central locations in the city and from areas 14, 64, 66, and 68 in the north-west area of the city.

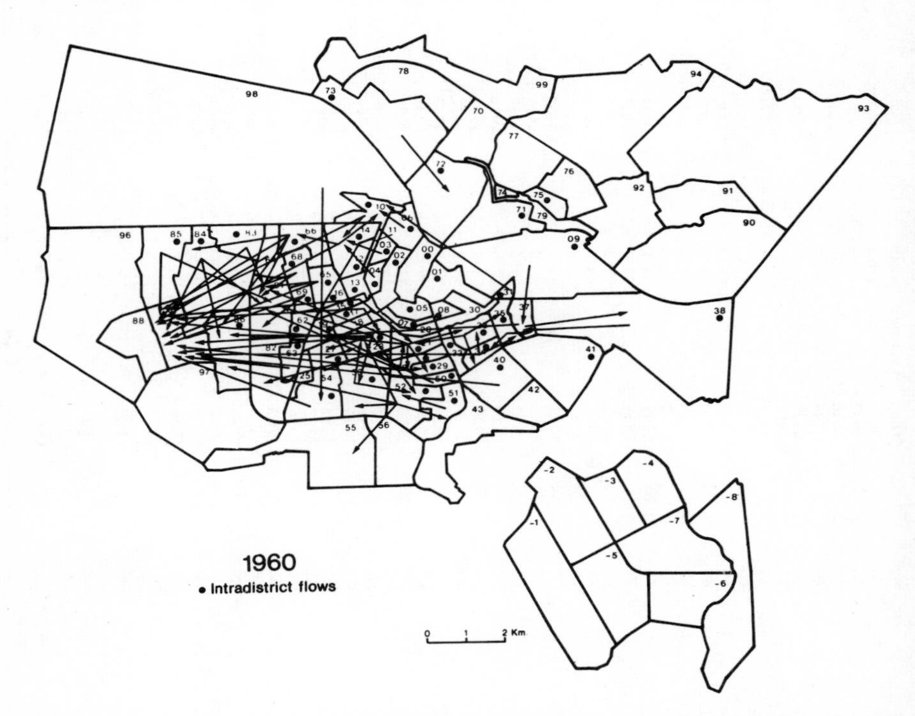

FIGURE 4.3. Vectors of observed 1960 migration flows in Amsterdam of more than 90 persons

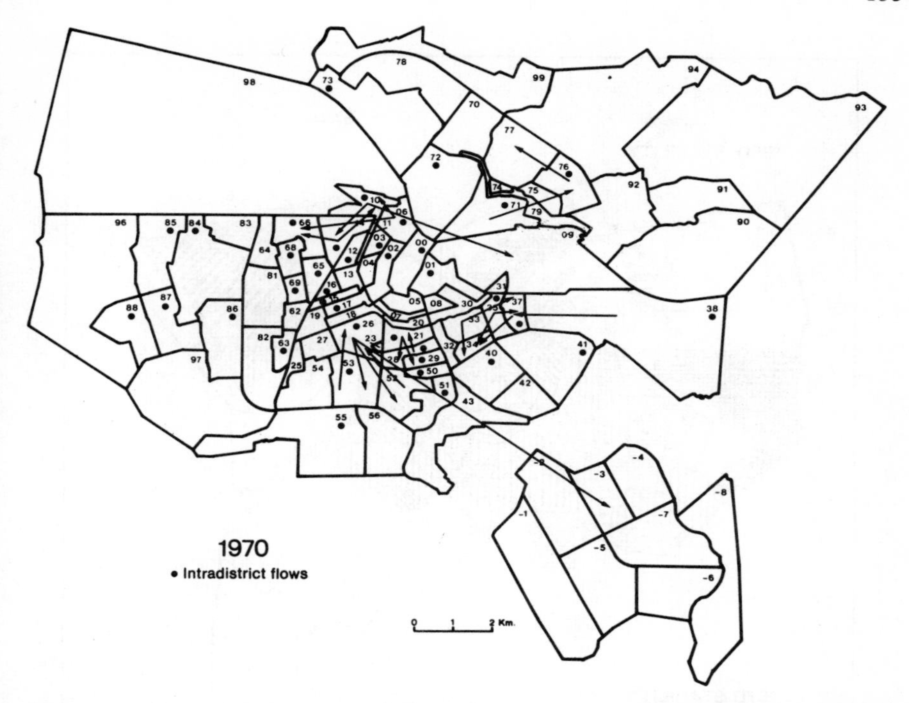

FIGURE 4.4. Vectors of observed 1970 migration flows in Amsterdam of more than 90 persons

Without any additional information it could be surmised that these flows represent the response of migrants to new housing opportunities in the city, and in fact a considerable housing development was constructed in the western subdistricts of Amsterdam in the early 1960s.

In 1970 the patterns are much more diffuse. There are significantly large flows out of 6, 10, 14, 21, 26, 33, and 35, although most of these flows are to adjacent areas and there are none of the dramatically biased patterns of the 1960 map. The flows from subdistrict 26 to the Bijlmermeer (subdistrict-3) represent the development of new housing. The out-migration from areas 21, 26, 33, and 35 is from housing built in the last century, and potentially represents the desire for more modern, convenient apartments. At best, the 1970 map creates an impression of movement. It is difficult to discern any outstanding trends in the flows from a subjective interpretation of the map.

The maps in Figure 4.5 depict the amount of intradistrict movement expressed as a percentage of the total migration originating in a district. The proportion of movers who choose to move locally has declined remarkably. Whereas some seventeen districts had 15 per cent. or more of the population moving within the district of origin in 1960, only three districts had percentages of internal movement which were this high in 1970. In 1970 most of the subdistricts had percentages of internal migration which ranged in the interval from 5 to 20 per

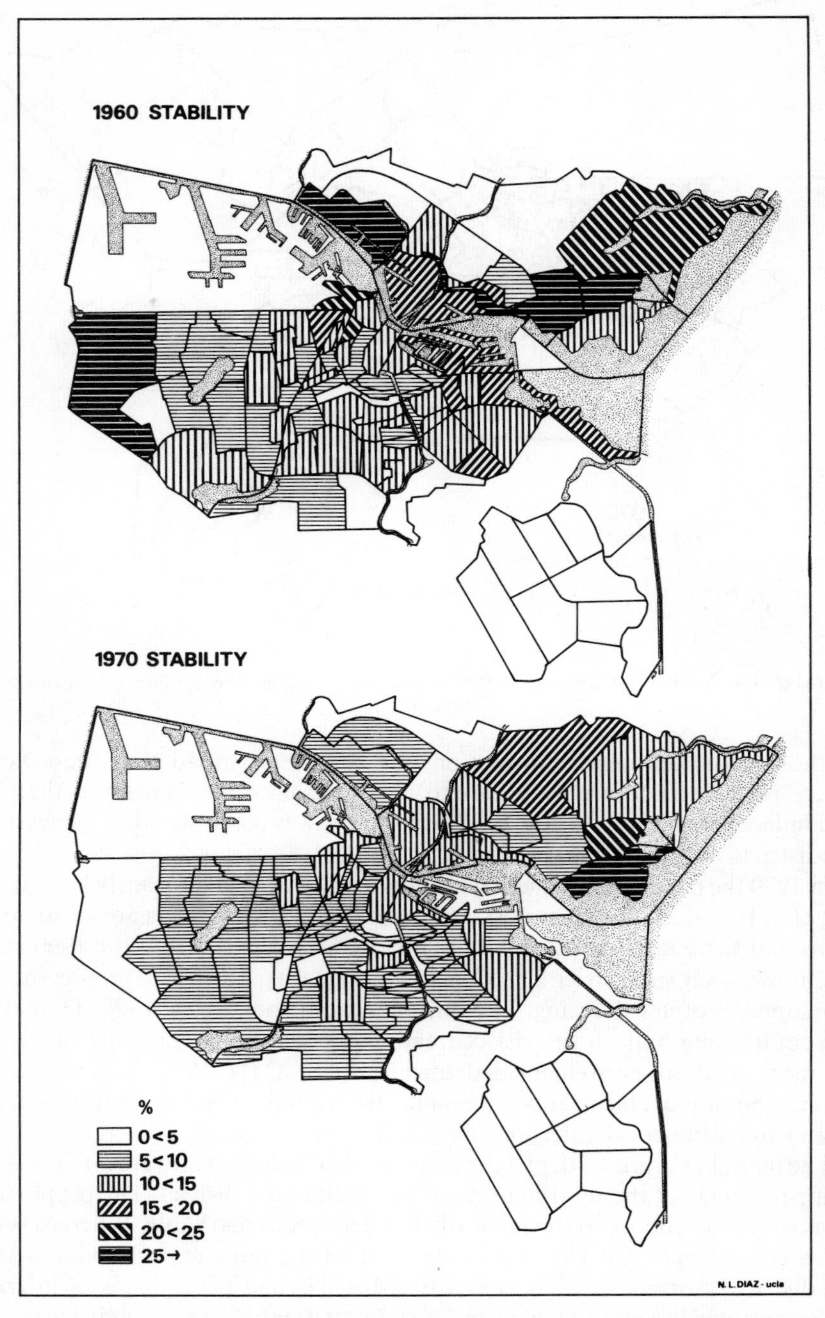

FIGURE 4.5. Percentage of movers who move within the originating district

cent. The higher percentages of internal movement were in the more newly developed areas in the north of the municipality. There are numerous implications to be drawn from this temporal change, including the observations that fewer migrants are moving locally and the speculation that the newer residential areas with higher rates of mobility reflect the internal adjustment of new movers. However, even though we can learn a great deal from discussions of the population flow maps and cartographic presentation of percentages of internal movements, none of these approaches statistically analyses the complex quantitative information which is available in the migration matrices. The strengths of the entropy techniques which are used in this study are that they are quantitative summary measures which can express many of the subtleties of the patterns of migration which cannot be addressed via a cartographic analysis.

In concluding the description of the aggregate flows and the methods which might be used to analyse the patterns reflected in the migration matrices, it is useful to compare the Markov approaches already discussed in the literature review with the entropy measures to be developed in the remainder of the paper. In fact, the Markov and entropy approaches are both concerned with the analyses of the probabilities of moving from state i to state j and the Pij values are those which represent these movements in probability terms. However, whereas the Markov model is a dynamic model of the movement process and requires assumptions about the process of mobility (including those of stationarity and homogeneity in the matrices) the entropy statistics and the entropy maximizing approach are much less demanding in their requirements and assumptions. Because we can use the entropy measures in a fashion similar to the use of descriptive and inferential statistics, they appear potentially powerful in the analysis of large data matrices.

ENTROPY

Entropy has received a great deal of attention in urban and regional studies during the past decade. In particular, the entropy maximizing methodology has proved immensely popular for spatial interaction modelling. Defined variously as a measure of uncertainty, organization, order, disorder, choice, or expected information, entropy is, not surprisingly, a concept which can cause and has caused some confusion in the past. The intent of this section is to describe the separate derivations of the entropy concept in statistical mechanics and information theory and to show how the two interpretations are related. This brief review will provide the basis for expanded discussions and applications of entropy measures of homogeneity and of the entropy maximizing methodology for modelling spatial interaction.

Entropy and statistical mechanics

Entropy has its origins in statistical mechanics and is related to the second law of thermodynamics which says, essentially, that a natural process which starts in one equilibrium state and ends in another will go in the direction that causes the entropy of the system to increase. Entropy is a measurable thermodynamic variable which may be thought of as the 'unavailability' of energy to the system. To illustrate what this means, let us assume that the state of a system of molecules, for instance, is described in terms of the energy levels of those molecules. If the distribution of probabilities p_i of a system's energy levels is known, the calculation of the entropy (S) of that system state is derived from the theory of ensembles and is expressed as

$$S = -k \sum_{i=1}^{n} p_i \ln p_i \tag{4.6}$$

As the distribution of energy levels in the system becomes more homogeneous (through heat exchange, for instance), entropy increases, since energy is becoming more unavailable. Maximum entropy is achieved when every molecule in the system attains the same energy level.

Entropy and information theory

A concept equivalent in mathematical form to that of thermodynamic entropy appeared in the literature of information theory as a means of determining how much information is produced by a discrete information source modelled as a Markov process (Shannon, 1948). The problem was to find a unique, unambiguous measure of the uncertainty of the distribution of probabilities p_i associated with a set of events x_i. Shannon proposed that it was necessary to find a measure H which is continuous in the p_i, is a monotonic increasing function of the number of events if all the p_i are equal, and is additive for independent sources of uncertainty. The only measure satisfying these three criteria is

$$H = -k \sum_{i=1}^{n} p_i \ln p_i \tag{4.7}$$

where k is a constant amounting to a choice of unit of measure. Shannon notes the similarity of H to the entropy of statistical mechanics and refers to H variously as a measure of choice, uncertainty, or entropy.

Two important characteristics of the information theoretic uncertainty measures have been noted. The quantity H attains a minimum of zero when one p_i equals one and the rest are zero. In this case the outcome of the event is certain and the set of p_i values has maximum order. At the other extreme, H attains its maximum value of $\ln(n)$ when the outcome is completely uncertain or disordered, i.e. when $p_1 = p_2 = \ldots = p_n$.

Statistical mechanics and information theory

Comparison of equations (4.6) and (4.7) indicates that the entropy of statistical mechanics is equivalent in form to that of the uncertainty or entropy of information theory. But as Jaynes (1957, p. 621) has noted, 'The mere fact that the same mathematical expression for entropy occurs both in statistical mechanics and in information theory does not in itself establish any connection between these fields'. Nonetheless, Jaynes has suggested an important reinterpretation of statistical mechanics which allows thermodynamic entropy and information theoretic entropy to be viewed as the same concept and not merely as the same mathematical expression. Jaynes' argument is based on the consideration of statistical mechanics not as a physical theory but rather as a form of statistical inference, the object of which, for any given problem, is to find the most likely distribution of the probabilities of the occurrence of an event in the absence of complete information about the event. The derivation of this most likely distribution follows Shannon's proof that the solution to the problem is to find the distribution which maximizes entropy. By accepting the information theoretic view that entropy is a unique, unambiguous measure of the amount of uncertainty in a probability distribution, Jaynes maintains that entropy becomes a primitive concept, more basic than energy. Statistical mechanics may now be seen as a form of statistical inference, and the prediction problem is freed from the constriction of physical theory based on the laws of motion. The maximization of entropy becomes 'not an application of a law of physics, but merely a method of reasoning which ensures that no unconscious arbitrary assumptions have been introduced' (Jaynes, 1957, p. 630).

ENTROPY MEASURES

Entropy measures of matrix structure have been derived either directly or indirectly from Shannon's (1948) formulation of the entropy of two events. Letting $p(i, j)$ be the probability of the joint occurrence of i for the event x and j for the event y, such that $\sum_{i=1}^{m} \sum_{j=1}^{n} p(i,j) = 1.0$, the entropy of the joint event is

$$H(x,y) = -\sum_i \sum_j [p(i,j) \log p(i,j)] \tag{4.8}$$

while

$$H(x) = -\sum_i \sum_j \left[p(i,j) \log \sum_j p(i,j) \right] \tag{4.9}$$

and

$$H(y) = -\sum_i \sum_j \left[p(i,j) . \log \sum_i p(i,j) \right] \tag{4.10}$$

The relationship between the entropy of the joint event and the entropies of the individual events is expressed as

$$H(x,y) \leqslant H(x) + H(y) \tag{4.11}$$

with equality only if the events x and y are independent. If the two events are not independent, then for any value i of x there is a conditional probability $p_i(j)$ that y has the value j. The conditional probability $p_i(j)$ is expressed as

$$p_i(j) = \frac{p(i,j)}{\sum_j p(i,j)} \tag{4.12}$$

and the conditional entropy of y, $H_x(y)$, is defined as the weighted average of the entropy of y for each value of x. Thus

$$H_x(y) = -\sum_i \sum_j [p(i,j) \log p_i(j)] \tag{4.13}$$

The relationship between the conditional entropy, the joint entropy, and the entropy of the event x can be obtained by substituting the value of $p_i(j)$ given in equation (4.12) into equation (4.13) such that

$$H_x(y) = -\sum\sum\left[p(i,j) \log \frac{p(i,j)}{\sum_j p(i,j)} \right]$$

$$= -\sum_i \sum_j [p(i,j) \log p(i,j)] + \sum_i \sum_j [p(i,j) \log \sum_j p(i,j)]$$

or $$H_x(y) = H(x,y) - H(x) \tag{4.14}$$

Thus the entropy of the joint event (x,y) is the sum of the entropies of x and of y when x is given.

The translation of Shannon's formulations based on joint events to the analysis of two-dimensional matrices is simple and direct, and has been described in greatest detail by Sonis (1968). However, Sonis' work and subsequent applications, particularly those by Berry and Schwind (1969) and Medvedkov (1970), have introduced some confusion into the study of matrix entropy measures through the use of varying methods of mathematical notation and the inconsistency of names given to the derived measures. The following discussion indicates the correspondences among the measures used by Sonis, Berry and Schwind, and Medvedkov and describes the ways in which these measures have been used to analyse migration matrices. The notation and formulae are summarized in Table 4.5, and the connections among the measures used in this analysis and their counterparts in the studies of Shannon, Sonis, Berry and Schwind and Medvedkov are shown.

Joint entropy

The entropy of the joint event (denoted here as $H(p_{ij})$ and equivalent to $H(x,y)$ in equation 4.8) measures the homogeneity of the entire matrix of probabilities. It varies between a maximum log nm when all p_{ij} are equivalent and a minimum of zero when one p_{ij} equals 1.0 and the rest equal zero. Medvedkov suggests that $H(p_{ij})$ measures the entropy of the linkages between the initial and resulting states of the matrix.

Initial-and final-state entropies

The entropy of the initial states, $H(p_{i\cdot})$ (that is $H(x)$ in equation 4.9), and the entropy of the final states, $H(p_{\cdot j})$ (that is $H(y)$ in equation 4.10), can be thought of as measuring, respectively, the homogeneity of the total flows from all

TABLE 4.5. Notations and definitions appearing in selected studies of entropy measures of homogeneity

Shannon (1948)	Sonis (1968)	Berry and Schwind (1969)	Medvedkov (1970)	Present Paper
	$M = \sum_{ij} m_{ij}$			$M = \sum_{i=1}^{m} \sum_{j=1}^{n} m_{ij}$
	$n_i = \sum_{j=1}^{n} m_{ij}$		$x_i = \sum_{r=1}^{n} (x_i y_r)$	$m_{i\bullet} = \sum_j m_{ij}$
	$k_j = \sum_{i=1} m_{ij}$		$y_r = \sum_{i=1}^{n} (x_i y_r)$	$m_{\bullet j} = \sum_i m_{ij}$
$p(i,j)$	$P_{ij} = \frac{m_{ij}}{M}$	p_{ij}	$p(x_i y_r) = \frac{x_i y_r}{\sum_i \sum_r x_i y_r}$	$p_{ij} = \frac{m_{ij}}{M}$
	$P_i = \frac{n_i}{M} = \frac{\sum_j m_{ij}}{M} = \sum_j P_{ij}$	$p_{i\bullet} = \sum_j p_{ij}$	$p(x_i) = \sum_{r=1}^{n} p(x_i y_r)$	$p_{i\bullet} = \sum_j p_{ij} = \frac{m_{i\bullet}}{M}$
	$Q_j = \frac{k_j}{M} = \frac{\sum_i m_{ij}}{M} = \sum_i P_{ij}$	$p_{\bullet j} = \sum_i p_{ij}$	$p(y_r) = \sum_{i=1}^{n} p(x_i y_r)$	$p_{\bullet j} = \sum_i p_{ij} = \frac{m_{\bullet j}}{M}$
$p_i(j) = \frac{p(i,j)}{\sum_j p(i,j)}$	$P_{j\|i} = \frac{m_{ij}}{n_i} = \frac{P_{ij}}{P_i}$		$p(y_r \| x_i) = \frac{p(x_i y_r)}{p(x_i)}$	$p_{j\|i} = \frac{p_{ij}}{p_{i\bullet}} = \frac{m_{ij}}{m_{i\bullet}}$
	$Q_{i\|j} = \frac{m_{ij}}{k_j} = \frac{P_{ij}}{Q_j}$		$p(x_i \| y_r) = \frac{p(x_i y_r)}{p(y_r)}$	$p_{i\|j} = \frac{p_{ij}}{p_{\bullet j}} = \frac{m_{ij}}{m_{\bullet j}}$
$H(x,y) = -\sum_i \sum_j p(i,j) \log p(i,j)$ entropy of the joint event	$H^* = -\sum_i \sum_j P_{ij} \log P_{ij}$ measure of homogeneity	$H(p_{ij}) = -\sum_i \sum_j p_{ij} \log p_{ij}$ joint entropy	$H(X,Y) = H_{(x,y)} = -\sum_i^{n} \sum_r^{m} p(x_i y_r) \log p(x_i, y_r)$ entropy of the linkages between initial and resulting states	$H(p_{ij}) = -\sum_i \sum_j p_{ij} \log p_{ij}$ joint entropy

TABLE 4.5. *contd.*

Shannon (1948)	Sonis (1968)	Berry and Schwind (1969)	Medvedkov (1970)	Present Paper
$H(x) = -\sum_i \sum_j p(i,j) \log \sum_j p(i,j)$ entropy of the event x	$H_n^* = -\sum_i P_i \log P_i$ homogeneity of the initial distribution	$H(p_{i\cdot}) = -\sum_i p_{i\cdot} \log p_{i\cdot}$ row entropy	$H(X) = H_{(x)} = -\sum_i^n p(x_i) \log p(x_i)$ entropy of initial states	$H(p_{i\cdot}) = -\sum_i p_{i\cdot} \log p_{i\cdot}$ entropy of initial states
$H(y) = -\sum_i \sum_j p(i,j) \log \sum_i p(i,j)$ entropy of the event y	$H_k^* = -\sum_j Q_j \log Q_j$ homogeneity of the final distribution	$H(p_{\cdot j}) = -\sum_j p_{\cdot j} \log p_{\cdot j}$ column entropy	$H(Y) = H_{(y)} = -\sum_r^m p(y_r) \log p(y_r)$ entropy of resulting states	$H(p_{\cdot j}) = -\sum_j p_{\cdot j} \log p_{\cdot j}$ entropy of final states
	$I^* = (H_n^* + H_k^*) - H^*$ non-homogeneity of the redistribution process	$H(\hat{p}_{ij}) = H(p_{i\cdot}) + H(p_{\cdot j}) - H(p_{ij})$ expected joint entropy	$H(Y \leftrightarrow X) = H(X) + H(Y) - H(X,Y)$ joint entropy	$H(\hat{p}_{ij}) = H(p_{i\cdot}) + H(p_{\cdot j}) - H(p_{ij})$ expected joint entropy
	$h_i^- = -\sum_{j=1} P_{j\|i} \log P_{j\|i}$ homogeneity of a row		$H(Y\|x_i) = \sum_{r=1}^m p(y_r\|x_i) \log p(y_r\|x_i)$ entropy of output states with respect to a single input state	$H(p_{j\|i}) = -\sum_j p_{j\|i} \log p_{j\|i}$ conditional row entropy
	$H_i^- = P_i h_i^- = -\sum_j P_{ij} \log P_{j\|i}$ $= -P_i \sum_j P_{j\|i} \log P_{j\|i}$ measure of homogeneity of expulsion from i			$H_i(p_{j\|i}) = p_{i\cdot} H(p_{j\|i})$ $= -\sum_j p_{ij} \log p_{j\|i}$ weighted conditional row entropy
$H_x(y) = -\sum_i \sum_j p(i,j) \log p_i(j)$ conditional entropy of y	$H^- = \sum_{i=1}^n H_i^- = -\sum_{i=1}^n P_i h_i^-$ $= -\sum_i \sum_j P_{ij} \log P_{j\|i}$ measure of expulsion of entire matrix		$H(Y\|X) = -\sum_{i=1}^n p(y_r) H(Y\|x_i)$ average entropy of the output states in respect to the input states	$H^*(p_{j\|i}) = \sum_i H_i(p_{j\|i})$ $= -\sum_i \sum_j p_{ij} \log p_{j\|i}$ weighted conditional row entropy of entire matrix

TABLE 4.5. *Contd.*

Shannon (1948)	Sonis (1968)	Berry and Schwind (1969)	Medvedkov (1970)	Present Paper
				$H(p_{i\|j}) = -\sum_i p_{i\|j} \log p_{i\|j}$ conditional column entropy
	$H_j^+ = Q_j h_j^+ = \sum_i P_{ij} \log Q_{i\|j}$ $= -Q_j \sum_i Q_{i\|j} \log Q_{i\|j}$ measure of homogeneity of attraction of j			$H_j(p_{i\|j}) = p_{\cdot j} H(p_{i\|j})$ $= -\sum_i p_{ij} \log p_{i\|j}$ weighted conditional column entropy
	$H^+ = \sum_j H_j^+$ $= -\sum_i \sum_j P_{ij} \log Q_{i\|j}$ measure of attraction of entire matrix			$H^*(p_{i\|j}) = \sum_j H_j(p_{i\|j})$ $= -\sum_i \sum_j p_{ij} \log p_{i\|j}$ weighted conditional column entropy of entire matrix

origins and the homogeneity of the total flows into all destinations. Sonis speaks of this as the homogeneity of the initial and final distributions, while Berry and Schwind refer to measures of row and column entropy.

Expected joint entropy

As indicated in equation (4.11), the joint entropy is always less than the sum of the entropies of the initial and final states if the events x and y are not independent. The difference between the left- and right-hand sides of equation (4.11) is called by Berry and Schwind the 'expected joint entropy' and can be given as

$$H(\hat{p}_{ij}) = H(p_{i\cdot}) + H(p_{\cdot j}) - H(p_{ij}) \tag{4.15}$$

Sonis suggests that since $H(\hat{p}_{ij})$ equals zero when the initial and final states are independent, or 'undisturbed', a value of $H(\hat{p}_{ij})$ greater than zero reflects the non-homogeneity, or disturbance, attributable to the process of redistribution. Thus the expected joint entropy diverges from zero when $p_{ij} \neq p_{i\cdot} p_{\cdot j}$; i.e. when 'there is a system to the flows apart from ordering effects that may have been imposed by concentration among the initial and final states' (Berry and Schwind, 1969, p. 9).

Conditional row and column entropy measures

The entropy of the final states with respect to a single initial state can be written as

$$H(p_{j/i}) = -\sum_j p_{j/i} \log p_{j/i} \tag{4.16}$$

which is a measure of the homogeneity of a single row of the probability matrix, based on the conditional probabilities $p_{j/i}$.

Sonis suggests weighting $H(p_{j/i})$, the conditional row entropy, by $p_{i\cdot}$, the probability of a flow originating in state i, to obtain $H_i(p_{j/i})$, which he terms a measure of the homogeneity of expulsion from state i. This weighted conditional row entropy is given as

$$H_i(p_{j/i}) = p_{i\cdot} H(p_{j/i}) = \sum_j p_{ij} \log p_{j/i} \tag{4.17}$$

More commonly, $H_i(p_{j/i})$ is summed over all i to obtain the weighted conditional row entropy of the entire matrix, written as

$$H^*(p_{j/i}) = \sum_i \sum_j p_{ij} \log p_{j/i} \tag{4.18}$$

Note that $H^*(p_{j/i})$ is equivalent to equation (4.13), which Shannon calls the conditional entropy of the event y.

The conditional column entropy, or the entropy of the initial states with respect to a single final state, is

$$H(p_{i/j}) = -\sum_i p_{i/j} \log p_{i/j} \tag{4.19}$$

Weighting $H(p_{i/j})$ by $p_{.j}$ yields

$$H_j(p_{i/j}) = p_j H(p_{i/j}) = \sum_i p_{ij} \log p_{i/j} \tag{4.20}$$

which is, in Sonis' terms, a measure of the homogeneity of attraction of state j. Summing equation (4.20) over all j gives a measure of attraction, or the weighted conditional column entropy, of the entire matrix,

that is,
$$H^*(p_{i/j}) = \sum_i \sum_j p_{ij} \log p_{i/j} \tag{4.21}$$

The nature of homogeneity in migration matrices

Before discussing the kinds of information generated in the application of matrix entropy measures to case studies of migration, it is useful to consider in greater detail what is meant by the term 'homogeneity' in reference to matrices of migration flows or probabilities. It has already been stated that the measure of joint entropy, for instance, attains a maximum value when all of the migration flow probabilities are equivalent. This accords well with an intuitive notion of maximum homogeneity of the probability matrix. It may be expected, then, that a measure of homogeneity would indicate how *similar* the elements of a matrix are with respect to one another. Imagine, for example, three 2×2 matrices with the following p_{ij} elements:

Case I: (0.25, 0.25, 0.25, 0.25)
Case II: (0.30, 0.25, 0.25, 0.20)
Case III: (0.60, 0.30, 0.10, 0.0)

It is not difficult to see that the elements of case I are most similar, or homogeneous, while cases II and III represent decreasing levels of internal homogeneity. But what of more complex matrices? Comparison of the following two sets of p_{ij} does not readily lead to an intuitive assessment of relative homogeneity:

Case IV: (0.29, 0.27, 0.23, 0.21)
Case V: (0.28, 0.27, 0.27, 0.18)

As Gurevich (1969b, p. 415) points out, in these 'more complicated situations that may not be self-evident... intuition must be replaced by a reasonable formal criterion, namely, a measure of homogeneity'. While there exist several such possible measures, the entropy-based ones possess a number of attractive properties (Gurevich, 1969a, pp. 408–409):

1. For a given number mn of the p_{ij}, the entropy measure attains a maximum of $\log mn$ if and only if all p_{ij} are equal.
2. For a given mn and given that $\sum_i \sum_j p_{ij} = 1.0$, a 'smoothing' of the magnitudes of the p_{ij} leads to an increase in the magnitude of the entropy, such that as the p_{ij} approach complete smoothing, entropy approaches $\log mn$.
3. A positional change of any elements of the subset of the p_{ij} being used to

calculate a particular entropy measure changes the structure of the matrix but does not alter the value of the entropy.

4. If $mn = 1.0$, entropy equals zero in only one case, i.e. when one p_{ij} equals 1.0 and the rest are zero.

Gurevich (1969a, pp. 409–410) introduces the concept of a limitator of homogeneity, L^*, which 'represents the numerical integral valuation of the aggregate of all factors... that restrict the greatest possible, complete homogeneity of the magnitudes $[p_{ij}]$ characterized by the measure [maximum entropy = log mn]'. Property (1) indicates that for a given mn, an entropy measure H can be written as

$$H = \log \lambda^* mn \tag{4.22}$$

where the multiplier λ^* satisfies the inequality

$$\frac{1}{mn} \leqslant \lambda^* \leqslant 1$$

Solving equation (4.22) for λ^* gives

$$\lambda^* = \left(\frac{1}{mn}\right) 10^H \tag{4.23}$$

The limitator L^* is defined as

$$L^* = 1 - \lambda^* = 1 - \left(\frac{1}{mn}\right) 10^H \tag{4.24}$$

so that
$$0 \leqslant L^* \leqslant \frac{mn - 1}{mn}$$

When the limitator L^* equals zero, there is no limitation of homogeneity, and $H = \log mn$ (i.e. entropy reaches a maximum). When $L^* = (mn - 1)/mn$, the limitation of homogeneity is complete and H equals zero.

Obviously, the upper bound of the limitator is dependent on the magnitude of mn, though for very large matrices the maximum value of L^* approaches 1.0. It is useful to fix the bounds of the limitator so as to facilitate comparisons of matrices of different sizes. Therefore, we define very simply a value L as

$$L = \frac{L^*}{L^*_{\max}} \times 100\% \tag{4.25}$$

This L value can be thought of a measure of relative homogeneity, varying between 0 (maximum homogeneity) and 100 (minimum homogeneity) per cent., and can be used for each (joint, initial, final, expected, and conditional row and column) entropy measure.

Interrelationships of entropy measures and matrix structure

Given such a plethora of entropy measures, one may easily lose sight of the interconnections among them and of their relationship to actual origin–destina-

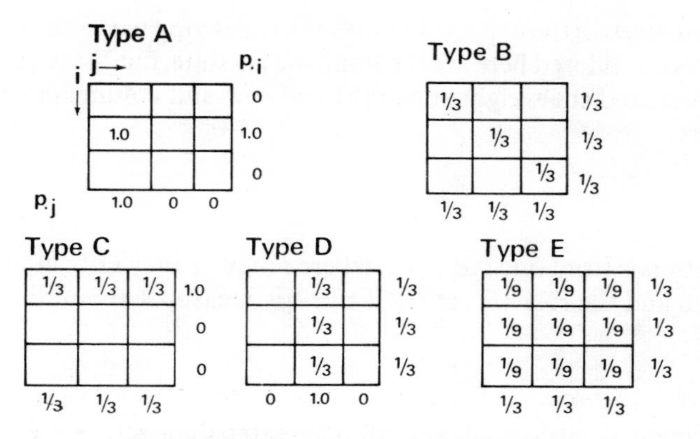

FIGURE 4.6. Hypothetical matrix structures

tion matrices of migration probabilities. It is useful to consider what their expected values might be given certain specific spatial patterns of migration. The following typology of hypothetical matrices is a useful pedagogic device and helps to clarify some of the relationships described in the preceding paragraphs. Figure 4.6 illustrates the kinds of matrix associated with each type, and

TABLE 4.6. Expected values of selected entropy measures conforming to hypothetical matrix types

Matrix type	A	B	C	D	E
Joint entropy, $H(p_{ij})$	0	$\log n$	$\log n$	$\log n$	$\log n^2$
L	100%	$\frac{n^2-n}{n^2-1} \times 100\%$	$\frac{n^2-n}{n^2-1} \times 100\%$	$\frac{n^2-n}{n^2-1} \times 100\%$	0%
Initial-state entropy, $H(p_{i\cdot})$	0	$\log n$	0	$\log n$	$\log n$
L	100%	0%	100%	0%	0%
Final-state entropy, $H(p_{\cdot j})$	0	$\log n$	$\log n$	0	$\log n$
L	100%	0%	0%	100%	0%
Expected joint entropy, $H(\hat{p}_{ij})$	0	$\log n$	0	0	0
Weighted conditional row entropy of matrix, $H^*(p_{j\mid i})$	0	0	$\log n$	0	$\log n$
L	100%	100%	0%	100%	0%
Weighted conditional column entropy of matrix, $H^*(p_{i\mid j})$	0	0	0	$\log n$	$\log n$
L	100%	100%	100%	0%	0%

Table 4.6 summarizes the expected values of the entropy measures for each type. The measures considered here are the joint, initial-state, final-state, and expected joint entropies, and the weighted conditional row and column entropies of the entire matrix.

Type A

All migration is from one i to one j, where i may or may not equal j. Thus one p_{ij} equals 1.0 and the rest are zero. All entropy measures are minimized.

Type B

All movement is intrazonal, and all p_{ij} greater than zero are equal. That is, $p_{ij} = 0$ if $i \neq j$, and $p_{11} = p_{22} = \ldots = p_{nn}$. Initial-state, final-state, and expected joint entropies are maximized, joint entropy equals log n, and the conditional entropies are minimized.

Type C

All movement begins in one origin i and is distributed evenly among all destinations j. For one i, $p_{i1} = p_{i2} = \ldots = p_{in}$; for all other i, p_{ij} equals zero. The final-state entropy and conditional row entropy of the entire matrix are maximized, joint entropy equals log n, and the initial-state, expected joint, and conditional column entropies are minimized.

Type D

This is the converse of type C, with all movement ending in one j and being derived equally from all i. For one j, $p_{1j} = p_{2j} = \ldots = p_{nj}$; for all other j, p_{ij} equals zero. The initial-state entropy and conditional column entropy are maximized, joint entropy equals log n, and the other measures equal zero.

Type E

All p_{ij} are equal and all measures are maximized, with the exception of the expected joint entropy which equals zero.

It is clear that seldom, if ever, will any of these five types of origin–destination matrices be observed in actual practice. However, it is not difficult to imagine intermediate situations which are combinations of one or more of the five hypothetical types, particularly if these types are thought of in terms of the spatial biases in migration which they imply. Probably much intraurban migration, for instance, combines elements of types B, C, D, and E with an origin–destination matrix tending towards the following characteristics: (1) no empty cells (type E); (2) a bias in favour of short distance moves—i.e.

higher p_{ij} values along the diagonal (type B); (3) a bias in favour of migration to a restricted number of destinations (type D); and (4) a bias in favour of migration beginning in a restricted number of origins (type C). For such a matrix, expected joint entropy approaches zero, while the other five measures considered in this section approach their respective maxima.

Previous applications of entropy measures in migration studies

While the concept of entropy has received a fair amount of attention in the geographic literature, few studies, save those of Sonis (1968) and Berry and Schwind (1969), have dealt empirically with applications to migration analysis. Sonis' study is concerned with the temporal stability of the entropy measures as applied to matrices of the annual migration of total and non-white populations among four regions of the United States during the period March 1963 to March 1966. He notes that for the three migration matrices for the entire population, the values of the joint entropy, the entropies of the initial and final states, and the weighted conditional row and column entropies are very stable over time. Furthermore, the entropies of the initial and final states are almost equivalent, as are the weighted conditional row and column entropies. He maintains that this equivalence is not surprising, as the relationship $H(p_{i\cdot}) = H(p_{\cdot j})$ always follows from the equality $H^*(p_{j/i}) = H^*(p_{i/j})$. In other words, 'it is found that the homogeneity of the initial and final distributions of migrants is directly associated with the homogeneity of attraction and expulsion of the migratory stream as a whole' (Sonis, 1968, p. 61).

Berry and Schwind consider the interpretation of values of joint, expected joint, initial-state, and final-state entropies of *a priori* (expected) and *a posteriori* (observed) migration matrices. They suggest that an organization or concentration in the migrant origins or destinations may represent systematic regularity that is present in the p_{ij} values. Further, they consider the meaning of cases in which joint and expected joint entropies are, or are not, equivalent. If initial- and final-state entropies are maximized, 'equality of joint entropy and expected joint entropy reveals pure random motion. When joint and expected joint entropies are unequal, there is a system to the flows apart from ordering effects that may have been imposed by concentration in the initial or final states' (Berry and Schwind, 1969, p. 9). To demonstrate these points, entropy measures are calculated for a matrix of migration flows among the twelve state economic areas of Iowa from 1955 to 1960 and for two matrices of model-predicted flows. Inequality of the initial- and final-state entropies of the observed flows and deviations of the observed flow measures from the predicted flow measures are explained in terms of four systematic elements which are thought to be spatially biasing the migration flows.

The potential of the matrix entropy measures described by Sonis and by Berry and Schwind is discussed by Medvedkov (1970), who notes the similarity of these two independent studies. Medvedkov provides a review of entropy measures and a useful discussion of the role of information theory in geography.

These papers appear to represent the sum total of research on geographic aspects of migration which apply matrix entropy measures. Of these, only two are empirical studies and both are concerned with relatively small matrices of migration flows among large areas. In addition, each deals largely with the application of the entropy measures to answer specific questions about migration (e.g. temporal stability of migration flows and the validity of the gravity model of migration). Neither gives an extensive analysis of the utility of the information gained from the wide assortment of matrix entropy measures.

The analysis of intraurban migration in Amsterdam

The purpose of this study is to examine the utility, in terms of the range and interpretability of information gained, of the application of entropy measures of homogeneity to large matrices of intraurban migration. The research is not focused on the explanation of substantive aspects of migration in a particular case study but rather on the use of a specific empirical data set for the illustration and assessment of a relatively unused analytic technique in order to determine its potential for substantive studies.

As we have noted, the Bureau of Statistics in Amsterdam has prepared population flow tables for the period 1960–1970 for some 80 or 89 small districts in the municipality. The raw data on numbers of moves between regions have been converted to probabilities of the form $p_{ij} = m_{ij}/M$, where $\Sigma_i \Sigma_j p_{ij} = 1.0$ (Table 4.5). For each of the eleven probability matrices, the following entropy measures of homogeneity have been calculated: joint entropy, initial-state and final-state entropies, expected joint entropy, conditional row and column entropies, and weighted conditional row and column entropies of the entire matrix. Since the number of cells in the matrices varies from 80^2 during 1960–1965 to 89^2 during 1966–1970, the corresponding L values of the measures are also given, where appropriate, in order to facilitate cross-temporal comparisons.

Joint, initial-state, final-state, and expected joint entropies

The joint, initial-state, and final-state entropies and their corresponding L values, as well as the expected joint entropy, are given in Table 4.7, and the L values are graphed in Figure 4.7.

An examination of the table and figure reveals that there is considerable heterogeneity in the p_{ij} values, although the L value of joint entropy varies by only about 9 percentage points. However, this unevenness of the distribution of flows tends to decrease over time (entropy is increasing). The addition of units to the study area in 1966 has the effect of initially raising the L value of the joint entropy, as there is little migration to or from the units of the Bijlmermeer district until the close of the decade.

The distributions of the proportions of out-migrants from each origin and of in-migrants to each destination (the $p_{i\cdot}$ and $p_{\cdot j}$) are much more homogeneous than the p_{ij} values. The homogeneity of the initial-state distribution generally

TABLE 4.7. Joint, initial-state, and final-state entropies and L values

Year	Joint entropy $H(p_{ij})$	L(%)	Initial-state entropy $H(p_{i\cdot})$	L(%)	Final-state entropy $H(p_{\cdot j})$	L(%)	Expected joint entropy $H(\hat{p}_{ij})$
1960	3.297	69.1	1.759	28.6	1.765	27.6	0.227
1961	3.301	68.8	1.756	29.1	1.767	27.2	0.222
1962	3.307	68.4	1.764	27.8	1.755	29.3	0.213
1963	3.322	67.2	1.772	26.4	1.769	26.9	0.218
1964	3.336	66.2	1.775	25.9	1.782	24.7	0.221
1965	3.368	63.6	1.773	26.2	1.766	27.4	0.171
1966	3.391	69.0	1.777	33.1	1.779	32.8	0.164
1967	3.397	68.5	1.785	31.9	1.794	30.4	0.182
1968	3.423	66.6	1.787	31.6	1.809	27.9	0.173
1969	3.447	64.7	1.795	30.3	1.823	25.9	0.171
1970	3.464	63.3	1.800	29.4	1.824	25.4	0.160

$\log 80 = 1.9031$ $\quad \log 80^2 = 3.8062$
$\log 89 = 1.9494$ $\quad \log 89^2 = 3.8988$

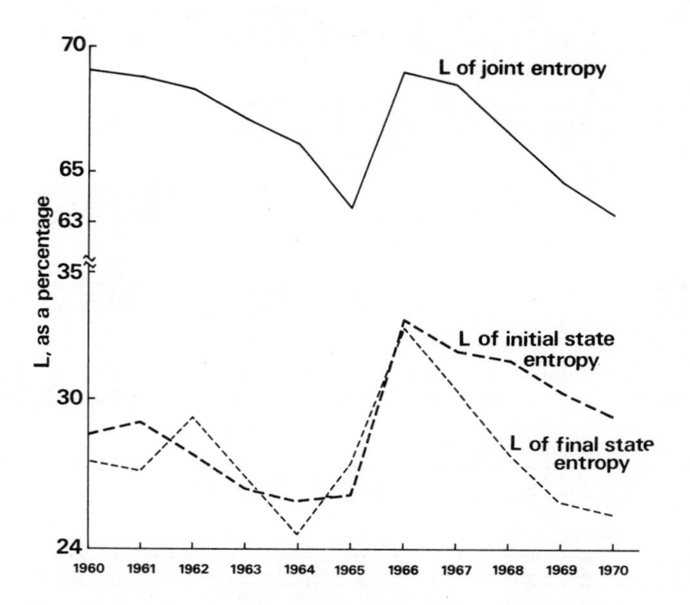

FIGURE 4.7. Graphs of L value for joint, initial-state, and final-state entropies

increases (entropy is increasing) during the first half of the period, decreases sharply in 1966, and gradually increases through the rest of the period without ever attaining its earlier levels. The homogeneity of the final-state distribution fluctuates more in the earlier years than does that of the initial-state distribution,

TABLE 4.8. L values of conditional row entropy

	1960	1961	1962	1963	1964	1965	1966	1967	1968	1969	1970
00	52.8	53.4	51.7	53.1	50.4	45.3	49.9	50.0	50.0	44.7	49.1
01	54.1	49.8	51.2	47.9	49.6	46.3	46.3	45.6	42.1	41.6	45.9
02	41.4	39.9	40.6	40.2	40.1	39.8	42.9	43.0	44.9	40.4	42.7
03	63.1	61.5	66.4	66.7	62.8	56.1	55.7	56.6	51.4	53.9	49.9
04	49.4	49.6	56.0	47.3	47.2	47.1	48.0	50.3	48.0	45.2	44.0
05	45.5	44.0	56.2	45.5	42.4	43.0	46.1	45.6	51.4	42.7	44.4
06	55.6	55.2	55.1	59.8	57.9	52.0	53.2	51.9	50.5	44.4	40.4
07	43.9	45.9	43.0	46.0	45.6	41.8	46.0	47.2	43.4	42.3	42.0
08	41.0	46.1	43.2	42.7	41.0	44.0	46.5	45.9	46.7	45.9	44.1
09	69.8	70.5	65.6	57.7	51.5	48.6	50.4	49.0	51.2	55.8	47.8
10	66.0	66.2	64.1	65.2	63.0	59.6	61.7	58.6	57.9	52.2	50.3
11	52.4	58.6	63.8	61.4	53.7	51.5	59.8	56.1	56.4	51.5	49.7
12	51.7	48.0	51.2	51.7	46.8	48.9	47.1	52.6	43.6	47.7	48.1
13	45.6	45.9	44.9	50.6	39.6	40.6	48.7	46.5	45.2	43.8	35.5
14	59.6	59.0	61.4	61.9	60.7	55.2	54.8	53.9	51.3	47.2	47.1
15	54.4	57.1	57.4	54.3	52.4	46.7	53.1	49.1	48.1	48.6	42.8
16	53.9	59.0	53.6	49.8	50.8	45.9	53.2	44.1	41.5	47.3	47.2
17	43.6	44.2	45.8	41.0	43.0	40.5	44.2	48.1	42.0	40.2	37.4
18	59.6	53.5	50.4	48.3	50.9	47.0	47.6	49.4	48.7	47.6	54.2
19	47.7	48.5	49.7	50.2	44.4	47.3	45.3	46.2	45.9	39.8	41.9
20	50.8	48.9	47.8	56.8	49.9	44.7	53.2	52.0	55.4	53.3	35.9
21	51.8	50.9	54.0	52.1	48.5	49.3	47.9	47.9	46.4	41.6	44.9
23	52.5	59.0	62.0	65.7	63.0	53.1	60.4	57.8	49.0	58.0	62.3
25	59.5	58.8	53.2	54.8	60.5	42.7	53.4	55.4	49.9	47.1	47.4
26	58.6	58.8	59.6	57.8	61.6	54.2	52.7	56.3	47.8	49.6	48.7
27	54.7	51.5	59.1	57.9	55.3	51.6	56.0	55.4	50.3	48.0	41.2
28	51.8	56.7	49.3	51.1	50.6	45.8	48.0	48.1	48.4	44.5	43.8
29	50.3	54.9	55.0	50.8	47.5	43.8	51.8	48.4	47.3	42.6	40.0
30	46.1	38.0	44.0	46.9	41.6	42.7	47.7	45.0	39.5	43.7	40.7
31	68.9	63.7	78.1	69.0	65.6	62.0	62.7	64.6	62.9	55.2	52.2
32	43.9	45.3	48.1	44.0	40.2	43.8	49.4	47.8	43.1	43.2	35.8
33	52.1	49.4	49.9	50.9	51.0	48.3	53.3	45.9	45.5	45.3	42.3
34	53.1	49.9	52.5	55.3	49.3	47.5	52.8	51.7	45.0	47.5	46.9
35	56.0	55.5	57.3	57.5	56.2	53.1	54.5	51.4	50.3	49.3	48.8
37	56.8	56.8	57.9	56.2	54.6	54.9	60.6	50.7	51.2	50.4	47.6
38	56.4	60.1	53.5	56.9	54.1	53.0	59.2	56.3	53.7	49.6	50.6
40	59.3	57.3	52.5	53.8	50.6	50.3	52.3	54.3	48.7	53.9	46.8
41	59.8	59.1	60.1	61.2	56.3	52.9	55.1	56.1	51.3	49.7	55.7
42	61.5	62.3	64.4	66.0	67.0	58.0	68.8	65.9	59.4	48.3	60.6
43	76.5	83.4	89.6	84.8	90.0	91.6	93.5	92.5	72.1	70.9	74.2
50	54.0	53.4	51.9	58.2	54.9	49.2	56.9	53.4	43.4	46.1	50.8
51	61.3	58.0	53.4	57.7	57.2	46.6	54.8	52.8	54.6	46.7	42.9
52	59.2	61.5	57.7	59.6	58.7	48.3	52.8	54.6	51.2	50.3	48.3

53	72.4	73.1	71.9	71.7	71.3	67.8	65.9	71.6	62.1	63.8	64.1
54	60.3	60.6	54.3	54.8	59.8	51.4	57.7	53.6	45.7	45.5	42.5
55	65.2	71.0	77.6	63.7	57.1	63.7	61.4	65.1	67.8	71.2	67.2
56	94.1	87.3	83.1	72.9	72.4	72.2	76.1	72.5	83.6	64.5	64.8
62	57.9	48.4	50.6	50.0	47.1	46.0	49.9	48.4	43.4	47.8	39.1
63	56.9	59.6	50.2	54.6	49.2	48.0	50.3	51.5	50.6	44.3	39.6
64	70.3	65.1	66.1	47.6	58.9	50.6	53.0	57.0	55.2	50.8	47.6
65	52.4	46.4	48.9	43.0	47.0	40.6	43.6	44.5	43.4	43.1	40.9
66	55.5	57.2	56.6	47.9	45.1	44.1	49.9	50.5	43.1	45.3	45.0
68	56.0	53.8	50.6	50.2	50.7	45.1	43.4	47.8	45.3	44.6	46.8
69	57.3	51.4	49.7	44.7	47.3	44.5	45.8	48.2	44.8	45.6	43.5
70	75.1	74.7	80.3	76.6	75.5	81.8	81.2	69.1	68.9	66.6	51.8
71	69.5	69.4	69.6	70.2	63.9	71.7	72.9	77.0	70.8	60.9	63.6
72	63.3	67.5	70.1	68.2	73.7	67.3	70.4	73.6	71.9	64.8	61.1
73	74.7	77.7	66.5	76.4	69.8	72.0	66.4	62.1	64.8	68.4	54.6
74	64.1	63.4	67.5	75.3	73.4	69.7	74.4	66.1	73.8	66.5	71.8
75	69.3	69.1	68.2	71.1	71.2	70.3	72.3	63.6	62.9	61.2	61.5
76	92.9	95.1	90.3	89.0	92.0	80.1	57.6	59.9	55.9	56.6	62.4
77							100.0	88.9	65.8	56.0	68.0
78							93.6	80.4	78.0	55.4	61.1
79	94.5	94.6	96.7	94.9	95.3	98.0	95.5	79.4	78.4	78.8	78.9
81	77.0	58.8	52.0	54.4	47.0	48.1	60.9	63.4	55.7	51.1	47.9
82	72.0	66.2	51.4	53.8	63.1	54.0	58.0	56.3	62.2	59.4	51.1
83	70.4	67.1	61.0	59.2	62.6	49.5	54.4	51.6	52.9	49.1	50.0
84	61.6	58.7	63.9	54.8	58.4	52.2	54.0	54.4	53.6	56.2	46.7
85	56.6	57.4	58.3	60.5	53.4	52.9	59.5	58.0	53.6	53.5	51.2
86	62.7	57.9	59.4	64.0	61.4	55.5	55.7	66.4	60.8	57.7	52.9
87	70.8	47.2	54.2	48.4	56.1	48.8	65.0	65.6	63.8	59.1	52.1
88	100.0	82.8	53.3	53.9	47.5	42.9	55.6	61.8	55.3	49.4	53.5
90	96.0	94.7	95.5	91.5	92.1	93.9	97.7	95.2	94.8	96.8	97.0
91	91.6	95.3	98.5	97.9	97.3	95.3	93.2	96.0	92.9	95.6	92.9
92	92.6	91.8	85.8	92.5	91.2	91.9	88.9	92.7	90.0	92.5	85.0
93	98.7	98.8	98.4	93.6	97.7	97.0	98.2	98.5	97.9	96.8	95.0
94	97.0	92.4	95.2	98.1	98.8	96.8	98.3	96.5	97.9	96.5	95.6
95	78.0	77.8	78.5	84.6	86.5	84.3					
96	89.3	88.4	84.1	89.6	72.6	85.7	82.4	89.1	84.1	84.0	82.5
97	83.1	83.3	76.9	85.9	88.5	88.5	88.3	88.0	84.6	83.0	81.2
98	84.0	79.0	83.1	87.9	84.7	87.7	72.5	62.3	77.7	91.8	78.4
99	86.6	94.0	88.6	90.8	87.6	94.9	89.0	92.3	96.5	90.8	92.1
-1							97.1	94.7	95.1	96.0	95.3
-2							99.0	85.4	93.3	79.7	78.5
-3							100.0	100.0	100.0	96.2	72.2
-4							100.0	100.0	96.2	97.2	82.9
-5							100.0	98.9	95.1	100.0	98.2
-6							100.0	100.0	99.4	100.0	100.0
-7							100.0	99.6	98.0	97.9	94.2
-8							98.8	92.9	95.1	94.5	95.2

and increases much more rapidly from 1966 to 1970. The expected joint entropy is low, indicating that the p_{ij} do not vary greatly from the marginal product $p_{i\cdot}p_{\cdot j}$.

Conditional row entropies

The conditional row entropy of each of the 89 origins has been calculated, and the L values are given in Table 4.8. While the time series of the L values of all of the districts have been graphed, only a representative sample of five has been selected for discussion here (Figure 4.8). The temporal trends in L for most of the 89 districts approximate one or another of the sample cases. For many of the districts (perhaps one-third), the level of homogeneity of the out-migration pattern shows relative stability over time and tends to be either high, as in district 07, or very low, as in district 92. The extreme L values of district 92 and of the other units in the Bijlmermeer are due to the fact that for most of these units the number of out-migrants is less than the number of possible destinations during each time period. In such cases, it is difficult to give meaningful interpretations to entropy measures of homogeneity. Another

L Values of Conditional Row Entropy for Total Flows for a Sample of Five Small Districts

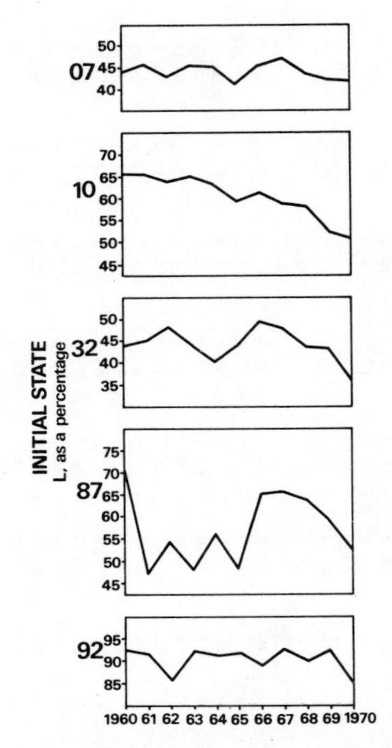

FIGURE 4.8. Graphs of L values of conditional row entropy for total flows for a sample of five small subdistricts

source of error is introduced when the flows are very small, namely, that Stirling's approximation to the factorial, on which the derivation of the entropy measure is based, is not accurate when the flows are small (Pielou, 1969, p. 232).

The majority of the remaining districts exhibit time series of conditional row entropy L values similar in form to those shown for areas 10 and 32. Homogeneity is moderate throughout the period, and the overall trend is in favour of increasing evenness of out-migration. Peaks in L are not uncommon, particularly in 1962 or 1963 and again in 1966. The decrease in entropy in 1966 is attributable to the increase in the number of destinations from 80 to 89. Subdistrict 87, while not directly representative of any other cases, is included in Figure 4.8 because it demonstrates the large year-to-year fluctuations in homogeneity which are observed in some cases.

Conditional column entropies

The conditional column entropy, which measures the organization of the in-migration pattern, has been calculated for each destination, or final state, and the L values are given in Table 4.9. The *types* of temporal trends in L observed for each of the 89 destinations are not unlike those already examined in Figure 4.8, but there is not much similarity between the out-migration and in-migration plots of each district taken in turn. Nonetheless, much of the discussion of the trends of the L values of the conditional row entropies is generally applicable to the conditional column entropies as well.

The time series of the L values of the weighted conditional row and column entropy measures of the entire matrix are plotted in Figure 4.9, while the entropy measures themselves are given in Table 4.10. The degrees of homogeneity of the overall patterns of out- and in-migration are very similar in terms of magnitude, range, and temporal variations. Neither pattern exhibits extremely high or low levels of homogeneity. Each shows a tendency towards

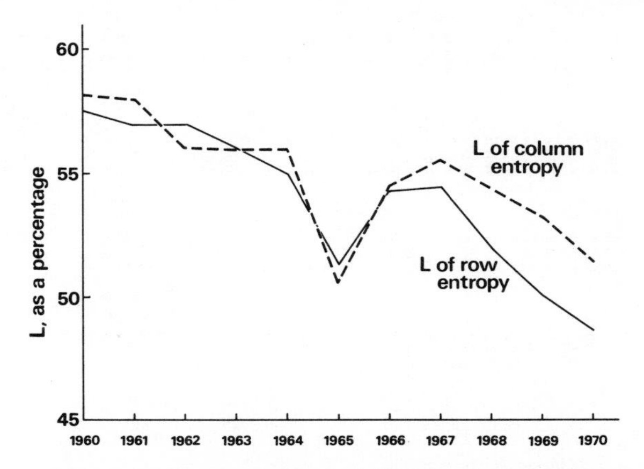

FIGURE 4.9. Graphs of L values for weighted conditional row and column entropies for the entire matrix

TABLE 4.9. L values of conditional column entropy

	1960	1961	1962	1963	1964	1965	1966	1967	1968	1969	1970
00	63.3	67.1	62.9	58.5	52.2	54.5	59.3	57.0	57.9	54.7	53.0
01	66.1	60.9	59.3	56.0	63.1	55.1	57.4	60.2	54.3	51.2	51.9
02	49.9	49.1	45.7	48.8	49.3	43.4	47.6	44.2	47.4	49.6	48.4
03	74.7	72.5	72.2	71.5	70.7	62.4	65.6	59.3	62.3	56.1	56.2
04	58.2	58.9	57.8	54.9	52.9	50.6	54.3	58.4	53.9	49.9	50.0
05	55.8	53.7	46.8	45.4	48.6	52.5	51.0	53.7	53.8	48.7	44.7
06	65.1	65.1	61.5	65.0	62.5	55.7	56.8	59.9	51.1	60.1	53.0
07	50.0	55.9	49.1	49.0	48.0	46.9	53.3	49.5	47.7	47.7	48.5
08	51.7	51.3	48.1	47.3	42.2	41.0	43.7	46.8	46.2	45.6	44.3
09	79.2	80.2	77.4	66.0	67.0	63.9	64.5	61.2	65.6	62.2	58.6
10	74.4	75.5	71.4	71.9	67.5	58.2	66.6	68.8	62.5	58.3	60.4
11	62.5	60.5	58.0	59.4	55.9	54.7	56.8	56.5	58.6	52.7	52.4
12	56.6	56.8	52.8	54.1	56.1	50.2	54.1	53.9	52.4	53.0	50.7
13	46.7	50.3	41.6	46.5	41.2	41.7	54.3	54.1	53.6	50.1	51.2
14	66.6	66.7	65.0	64.1	63.8	56.7	61.4	58.8	57.0	53.0	54.4
15	57.1	61.0	57.8	56.5	51.8	45.9	53.3	51.2	52.8	50.1	44.3
16	57.9	65.5	58.6	55.8	58.6	46.7	53.6	53.0	48.0	57.3	55.0
17	46.1	46.8	46.9	42.5	41.1	40.2	46.8	46.7	47.3	45.4	41.3
18	56.7	53.6	49.8	54.2	57.3	51.9	53.9	50.3	50.8	54.7	58.1
19	45.7	48.8	50.9	50.2	44.0	49.2	47.6	48.9	47.6	47.4	48.9
20	53.6	51.6	54.8	54.6	45.8	50.4	65.1	57.4	54.5	51.7	55.2
21	56.1	57.8	55.0	51.9	52.8	50.7	53.0	51.9	52.5	46.8	50.3
23	60.6	53.3	51.5	62.9	64.7	55.5	62.2	59.0	57.3	66.5	62.2
25	57.4	53.6	55.3	51.1	52.6	47.7	51.5	56.2	52.4	51.1	50.1
26	64.0	59.4	59.3	59.5	59.4	56.3	55.7	59.1	53.7	54.1	54.2
27	54.3	49.2	54.3	52.6	51.0	43.7	54.1	51.3	51.2	52.3	50.1
28	58.9	54.0	51.1	55.8	51.1	52.9	52.1	55.4	53.0	50.3	51.0
29	57.5	57.0	56.3	49.2	48.0	46.4	53.2	53.0	54.9	51.3	49.6
30	48.2	45.0	42.1	44.4	40.1	41.0	46.1	47.5	39.0	49.2	39.7
31	77.9	77.1	78.6	69.7	68.0	64.2	62.9	59.7	63.3	57.8	56.6
32	49.1	55.5	44.7	45.9	45.9	47.2	53.3	50.3	51.9	50.6	45.3
33	58.0	59.8	58.0	56.7	54.9	51.3	55.6	53.4	55.3	52.7	51.5
34	62.2	58.9	60.4	63.9	56.9	55.2	54.1	60.0	57.3	61.5	56.7
35	64.4	61.2	59.8	62.7	61.0	48.1	54.5	54.7	57.3	54.1	52.9
37	61.8	66.5	61.9	66.1	61.3	58.9	61.8	59.4	58.7	62.1	54.8
38	66.9	69.2	61.1	63.0	61.7	55.0	63.6	63.1	64.8	58.5	60.9
40	61.2	59.9	51.9	52.3	50.1	50.4	58.4	59.6	54.2	56.3	50.6
41	60.3	55.9	59.0	54.8	52.8	50.4	56.3	57.2	55.7	53.1	54.5
42	67.2	65.6	70.2	70.9	70.3	64.7	70.0	75.6	72.3	63.3	67.2
43	84.4	93.3	93.1	90.6	88.4	88.3	88.6	78.8	69.0	70.2	82.1
50	53.7	49.6	50.7	54.3	48.7	43.5	52.8	52.0	48.8	46.0	50.4
51	56.9	56.0	50.1	52.3	51.5	44.3	51.4	50.4	56.3	50.1	49.7
52	57.1	57.4	54.6	53.5	58.4	49.1	50.7	51.6	50.4	52.4	52.0

53	76.8	76.6	76.0	74.6	72.6	68.5	69.9	73.1	64.7	68.9	71.7
54	50.5	50.3	44.6	51.5	51.3	42.4	49.4	54.7	47.3	46.0	44.7
55	58.3	55.7	52.8	36.9	47.7	40.4	52.3	54.1	56.8	56.3	59.0
56	70.4	76.7	38.3	40.8	54.8	53.9	59.3	55.6	61.8	60.9	59.0
62	46.3	44.8	45.3	52.1	47.8	45.5	48.7	54.2	51.3	50.6	47.1
63	50.8	47.0	47.4	46.4	46.1	46.5	49.7	49.6	51.6	47.1	41.8
64	54.3	50.3	45.6	48.0	55.8	50.8	49.7	56.5	54.2	48.5	55.1
65	47.5	49.5	49.3	46.3	45.4	46.9	46.1	50.1	54.2	49.9	48.3
66	53.3	50.0	48.6	45.2	50.0	47.3	52.7	52.2	51.8	54.0	53.2
68	54.9	54.6	51.3	47.9	51.4	53.5	50.4	52.0	53.7	54.5	56.1
69	59.6	53.9	50.1	46.8	52.6	46.1	55.6	56.0	50.3	55.3	49.0
70	81.0	84.8	84.4	80.3	82.6	50.2	45.0	42.0	36.9	43.9	56.9
71	72.9	74.3	70.9	67.7	69.8	62.5	66.6	71.1	68.0	66.0	63.4
72	75.4	76.0	78.1	66.7	79.0	67.1	69.1	76.5	74.5	68.5	58.5
73	82.5	73.6	70.3	77.6	79.2	67.7	65.3	72.0	74.2	70.8	60.8
74	81.0	79.4	77.6	82.7	80.1	71.2	80.9	77.4	85.5	76.4	75.3
75	80.8	73.9	78.8	79.7	78.8	63.4	80.5	76.2	74.0	68.9	73.1
76	91.1	98.7	94.5	98.0	50.3	36.2	38.9	39.0	34.0	45.4	46.1
77							57.6	37.9	40.2	34.6	38.1
78							88.8	85.8	43.0	39.5	63.0
79	93.8	97.7	96.8	96.7	95.5	98.7	95.6	82.4	77.2	85.5	81.2
81	39.8	45.2	48.4	48.0	41.9	50.0	51.8	55.0	53.6	51.3	48.3
82	40.5	36.2	61.2	61.9	55.6	44.2	53.2	48.1	48.3	49.3	50.0
83	51.7	51.1	49.7	46.7	56.2	45.7	46.3	51.9	54.3	49.8	48.0
84	48.3	47.3	44.9	47.7	51.8	45.1	46.8	49.4	51.3	51.3	50.4
85	45.6	52.9	50.1	57.6	51.4	45.3	52.6	54.9	51.8	55.8	52.1
86	34.8	46.3	48.9	45.8	47.5	45.9	49.4	56.2	50.8	49.0	45.1
87	35.1	37.3	39.3	39.0	34.6	40.1	47.3	44.1	44.5	47.6	42.9
88	51.1	34.4	36.5	36.3	43.6	38.6	44.3	45.2	46.8	48.3	46.7
90	96.7	96.7	97.7	92.2	97.7	97.4	94.7	95.7	95.8	94.6	94.7
91	89.7	98.0	98.7	94.8	95.2	93.3	97.9	93.9	93.9	91.1	96.1
92	89.4	87.8	85.5	93.8	64.4	95.1	89.1	96.3	89.7	90.4	91.4
93	94.2	94.0	96.4	95.4	96.6	96.2	98.5	97.0	100.0	96.0	92.7
94	98.9	98.7	95.2	97.2	94.9	96.9	93.1	93.1	98.4	92.3	93.6
95	86.8	85.1	90.0	91.2	81.4	86.3					
96	92.3	87.2	86.2	91.4	88.3	84.7	83.9	85.6	86.3	83.3	78.8
97	81.9	86.0	85.7	83.7	83.2	83.7	88.7	87.0	85.3	76.0	81.8
98	80.0	87.0	84.3	94.2	90.8	92.9	68.1	69.0	78.9	77.5	82.7
99	85.1	85.8	86.1	90.2	87.8	90.4	85.6	89.4	93.2	90.3	87.9
-1							97.8	97.8	97.0	99.3	96.8
-2							97.7	96.3	59.2	47.5	35.0
-3							100.0	100.0	100.0	40.3	32.7
-4							100.0	100.0	98.9	83.0	35.1
-5							99.0	100.0	100.0	100.0	100.0
-6							100.0	98.2	99.3	100.0	98.2
-7							100.0	95.9	98.9	98.4	98.2
-8							97.3	93.3	98.0	95.5	91.7

TABLE 4.10. Weighted conditional row and column entropies of entire matrix and L values

Year	Row		Column	
	$H^*(p_{j|i})$	$L(\%)$	$H^*(p_{i|j})$	$L(\%)$
1960	1.538	57.6	1.532	58.2
1961	1.545	56.9	1.534	58.0
1962	1.544	57.0	1.552	56.1
1963	1.552	56.1	1.553	56.0
1964	1.562	55.1	1.554	56.0
1965	1.596	51.3	1.602	50.6
1966	1.615	54.3	1.613	54.5
1967	1.613	54.5	1.603	55.6
1968	1.637	51.9	1.614	54.4
1969	1.652	50.1	1.624	53.3
1970	1.664	48.7	1.640	51.5

$\log 80 = 1.9031$
$\log 89 = 1.9494$

increasing homogeneity during the first half of the decade and again at the close of the period, following the not-unexpected shift in 1966.

Summary of the analysis

Several entropy measures of homogeneity have been used to examine certain structural aspects of origin—destination matrices of annual intraurban migration of the adult population of Amsterdam during the period 1960–1970. The specific matrix characteristics which have been investigated with the entropy-based methodology are: (1) the overall homogeneity of the entire matrix; (2) the homogeneity of the marginal distributions of out-migrants and in-migrants; (3) the degree of organization of out-migration and in-migration patterns for individual origins and destinations; (4) the homogeneity of the overall out-migration and in-migration patterns; and (5) the deviation of the observed cell entries from those expected under the condition $p_{ij} = p_{i\cdot}p_{\cdot j}$.

It has been shown that the conversion of a calculated value of an entropy measure to its corresponding L value allows the comparison of migration matrices of different size. For the case study considered here, this latter characteristic has permitted cross-temporal comparisons of migration matrices. Cross-temporal comparisons of specific structural aspects of the matrices have facilitated the identification of both general and deviant trends in the organization of migration flows.

Perhaps the strongest point in favour of the entropy measures and the L values is that they are concise, easily interpretable measures which reduce a great deal of information contained in large matrices to a few numbers. Unfortunately, a price must be paid for the parsimony of this method of analysis; that much of the potentially interesting variability of the migration flows between pairs of districts is lost. Furthermore, different kinds of matrix structure may yield identical values of certain entropy measures. 'Twere ever thus. You can't have your cake and eat it, too.

This methodology based on the entropy measures of homogeneity is a useful first step in the analysis of spatial patterns of intraurban migration. It allows a relatively quick, objective identification of certain spatial and temporal regularities in flow patterns which is, of course, a necessary step in the analysis of the processes giving rise to those patterns. Further development of the methodology probably lies not so much in finding new ways of arranging the matrix entries in order to create new entropy measures but rather in altering the input to the analysis and in refining the means of interpreting the output. In the first case, for instance, it could be useful to weight the migration probabilities by the size of the origin population in order to assess the relative importance of similarly sized flows from areas of differing population sizes. In the second case, a systematic grouping of origins or destinations according to their scores on the conditional row and column measures could aid in identifying areal groupings of subdistricts having similar out- and in-migration patterns.

PREDICTIVE ENTROPY MODELS

The type of predictive interaction model which is the focus of this paper is Wilson's entropy-maximizing derivation of the gravity model. The importance of Wilson's contribution to spatial interaction modelling is primarily that the entropy-maximizing approach gives the 'gravity' model a statistical derivation which is no longer dependent on analogies to Newtonian physics. That the model and the methodology are conceptually appealing and readily adaptable to a variety of problems can be seen in the tremendous proliferation of the technique during the period 1970–1977. The main objective here is to consider a few aspects of the entropy-maximizing spatial interaction model and associated theoretical and empirical developments. Almost all the applications of entropy statistics are to trip distribution modelling, and for the purpose of simplicity and clarity this review of the technical aspects of the model will follow that body of knowledge. A brief outline of Wilson's derivation of his basic family of models is given in the next section, followed by short discussions of calibration techniques, the measurement of model performance, the interpretation of the model's balancing factors, and the form of the deterrence function. A separate section is devoted to extensions and applications of the basic model to the predictions of intraurban migrations in Amsterdam.

Derivation of the model

The entropy-maximizing approach to modelling is to make the fullest possible use of all available information without making any assumptions about that which remains unknown. Translating this into terms specifically applicable to interaction (e.g. trip distribution or migration distribution) models, the contention is that the best procedure for estimating a T_{ij} distribution in the absence of complete information is to define the possibilities unambiguously, define all the information available in terms of those possibilities, and find the particular distribution (T_{ij}) that is consistent with all this information but is maximally uncommitted in relation to what is unknown (Cordey Hayes and Wilson, 1971).

This amounts to finding the T_{ij} distribution which maximizes entropy subject to certain constraints. Wilson (1970) argues that three constraints are necessary for a good estimate of the distribution: marginal constraints on the total trip production by each origin and the total trip attraction to each destination, and a behavioural constraint on the total 'expenditure' on trips. These constraints are restated as follows:

$$\sum_j T_{ij} = O_i \tag{4.26}$$

$$\sum_i T_{ij} = D_j \tag{4.27}$$

$$\sum_i \sum_j T_{ij} c_{ij} = C \tag{4.28}$$

To estimate the T_{ij}, it is necessary to find the matrix $\{T_{ij}\}$ which has the greatest number of states (designated as $W(\{T_{ij}\})$ associated with it. This is given as

$$W(\{T_{ij}\}) = \frac{T!}{\prod_{ij} T_{ij}!} \tag{4.29}$$

where $T = \sum_i \sum_j T_{ij}$

To maximize W subject to the constraints, the Lagrangian L is maximized such that

$$L = \ln W + \sum_i \lambda_i^{(1)}(O_i - \sum_j T_{ij}) + \sum_j \lambda_j^{(2)}(D_j - \sum_i T_{ij}) + \beta(C - \sum_i \sum_j T_{ij} c_{ij}) \tag{4.30}$$

where $\lambda_i^{(1)}, \lambda_j^{(2)}$, and β are Lagrangian multipliers associated with equations (4.26), (4.27), and (4.28). This maximization involves the expressions:

$$\exp(-\lambda_i^{(1)}) = O_i \left[\sum_j \exp(-\lambda_j^{(2)} - \beta c_{ij}) \right]^{-1} \tag{4.31}$$

$$\exp(-\lambda_j^{(2)}) = D_j \left[\sum_i \exp(-\lambda_i^{(1)} - \beta c_{ij}) \right]^{-1} \tag{4.32}$$

which lead to the equation:

$$T_{ij} = A_i B_j O_i D_j \exp(-\beta c_{ij}) \tag{4.33}$$

where

$$A_i = \left[\sum_j B_j D_j \exp(-\beta c_{ij}) \right]^{-1} = \frac{\exp(-\lambda_i^{(1)})}{O_i} \tag{4.34}$$

$$B_j = \left[\sum_i A_i O_i \exp(-\beta c_{ij}) \right]^{-1} = \frac{\exp(-\lambda_j^{(2)})}{D_j} \tag{4.35}$$

How does this relate to entropy? In statistical mechanics, the entropy of the probability distribution $p_1, p_2, \ldots, p_n$ is defined as

$$h = -k \sum_i \sum_j p_{ij} \ln p_{ij} \tag{4.36}$$

Wilson shows that equation (4.36) is equivalent to

$$\ln W = T \ln T - T - \sum_i \sum_j (T p_{ij} \ln T p_{ij} - T p_{ij}) \tag{4.37}$$

$$= -T \sum_i \sum_j p_{ij} \ln p_{ij}$$

which is structurally equivalent to the entropy expression of equation (4.36), if we define:

$$p_{ij} = \frac{T_{ij}}{T}$$

Thus, maximizing $\ln W$ subject to the three constraints to find the most probable distribution of the T_{ij} is, in effect, equivalent to finding the entropy-maximizing solution.

Wilson goes on to show that the most probable distribution of trips, equation (4.33), is equivalent to the distribution derived from a gravity model modified to satisfy the constraints

$$\sum_j T_{ij} = O_i \tag{4.38}$$

and

$$\sum_i T_{ij} = D_j \tag{4.39}$$

Balancing factors A_i and B_j

$$A_i = \left[\sum_j B_j D_j f(c_{ij}) \right]^{-1} \tag{4.40}$$

$$B_j = \left[\sum_i A_i O_i f(c_{ij}) \right]^{-1} \tag{4.41}$$

are introduced to ensure that the constraints are satisfied, thus yielding

$$T_{ij} = A_i B_j O_i D_j f(c_{ij}) \tag{4.42}$$

where the cost c_{ij} is interpreted as a measure of distance. The modified gravity model of equation (4.42) is the same as the trip distribution model of equation (4.33) if the function $f(c_{ij})$ is replaced by the negative exponential function.

Since the model of equation (4.42) entails constraints on both trip productions and trip attractions, as given in equations (4.38) and (4.39), it is sometimes called the production–attraction-constrained, or doubly-constrained, model.

Cordey Hayes and Wilson (1971) have shown that a whole 'family' of spatial interaction models can be developed by adjusting the hypothesis which led to the entropy-maximizing derivation of the gravity model. If the D_j values are not known, a production-constrained model can be stated as

$$T_{ij} = A_i O_i W_j f(c_{ij}) \tag{4.43}$$

where W_j is some measure of 'attractiveness' and where

$$A_i = \left[\sum_j W_j f(c_{ij}) \right]^{-1} \tag{4.44}$$

A second singly-constrained model is used when the O_i values are not given independently. This attraction-constrained model is given as

$$T_{ij} = B_j D_j W_i f(c_{ij}) \tag{4.45}$$

where

$$B_j = \left[\sum_i W_i f(c_{ij}) \right]^{-1} \tag{4.46}$$

The W_i are an index substituting for the O_i. When neither the O_i nor the D_j values are known, an unconstrained model is appropriate and is stated as

$$T_{ij} = K W_i W_j f(c_{ij}) \tag{4.47}$$

which is not unlike the form of Reilly's (1931) retail gravitation model.

The choice of model from among this family depends, of course, not only on the amount of information available but also on the type of problem for which it is to be used. The production–attraction-constrained model is well suited for the analysis of journey-to-work flows, while the origin-constrained and destination-constrained variations are useful for modelling retail location and residential location and relocation respectively.

Balancing factors

It was mentioned earlier that the A_i and B_j values are balancing factors associated with the marginal constraints on the trip productions and attractions. As the model is calibrated, the balancing factors (also referred to as normalizing or adjustment factors) are assigned values such that the constraints on the origin and destination totals will always be satisfied. The calculation of the A_i and B_i values from equations (4.34) and (4.35) is straightforward, and their mathematical function is clear. Efforts to accord the balancing factors a substantive interpretation have not been easy, probably because of their interdependent relationship. Wilson suggests that the value $1/A_i$ is related to the accessibility to opportunities at the destination and that $1/B_j$ is related to the accessibility to opportunities at the origin. A different emphasis is given in the interpretation by Wagon and Hawkins (1970), who say that A_i measures the difficulty of leaving the origin while B_j measures the difficulty of getting to a destination. Cesario (1974) expresses it succinctly by calling A_i the emissiveness of an origin and B_j the attractiveness of a destination. Whatever their name or definition, the balancing factors have not attracted much attention in the way of empirical research. Certainly, a future potential research topic would be to relate the notions of 'emissiveness' and 'attractiveness' to some substantive studies of origin–destination ecological characteristics.

The form and calibration of the cost function

The specification and calibration of the cost function are critical parts of the entropy-maximizing trip distribution model. The popular interpretation of the role of the cost function can be readily perceived from the nature of the terms which are sometimes substituted for the word 'cost': deterrence, friction, impedance, resistance, and separation. The idea which is conveyed is that the number of trips between two places is an inverse function of the degree of difficulty of making the trip. The 'difficulty' or 'cost', of a trip can be measured in many ways, e.g. as consumer expenditure on the trip, road distance between two points, or actual travel time. Whatever the unit of measurement, the tacit assumption is that the form of the cost function expresses the way in which travellers respond to the perceived cost of making a trip.

The usual entropy-maximizing model is written with a negative exponential cost function, as in equation (4.33). This particular function arises from the widely used expression of the cost constraint as

$$\sum_i \sum_j T_{ij} c_{ij} = C \tag{4.48}$$

As Wilson (1970) notes, this assumes that the traveller's subjective perception of cost is identical to the way in which it is objectively measured. If a different assumption is made about the way in which travellers perceive costs, then $f(c_{ij})$ may take some form other than $\exp(-\beta c_{ij})$. For instance, if $\log c_{ij}$ is substituted for c_{ij} in equation (4.48), then $\exp(-\beta c_{ij})$ becomes $c_{ij}^{-\beta}$.

There is nothing inherently sacred about the negative exponential cost function to the entropy-maximizing trip distribution model, although there is ample evidence to support the hypothesis that the barrier effect of distance on the frequency of certain types of spatial interaction is often best described by a negative exponential function.

The form of the entropy-maximizing model given in equation (4.33) has become so familiar in the past decade that it is worth repeating, at the risk of belabouring the point, that the negative exponential function itself is not basic to the entropy-maximizing trip distribution model. Indeed, it is not even necessary to include a cost function at all if there is no sound theoretical reason for its inclusion (e.g. Chilton and Poet, 1973).

The calibration of the trip distribution model is the process of assigning optimal values to the model parameters, where the optimality of the parameter estimates is measured by a calibration statistic. In broad terms, calibration usually involves an iterative systematic search for those parameter value(s) which will optimize some prespecified criterion, or calibration statistic. Several calibration techniques have been suggested; some of the more widely known ones are outlined very briefly here.

Hyman (1969) has shown, via a Bayesian approach, that the best calibration statistic is the mean trip cost, if the cost function is expressed in negative exponential form. Calibration, then, involves adjusting the parameter of the cost function until the mean trip cost of the predicted trip distribution equals the survey mean trip cost. If a different cost function is specified, the calibration statistic must be chosen accordingly. For instance, if the cost constraint is

$$\sum_i \sum_j T_{ij}(\log c_{ij}) = C \tag{4.49}$$

then the mean of the log of the cost of travel should be used for calibration.

An alternative justification for the mean trip cost as a calibration statistic has been derived from a maximum likelihood methodology by Evans (1971). The method is based on finding that parameter value which has the highest probability of reproducing the observed trip distribution, after satisfying the row and column constraints. Kirby (1974) notes that this method requires a knowledge of the sampling distribution from which the observed trips are drawn. If the sampling distribution is not known, some other method of calibration, such as non-linear least squares, may be more appropriate. The non-linear least squares method seeks that parameter value which minimizes the sum of squares of the differences between the observed and predicted trip distributions. While this method makes no assumptions about the form of the sampling distribution, the estimated parameters will not necessarily satisfy the entropy-maximizing model's cost constraint (Openshaw, 1976).

Several other methods of parameter estimation are feasible but have received less attention. Openshaw (1976) discusses the chi-square and minimax estimators. Ordinary least squares may also be used to estimate the model parameters, if, as Stetzer (1976) suggests, appropriate means of linearizing the model are used. Nakanishi and Cooper (1974) discuss the circumstances under which generalized least squares may be used.

A wide variety of techniques can be used to optimize the calibration statistic, including both numerical methods, such as first-order iteration or the Newton–Raphson technique, and search procedures, of which the methods based on Fibonacci numbers are perhaps most often used for this type of problem. These techniques are well documented elsewhere (especially Batty, 1971; Batty and Mackie, 1972; Openshaw, 1976) and will not be elaborated here.

Model performance

The ultimate test of this type of model is, of course, how well the model predictions agree with what is observed in reality. The most common method of measuring model performance is to use a goodness-of-fit statistic which is some function of the deviation between the observed data and the model predictions. Other means of assessing model performance are possible, including the examination of the residuals for indications of specification errors or the estimation of trip assignment confidence limits resulting from calibration error (Openshaw, 1976). Only true goodness-of-fit measures are discussed in this paper.

The choice of a goodness-of-fit test for the purpose of measuring model performance is not clear-cut. A variety of measures have been suggested, analysed in terms of utility and limitations, and tested (Batty, 1970a, 1970b, 1971; Hathaway, 1975; Openshaw, 1976; Wilson *et al.*, 1969). Among the more popular ones are the coefficient of determination (R^2), the root mean square error (RMSE), the chi-square statistic, and the mean percentage error. Each has its own drawbacks. The chi-square statistic, for instance, should not be used if any of the predicted or observed flows is of a magnitude less than six; R^2 is not especially meaningful unless the slope and intercept of the plot of the predicted flows against the observed flows are also evaluated; and the statistics may be biased if the distributions are not normal. The sensitivity of any of the statistics to parameter variation is not very good, and there is some evidence to support the contention that the choice of test is not especially critical, since none of them is overwhelmingly superior in all situations (Openshaw, 1976).

The prediction of intraurban migration

The object of this section is to demonstrate the adaptation and use of a simple version of Wilson's entropy-maximizing trip distribution model for the prediction of intraurban migration flows. The model is a straightforward doubly-constrained trip distribution model of the form

$$M_{ij} = A_i O_i B_j D_j f(c_{ij}) \tag{4.50}$$

subject to the constraints in equations (4.26), (4.27), and (4.28), where M_{ij} equals the number of people moving from cell i to cell j. The O_i and D_j values were obtained from the survey data described earlier in the paper. The 'cost' variable c_{ij} is measured as the straight-line distance between centroids of districts.

The generalized cost function $f(c_{ij})$ has been replaced by $\exp(-\beta c_{ij})$, which arises from the cost constraint of equation (4.28). Given a reasonable *a priori* justification, some function other than the negative exponential could have been specified. In order to evaluate other forms of the cost function, several different distance decay functions were fitted to the observed data for 1960 and 1970. Those selected included the negative exponential, the Pareto, the log-normal, the normal, and the square root. The goodness of fit of each to the observed trip distribution was measured by the coefficient of determination. No one model was superior (Table 4.11). Given that there is no information to contradict the validity of the cost constraint of equation (4.28) and given that the negative exponential distance decay function (derived from the cost constraint via entropy maximization) described the observed distance decay as well as the other functions, the negative exponential function is used to replace $f(c_{ij})$ in our model (equation 4.50).

TABLE 4.11. R^2 of fit of selected distance decay functions to observed data

Function	1960	1970
Negative exponential	0.309	0.309
Pareto	0.275	0.272
Lognormal	0.337	0.327
Normal	0.222	0.238
Square root	0.342	0.334

The method of calibration chosen for this case study is based on an iterative procedure suggested by Hyman (1969) and requires adjusting the value of the parameter β such that the model-predicted mean trip cost $\bar{c}$ is equal to the observed mean trip cost $\bar{c}_{\text{obs}}$. In actual practice, calibration entails varying β until the quantity $\bar{c} - \bar{c}_{\text{obs}}$ is less than some small predetermined amount. The calibration statistic is given as

$$\bar{c}_{\text{obs}} = \frac{\sum_i \sum_j M_{ij} c_{ij}}{\sum_i \sum_j M_{ij}} \tag{4.51}$$

The first step in the calibration procedure is to establish a reasonable starting point for β. Baxter (1972) has shown that the mean value ($\bar{c}$) of the continuous function $y = \exp(\beta c_{ij})$ where $\beta < 0$ is

$$\bar{c} = \frac{\int_0^{-\infty} c_{ij} \exp(\beta c_{ij})\, dc_{ij}}{\int_0^{\infty} \exp(\beta c_{ij})\, dc_{ij}} = -\frac{1}{\beta} \tag{4.52}$$

Allowing for the fact that in practice $\bar{c}_{\text{obs}}$ is not calculated from a continuous function, the value $-1/\bar{c}_{\text{obs}}$ provides an adequate first approximation of β. The initial (zero) value of the cost-function parameter is set at $\beta_0 = 1/\bar{c}_{\text{obs}}$. Following Hyman's procedure, the first iteration calculates β_1 according to

$$\beta_1 = \frac{\beta_0 - \bar{c}_0}{\bar{c}_{\text{obs}}} \tag{4.53}$$

while succeeding iterations use the formula

$$\beta_{m+1} = \frac{(\bar{c}_{\text{obs}} - \bar{c}_{m-1})\beta_m - (\bar{c}_{\text{obs}} - \bar{c}_m)\beta_{m-1}}{\bar{c}_m - \bar{c}_{m-1}} \tag{4.54}$$

where the subscript m refers to the number of the iteration. For each successive estimate of β, the balancing factors, which ensure satisfaction of the constraints (4.26) and (4.27), are calculated as follows:

$$A_i = \left[\sum_j B_j D_j \exp(-\beta c_{ij}) \right]^{-1} \tag{4.55}$$

$$B_j = \left[\sum_i A_i O_i \exp(-\beta c_{ij}) \right]^{-1} \tag{4.56}$$

The values of A_i and B_j are adjusted so that they remain within approximately the same range, whereupon the mean trip cost is calculated and its divergence from $\bar{c}_{\text{obs}}$ is measured. If the difference $|\bar{c}_m - \bar{c}_{\text{obs}}|$ is not sufficiently small, β and the balancing factors are readjusted.

The model has not been used in this study to predict intradistrict movement, because there was no reasonable way to estimate intradistrict travel cost (i.e. distance) in a manner consistent with the method used for measuring interdistrict travel cost. The model has been calibrated for each year of the period 1960–1970. Input to the model includes the marginal totals of the migration matrix minus the intradistrict movement, a matrix of travel costs c_{ij}, and the observed mean trip cost. For this case study, the spatial system consists of 79 districts during 1960–1965 and 89 districts during 1966–1970 (subdistrict 95 was eliminated from the calculations for 1960–1965). For each year, the model allocates approximately 58000 to 76000 migrants to 79 × 78 (for 1960–1965) or 89 × 88 (for 1966–1970) origin–destination pairs. The cost-function parameter is adjusted until the model mean trip cost differs from the observed mean by no more than 0.01 per cent. Using $1/\bar{c}_{\text{obs}}$ as a first approximation of β, the program usually converges to an acceptable estimate of the observed mean trip cost in less than 30 CPU seconds on the IBM system 360/model 91.

The goodness of fit of the predicted migration pattern to the observed distribution has been measured with the coefficient of determination (R^2) and the residual standard deviation. A linear regression model of the form

$$\hat{M}_{ij} = a + bM_{ij}$$

where $\hat{M}_{ij}$ is the number of migrant trips predicted by the model, was fitted for each year. The parameters of the regression equations and R^2 are given in Table 4.12. R^2 is fairly high for each year, and a high correlation between the observed and predicted flows has been interpreted as indicating a good level of model performance (Batty, 1970c; Wilson *et al.*, 1969). However, an inspection of the parameters a and b of the regression equations clearly reveals that

TABLE 4.12. Parameters of $M_{ij} = a + bM_{ij}$ and R^2

Year	a	b	R^2
1960	3.368	0.726	0.716
1961	3.312	0.724	0.708
1962	2.959	0.723	0.702
1963	3.137	0.667	0.656
1964	3.181	0.663	0.660
1965	2.710	0.734	0.718
1966	2.205	0.750	0.733
1967	2.663	0.703	0.688
1968	2.578	0.717	0.713
1969	2.694	0.709	0.716
1970	2.516	0.729	0.729

the model overestimates small magnitude migration flows and underestimates large flows.

A second goodness-of-fit measure, the residual standard deviation (RSD), has been calculated according to the equation

$$\text{RSD} = \left[\frac{1}{N}\sum_i\sum_j(\hat{M}_{ij} - M_{ij})^2\right]^{1/2}$$

where N is the number of trip pairs. The values of the residual standard deviation for each year are given in Table 4.13. For about 68 per cent. of the cases, the observed number of trips will differ from the predicted number of trips within a range of plus or minus the residual standard deviation. Obviously, the residual standard deviation cannot be used as a measure of model performance without a consideration of the frequency distribution of trip sizes. The distributions for 1960 and 1970 are given in Table 4.14. The majority of cells of the predicted trip distribution matrices were assigned a number of trips smaller in magnitude

TABLE 4.13. Residual standard deviation

Year	RSD
1960	10.948
1961	10.481
1962	10.197
1963	8.951
1964	8.548
1965	8.650
1966	8.288
1967	8.495
1968	7.732
1969	7.730
1970	7.331

TABLE 4.14. Frequency distribution of M_{ij}

Year	Number of migrants						
	0	1–10	11–20	21–30	31–40	41–50	> 50
1960	1 970	2 091	893	493	254	143	318
1961	2 000	2 055	923	497	254	169	264
1962	1 921	2 314	962	408	243	115	199
1963	1 986	2 318	999	437	179	96	147
1964	1 890	2 409	983	451	187	113	129
1965	1 812	2 418	1 012	445	205	106	164
1966	3 253	2 411	1 073	532	248	122	193
1967	3 069	2 605	1 058	496	261	147	196
1968	2 921	2 576	1 156	551	283	145	200
1969	2 736	2 740	1 200	571	280	125	180
1970	2 634	2 806	1 218	577	275	162	160

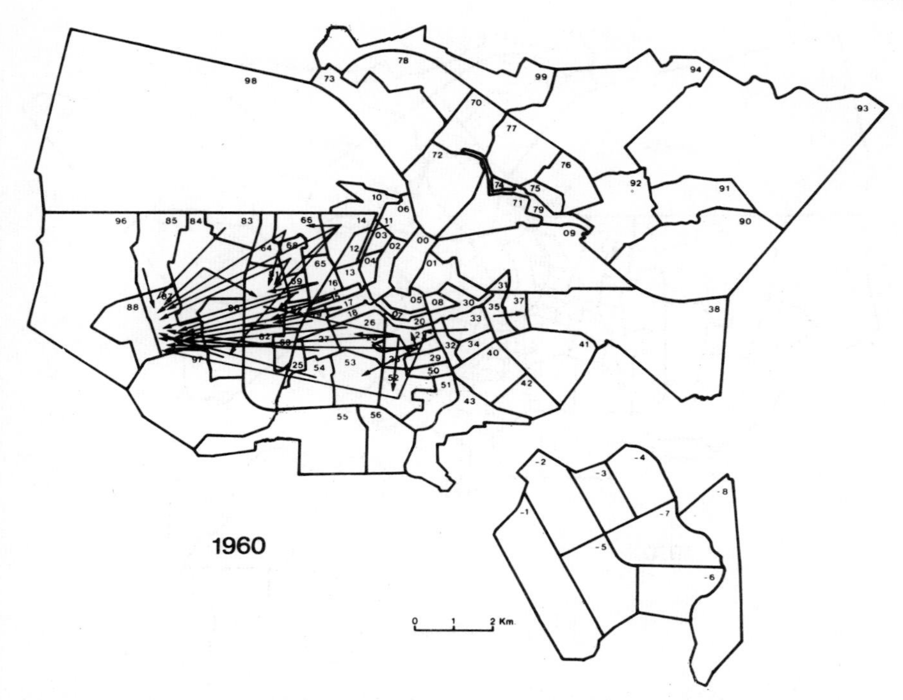

FIGURE 4.10. Vectors of predicted 1960 migration flows in Amsterdam of more than 90 persons

than the size of the residual standard deviation. This cannot be interpreted as indicating a very good fit of the predicted trip distribution to the observed.

In light of the not-especially encouraging results of the goodness-of-fit tests, it is interesting to see how well the model predicts the directional biases of the flows, if not their magnitudes. Figures 4.10 and 4.11 depict, in the form of vectors, the predicted origins and destinations of all flows exceeding 90 persons for the years 1960 and 1970. In fact, the results predicted from the model are more encouraging when we examine their presentation in cartographic form. The 1960 and 1970 observed and predicted patterns are not dissimilar in their overall structure. The basic striking westward directional bias in the 1960 map (Figure 4.3) is reflected quite well in the predicted results. Thus we can argue that to a large extent the model is adequately reproducing the observed *pattern* of flows, and the poor fit is almost totally due to the problem of incorrectly estimating the magnitudes of the flows. The 1970 predicted map, at first glance dissimilar to Figure 4.4, is also representative of the pattern of observed flows. While there are not as many of the 1960 vectors reproduced in the 1970 map, again this is because of the underestimation of the magnitudes of the flows. Several of the major directional vectors—to the Bijlmermeer (–3), to 28, to 66, and between 21 and 28—are represented.

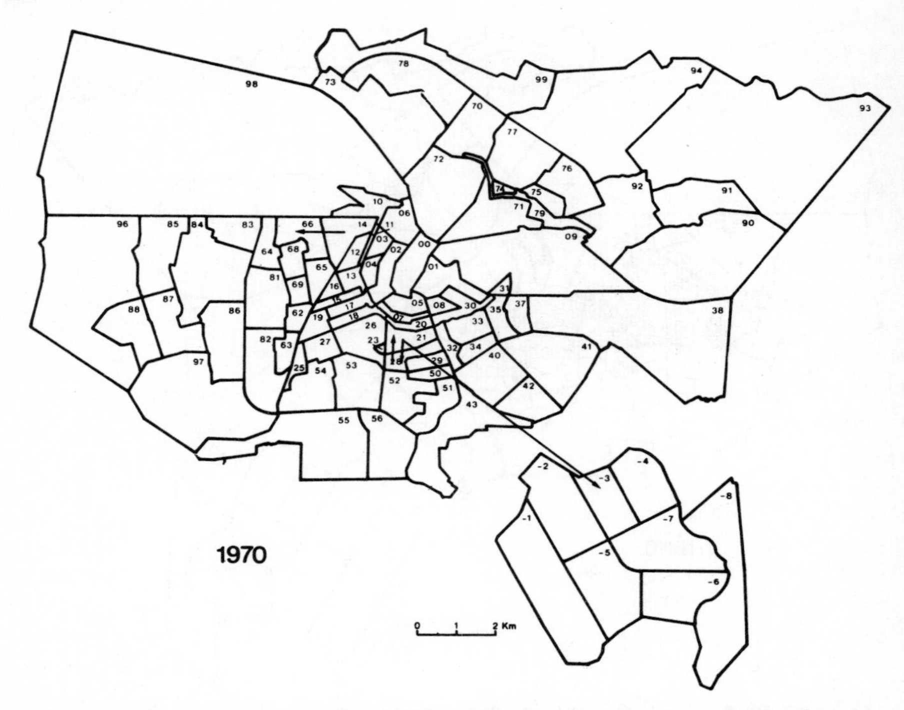

FIGURE 4.11. Vectors of predicted 1970 migration flows in Amsterdam of more than 90 persons

It is obvious that the problem implicit in the model is a better estimation of the magnitudes of the flows and of the, as yet, unpredicted internal flows. Given the small amount of information which is used as input to the model, the predictions which we have obtained seem reasonable. To get a good notion of how reasonable the estimates actually are, we would need to compare them with the estimates derived from other models applied to this data. Beyond increasing the input to the model, perhaps via disaggregation by migrant type, the most obvious areas of improvement of the model are the form of the cost function and the measurement of the cost of migration. Some final evaluative remarks will be included in the conclusion.

CONCLUSION

We have had four major goals in this paper. First, we have argued a philosophical distinction between micro- and macroanalysis of intraurban migration. Second, we have reviewed the extensive literature on the macroanalytic approaches to intraurban migration, emphasizing particularly those studies which have attempted an explicitly spatial approach to the structure of migration within cities. Third, we have demonstrated and evaluated the application of several entropy-based measures of homogeneity to migration matrices. Fourth, we have examined the adaptation of the entropy-maximizing trip distribution model for the prediction of intraurban migration flows.

The results of the empirical sections of the paper are not totally unambivalent. We were able to show quite clearly that the L values are adequate descriptive summaries of the changing population flows over time. These values declined over the ten-year period, indicating that entropy was increasing and the matrix of flows was tending to a homogeneous interchange of population. The values also reflected the increase in the number of spatial units which took place in 1965–1966. While there is considerable variation from subdistrict to subdistrict with respect to the increase in entropy, wide variations from year to year in the homogeneity values are relatively rare. In sum, the joint, expected, conditional row and conditional column entropies all yield similar conclusions. However, two speculations are possible at this point. First, a large-scale generalization is that as the region achieves a balance in population and ceases to grow (or is even losing population slowly) the population flows within the city tend to settle down to an approximately equal interchange between subdistricts. The second speculation is potentially more important. When we consider the L values for the small subdistricts we are able on the basis of these values to categorize the subdistricts into types according to the temporal trend of the L values. Thus districts which have a steady trend are easily identified as those which are likely to have similar numbers of in- and out-migrants each year, and planning for the infrastructure of those subdistricts becomes that much simpler. Regions which exhibit decreasing entropy for in-migration but increasing entropy for out-migration are districts which are sending migrants widely throughout the city but which are receiving migrants from only one or two sources—perhaps from restricted areas of the city. Such districts are anomalous within a system in which the basic structure is of nearly equal interchanges within the city. The most potentially interesting subdistricts are those which have large year-to-year fluctuations in the entropy values. This may reflect fluctuating opportunities—the construction or demolition of housing within the subdistrict or the invasion of neighbourhoods by minority populations. In any case, the ability to identify subdistricts which have anomalous patterns in the L values (i.e. values different from the overall matrix pattern) is a useful device for planning and policy analyses.

The ability to predict population movements is of fundamental importance to urban governments. The provision of public services such as schools, water, police, and fire protection is closely related to the distribution of population. Thus, to have some notions of the changing population distribution is crucial to efficient urban government. The entropy-maximizing model outlined in this paper goes some way towards providing such an analysis of the streams of migration. Although the model outlined in the paper is an adequate representation of the basic structure of the population flows, it still requires improvement in the estimation of the magnitudes of the flows. However, given the difficulties of finding an adequate cost function for movements between small areas of a city, the model is useful. The development of a method for estimating internal flows and an improvement in the magnitudes of prediction will make the model more generally applicable.

Although the entropy-maximizing model is now well developed, there are still insufficient studies to evaluate its long-term potential in predicting migration. There have been more applications in transportation modelling, but even in those cases, as in the examples presented in this paper, the evidence is far from conclusive.

ACKNOWLEDGMENTS

The authors would like to thank Dr. Frans Dieleman of the Free University of Amsterdam for help in collecting the data on which this study is based and the Bureau of Statistics of Amsterdam for making the data available. The support of the campus computing network at U.C.L.A. and of NSF Grant SOC 76–19634 is gratefully acknowledged.

REFERENCES

Adams, J. S. (1969). Directional bias in intra-urban migration. *Economic Geography*, **45**, 302–323.

Albig, W. (1933). The mobility of urban population, a study of four cities of 30,000 to 40,000 population. *Social Forces*, **11**, 351–367.

Barrett, F. A. (1973). *Residential Search Behavior*. Geographical Monographs, York University, Toronto.

Batty, M. (1970a). An activity allocation model for the Nottinghamshire–Derbyshire subregion. *Regional Studies*, **4**, 307–332.

Batty, M. (1970b). Models and projections of the space economy: a subregional study in North West England. *Town Planning Review*, **41**, 121–148.

Batty, M. (1970c). Some problems of calibrating the Lowry model. *Environment and Planning*, **2**, 95–114.

Batty, M. (1971). Exploratory calibration of a retail location model using search by golden section. *Environment and Planning*, **3**, 411–432.

Batty, M., and Mackie, S. (1972). The calibration of gravity, entropy, and related models of spatial interaction. *Environment and Planning*, **4**, 205–233.

Baxter, R. (1972). *Program Entropy: Documentation and Test Output*. Geography Program Exchange, Computer Institute for Social Science Research, Michigan State University, East Lansing.

Berry, B. J. L., and Schwind, P. J. (1969). Information and entropy in migrant flows. *Geographical Analysis*, **1**, 5–14.

Brown, L. A., and Holmes, J. (1971). Intra-urban migrant lifelines: a spatial view. *Demography*, **8**, 103–122.

Brown, L. A., and Longbrake, D. B. (1969). On the interpretation of place utility and related concepts: the intra-urban migration case. In K. R. Cox and R. Golledge (Eds.), *Behavioral Problems in Geography: A Symposium*. Studies in Geography No. 17. Northwestern University, Evanston.

Brown, L. A., and Longbrake, D. B. (1970). Migration flows in intra-urban space: place utility considerations. *Annals, Association of American Geographers*, **60**, 368–384.

Brown, L. A. and Moore, E. (1970). The intra-urban migration process: a perspective, *Geografiska Annaler*, *B*, **52**, 1–13.

Burgess, E. W. (1925). The growth of the city. In R. E. Park, E. W. Burgess and R. D. McKenzie (Eds.), *The City*, University of Chicago Press, Chicago.

Butler, E. W., Chapin, F. S. Jr., Hemmens, G. C., Kaiser, E. J., Stegman, M. A., and Weiss, S. F. (1969). *Moving Behavior and Residential Choice: A National Survey*. National Cooperative Highway Research Program Report No. 81, Highway Research Board, Washington.

Caplow, T. (1949). Incidence and direction of residential mobility in a Minneapolis sample. *Social Forces*, **27**, 413–417.

Cesario, F. J. (1974). The interpretation and calculation of gravity model zone-to-zone adjustment factors. *Environment and Planning*, **6**, 247–257.

Chilton, R., and Poet, R. R. W. (1973). An entropy maximizing approach to the recovery of detailed migration patterns from aggregate census data. *Environment and Planning*, **5**, 135–146.

Clark, W. A. V. (1970). Measurement and explanation in intra-urban residential mobility. *Tijdschrift voor Economische en Sociale Geografie*, **61**, 49–57.

Clark, W. A. V. (1971). A test of directional bias in residential mobility. In H. McConnell and D. Yaseen (Eds.), *Models of Spatial Variation*, Northern Illinois University Press.

Clark, W. A. V., and Cawallader, M. (1973). Locational stress and residential mobility. *Environment and Behavior*, **5**, 29–41.

Clark, W. A. V., and Huff, J. O. (1977). *Some Empirical Tests of Duration of Stay Effects in Intraurban Migration.* Environment and Planning, A9.

Cordey Hayes, M., and Wilson, A. G. (1971). Spatial interaction. *Socio-Economic Planning Sciences*, **5**, 73–95.

Evans, A. W. (1971). The calibration of trip distribution models with exponential or similar cost functions. *Transportation Research*, **5**, 15–38.

Ginsberg, R. B. (1971). Semi-Markov processes and mobility. *Journal of Mathematical Sociology*, **1**, 233–262.

Ginsberg, R. B. (1972a). Critique of probabilistic models: application of the semi-Markov model to migration. *Journal of Mathematical Sociology*, **2**, 63–82.

Ginsberg, R. B. (1972b). Incorporating causal structure and exogenous information with probabilistic models: with special reference to choice, gravity, migration, and Markov chains. *Journal of Mathematical Sociology*, **2**, 83–103.

Ginsberg, R. B. (1973). Stochastic models of residential and geographic mobility for heterogeneous populations. *Environment and Planning*, **5**, 113–124.

Goldstein, S. (1958). *Patterns of Mobility, 1910–1950 (The Norristown Study)*, University of Pennsylvania Press, Philadelphia.

Goldstein, S., and Mayer, K. (1961). *Residential Mobility, Migration and Commuting in Rhode Island.* Publication No. 7, Planning Division, Rhode Island Development Council, Providence.

Green, H. W. (1934). Movements within the Cleveland Metropolitan District, Reports Nos. 3, 5, 7, 9, 11. *Cleveland Real Property Inventory*.

Gurevich, B. L. (1969a). Geographical differentiation and its measure in a discrete scheme. *Soviet Geography: Review and Translation*, **10**, 387–413.

Gurevich, B. L. (1969b). An operator of smoothing and measures of homogeneity of linearly ordered geographical structures. *Soviet Geography: Review and Translation*, **10**, 413–420.

Hathaway, P. J. (1975). Trip distribution and disaggregation. *Environment and Planning*, **7**, 71–97.

Henry, N. W., McGinnis, R., and Tegtmeyer, H. W. (1971). A finite model of mobility. *Journal of Mathematical Sociology*, **1**, 107–118.

Hoyt, Homer (1939). *The Structure and Growth of Residential Neighborhoods in American Cities*, U. S. Government Printing Office, Washington, D. C.

Hyman, G. (1969). The calibration of trip distribution models. *Environment and Planning*, **1**, 105–112.

Jaynes, E. T. (1957). Information theory and statistical mechanics. *Physical Review*, **106**, 620–680.

Johnston, R. J. (1969a). Population movements and metropolitan expansion: London 1960–1961. *Transactions, Institute of British Geographers*, **46**, 69–91.

Johnston, R. J. (1969b). Some tests of a model of intra-urban population mobility: Melbourne, Australia. *Urban Studies*, **6**, 34–57.

Kirby, H. (1974). Theoretical requirements for calibrating gravity models. *Transportation Research*, **8**, 97–104.

Kulldorf, G. (1955). *Migration Probabilities*. Lund Studies in Geography, No. 14, C. W. K. Gleerup, Lund.

Land, K. C. (1969). Duration of residence and prospective migration: further evidence. *Demography*, **6**, 133–140.

Lansing, J. B. (1966). *Residential Location and Urban Mobility: The Second Wave of Interviews*, University of Michigan Survey Research Center, Ann Arbor.

Lansing, J. B., *et al.* (1964). *Residential Location and Urban Mobility: A Multivariate Analysis*, Survey Research Center, Institute for Social Research, The University of Michigan.

Medvedkov, Y. V. (1970). Entropy: an assessment of potentialities in geography. *Economic Geography*, **46**, 306–316.

McFarland, D. D. (1970). Intragenerational social mobility as a Markov process: including a time stationary Markovian model that explains observed declines in mobility rates over time. *American Sociological Review*, **35**, 463–476.

McGinnis, R. (1968). A stochastic model of social mobility. *American Sociological Review*, **23**, 712–722.

MacKinnon, R., and Skarke, M. (1975). *Exploratory Analysis of the 1966–1971 Austrian Migration Table*, Research Report No. 31, International Institute for Applied Systems Analysis, Haxenburg, Austria.

Moore, E. G. (1966). Models of migration and the intra-urban case. *The Australian and New Zealand Journal of Sociology*, **2**, 16–37.

Moore, E. G. (1969). The structure of intra-urban movement rates: an ecological model. *Urban Studies*, **6**, 1, 17–33.

Moore, E. G. (1971). Comments on the use of ecological models in the study of residential mobility in the city. *Economic Geography*, **47**, 73–85.

Moore, E. G. (1972). *Residential Mobility in the City*. Commission on College Geography Resource Paper No. 13, Association of American Geographers, Washington, D. C.

Moore, E. G. (1973). *Models of Residential Location and Relocation in the City*, Northwestern University, Evanston, Illinois.

Morrill, R. L. (1963). The distribution of migration distances. *Papers, Regional Science Association*, **11**, 75–84.

Morrill, R. L. (1965). *Migration and the Spread and Growth of Urban Settlement*. Department of Geography, Royal University of Lund, C. W. K. Gleerup, Lund, Sweden.

Morrill, R. L., and Pitts, R. R. (1967). Marriage, migration, and the mean information field: a study in uniqueness and generality. *Annals, Association of American Geographers*, **57**, 401–422.

Morrison, P. A. (1967). Duration of residence and prospective migration: the evaluation of a stochastic model. *Demography*, **4**, 533–561.

Myers, G. C., McGinnis, R., and Masnick, G. (1967). The duration of residence approach to a dynamic stochastic model of internal migration: a test of the axiom of cumulative inertia. *Eugenics Quarterly*, **14**, 121–126.

Nakanishi, M., and Cooper, L. G. (1974). Parameter estimation for a multiplicative competitive interaction model—least squares approach. *Journal of Marketing Research*, **11**, 303–311.

Openshaw, S. (1976). An empirical study of some spatial interaction models. *Environment*

and Planning, A, **8**, 23–41.
Pielou, E. C. (1969). *An Introduction to Mathematical Ecology*, John Wiley, New York.
Price, D. O. (1948). Distance and direction as vectors of internal migration, 1935–40. *Social Forces*, **27**, 48–53.
Quigley, J. M. (1976). Housing demand in the short run: an analysis of polytomous choice. *Explorations in Economic Research*, **3**, No. 1, 76–102.
Reilly, W. J. (1931). *The Law of Retail Gravitation*, G. P. Putnam, New York.
Rogers, A. (1968). *Matrix Analysis of Interregional Population Growth and Distribution.* University of California Press, Berkeley.
Rossi, P. H. (1955). *Why Families Move: A Study in the Social Psychology of Urban Residential Mobility*, The Free Press, Glencoe, Illinois.
Schnore, L. F. (1957). Metropolitan growth and decentralization. *American Journal of Sociology*, **63**, 171–180.
Schnore, L. F. (1963). The socio-economic status of cities and suburbs. *American Sociological Review*, **28**, 76–85.
Shannon, C. E. (1948). Mathematical theory of communication. *Bell System Technical Journal*, **27**, 379–423 and 623–656.
Shaw, R. P. (1975). *Migration Theory and Fact.* Regional Science Research Institute Bibliography Series No. 5, Philadelphia, Pennsylvania.
Simmons, J. W. (1968). Changing residence in the city: a review of intra-urban mobility. *Geographical Review*, **58**, 622–651.
Simmons, J. W. (1974). *Patterns of Residential Movement in Metropolitan Toronto*, University of Toronto Department of Geography Research Publications.
Sonis, M. G. (1968). An application of entropic measures of uniformity to the analysis of population redistribution (in Russian) (title transliteration: 'Znachenie Entropiinykh Mer Odnorodnasti Dlya Analiza Pereraspredelenii Naseleniya'). *Mathematics v Economicheskoi Geografii, Voprosy Geografii*, No. 77, Moscow.
Speare, A. (1970). Home ownership, life cycle state, and residential mobility. *Demography*, **7**, 449–458.
Speare, A., Goldstein, S., and Frey, W. H. (1974). *Residential Mobility, Migration and Metropolitan Change*, Ballinger, Cambridge, Massachusetts.
Spilerman, S. (1972). The analysis of mobility processes by the introduction of independent variables into a Markov chain. *American Sociological Review*, **37**, 277–294.
Spilerman, S. (1973). Extensions of the mover–stayer model. *American Journal of Sociology*, **78**, 599–626.
Stetzer, F. (1976). Parameter estimation for the constrained gravity model: a comparison of six methods. *Environment and Planning, A*, **8**, 673–683.
Stewart, J. Q. (1947). Empirical mathematical rules concerning the distribution and equilibrium of population. *Geographical Review*, **37**, 461–485.
Stouffer, S. A. (1940). Intervening opportunities: a theory relating mobility and distance. *American Sociological Review*, **5**, 845–867.
Tarver, J. D., and Skees, P. M. (1967). Vector representation of interstate migration streams. *Rural Sociology*, **32**, 178–193.
Taeuber, K. E., and Taeuber, A. F. (1964).White migration and socio-economic differences between cities and suburbs. *American Sociological Review*, **29**, 718–729.
Tobler, W. (1975). *Spatial Interaction Patterns.* Research Report No. 19, International Institute for Applied Systems Analysis, Laxenburg Austria.
Wagon, D., and Hawkins, A. (1970). The calibration of the distribution model for the SELNEC study. *Transportation Research*, **4**, 103–112.
Whitelaw, J. S., and Robinson, S. (1972). A test for directional bias in intraurban migration. *New Zealand Geographer*, **28**, 181–193.
Wilson, A. G. (1970). *Entropy in Urban and Regional Modelling*, Pion, London.
Wilson, A. G., Hawkins, A. F., Hill, G. J., and Wagon, D. J. (1969). Calibration and testing

of the SELNEC transport model. *Regional Studies*, **3**, 337–350.

Wolpert, J. (1965). Behavioral aspects of the decision to migrate, *Papers and Proceedings, Regional Science Association*, **15**, 159–169.

Wolpert, J. (1967). Distance and directional bias in inter-metropolitan migration streams, *Annals, Association of American Geographers*, **57**, 605–616.

Zipf, G. K. (1949). *Human Behavior and the Principle of Least Effort: An Introduction to Human Psychology*, Addison-Wesley, Cambridge, Massachusetts.

Chapter 5

Values and Perceptions in Descriptive Approaches to Urban Social Geography

Paul L. Knox and Andrew MacLaran

The starting point for this study rests on the almost tautological observation that social scientists, administrators, decision-makers and planners have, like the rest of the middle classes, consistently failed to appreciate the narrowness of their own judgements. In this context, the ideal type (in the Weberian sense) is represented by Davies' (1972) 'evangelistic bureaucrat', but there are many species of those 'who know best' and are eager to say so. Between them they have for many years (for the most part unwittingly) practised a kind of cultural imperialism, imputing their own ideals and reasoning to others while subscribing to the value-free assumptions of positivism. Recently, however, the dialectic of philosophical thought within the social sciences has produced several critiques of such transgressions, some of which have gone on to present lucid expositions of alternative methodological frameworks within which to accommodate both our own values and perceptions and those of the people whose attributes or behaviour are under consideration (Buttimer, 1974; Donnison, 1972; Gans, 1968; Harvey, 1973; King, 1976; Rein, 1973; Vickers, 1973).

In this paper we are concerned more with other people's attitudes, adopting a neo-positivistic perspective which is broadly similar to the 'value-critical' approach favoured by Rein (1973) and King (1976). Our particular concern is with the apparently simple problem of describing intraurban variations in social conditions. The most appropriate device for such a task would appear to be some form of social indicator—or series of indicators—which could provide 'objective' measures of housing conditions, educational facilities and opportunities, environmental quality, social pathologies, and so on, for different parts of the city (Smith, 1973). Fostered by a growing concern with social 'problems', the so-called 'social indicators movement' has attracted a substantial research effort since its inception in 1966, including the development of a wide range of territorial indicators at both the regional and metropolitan levels (see, for example, Coates, Johnston, and Knox, 1977; Smith, 1977). Several persistent stumbling-blocks have hampered the full development of this approach, however. Broadly speaking, they centre on the twin problems of weighting and analysing objective data so that the indicators are as sensitive as possible to *social* well-being rather than to the professional preoccupations, fashions, and predispositions of academics or administrators (Biderman, 1966; Hall, 1972; Knox, 1975). It is here, of course, that people's values and perceptions come in. Much of the literature on social indicators in fact begins or ends with pleas for more intensive and purposeful gathering of 'subjective' data and for more research into people's aspirations, priorities, and perceptions. The contention is that this sort of information not only helps increase the sensitivity of social indicators but also helps to avoid or reduce the ambiguities associated with some commonly used objective data. Smith (1975), for instance, has demonstrated the fragility of crime rates as territorial social indicators, showing that many crime statistics are open to quite different interpretations and emphasizing that 'crime' is, to a large extent, in the eye of the beholder. Moreover, there is also—as we shall see—a strong case to be made for accepting subjective feelings, perceptions and personal interpretations of local conditions and personal circumstances as quite independent and distinctive elements of individual and community well-being. In the research reported here, we explore the problems, possibilities and effects of (1) modifying 'objective' indicators of local conditions according to prevailing local values; and (2) complementing these indicators with measures of perceived local conditions.

SOCIAL VALUES IN THEORY AND REALITY

It is not difficult to justify our implicit assumption that preferences for major domains of life vary in intensity between different groups, classes, and communities. As Rokeach and Parker (1970) point out, our current values are broadly determined by personality factors, on the one hand, and by antecedent cultural and social experience, on the other, so that we may expect variations in values to occur by subcultural membership, age, sex, religion, race, ethnic identification, life-style, socioeconomic status, intelligence, authoritarianism, and so on. It follows that values will also vary in social and physical space according to the clustering and segregation of people along these dimensions. In the United States, interurban variations in priorities have been catalogued by Fowler (1974) and by Bryant (1975), who found the residents of older, 'core' cities to be most concerned with transport, housing, and urban planning, whereas the residents of 'suburban' settlements were more concerned with the provision of urban services. Priorities also vary by city size. Fischer (1975), for example, shows that there is less attachment to 'traditional' values in larger urban areas; and Blake, Weigl, and Perloff (1975) show that while the importance attached to personal and kinship relationships tends to be consistently high, the importance attached to health, employment, education, and recreation increases with community size. Several structural variations in the strength and ordering of preferences have also been established. Lovrich (1974), for example, has described the very different priorities of Anglo, Black, and Mexican American voters in Denver. In Britain, Douglas's (1964) findings on social class differences in attitude to education have become part of the conventional wisdom of a whole generation of educationalists; and Knox (1976a) has analysed variations in priority preferences for a number of major life domains, showing that attitudes to health, housing conditions, neighbourhood, job satisfaction, education, money, social status, family life, leisure, and social stability vary significantly according to a wide range of structural variables which includes occupation, educational achievement, income, tenure, age, marital status, and household size.

Reasons for intergroup differences in values

The explanations advanced for these differences are rarely more than tentative, although existing social, psychological, and geographic theory points to several reasons for interpersonal and intergroup variation in values. As Engels observed, the poor are unlikely to value environmental quality highly because they have more urgent needs to satisfy. In terms of economic analysis, environmental quality is thus highly income-elastic. On similar grounds it may be argued that other higher order life-domains will also be highly income-elastic; i.e. that successive increases in people's incomes will bring about marked increases in the intensity with which the domains are valued. In terms of psychological theory, the hierarchy of human needs proposed by Maslow (1970) provides a useful conceptual framework here. Briefly, Maslow's argument is that as man's basic needs for nutrition, shelter, and safety are satisfied, motivation turns towards the higher goals of affection and 'belongingness', followed at successively higher levels by the desire for prestige, status, and dominance, and for personal achievement or 'self-actualization'. Accepting this model of behaviour, it follows that those with low levels of material provision will value materialistic domains more than the aesthetic, spiritual, or cultural domains of life. We could thus expect to find, for example, that low-income groups attach a particularly low level of importance to social status. This translates conveniently into marginalist economic theory, with the priorities of different groups reflecting marginal utilities that are directly related to the group's position on the hierarchy of motivation. Zelinsky (1975, p. 109) has articulated this reasoning in a spatial context, suggesting that, as economic and social constraints on people are relaxed, America will witness 'the self-realisation of the highly mobile, atomistic individual searching out what he or she believes to be an optimal location in physical and social space'. Here, of course, the assumption is that changes in priorities will be of sufficient magnitude to precipitate change in behavioural patterns. In support of his hypothesis, Zelinsky is able to identify several emergent 'voluntary regions', including educational subregions at the intraurban scale. It is worth noting that there is also a corpus of evidence which supports the hierarchical–marginalist hypothesis in general terms. Rokeach and Parker (1970), for instance, found that the domain which best distinguished rich and poor in the United States was that of a 'comfortable' (i.e. prosperous) life, with the rich attaching much less importance to it than the poor. Similarly, Lovrich (1974) found that while the more prosperous Anglo population of Denver was most concerned with the environment, Black and Mexican American minorities were more concerned with helath, housing, and welfare programmes.

Quite different hypotheses can be generated from other perspectives on society. If it is accepted, for example, that major cultural or ideological differences exist between racial, religious, or socioeconomic groups, then variations in values ought to exist as a result of fundamentally different perspectives on life-domains. Perhaps the most familiar idea in this context is the concept of a 'culture of poverty' dominated by present-oriented, hedonistic values. Advocates of this concept would thus hypothesize, for example, that those in the lowest income groups place a particularly high value on leisure and recreation and particularly low values on job satisfaction and education (Lewis, 1959,1966; Banfield, 1970, 1974). There seems to be little doubt that antecedent conditions of inequality generate differences in aspirations and expectations but, notwithstanding the broad appeal of the concept, the available evidence (albeit fragmentary) does not entirely support the proposition that the *values* of the poor are particularly present-oriented or hedonistic. Thus, although Knox (1976a) found that the importance attached to education and job satisfaction increased markedly with increases in income, an equally striking linear relationship was found to exist between income and the importance attached to leisure and recreation. In the United States, Davidson and Gaitz's (1974) investigation of work behaviour and attitudes casts serious doubts on the notion of a culture of poverty, supporting Rokeach and Parker's conclusions, which were based on a survey of attitudes towards a wide range of life-domains. They did find differences between the values of the rich and the poor, but not in terms of the propensity to value immediate gratification. Moreover, the differences they found were not expressed in any dichotomous way, but in terms of a continuum of status: 'Strictly speaking, it is not correct to speak of a "culture of poverty" and a "culture of affluence". It would be more accurate to speak of variations of value systems associated with variations of status' (Rokeach and Parker, 1970, p. 209).

Other hypotheses concerning variations in preferences are not difficult to formulate. Viewed in terms of psychological responses to objective circumstances, it could be hypothesized that some people value (or say they value) what they know (or think) they are best at or have most of, whereas others may value what they do not have or cannot get. Alternatively, values may be seen as the product of cognitive processes dominated by the type, quantity, and bias of information received—whether from newspapers, colleagues at work, or advertisements. Viewed from a demographic angle, it seems reasonable to expect that values will be related to a stage in the family cycle. Family life, for instance, is conceivably of different importance to young, single people than it is to couples with young children or to the very old; and housing conditions may be expected to be more highly valued by married couples than by single persons. Indeed, such variations in priority preferences are central to Abu-Lughod and Foley's classic model of intraurban mobility (Foote *et al.*, 1960). If the model has any authenticity, it seems logical to expect a consequent spatial differentiation in preferences reflecting, in effect, the familism dimension of urban areas. However, spatial variations in preferences may not be entirely attributable to the spatial expression of structural factors. Coates, Johnston, and Knox (1977) point to the importance of neighbourhood effects in shaping and modifying attitudes. In this process, people tend to conform to what they perceive as community norms in order to gain the respect of their peers. The 'suburban poverty' syndrome identified by Hoivik (1973) is largely a product of neighbourhood effects whereby the consumption patterns and commodity fetishism of the lower middle classes is 'imposed' on incoming and aspirant families who in fact have incomes insufficient to sustain their hedonistic materialism. There is also evidence of the operation of neighbourhood effects in relation to attitudes towards education (Robson, 1969; Wilson, 1959), delinquency (Baldwin and Bottoms, 1976), and political parties (Johnston, 1974), and it seems fair to expect the importance attached to a wide range of life-domains to be subject to similar processes.

Social values and social welfare

We are thus presented with a complex of value-shaping systems which does not appear to be mutually exclusive. Moreover, it is probably the overlapping and interaction of these systems which account for many of the apparent contradictions of personal values observed in empirical studies of values. In addition to these complexities and contradictions, there often exists an ambiguity or ambivalence of values which results from man's tendency to polarize feelings around primitive concepts (Tuan, 1973). How then can values be adequately taken into account in describing personal, social, or territorial well-being? The difficulties of reconciling conflicting social values have occupied welfare economists, decision theorists, and statisticians for a number of years. Broadly speaking, their objective has been to specify algebraically an overall 'welfare function' capable of describing an optimal combination of goods and services. Assuming the welfare of an individual to be a function of the quantity and importance of goods, services, and externalities 'consumed', the welfare function can be written

$$W_i = f(a_i A, b_i B, c_i C, \ldots, n_i N)$$

where W_i is the welfare of individual i, and $a_i, b_i, c_i, \ldots, n_i$ are importance weights for quantities of various goods, services, and externalities $A, B, C, \ldots, N$. For social or territorial groups, the summation of W could then give a cardinal measure of social welfare (= 'utility', in the jargon of welfare economics). The conventional wisdom of welfare economists, however, holds that utility cannot be measured in absolute terms, so that the bulk of recent literature has been concerned with devising a social welfare function couched in terms of ordinal utility. A major stumbling block has been the 'paradox of majority rule' expounded by Arrow (1951), whereby 'rational' interpretation of individually-ordered priorities produces a majority solution which is highly ambiguous. This is best illustrated by Arrow's (1951, p. 3) original argument, using the example of three people ranking the importance of three alternatives and assuming that the rational way of passing from individual to collective values is to accept that one alternative is preferred to another if a majority of the community rank it highest of the two:

> Let A, B and C be the three alternatives and 1, 2 and 3 the three individuals. Suppose individual 1 prefers A to B and B to C (and therefore A to C), individual 2 prefers B to C and C to A (and therefore B to A), and individual 3 prefers C to A and A to B (and therefore C to B). Then a majority prefer A to B, and a majority prefer B to C. We may therefore say that the community prefers A to B and B to C. If the community is to be regarded as behaving rationally, we are forced to say that A is preferred to C. But in fact a majority of the community prefer C to A.

Attempts to avoid this impasse have generated a considerable volume of literature, most of which accords with Rothenberg's (1961, p. 309) observation that, in terms of ordinalist theory, 'no suggested method of aggregation [of values], short of unanimity, renders a *demonstrably* "correct" solution'. As we have seen, the likelihood of finding complete unanimity of values, even among a small group of people, is remote. The intractability of this situation has led to the emergence of a more pragmatic approach to the construction of a social welfare function. Rothenberg (1961) concludes that it is quite reasonable to think, in practical terms, of a social welfare function derived from an empirical consensus of values prevailing in the community, a possibility which Minas and Ackoff (1964) have explored and which Harvey (1973, p. 80) has endorsed. Similarly, Nath (1969) has argued for the development of 'realistic' and 'decision-making' social welfare functions. To follow this approach is to forfeit the possibility of describing and analysing social well-being with the elegant clarity of algebra, but, as Smith (1973, p. 47) observes, 'the imperative of empirical analysis in welfare geography means that we must be prepared to move in where the angels fear to tread'. This includes embracing the theoretically distasteful cardinalist assumption by adopting relatively simple methodologies based on the aggregation of individuals' weighted experience. This is the approach which is followed in much of this paper.

Identifying social values

How, then, do we derive quantitative measures of the importance attached to different aspects of life? Adherents to neo-classical economic theory, assuming marked demand to be a reflection of collective preferences, would propose that the simplest way of obtaining measures of people's values is to observe their behaviour in the 'market-place' of the real-world environment. Evidence of people's valuation of different aspects of housing and neighbourhood, for example, could be inferred from an analysis of house-purchase activities; their valuation of leisure time might be derived by analysis of overtime working, modal choices in transport, and so on. Zelinsky's (1974) use of the sales of 'personality-sensitive' goods and services such as specialized book clubs, records, gadgetry, pets, and magazines is a recent example of this type of approach, and it certainly seems to be justified by Raban's (1974) acute observations on urban life-styles, values, and consumer patterns in *Soft City*. But although some indication of people's priorities can be deduced from behaviour in the market-place, the approach is inadequate—for our purposes—and can be misleading. Market-place behaviour can only reflect effective demand and, moreover, an effective demand that is subject to the influence of powerful advertising campaigns, the availability of goods and services, and the influence of habit, loyalty, novelty, and other quirks of consumer behaviour. In addition, we shall be concerned with public goods (both pure and impure) for which it would be extremely difficult to gauge even effective demand through market behaviour alone.

These shortcomings have for some years provided a case for the paternalism which has often resulted in the cultural imperialism of 'experts'. It is argued that, since market demand is an inadequate guide, the experience and expertise of politicians and professional policy-makers should be relied upon to gauge collective preferences—a sort of 'experts rule OK' approach (see, for example, Tinbergen, 1956). Adopting the classical Burkean philosophy that they are elected as those most able to make the wisest choices possible on behalf of their constituents and their real interests, politicians have always assumed this ability. In practice, however, many of their decisions are based on alternatives which already have others' interpretations of social values built into them. Planners, in particular, require evidence of priorities in order to discriminate between different policy proposals. Sophisticated plan-evaluation techniques such as cost-benefit analysis, planning balance sheets, and goals achievement matrices require such information in order to weight the constituent components (e.g. roads, shops, environment, landscape) of structure plan strategies and subregional strategies (Lichfield, Kettle, and Whitbread, 1975; Self, 1976), and as a result it has become common practice for planners to weight or order societal preferences themselves (well-documented examples can be found in the Coventry–Solihull–Warwickshire study team's *Subregional Study*, 1971, and in the Strategic Plan for the North West, 1974). Accepting the experience and expertise of politicians and policy-makers in these roles, it would be possible to derive a series of weights for any set of life-domains by way of structured interviews with either or both, perhaps using the Delphi technique, which is based on the iterative questioning of a selected panel of experts (Dalkey *et al.*, 1972). But, as Hall (1972) points out, there is no real evidence to show that the preferences and priorities of either politicians or professionals resemble those of people in general, apart from the rather attenuated expression of the ballot box in the case of politicians. Politicians are able to see only a small cross-section of their electorate, most of whom are concerned with particular grievances (Heclo, 1969), and experience has shown that few of the priorities discussed at the hustings bear much resemblance to what happens once the elections are over. Local councillors in urban areas often have no particular personal association with the ward they 'represent', preferring to see their public role mainly in terms of responsibility for the city as a whole or in terms of their specialisms as committee members (Batley, 1972; Newton, 1976). Davies (1976, p. 352) suggests that, after election, 'a councillor's perceptions become increasingly socialised into ways of looking at things dominated by other councillors, and his views become more similar to others in his stratum of the political elite'. It is therefore not surprising to find that what hard evidence there is suggests a marked discrepancy between the priorities of local electorates and those of their representatives (see, for example, Bryant, 1975).

Professional policy-makers, whose values are derived from ideologies which have principally centred around the trinity of beauty, safety, and efficiency, are apparently grossly insensitive to the values of the public (Davies, 1972; Gans, 1969; Goodman, 1972). This insensitivity should not be surprising since, apart from the influence of any underlying professional ideology, policy-makers' conceptions of social values must stem largely from personal intuition, since many of the official channels of the planning process are geared exclusively to the views of issue-oriented pressure groups and vociferous and articulate individuals through demonstrations, protests, and public inquiries. Attempts to broaden the flow of information to officials about the public's values by way of public consultation and participation exercises have so far been disappointing. White-collar classes are much better able to operate within the legal, professional, and administrative framework that exists for participation and consultation than are blue-collar workers (Stringer and Taylor, 1974). Moreover some officials apparently regard the objective of public consultation as being 'to tell the people what you are going to do ... so as to carry them along with you' (Batley, 1972, p. 107). Even where vigorous and sincere attempts are made to involve the public, many authorities find that the 'silent majority' remains silent even when assailed by expensive displays, broadsheets, and publicity campaigns. However well-intentioned they may be, politicians and policy-makers are thus liable to impose preferences rather blindly from above, perhaps inflicting heavy costs on large but relatively silent sections of society. By way of elimination, then, we are left with the views of the people themselves as a means of identifying social values, and it therefore seems that a more direct, survey-based method of measuring social values is necessary.

It is worth noting, however, that the utility of survey-based information about priorities has been questioned by some administrators and planners. Eagland (1973) writes that asking the public directly about priority preferences would be like 'a blindfolded man picking his football pool selection with a pin', the implication being that people are not well-enough informed to take decisions about their own lives for themselves. Others, such as Powell (1973), feel that surveys of social values would be a waste of resources, arguing that the preferences of different people will cancel each other out or, at best, produce only a broad and indecisive ranking. There is a complacent vanity in these sentiments which fits in well with Davies' (1972) image of the evangelistic bureaucrat. The idea that the public must be educated before it can be consulted about its own welfare is understandably attractive to the meritocracy of local government (*c.f.* white Rhodesia), but in what is purportedly a democratic environment it should be clear that even a broad ranking of priorities based on what people actually feel (or say they feel) is more acceptable than an unqualified ordering made by someone 'who knows best' (or thinks he does). This argument clearly has important implications for policy making and decision taking—in the virtually non-participatory societies of Britain and the Western world, at any rate. Even though we may not be able (in the foreseeable future) to operate within a socialist framework, it suggests that policy making and decision taking should at least be more overtly influenced (i.e. weighted) by the needs felt by people. Such weighting does not require that the experience and judgement of administrators, planners, or politicians should be completely removed or replaced, for, once these needs have been articulated and built into descriptive social indicators, plan evaluation techniques, and so on, there is still a case for presiding over the 'public interest' which lies behind the conflicts and ambiguities of priorities expressed without constraint. In any event, we are concerned here only with the problem of how best to take account of social values in describing people's well-being, and the question remains as to how these values should actually be measured. Several methods exist for eliciting people's priorities by way of social surveys, although most are unsuitable for present purposes. Methods which are based on preferred levels of spending, for example (see Lovrich, 1974), are unable to cope with life-domains which are not entirely 'market-place' commodities; and methods which are based on hypothetical games (e.g. Hoinville, 1971) do not provide measures of the *intensity* of values. Others (e.g. Allport, Vernon, and Lindzey, 1970) Kluckhohn and Strodtbeck, 1961; Morris, 1956; are elaborate and time-consuming, and therefore inappropriate for use with large samples. The basic tool selected for use in this study is the relatively simple eleven-point ladder scale (after Kilpatrick and Cantril, 1960) with a semantic differential of 'completely unimportant' and 'overwhelmingly important' at the polar values 1 and 10. Apart from simplicity and economy in use, the main advantage of this method is that respondents' ratings are self-anchored (in that the top and bottom of the ladder are defined in their own frame of reference), so that it is possible to make direct comparisons (both between people and between life-domains) of quantified levels of importance. This is an important attribute in the present study, since a major aim is to derive overall parameters of values within urban subareas which can be used to qualify the evidence of 'objective' measures of spatial variations in major aspects of life. The city in which this task was undertaken is Dundee, which, although it is by no means representative of British cities, is not atypical of medium-sized British industrial cities in its social and ecological structure.

SOCIAL VALUES AND SOCIAL INDICATORS IN DUNDEE

The city

In 1971, Dundee was Scotland's third largest city, with a population of 182 204 including a workforce of 86 870, employed mainly in textile, engineering, and electrical industries, and a relatively undeveloped service sector. Since mushrooming as a working-class town during the textile boom of the 1820s, the city has been unable to offer more than a narrow range of employment opportunities in which low wages have been endemic, and it has consequently lacked the tax base and the spending power to create much more than a minimum of urban amenities. There has been some recent expansion in electronics and light engineering industries, but this is dominated by a few large and externally controlled (i.e. U.S.) firms and has proved very vulnerable to economic recession. As a result, Dundee remains a relatively poor city: a recent survey by the Department of the Environment found that over 13 per cent. of the city's 533 enumeration districts were 'multiply deprived' (in terms of the overlap of the incidence of overcrowding, the lack of basic plumbing amenities, and unemployment) in 1971 (Holtermann, 1975).

Dundee's morphological structure is basically linear, stretching along the north bank of the Tay estuary and dominated by the steep-sided Law hill. Early development was radial in form, with five main axes based on industrial and commercial development extending from a central area located near the shore line. Between the jute mills and factories strung along these axial belts are the hurriedly built tenements dating from the mid-nineteenth century. These stone and brick-built dwellings are between three and five storeys high, with an external common access at the rear by way of staircases leading to platforms running the whole length of the building on each of the floors. On each platform is a common toilet in a brick-built stack appended to the staircase shortly after construction. The tenements were conventionally laid out in large rectangular blocks, with the main doors on the platforms facing inwards to a central open space which originally contained a wash-house. Built at extremely high densities, some tenement blocks subsequently lost even these central areas to infilling with smaller tenement buildings before the practice was proscribed by nineteenth century public health by-laws. Inside, the tenements typically consist of only one or two rooms, with rudimentary plumbing and cooking facilities. Not surprisingly, much of this housing is obsolescent, and has been the focus of the city's rehabilitation and renewal schemes, the latter in particular accounting for the demolition of 19 377 dwellings between 1950 and 1975. Nevertheless, in 1975 over 13 500 tenement dwellings remained, providing a highly distinctive inner zone to the city. Many of the more spacious and substantially built dwellings of the same period also remain, providing distinctive leafy and sequestered environments on the fringe of this zone and in substantial parts of the eastern and western suburbs of the city. Originally constructed as mansions and villas for the jute 'barons' and their senior managers, many have been subdivided into large apartments as they have filtered down the housing market, but nevertheless they constitute the nuclei of the most well-to-do neighbourhoods in the city.

The bulk of post–1918 residential development has been provided by the local authority, together with the Scottish Special Housing Association—to the extent that nearly 60 per cent. of the city's housing stock consisted of public housing in 1971. Most of the inter-war housing schemes and estates are located to the south of the Kingsway (an outer ring road constructed during the 1920s along which the majority of the city's industrial estates are situated) and are relatively small, only two out of ten exceeding 1000 units. In contrast, the post-war schemes to the north of the Kingsway have been large-scale enterprises, creating sprawling estates with few local amenities. Latterly these have been accompanied by multistorey housing schemes in the inner city, products of the *zeitgeist* of British town planning in the 1960s. Towards the south-west of the city, along the central part of the Kingsway, and in parts of the eastern suburbs are the main areas of private inter-war housing, many of them dominated by bungalow developments. Finally, there are the uniform suburbs of private post-war development, constructed mostly by one building firm and optimistically described by estate agents as 'Dundee's Little California'; these are situated in the east of the city, with small outliers on the northern and north-western boundary.

The ecological context

The ecological structure associated with this morphology forms the basis of the sampling frame used for the survey of social well-being reported here. While a clustering of subareas (enumeration districts, in this case) on the basis of social, demographic, housing, and household characteristics may not be completely congruent with communities of interest (Palm, 1973), it does provide a comprehensive classification of neighbourhoods which constitutes an effective sampling frame for more detailed research on people's attributes and behaviour as well as their attitudes (Herbert and Evans, 1974; Rees, 1970; Robson, 1969)—and our research strategy required information on all three. The input variables for the ecological classification of Dundee (Table 5.1) encompass those census variables which have proved highly diagnostic in ecological studies of other British cities. The danger of circular argument here is obvious, as are the dangers of relying on the rather limited cover provided by census data, the uncertainties involved in the implied assumption that enumeration districts define relatively homogeneous socioeconomic units, and the familiar hazards associated with the multivariate analysis of spatial data of any kind (Cliff and Ord, 1973; King, 1969). They are, nevertheless, worth a gentle reminder. The algorithm selected in order to cluster the enumeration districts into neighbourhood types was Ward's 'error sum of squares' method, since it was essential that the sampling strata should be relatively homogeneous in their internal characteristics (see Everitt, 1974, for a detailed discussion of clustering procedures in this context).

TABLE 5.1. Input variables for cluster analysis of Dundee enumeration districts

District	Input variables
1	Percentage of economically active in socioeconomic groups I–IV
2	Percentage of economically active unemployed
3	Percentage with ONC/A-levels
4	Female activity rate
5	Percentage aged 60 or more
6	Percentage aged 15–44
7	Percentage of females
8	Female marriage rate
9	Percentage of households consisting of 1 or 2 persons
10	Percentage of households living at a density of more than 1 person per room
11	Percentage of households with children under 15
12	Mean household size
13	Percentage of dwellings owner-occupied
14	Percentage of dwellings privately rented
15	Percentage of dwellings with all three basic amenities (hot water, fixed bath or shower, and an inside WC)
16	Percentage of dwellings with 6 or more rooms
17	Percentage of dwellings vacant

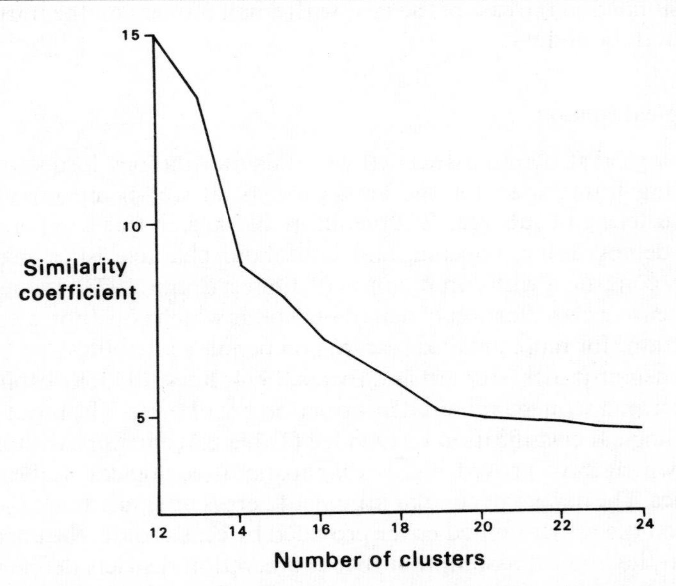

FIGURE 5.1. Similarity coefficients derived from the cluster analysis of E.D. data

Applied without contiguity constraint on normalized data for the 533 enumeration districts, the fusion process resulted in a considerable loss of detail in the transition from 14 to 13 clusters (Figure 5.1), and so this point was taken as the cut-off for the procedure. The salient characteristics of each of the

TABLE 5.2. Dominant characteristics of each neighbourhood type

Neighbourhood type	Dominant characteristics[a]
1	Privately rented dwellings, persons aged 15–44
2	Privately rented dwellings, lack of basic amenities, 1 or 2-person households
3	Privately rented dwellings, lack of basic amenities, unemployment, low educational achievement, vacant dwellings
4	Low marriage rate, low unemployment
5	Persons aged 60 or more
6	1-or 2-person households, persons aged 60 or more, few persons aged 15–44, few households with children, females, low incidence of overcrowding, low marriage rate
7	Owner-occupied dwellings, persons in socioeconomic groups I–IV, low incidence of overcrowding, high educational achievement, large dwellings
8	Owner-occupied dwellings, households with children, high marriage rate, few people aged 60 or over, high educational achievement, large dwellings, persons in socioeconomic groups I–IV
9	Few owner-occupied dwellings, few privately rented dwellings[b]
10	Overcrowded dwellings
11	Households with children, overcrowded dwellings, large families
12	Low educational achievement
13	Households with children, few persons aged 60 or more, high marriage rate, vacant dwellings, persons aged 15–44
14	Few households with children, low unemployment, low educational achievement, small households, females, persons aged 60 or more, low marriage rate, low overcrowding, low female activity rates

[a] Variables for which the mean score is more than one standard deviation from the mean of the 533 enumeration districts.
[b] Variables for which the mean score is more than 0.75 of a standard deviation from the mean of the 533 enumeration districts.

fourteen neighbourhood types thus produced are summarized in Table 5.2; their spatial expression is shown in Figure 5.2(a), (b), and (c). Most of the neighbourhood types are highly disaggregated, reflecting the fragmentation of urban subareas prompted by topography, industrial land use, and highways, as well as the compartmentalization resulting from sociospatial processes and institutional filtering. Types 1, 2, and 3 are inner-city districts of privately rented tenements, differentiated one from another mainly by the social and demographic attributes of their occupants. Type 4 also consists predominantly of inner-city districts, but has a mixed tenure structure of rather less-inadequate dwellings and is characterized by particularly low levels of unemployment. These are surrounded by other local authority housing (neighbourhood types 5, 6, and 14) occupied by populations of different kinds; type 5 contains residents whose social and demographic characteristics are more or less 'average', whereas types 6 and 14 contain an aging population of small households. The owner-occupied housing of the educated middle classes (types 7 and 8) is also

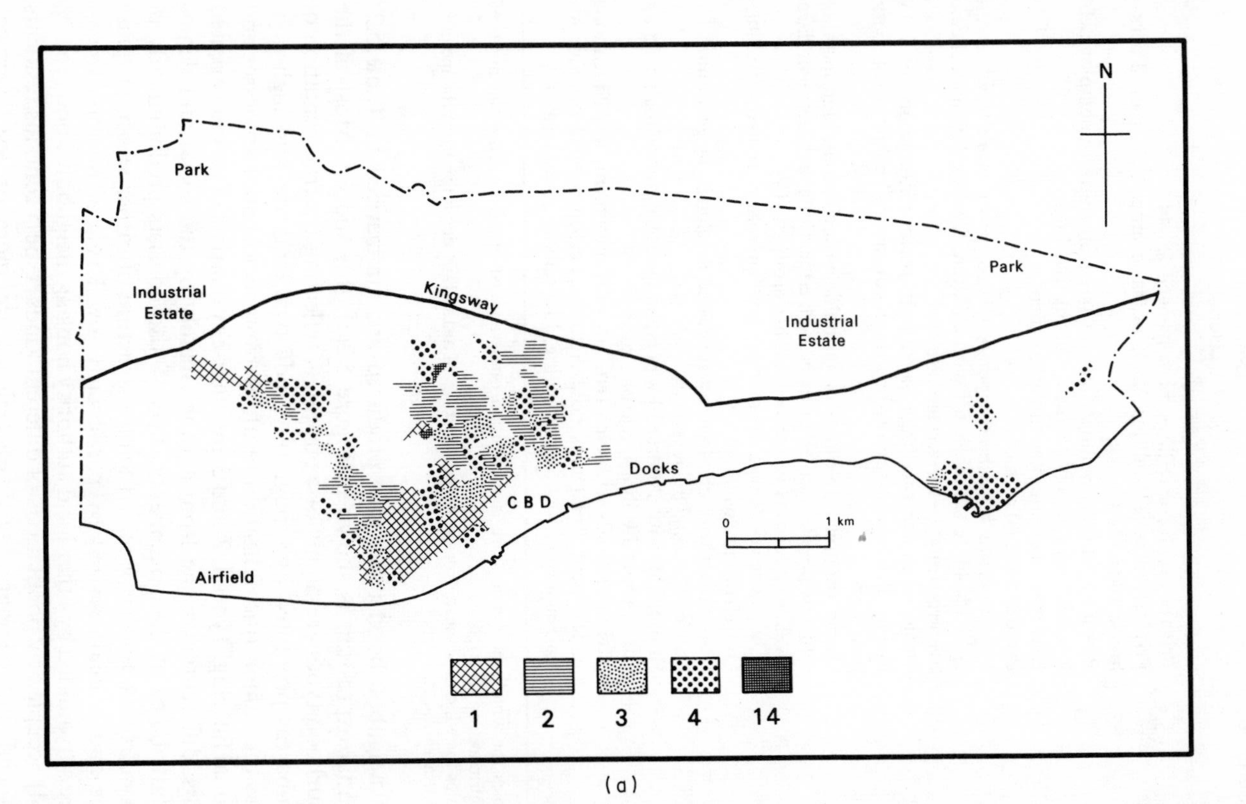

FIGURE 5.2(a). The ecological context: neighbourhood types 1, 2, 3, 4, and 14. The dominant characteristics of each type of area are listed in Table 5.2

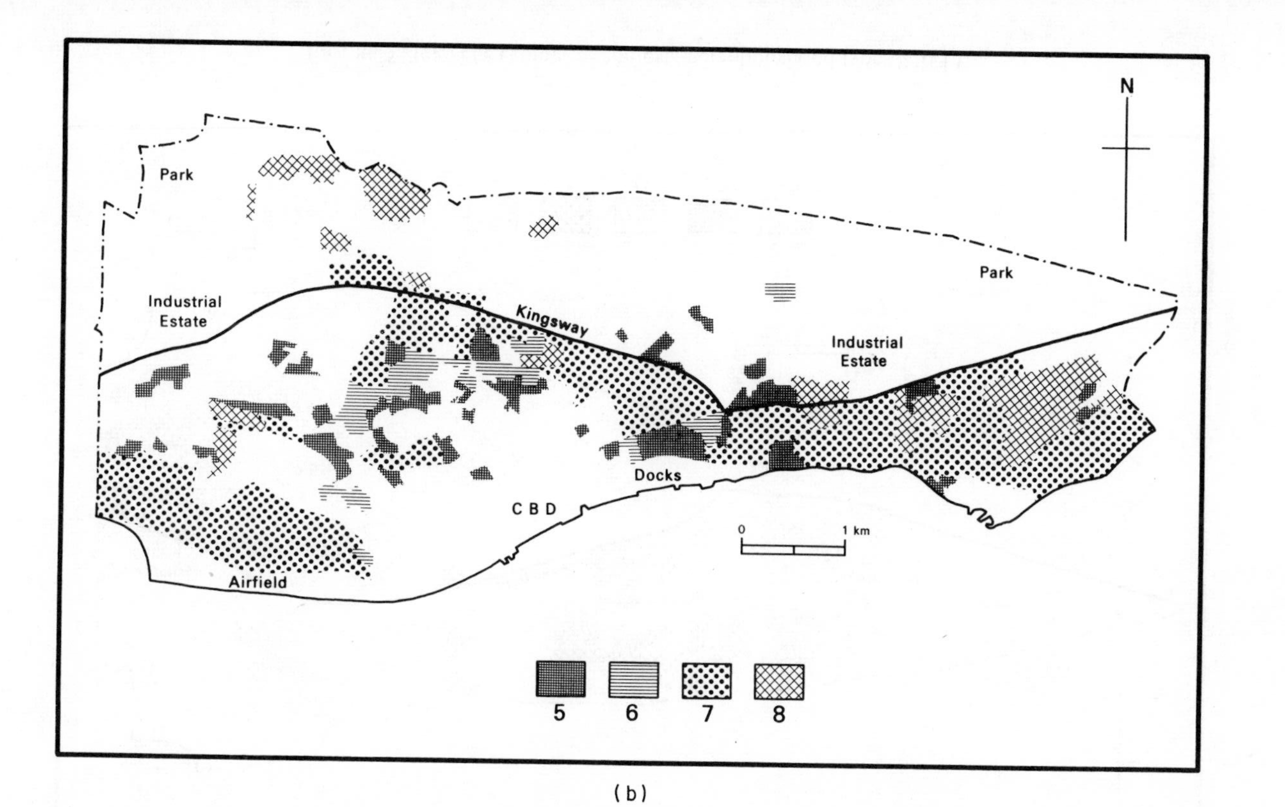

(b)

FIGURE 5.2(b). The ecological context: neighbourhood types 5 to 8

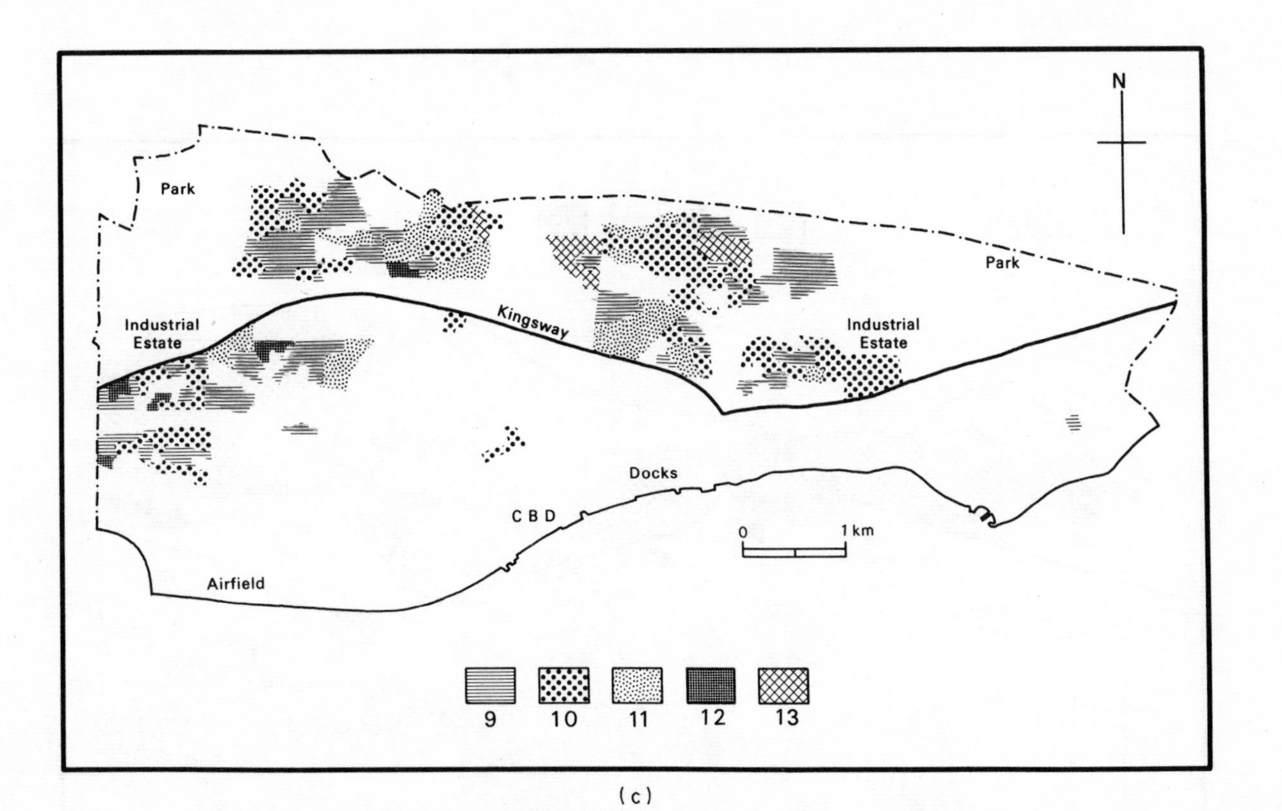

(c)

FIGURE 5.2(c). The ecological context: neighbourhood types 9 to 13

differentiated by life-cycle characteristics, but the extensive areas of local authority housing in the north and west of the city which comprise types 9 to 13 are finely differentiated in terms of social composition and housing characteristics as well as by life-cycle attributes.

The survey: objective conditions

A survey was conducted between August and November 1974, sampling private households within the fourteen strata at random from the valuation roll, which is the most comprehensive and up-to-date list of private households available. With an overall response rate of nearly 70 per cent., an effective sample size of around 35 for each neighbourhood type was achieved. Questionnaires were addressed to the head of each household (or the joint head of the household if he or she was in full-time paid employment or actively seeking work) and were designed to elicit information not only on people's priorities but also on their 'objective' circumstances on various domains of life. Both themes of inquiry were concerned with eleven life-domains which relate to people's well-being in an urban environment: health, housing, employment, education, personal security, family and neighbourhood stability, consumption/finance, leisure, participation, access to urban amenities, and environmental quality. It should be admitted at the outset that these domains were not selected on the basis of any particular social or psychological survey—a task well beyond our resources. In mitigation, however, there is some precedent for believing them to represent important (although not completely exhaustive) aspects of well-being for most people (Abrams, 1973; Campbell and Converse, 1972; Coates, Johnston, and Knox, 1977; Smith, 1973). Our interest, therefore, is not so much in whether or not people value these life-domains, but rather in how the intensity of feelings attached to them varies between individuals and neighbourhood types.

In administering the survey, questions relating to people's objective circumstances on the eleven domains were asked first, in order to enhance respondents' understanding of the nature and scope of each domain. It is useful to preface our examination of intraurban variations in values with some indication of the results of these questions, since a brief summary of the 'objective' geography of social well-being in Dundee will provide a benchmark for subsequent discussion of both attitudes to and perception of different life-domains. A full list of the 50 variables employed to gauge objective conditions for each domain is given in the Appendix to this chapter. For each respondent, the scores for these variables were aggregated, averaged, and transformed to a scale of 0 (the worst possible) to 100 (the best possible), in order to provide summary social indicators of objective circumstances for each domain (a full description of the methodology is given by MacLaran, 1977). Subsequently, the domain indicators were also aggregated to give a global measure of social well-being which we have called an index of levels of living. By averaging these scores, approximations of the relative conditions prevailing at the neighbourhood level can be obtained.

These are presented in full in Table 5.11 in the Appendix. The best areas, as we would expect, are the owner-occupied districts which comprise neighbourhood types 7 and 8. The former has above-average scores for each of the eleven domains, whereas the latter is below average in terms of leisure, access to local amenities, and participation; both emerge with overall level of living scores of around 73. Some way behind these areas, with an index score of 65, is neighbourhood type 6, which consists of the most stable and sought-after of the older local authority estates. Without achieving outstanding scores for any of the domains, there is a broad consistency of well-being in these districts; only levels of health and housing conditions fall below the respective Dundee means, and then only by a small margin. At the other end of the spectrum of well-being, there is a number of different neighbourhood types with scores of between 50 and 55. These include both inner-city districts (types 2 and 3; index scores 54 and 50 respectively) and outlying suburbs of more recent public housing schemes (types 9, 10, 11, and 13; index scores 52, 55, 49, and 55 respectively). For these districts, average scores are rarely matched on any of the domains, their low index scores thus resulting from multiple deprivation rather than from particularly poor conditions in only a few life-domains. In relative terms, the inadequacies of inner-city districts are least marked in relation to leisure and access to local amenities, whereas in the local authority estates the most redeeming feature of life is the adequacy of housing conditions. Between these extremes are the remainder of the neighbourhood types, with intermediate index scores: types 1 and 12, as a result of a rather variable collection of domain scores, and types 4, 5, and 14 as a result of consistently near-average scores on most domains.

Local values

Against this background, then, we may briefly catalogue the main features of distribution of scores (from 0 to 10 on the ladder scale) attached to each domain within Dundee. Table 5.3 shows the frequency distribution of value scores on each of the life-domains for the overall sample of 462 respondents. There is clearly a pronounced positive skew to each of these distributions but, as Knox (1976a) points out, there is no social or psychological theory which requires that priority preferences should be normally distributed or otherwise. Moreover, it is not surprising that domains which have been selected because they were, *a priori*, believed to be important to most people should attract valuations which reflect this assumption. Some idea of the relative importance of each domain is afforded by the final column of Table 5.3, which lists the overall adjusted mean value attached to each domain. In calculating this value, the overall sample means have been weighted to correct for the bias introduced by the different sampling fractions associated with the fourteen strata. In practice, this procedure did not alter any of the 'raw' cluster means by more than 0.2 of a point, so that the figures listed in Table 5.3 reflect a relatively stable expression of the intensity of feelings associated with each domain. Health

TABLE 5.3. Mean domain scores and percentage distributions of importance ratings; overall sample

Domain	Value score: percentage giving											$\bar{x}$
	0	1	2	3	4	5	6	7	8	9	10	(adjusted)
Health	0	0	0	*	0	*	1.5	6.2	16.2	33.1	42.4	9.1
Housing	0	0	*	*	1.1	*	8.4	25.5	31.4	27.5	5.4	7.9
Employment	0	0	*	*	1.3	4.1	8.9	16.7	21.7	29.9	16.9	8.2
Education	*	*	0	1.3	6.7	1.1	27.3	22.1	20.1	13.9	7.1	7.1
Security	0	0	*	*	7.1	6.1	26.2	25.5	19.1	11.3	4.3	7.1
Consumption/finance	0	0	0	*	2.1	2.3	17.8	30.3	32.0	11.9	3.0	7.4
Leisure	0	0	1.9	1.3	11.9	2.6	27.5	24.9	20.1	7.5	1.7	6.7
Participation	3.0	2.0	11.3	6.3	10.4	3.7	22.1	23.2	13.6	3.7	*	5.4
Access	1.3	*	5.1	4.8	8.6	3.0	17.8	21.4	21.4	12.3	4.1	6.6
Environmental quality	0	0	*	1.1	1.1	*	10.8	22.7	28.4	27.7	6.9	7.8
Stability	0	0	*	*	1.1	*	5.6	8.4	18.8	30.1	34.4	8.6

*Less than 1 per cent.

emerges clearly as the most important domain in overall terms with an average rating approaching 'overwhelmingly important'. This is followed by stability (8.6 points) and then employment, housing, and environmental quality, all of which are given overall mean ratings of around 8.0 points. The finance/consumption domain occupies the median position with 7.4 points, and this is followed at successively lower levels of importance by education and security (both at around 7.0 points), by leisure and access (both at around 6.6 points), and, finally, by participation, which is only given a rating of 5.4 points. This ordering accords fairly well with the evidence on priorities for major life-domains derived from various national and 'urban' samples in Britain (Abrams, 1973; Hall and Perry, 1974; Knox, 1976a), although direct comparisons are hampered by differences in the labelling and definition of the different sets of life-domains. What is clear is that the relative importance attached to health, stability, housing, education, and leisure is consistent, whereas the importance attached to the employment domain appears to be relatively greater in Dundee. Our initial reaction to this anomaly is that it is related to the vulnerable structure of Dundee's economy.

In general terms the consistency of value intensities extends to the level of neighbourhood types within Dundee. Table 5.4 shows the rank position of each domain by neighbourhood type (based on the mean scores allocated by respondents from each type) and illustrates this consistency well. It is worth noting, however, that this consistency is greatest at the extremes of the rankings. This may, of course, be an artifact of small absolute differences in the mean scores on which the rankings are based, but merits further attention because of the possibility that there are marked differences in the degree of consensus in the values attached to different domains. Some indication of consensus could be obtained from distributional parameters such as the best-estimate of the

TABLE 5.4. Local values; rank order of mean domain scores by neighbourhood type

Domain	Neighbourhood type													
	1	2	3	4	5	6	7	8	9	10	11	12	13	14
Health	2	1	1	1	1	1	1	2	1	1	1	2	2	1
Housing	4	3	3=	5	5	5	4	5	3	4	4	5	3	5
Employment	3	6	3=	4	4	3	2	3	5	3	3	3	4	3
Education	5	9	6	8	7	6	6	7	9	10	8	9	9	7
Security	10	5	9	9	8	9	7	8	8	7	7	7	7	8
Consumption/finance	7	7	7	7	6	7	8	6	6	5	5	6	6	6
Leisure	8	10	8	10	10	11	9=	9	7	8	9	8	10	9
Participation	11	11	11	11	11	10	11	10	11	11	11	11	11	11
Access	9	8	10	6	9	8	9=	11	10	9	10	10	7	10
Environmental quality	6	4	5	3	3	4	3	4	4	6	6	4	5	4
Stability	1	2	2	2	2	2	5	1	2	2	2	1	1	2

TABLE 5.5. Degree of consensus about the importance of life-domains, by neighbourhood type

Neighbourhood type	Domain										
	Health	Housing	Employment	Education	Security	Consumption/finance	Leisure	Participation	Access	Environment	Stability
1	92.2	81.2	83.4	74.2	66.5	72.0	86.4	40.0	53.3	85.1	77.6
2	95.9	76.9	63.0	77.6	73.8	83.2	66.6	11.7	64.7	76.7	86.1
3	96.5	79.9	79.2	89.3	81.3	80.1	75.6	52.0	42.1	76.3	96.3
4	96.1	92.2	79.4	76.4	83.2	89.2	88.0	46.1	78.8	79.9	93.8
5	86.0	79.4	80.5	76.4	73.3	79.9	71.0	44.8	57.6	84.2	81.3
6	91.8	81.2	81.2	77.6	74.2	76.7	58.1	59.9	63.0	77.6	83.4
7	92.2	87.1	85.1	83.2	88.5	69.9	68.4	35.5	69.6	91.0	81.2
8	84.2	79.4	83.5	74.5	81.2	83.0	77.7	75.1	67.8	88.0	88.8
9	95.0	84.8	68.2	80.1	86.0	68.2	81.5	18.4	41.3	70.0	76.2
10	95.6	86.0	80.3	80.4	77.2	81.2	81.0	33.8	70.5	78.2	84.3
11	99.5	83.5	80.0	76.2	69.0	79.1	72.3	40.0	53.2	86.4	82.0
12	95.3	82.6	76.4	78.4	85.4	78.4	80.1	34.6	54.9	76.4	81.3
13	94.7	84.3	77.1	76.3	76.1	82.1	79.8	38.9	56.1	79.9	80.0
14	90.1	80.7	73.4	77.0	73.2	72.1	65.4	49.3	60.3	77.6	83.3

standard deviation and the coefficient of variation, but their sensitivity with highly skewed data is obviously limited. We have therefore used Knox's (1976a) measure of consensus which is based on the ratio of the interquartile range to the mean of each distribution, giving an index ranging from 0, representing 'complete disagreement' (i.e. an even distribution of importance ratings resulting from an equal allocation of high, medium, and low importance ratings by respondents), to 100, representing the greatest possible degree of consensus. As Table 5.5 shows, the consensus of attitudes towards the five domains of life which are generally regarded as most important—health, stability, employment, housing, and environmental quality—is consistently strong. There is no such widespread consensus, however, as to the relative importance of domains which are consistently ranked lowest in importance by different neighbourhoods. Indeed, consensus within neighbourhood types varies a good deal for all of the other six domains except education, about which the *consensus* of feelings is consistently high, despite the apparent variations in the *intensity* of local feelings towards it. Table 5.5 thus reveals that consensus as to the importance of at least half of the domains varies a good deal between the fourteen neighbourhood types, suggesting that there may in fact be important differences in the structure of priority preferences expressed in different types of neighbourhood. We have therefore employed chi-square tests to evaluate the null hypothesis that there is no significant difference between neighbourhood types in the frequency that different importance ratings are allocated to each domain. The results of these tests prompted the null hypothesis to be rejected at the 1 per cent. level for seven out of eleven domains. Of the remaining four, the null hypothesis could be rejected at the 2 per cent. level for education and at the 5 per cent. level for access, but for leisure and the finance/consumption domain the null hypothesis had to be accepted. For all but two of the domains, then, significant differences in the way they are valued do exist between neighbourhood types. Closer examination of the strength and consensus of value scores attached to each domain by the neighbourhood types suggests that this variation is usually attributable to two or three 'deviant' neighbourhood types rather than to more widespread differences (Figure 5.3). Health, for example, is consistently rated as the first or second most important domain, with a range of less than 1 point in the mean scores by neighbourhood type; but for neighbourhood types 1, 3, and 5 there is an atypical spread of responses into the relatively lower responses between 5 and 7 points.

Attempts to explain such deviant cases must, at this stage, remain speculative. The generally high level of importance attached to the 'stability' domain is disrupted only by the consensus among residents of 'older' owner-occupied neighbourhoods (type 7) that it is of moderate importance, prompting us to invoke the conventional wisdom that family and neighbourhood stability is less important in ecologically middle-class districts where friendship patterns are traditionally diffuse. This, however, does not hold for neighbourhood type 8, the other 'owner-occupied' class of districts; respondents from this type of neighbourhood attach the highest average score of all on this domain. Since the

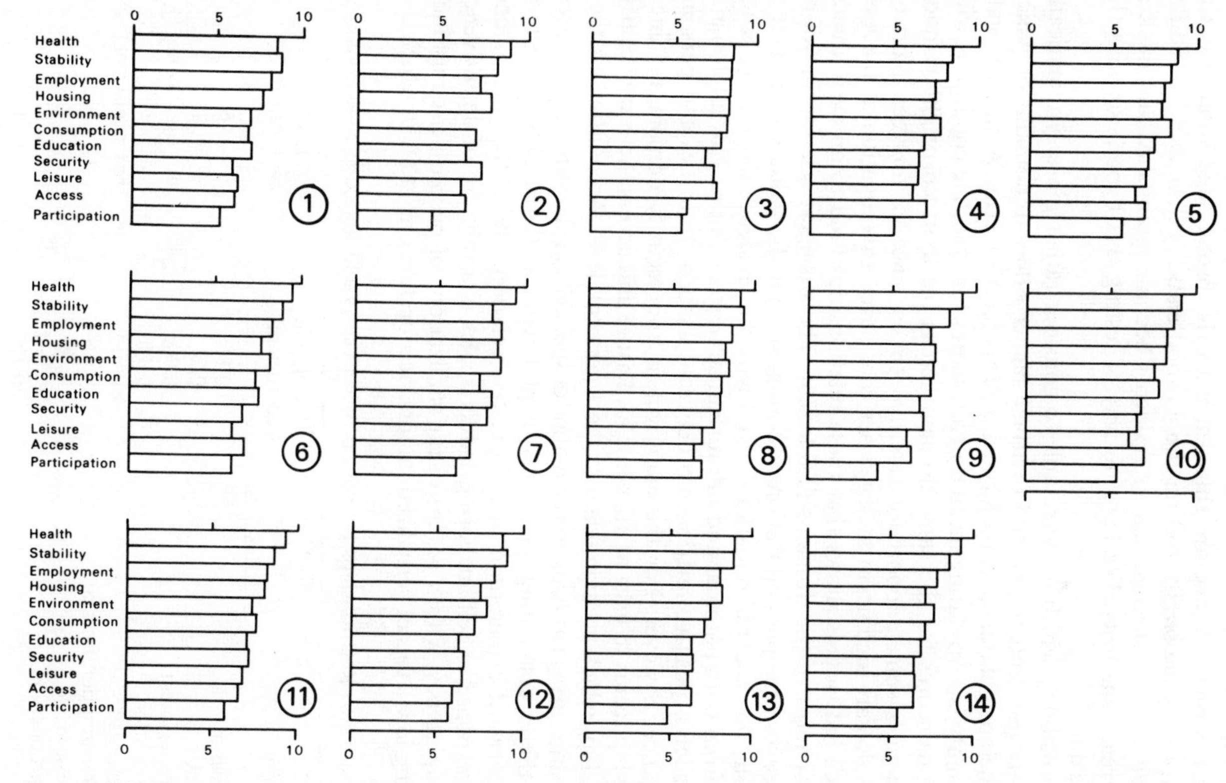

FIGURE 5.3. Mean importance ratings for each life-domain allocated by respondents from the fourteen neighbourhood types

essential difference between the types is that of life-cycle, it might be suggested that this is the key factor rather than a 'middle-class' ecology, but this is not at all convincing in the light of the ratings given by other neighbourhoods with aging population structures. We are thus left with the broad suggestion that the propensity to value family and neighbourhood stability decreases in middle-class environments *through time* as residents become established and nuclear families reach maturity. We have no way of testing this hypothesis with the available data.

One possibility which we were able to consider rather more systematically was that respondents might tend to attach higher values to domains on which they or their neighbourhood 'performed' well in objective terms. At the aggregate level of analysis, correlating mean domain scores for objective conditions with mean value scores for the same domain across the fourteen neighbourhood types, there is some support for this hypothesis, since all fourteen pairwise relationships are significant at the 5 per cent. level. Investigation at the level of the 462 individuals shows that these relationships hold to an even greater extent for most of the domains (Table 5.6). The strongest relationship of all exists between people's educational attainment and the value they attach to education; this accords remarkably well with the evidence derived by Knox (1976a) from both national and intraurban surveys of values. Not all domains exhibit such a positive relationship between personal priorities and personal performance, however. For the employment and security domain, no linear relationship seems to exist at all, while for leisure and access there are negative relationships which are significant at the 1 per cent. level. Accounting for these relationships brings us back to the realms of speculation. Turning to the battery of hypotheses concerning variations in preference outlined above, the most straightforward explanation of the positive relationships is that the psychological response to self-anchoring ladder scales is a mixture of defensiveness and complacency, with *a posteriori* rationalizations of people's circumstances producing low levels of verbalized importance for domains of life in which they

TABLE 5.6. Relationships between people's values and objective conditions

Domain	Correlation coefficient	Level of significance (%)
Health	0.115	5
Housing	0.212	1
Employment	0.066	not significant
Education	0.440	1
Security	0.015	not significant
Consumption/finance	0.232	1
Leisure	– 0.281	1
Participation	0.290	1
Access	– 0.122	1
Environmental Quality	0.255	1
Stability	0.119	1

have been relatively unsuccessful, and vice versa. On the other hand, these positive relationships may reflect a modified version of the hierarchical/marginalist model outlined above. Thus, although not conforming to a hierarchy of motivations which is necessarily Maslovian (i.e. ascending from nutrition, shelter, and safety to affection, belongingness, prestige, status, dominance, and, finally, self-actualization), people may tend to strive hardest towards fulfilment on the domains they value most. In either case, the two negative relationships between people's values and their objective conditions must be seen either as special cases or as artifacts of the systems of measurement used. The fact that those who enjoy relatively high levels of access to urban amenities fail to accord the domain as high a degree of importance as those who are obliged to travel considerable distances to them may have something to do with the negative externalities associated with living near busy shops, cinemas, community centres, public houses, and so on, and with the possibility that those who live in neighbourhoods where amenities are accessible tend to take proximity for granted and so undervalue it. Similarly, the relatively low value accorded to leisure by those with plenty of leisure time (especially the aged and the unemployed) may result from diminishing returns which bring boredom and restlessness. In contrast, of course, the busiest people and those for whom sport, culture, and entertainment facilities are least accessible are most likely to be the ones who will value leisure the most.

As Johnston (1976) points out, this kind of 'area' analysis, even when conducted with powerful statistical techniques such as multiple regression and factor analysis, cannot do more than *suggest* which processes underlie the observed spatial patterns of phenomena. An alternative methodology elaborated by Johnston, however, facilitates the identification of one set of processes—'structural' or 'neighbourhood' effects—which we have already noted as being potentially relevent to intraurban variations in attitudes. Although we are mainly concerned in this paper with the role of values in providing more sensitive descriptions of the social geography of urban areas, it is nevertheless singularly unfortunate that our data do not fulfil the criteria needed to test for the existence of neighbourhood effects. It is clearly an essential avenue of investigation for any future research into intraurban variations in values. But, notwithstanding our inability to make use of this methodology, it is sufficient for our purpose here to have established that significant variations in priority preferences do exist within Dundee. We therefore turn now to an examination of the effects of weighting objective indicators with people's values.

Local values and local well-being

The most illuminating way of comparing local values with objective conditions is to compute McKennell's index of discrepancy (see Hall and Ring, 1974) for each neighbourhood type and each of the domains (Table 5.7). The index brings domains which are of low importance to the centre of the scale and produces high positive scores for 'good' objective scores and high negative

TABLE 5.7. An index of discrepancy between local priorities and local conditions

Neighbourhood type	Domain										
	Health	Housing	Employment	Education	Security	Consumption/finance	Leisure	Participation	Access	Environment	Stability
1	8	−3	4	−4	2	−4	−1	−1	3	−5	0
2	4	−5	5	−2	3	−1	2	1	4	−3	0
3	7	−2	7	−5	2	−2	0	−1	2	−4	6
4	−2	−3	2	−3	2	0	−1	−1	2	5	10
5	−4	1	0	−4	2	5	−1	−1	−1	9	4
6	−4	−1	4	−5	2	2	0	−2	0	8	6
7	−2	6	4	−4	3	4	−2	−1	−1	2	0
8	0	7	2	−1	2	4	−2	−2	−1	6	−4
9	2	7	0	−3	2	5	−3	−1	−1	8	−2
10	2	6	−2	−2	2	7	−2	−1	−1	0	6
11	4	6	−4	−3	−1	6	−2	−1	0	2	6
12	2	0	−2	−3	3	6	−2	0	−1	6	4
13	2	4	−2	−2	3	6	−1	−1	−2	6	0
14	−4	−4	2	−4	2	2	0	−1	0	6	10

scores for 'poor' objective scores on the important domains.

For a given area, i, and a specific domain, d, it is calculated as

$$D_{id} = \frac{\left(\frac{n+1}{2} - r_{oi}\right)(n + 1 - r_{vi})}{5}$$

rounded to the nearest integer, where

n = the number of domains
r_{oi} = the rank of the domain in area i according to objective criteria

and

r_{vi} = the rank of the domain in area i in terms of value scores

The denominator is arbitrary, and in this case has been set at 5 in order to give index values ranging between − 10 and + 10. Thus, with our data, a domain which happens to be the 'best' (in objective terms) in the context of a particular neighbourhood whose residents also feel it to be most important, an average, to them would obtain an index score of

$$\frac{\left(\frac{11-1}{2} - 1\right)(11 + 1 - 1)}{5} = 10$$

Viewed in this context, most neighbourhoods experience a net increase in well-being across the spectrum of life-domains, the greatest positive difference being for neighbourhood type 6, the well-established inner-city local authority schemes with aging populations. In contrast, the net influence of values on objective conditions in inner-city tenement districts of type 1 appears to balance out, with large 'gains' in welfare derived from the domains of health, employment, and access to local amenities being cancelled out by 'losses' in welfare due to residents attaching high levels of importance to several domains of life (housing, education, consumption/finance, leisure, and participation) for which their objective circumstances are below standard. In terms of the convenient and increasingly familiar division of neighbourhood types into tenure-based housing classes, it is possible to recognize a broad pattern of ecological effects; the well-bing of inner-city districts of privately rented tenements is enhanced by taking account of people's own values for the domains of employment and access to local amenities but is depressed when values are taken into account for housing conditions, consumption/finance, and environmental quality. Conversely, most of the neighbourhood types dominated by local authority estates fare better in terms of housing conditions, consumption/finance, and environmental quality but worse in terms of employment. Owner-occupied areas benefit particularly from residents attaching high levels of importance to housing conditions. In addition, it should be noted that areas with 'older' population structures—somewhat obscured by this threefold division—are rather anomalous in experiencing a marked decrease in levels of health when values are taken into account. In terms of other domains it is also interesting that making allowances for values brings about 'losses' on the educational component of welfare for all types of neighbourhood and losses for most of them on participation and leisure, while most gain on the security component.

One shortcoming of the index of discrepancy is that, since it is based on rank orderings, it does not represent a weighted score which could form the basis of a refined version of the level of living index outlined above for objective indicators. In order to arrive at such an index, some choice must be made as to how the weights (the raw value scores) are to be incorporated with the objective scores. In the absence of any relevant theoretical or practical precedent, we have proceeded under the rather conflicting criteria of simplicity and sensitivity, weighting *individuals*' objective domain scores by a straightforward multiplication and then *averaging* these to arrive at a weighted domain score for neighbourhood types. Weighted level-of-living indexes for *neighbourhood types* can then be calculated by *aggregating* these weighted domain scores. It is important to remember that this procedure embraces the common but simplistic assumptions that the domains are mutually exclusive yet additive, together being exhaustive of 'level of living'. The results of these calculations show that weighted description, although it is arguably more sensitive to variations in well-being as well as being more acceptable in terms of theory and equity, produces much the same picture, ecologically, as the conventional unweighted approach. Correlations between the two across the fourteen neighbourhood types exhibit positive relationships which are significant at the 0.1 per cent. level for each of the eleven domains and for the overall level-of-living index. In view of the broad parallels found between objective conditons and people's values this association is not at all surprising. Moreover, it is likely that it is compounded at the aggregate level as many of the observed differences in values are 'washed out' by variations in value consensus and in the communality of 'objective' experience. However, the positive relationship between weighted and unweighted solutions is by no means perfect (as the index of discrepancy showed), and a number of interesting anomalies emerge on closer scrutiny of the data. In terms of the health domain, for example, the relative performance of the most prosperous of each of the owner-occupied and local authority neighbourhoods, (types 6 and 7) is enhanced by weighting according to people's values, whereas the relative well-being of some inner-city neighbourhoods (types 1 and 4) is depressed. And in terms of the leisure domain, the relative positions of neighbourhoods dominated by an aging population (types 6, 7, and 14) are considerably reduced, despite the fact that no significant variation exists between neighbourhood types in the importance attached to the domain. Overall, the effect of weighting produces a relatively depressed performance by some inner-city districts (neighbourhood types 2 and 3) and some outlying local authority schemes (types 9, 11, and 13) on at least four of the eleven domains. This is not matched by any marked improvement in the well-being of other neighbourhood types; rather, the position

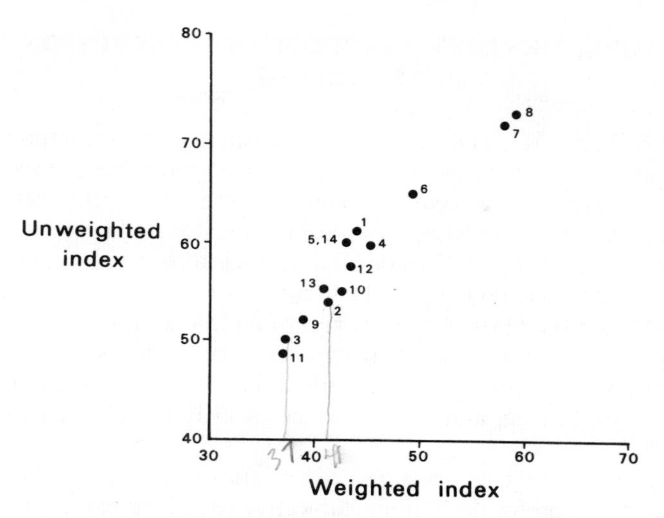

FIGURE 5.4. The relationship between weighted and unweighted 'objective' level-of-living scores for neighbourhood types

of owner-occupied districts (types 7 and 8) as the most advantaged is consolidated. This is also reflected in the weighted index scores for level of living (Figure 5.4). In overall terms, the owner-occupied suburbs stand clearly at the top, with index scores representing 58 and 59 per cent. respectively of the maximum possible score. These are closely followed by type 6 (index score of 49), which consist of older but much sought after local authority housing. The high index scores of the owner-occupied areas are the result of the above-average levels of (weighted) performance across all of the domains (with the exception of slightly below-average scores for type 8 on access and leisure), with their best relative performance being in terms of housing, followed by education, personal security, participation, consumption, and employment. Respondents from neighbourhood type 6 score well on the index because of consistently above-average performances on all except the housing domain. At the other extreme, residents of inner-city tenements comprising neighbourhood types 2 and 3 (index scores of 41 and 37 respectively) and of outlying local authority schemes comprising types 9, 11, and 13 (with index scores of 38, 36, and 41 respectively) experience below-average conditions on most domains of life, to the extent that they can only be interpreted as deprived in every sense of the word. Between these extremes the rest of the neighbourhood types emerge with intermediate index values which, as in the unweighted solution, are mostly the product of trade-offs between good and bad scores on different domains. The detailed social geography which emerges from fuller analysis of these data need not detain us here (a full exposition is given by MacLaran, 1977); rather, we turn to an examination of those aspects of well-being which objective indexes and indicators cannot—and do not attempt to—measure.

A COMPLEMENTARY PERSPECTIVE: PERCEPTION OF WELL-BEING

Abrams' (1972) observation that 'objective' prosperity may sometimes be linked with dissatisfaction whereas people living in poverty may declare themselves to be contented illustrates the central argument for extending the description or evaluation of well-being to 'subjective social indicators' which reflect perceived levels of well-being. The classic example of this paradox of satisfactions is implicit in the contrast between the popular stereotypes of working-class pensioners who enjoy the simple pleasures of life and of middle-class executives who reap only worry and frustration from their apparently comfortable life-style. In other words, an important component of individual well-being is the individual's own *sense* of well-being, and this is not necessarily correlated with objective reality.

It can be argued that the existence of variations in feelings of well-being is sufficient justification for developing subjective social indicators. This is essentially a phenomenological perspective, based on the belief that the emotions generated in relation to some aspect of a person's life, or in relation to his life as a whole, are themselves a significant reality. From this perspective it follows that any description of individual or social well-being must accommodate the views of the issue as seen through the eyes of the beholders. The objective world would thus be measured only indirectly, 'filtered through the individual's own perceptions and then weighed according to his expectations, experiences, attitudes and present circumstances' (Abrams, 1973, p. 35). In other words, the outputs of the social and economic system which are measured by conventional, objective social indicators become inputs to the physiological–psychological systems of individuals, and it is the extent to which they realize their perceptions of the good life which is the major criterion of whether the social and economic system is efficient or not. This, crudely, was the initial reasoning behind many of the pioneer attempts to develop subjective social indicators (Abrams, 1973; Allardt, 1973; Bradburn, 1969; Campbell and Converse, 1972), although current opinion (summarized by Abrams, 1976, and by Campbell, Converse, and Rodgers, 1976) is more disposed towards viewing perceived well-being as a distinctive facet of welfare which is complementary to the objective circumstances of life.

Accepting the logic of developing subjective indicators, there are several advantages to be gained from their use. One of these is that, since subjective indicators can be measured upon a common scale—'happiness' or 'satisfaction', for example—they allow direct comparisons to be made between different domains of life. Such comparisons are difficult to make with objective indicators without invoking a series of simplistic assumptions.

Another important advantage is that they do not attract the 'severe interpretative overload' often associated with 'objective' indicators which are really indirect measures of phenomena and therefore liable to unreliability (e.g. crime indicators; see Smith, 1975) or ambiguity (e.g. indicators of consumption; see

Mishan, 1967). These advantages have been clearly demonstrated in a number of surveys of the perceived well-being of national populations in Britain (Abrams, 1973), the United States (Andrews and Withey, 1974; Bradburn and Caplovitz, 1965; Campbell, Converse, and Rodgers, 1976; Cantril and Roll, 1971), and Scandinavia (Allardt, 1973). The preferred tool for measuring satisfaction in such surveys is a Cantril-type self-anchoring ladder scale. The general format is one in which the respondent is asked to imagine a 'best possible...' as one end of a 7-or 11-point scale and a 'worst possible...' as he envisages the domain at the other extreme. Then, with the scale meaning 'self-anchored' in this way, he is asked to locate his own current situation somewhere along the scale between these poles of complete satisfaction and dissatisfaction. The great advantage of this method is that it enables direct interpersonal and intergroup comparisons of quantified levels of satisfaction to be made, 'in that the scale level selected by one person or group (average of selections) can be specifically and meaningfully said to be higher, lower or equal to the scale level of some other individual or group, because the frames of reference of the replies are in fact similar psychologically' (Kilpatrick and Cantril, 1960, p. 161). Campbell (1972) has elucidated this argument by means of the analogy that satisfactions are equal in the sense that two vessels may be equally full even though they differ in size. Inferences made from such comparisons must be treated with caution, however, since the existence of variable aspirations within and between communities raises the question of whether someone with low expectations greatly fulfilled (the working-class pensioner?) is 'better off' than someone (the middle-class executive?) with high expectations poorly fulfilled. In addition, comparisons may be distorted to some degree by differences in cognition. As Abrams (1973, p. 36) observes, different people may place different meanings on the word 'satisfaction'—'from high elation to the mere absence of pain'. It follows that the affective response sought by means of ladder scales and the like may be modified by the effects of differential cognition. Similarly, class differences which exist in vocabulary and language structure may influence the sensitivity of semantic scales to people's true feelings. Bernstein (1959), for example, has identified a 'public' language of short, simple, and often unfinished sentences, and a 'formal' language in which a greater accuracy of meaning is maintained through grammatical order, syntax, and a wider vocabulary. Managerial and professional status groups, it is argued, use both formal and public languages, whereas the unskilled and semi-skilled possess only a public language. Thus, since public language discourages the verbalization of nuances of feeling, the formal language of questionnaire schedules and psychological tests may be unable to tap the true feelings of unskilled and semiskilled respondents. This, of course, becomes a more serious obstacle to the measurement of satisfaction as the elements of well-being under consideration become more specific. Finally, it should also be noted that ladder scales with polar values ranging from complete dissatisfaction to complete satisfaction necessarily combine positive and negative effects on one dimension, whereas one prominent social psychologist has suggested that positive and negative feelings represent independent dimensions of psychological well-being (Bradburn, 1969). Applying the combined criteria of sensitivity, robustness, and economy of effort, however, social psychologists in general seem to consider self-anchoring ladder scales to be the most appropriate available means of measuring satisfactions.

Sensitive to critics who might be sceptical of attempts to 'define the undefinable and measure the unmeasurable', the pioneers of subjective social indicators have themselves catalogued the areas where this methodology could give cause for concern, and have directed much of their initial research effort towards illuminating these concerns. Since subjective social indicators are relatively new to geographical inquiry, it is appropriate to summarize the issues here. What follows is drawn largely from the work of Andrews (1974; but see also Abrams, 1976), who has identified four distinct clusters of methodological concerns involving (1) validity, (2) interpretation, (3) completeness, and (4) utility. A frequently raised reservation about the *validity* of perceptual data is that people's perceptions of life will depend too much on their immediate circumstances, so that relatively unimportant events from the recent past may influence attitudes and render subjective indicators unstable. This is clearly a reservation which only repeated and in-depth attitudinal testing can remove, but there is already some evidence from American surveys that people's evaluations of major aspects of their lives do remain stable over the medium term (i.e. several months) at least (Andrews, 1974; Campbell, Converse, and Rodgers, 1976). A second cause for concern about the validity of perceptual data has been the fear that people may give biased answers amounting to a 'halo effect', as a result of responding in a way which they feel the interviewer wants or which they feel will put them in a better light. It might be anticipated, for example, that some people will tend to be more critical of those life-domains which lie clearly outside the influence of their own actions (e.g. environmental quality) than those for which they are more directly responsible (e.g. family life). However, tests conducted by both American teams are reassuring: Campbell, Converse, and Rodgers (1976) showed that the tendency to bias answers to make them appear more socially acceptable generally explained only 1.5 to 3.0 per cent. of the variance in people's answers; and Andrews and Withey (1974) have suggested that differences between people in their tendency to bias answers account for no more than 10 per cent. of the variance in their responses.

The main concern about the *interpretations* of levels of satisfaction is that, notwithstanding differences in aspirations and objective circumstances, different people may evaluate well-being—or some aspects of it—by different criteria, so that the comparability of responses is seriously weakened. Thus, as Knox (1976b) points out, some people may judge educational facilities by bricks and mortar while others include books, equipment, and the quality of teaching. Similarly, certain domains of life may be more prominent in some people's conception of a good life than in others'. Once again, the results of analyses of Americans' evaluations of well-being suggest that this concern is unfounded. Cantril (1965) and Andrews and Withey (1974) have shown that there are broad similarities between people both in the structure of their perceptions of life-domains and in the way they integrate these perceptions in evaluating well-being. And in Britain the results of a recent survey commissioned by the Survey Unit of the Social Science Research Council have similarly shown that 'in such matters as interpretations given to the phrase "quality of life" and the reference points used for assessing satisfaction all sub-groups of the population (middle class and working class, men and women, young and old, etc.) were using broadly the same criteria for evaluation' (Abrams, 1976, p. 7).

The third area of concern identified by Andrews—that of *completeness*—is something which applies equally to combinations of objective indicators. In relation to subjective indicators, empirical justification for rejecting this concern comes most convincingly from Andrews himself (1974, pp. 290–291):

> In the course of our work we have developed interview items which assess people's affective evaluations of about one hundred different aspects of their lives. The range of concerns is very broad and is itself based on a still larger list of some 800 concerns derived from 'free answer' questions in previous surveys and on series of structural interviews.... These items, in different overlapping subsets, have been administered to various national samples and local groups of the American population.... We find that about a dozen of these items, taken together and appropriately combined, can explain 50 to 60% of the variation in an index of perceived overall life quality (i.e., multiple correlations are in the range 0.7 to 0.8). Furthermore, of the approximately 100 concerns on which we have data, none is effective in raising this explanatory power.

The final area of concern centres on the *utility* of subjective indicators and brings us conveniently back to our introductory remarks. In this context, the most frequently articulated objection is that information on levels of satisfaction are irrelevant because people may well be ignorant about the true impact of various objective conditions. An example frequently cited in support of such claims is that of cigarette smoking: people may be very satisfied with the cigarettes they smoke as long as they remain ignorant of their chances on contracting cancer or bronchitis. In short, a satisfied customer is not always one who has been well served. But the fact that people may not know what is 'good' for them does not undermine the rationale of developing subjective social indicators. People's perceptions, however uniformed they may be, are real, and they often act on the basis of them. Subjective indicators cannot provide comprehensive descriptions or evaluations of well-being by themselves; they must be interpreted in conjunction with objective indicators. Both kinds of indicator are clearly subject to methodological qualifications which cannot be dismissed out of hand, but they should not be exaggerated to the point that we are fearful of using them.

Despite the vogue for perception studies which began in the late 1960s, geographers have been late in exploiting the potential of subjective social indicators. And although some applications of subjective social indicators have had an explicitly regional flavour (Institute for Environmental Studies, 1974; Knox, 1976b), none has examined intraurban variations in levels of satisfaction for more than a single life-domain (or subdomain; see, for example, Angrist, 1974; Eyles, 1976; Headey, 1972). We therefore enter somewhat cautiously an arena where there are few points of reference to anchor our findings, confining our attention to levels of satisfaction with each of ten major life-domains in order to facilitate direct comparisons with objective data and with people's values. (Questions relating to satisfaction with family and neighbourhood stability were dropped from the questionnaire after high rates of refusal and some hostility were encountered in pilot surveys.) The method used to measure people's satisfaction was an 11-point vertical ladder scale with a semantic differential of 'completely dissatisfied'/'completely satisfied' at the polar values 0 and 10. The relevant questions were located late in the questionnaire so as to avoid contaminating the importance ratings given to domains.

Satisfactions by neighbourhood types in Dundee

Figure 5.5 shows the average level of satisfaction with each of the ten life-domains in the fourteen neighbourhood types, and illustrates the marked variations which exist both between domains and between neighbourhood types. It is particularly striking to find that for some domains (consumption/finance, participation, and personal security) the average ratings of many neighbourhood types actually reflect *dissatisfaction* rather than satisfaction. Most dramatic of all, though, is the magnitude of the range in the average levels of satisfaction associated with the majority of domains. Satisfaction with environment, for instance, ranges from an average of 4.9 points for neighbourhood type 1 (inner-city tenement districts) to 8.8 points for neighbourhood type 7 (the longer established owner-occupied suburbs). Similarly, people's satisfaction with their level of consumption/financial position ranges from 4.2 in the peripheral local authority estates represented by neighbourhood type 11 to 7.5 in neighbourhood type 7; and from 6.3 to 9.8 for housing between the same extreme neighbourhood types. Not surprisingly, the frequency distribution of high (9 or 10 points) medium (7 or 8) and low (0 to 6) levels of satisfaction varies significantly between neighbourhood types for most domains (χ^2 test; 1 per cent. level). The two exceptions are the frequency distributions of scores allocated to education (significant at the 5 per cent. level) and participation (not significant at any level). Closer examination of people's individual levels of satisfaction with participation shows that there is a marked degree of variability within most of the neighbourhood types.

A brief examination of Figure 5.5 shows that, although there are no simple sociospatial patterns underlying these levels of satisfaction, there are several strong recurrent themes. Respondents from neighbourhood type 7, for example, are consistently well satisfied with most aspects of life, whereas those from types 1, 2, and 11 are almost as consistent in expressing lower values of satisfaction. Rather than risk excessive repetition in the elaboration of neighbourhood satisfactions on each domain, we shall base our description of intraurban

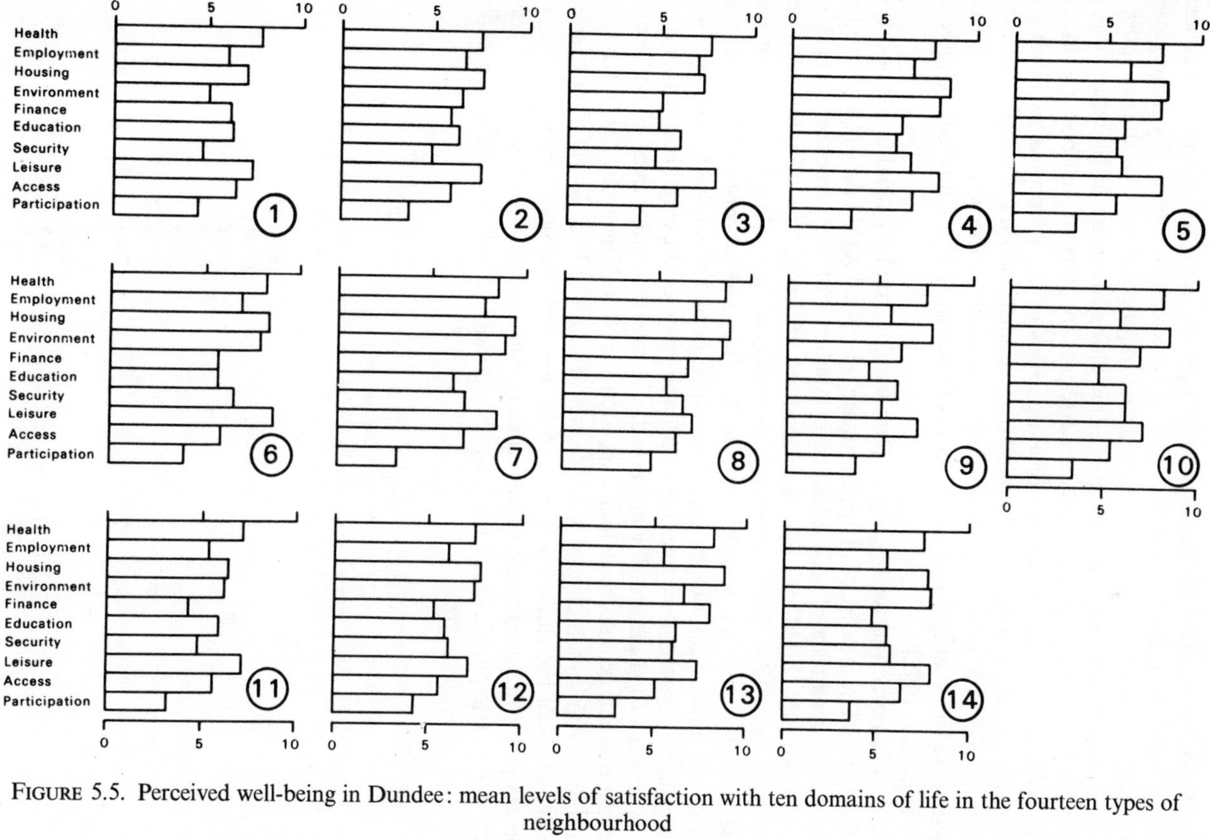

FIGURE 5.5. Perceived well-being in Dundee: mean levels of satisfaction with ten domains of life in the fourteen types of neighbourhood

variations in satisfaction around the expression of an *overall* measure of subjective well-being. Following the rationale used in constructing the index of objective levels of living, such a measure is conveniently derived for each individual from the mean-of-domain satisfaction levels, and for each neighbourhood type an index ranging from 0 to 100 can be obtained simply by aggregating individuals' subjective index scores and dividing by the number of respondents in each neighbourhood type. Although this global measure is, like the index of objective levels of living, a composite surrogate for overall well-being, evidence from both British and American investigations of the perceived well-being of various population subgroups shows that the mean score for people's satisfaction with their life *as a whole* is usually very close to the score obtained from calculating the average of domain scores (Abrams, 1976; Campbell, Converse, and Rodgers, 1976).

Levels of perceived well-being in Dundee are listed by neighbourhood type in Table 5.8. These scores fall approximately into a fivefold division centred on the overall mean score (63) which are labelled, for convenience, 'very high' (more than 70), 'high' (66–70), 'intermediate' (61–65), 'low' (56–60) and 'very low' (less than 56). Both extremes are occupied by solitary neighbourhood types. The best, not surprisingly, is type 7, which has a score of 74. Fewer than one in ten of the respondents from this stratum had individual subjective well-being scores less than the average of 63, and none of these fell below this figure by as much as 1 standard deviation (s.d.); conversely more than 40 per cent. of the respondents had scores which exceeded the overall mean by more than 1 s.d. Moreover, the very high global score is a product of high levels of satisfaction across most of the domains (Figure 5.5). For environment, employment, and consumption/finance the overall average is exceeded by more than 20 per cent.; only for participation does the neighbourhood's level of satisfaction fail to reach the overall mean.

TABLE 5.8. Index of perceived level of living by neighbourhood type

Neighbourhood type	Index score
1	61.3
2	62.0
3	59.4
4	66.9
5	63.9
6	67.3
7	74.0
8	69.2
9	58.9
10	62.5
11	54.4
12	63.2
13	61.8
14	63.2

The three neighbourhood types which express 'high' levels of perceived well-being constitute an unlikely mixture of inner-city districts (type 4), newer owner-occupied suburbs (type 8), and older public housing schemes (type 6). Within each type, perceived levels of well-being are consistently high, with over two-thirds of the respondents having scores greater than the Dundee average in each case. The high scores of all three neighbourhoods result from high levels of satisfaction with a majority of life-domains rather than from particularly high levels on just one or two, and none has a score of less than 90 per cent. of the overall mean for any domain. The differentiating factor between the three neighbourhoods lies in their tendency towards dissatisfaction with particular domains of life: respondents from the inner-city areas of type 4 were least satisfied with health, education, and participation; those from the older public housing schemes (type 6) were least satisfied with the accessibility of local amenities; and those from the newer private estates (type 8) were least satisfied with leisure and education.

Among the neighbourhood types with intermediate levels of perceived well-being, below-average levels of satisfaction are attached to a majority of life-domains. The group includes two kinds of inner-city districts (types 1 and 2) and five classes of public housing (types 5, 10, 12, 13, and 14) with quite diverse social and demographic characteristics, for all of which the overall mean scores are matched or exceeded on no more than three of the domains. Beyond this, there is no fixed pattern to the domain satisfactions; the intermediate global scores are mostly the product of various combinations of low and moderate domain satisfactions. The exception is neighbourhood type 14, respondents from which enjoyed near-average levels of satisfaction with a broad cross-section of life-domains. Their aggregate level of perceived well-being also happens to be coincident with the overall mean score of 63.

There are two neighbourhood types with 'low' levels of perceived well-being, one comprising inner-city districts dominated by the least attractive of the tenements (type 3) and one comprising local authority housing estates with large proportions of small households (type 9). In type 3, a large proportion of respondents had very low individual subjective well-being scores, whereas the low global score of type 9 can be attributed to a greater general prevalence of below-average conditions among respondents. In aggregate, both perform weakly over a wide range of domains. The satisfactions reported by respondents from neighbourhood type 3 match the overall averages on only three domains (education, employment, and leisure), and respondents from neighbourhood type 9 are less satisfied than the overall average with all domains except education and participation. Nowhere do neighbourhood domain scores rise above relevant overall mean by more than 10 per cent., although they decline to 72 per cent. of the overall mean satisfcation with environment in districts of type 3 and to 83 per cent. of the overall mean satisfaction with finance/consumption in districts of type 9.

Finally, we come to type 11 (peripheral council estates with a high incidence of large households and overcrowding) which, with a score of 54, has the worst overall level of perceived well-being of all. Three-quarters of the respondents from this stratum have individual subjective well-being scores amounting to less than the (Dundee) average score of 63 and almost half had scores which fell short of this figure by more than 1 s.d. Most daunting of all is the fact that their mean scores do not match the overall average on any of the domains, and only on education and leisure do their levels of satisfaction come within 10 per cent. of the overall averages.

Weighted levels of satisfaction

Comparing the domain satisfaction scores with the value scores outlined in earlier sections of this paper does not produce any major modifications to this broad pattern and structure of perceived well-being, although there are several interesting discrepancies in detail. The most striking of these is the decrease in welfare in terms of the finance and consumption and security components for almost all of the neighbourhood types (Table 5.9). These decreases are compensated by impressive across-the-board improvements in terms of health and housing, however. The influence of values is more variable on other domains. As we found with the objective domain scores, making allowances for prevailing local values results in losses of welfare in terms of the environmental quality component for inner-city districts and in terms of the employment component for peripheral local authority housing estates. And in the most prosperous districts of the city there is a pronounced discrepancy between people's educational achievements and opportunities and the importance they attach to to education as a major domain of life.

Nevertheless, the overall picture derived from the weighting procedure (following the same rationale as that used for the objective data, producing an index ranging from 0 to 100, with the latter representing the 'best-possible' score) must be regarded as a very clear reflection of the unweighted satisfaction scores. Correlations between individuals' weighted and unweighted domain satisfactions are strong, positive, and statistically significant (at the 1 per cent. level) for all domains, and these relationships are replicated at the aggregate level afforded by the fourteen neighbourhood types. In terms of the global scores computed as a measure of perceived well-being (Figure 5.6), correlation coefficients of +0.98 and +0.99 were established between weighted and unweighted scores for individuals and neighbourhood types respectively. Both relationships are statistically significant at the 0.01 per cent. level.

Subjective versus objective well-being

An issue of central importance to those concerned with social indicators—either as descriptive tools or as instruments of analysis and policy making—is the relationship between 'objective' and 'subjective' well-being. Apart from anything else, the existence of a simple, direct relationship (the sort we might expect to find from 'economic man') would render one or the other type of

Table 5.9. An index of discrepancy between local priorities and perceived local conditions

Neighbourhood type	Domain									
	Health	Housing	Employment	Education	Security	Consumption/finance	Leisure	Participation	Access	Environment
1	10	3	−3	−1	−2	4	2	−1	0	−3
2	6	9	2	0	−5	−2	2	−1	−1	1
3	8	5	3	1	−2	−3	4	−1	0	−2
4	3	7	1	−3	−1	−3	2	−1	1	5
5	3	7	1	−4	−1	−1	1	−1	−2	7
6	6	5	1	−3	0	−2	1	−2	−1	3
7	3	7	1	−5	−2	0	2	−1	−2	6
8	8	7	3	−4	−2	−1	0	−2	−1	4
9	8	9	−1	0	−2	−5	3	−1	−1	3
10	8	8	−3	0	1	−5	2	−1	−2	2
11	10	4	−3	0	−2	−5	3	−1	0	3
12	8	7	1	−1	−1	−5	1	−1	−1	4
13	8	9	−3	0	−1	−5	1	−1	−2	2
14	3	4	−5	−2	0	−5	3	−1	0	6

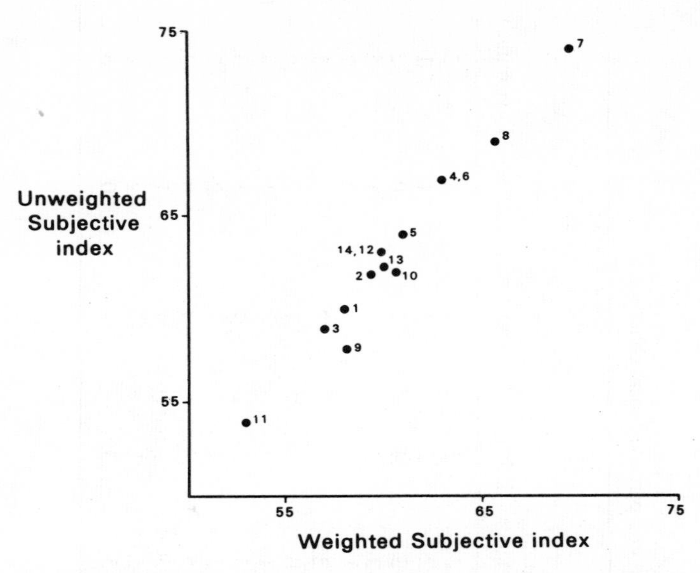

FIGURE 5.6. The relationship between weighted and unweighted perceived level-of-living scores for neighbourhood types

indicator superfluous. The generalized evidence of British and American surveys of life satisfaction tends to substantiate the presence of paradoxical self-evaluations in many circumstances, however. Abrams, having reviewed the findings of subjective social indicator studies between 1971 and 1975, goes so far as to assert (1976, p. 49) that:

> Of course, there will be some situations where the association is high; people living in damp, cold, overcrowded dwellings will usually record low levels of satisfaction with their housing. But the more typical situation is one where people with 'good' objective conditions (e.g. high incomes, higher education) express low levels of satisfaction.

In Dundee, correlations between objective and subjective scores were found to be positive and statistically significant (at the 1 per cent. level) for (1) individuals' index scores (both weighted and unweighted); (2) the mean index scores of neighbourhood types; (3) individuals' domain scores (except for education); and (4) the mean domain scores of neighbourhood types (except for education). Nevertheless, the existence of widespread contradictions within our matrix of life-domains and sociogeographical space is indicated in Table 5.10, which lists correlations *within* neighbourhood types for each domain. Although the general trend clearly remains one of positive association (and this is particularly pronounced in relation to housing, health, leisure, and access to local amenities), a statistically significant positive correlation was reported for only a minority of cases (albeit a large minority), thus lending qualified

TABLE 5.10. Relationships[a] between objective and subjective data within neighbourhood types

Neighbourhood type	Domain									
	Health	Housing	Employment	Education	Security	Consumption/finance	Leisure	Participation	Access	Environment
1	.379	.171	.467	.369	.341	.407	.375	−.259	.587	.337
2	−.030	.217	.658	.060	.289	−.105	−.016	.313	.084	.344
3	.624	.318	.197	.296	.325	.327	.385	−.142	.442	.022
4	.488	.453	.459	−.013	−.208	.210	.447	−.024	.626	.504
5	.400	.434	.235	−.126	−.043	.094	−.051	.402	.458	.389
6	.603	.691	.176	.284	.425	−.149	.534	.031	.469	.506
7	.371	.585	.147	.154	.118	.156	.062	−.035	.228	.131
8	.170	−.003	.149	−.080	−.156	.027	.458	.250	.237	−.004
9	.227	.618	−.088	.219	.209	.131	.238	.238	.242	.088
10	.271	−.349	.108	.040	.180	−.042	.355	.090	−.007	.796
11	.177	.197	.221	.087	.453	.126	.547	.275	.520	.478
12	.440	.800	.238	−.040	.299	.301	.382	.207	.309	.295
13	.439	.542	.271	−.111	.346	.189	.471	.307	.525	.432
14	.509	.346	.436	.139	.025	.015	.346	.117	.629	−.085

[a] Correlation coefficients greater than ± 0.350 are significant at the 5 per cent. level.

support to Abrams' assertions on the apparent paradox of satisfactions. At the ecological level, a comparison of the actual 'hard' and 'soft' domain scores of neighbourhood types (relative to the reference points provided by the two sets of overall average domain scores) provides some indication of the ecological expression of these paradoxical situations. In relation to housing conditions, for example, residents of inner-city districts (types 1 to 3) appear to be much more satisfied, on average, than might be anticipated from their objective circumstances, whereas the residents of newer private housing estates (type 8) and some public housing areas (particularly type 11) are less satisfied than might be expected. A similar situation obtains in relation to environmental quality, for the prevailing sense of satisfaction in inner-city tenement districts (especially types 2, 3, and 4) is considerably in excess of what might be 'warranted' by objective evaluations of environmental quality, while the residents of newer owner-occupied estates (type 8) and of local authority housing schemes consisting largely of multistorey blocks and/or maisonette dwellings (neighbourhood types 9 and 13) tend to be much less satisfied than their objective scores would suggest. The most striking differences between objective and subjective scores occur in the education domain, for which local satisfaction is broadly consistent in spite of widely divergent life-experiences. The disparity is dramatically illustrated by neighbourhood type 8, which has the best average objective score but the lowest average level of satisfaction with education. A rather less graphic but equally important generalization which can be drawn from such comparisons is the tendency for higher (i.e. higher than 'expected') levels of satisfaction to be expressed in neighbourhoods characterized by aging populations (types 6 and 7). In the owner-occupied sector, this is accentuated by the contrasting tendency for respondents from 'young' estates to be less satisfied.

We need not catalogue more instances of discrepancy between hard and soft evaluations of different aspects of well-being. The general lesson is clear enough: some of the objective outputs of society (wages, consumer goods, health services, housing, and so on) satisfy some groups of people whereas others do not and there is no simple structure to these discrepancies—at least at the intraurban level examined here. In most cases, it is possible to advance plausible explanations of such discrepancies without resorting to more surveys or to elaborate statistical analysis. The apparently universal propensity of the elderly towards higher levels of satisfaction, for example, has been attributed to a number of reasons: that today's old people were socialized to be happy with their lot; that they compare themselves with other elderly people; that they are less ready to express 'failure' when questioned by strangers; that they remember the severe and almost universal hardships of the inter-war depression; that older people will have had more time to filter away from unsatisfactory physical and social environments; and that older people will have learned the emotional advantages of 'dissonance reduction'—liking what they have and not liking what they have not got (Abrams, 1976; Campbell, Converse, and Rodgers, 1976). This list contains special cases of several key factors which seem, between them, to govern most instances of divergence between objective and subjective evaluations of well-being. The most widely recognized of these factors is the aspiration level of a person or social group, since it can be called upon to 'explain' the paradox of satisfaction on most occasions. People who appear to be relatively deprived in material terms yet express contentment with their situation are thus deemed to have unusually low expectations, whereas people who appear relatively deprived and also feel that way are deemed to have 'normal' expectations. Aspirations, in turn, depend on a whole series of factors, not least of which must be past experience of people in the 'objective' world. The sobering experience of the Depression would thus contribute to the lower aspirations of the elderly and, consequently, their tendency towards higher levels of satisfaction.

Similarly, our own results suggest that people who have enjoyed good educational opportunities and have been educated to a high standard also have aspirations towards education. Thus, areas in which individuals were found to attain the highest average objective domain scores were characterized by the greatest relative reduction in terms of the subjective measure; in contrast, essentially working-class districts in which conditions were objectively defined as below average were typified by increased levels of performance on the domain in terms of satisfaction. Aspirations will also be shaped by people's reference group. For the elderly, this may simply consist of other elderly people, but for other population subgroups the selection of reference groups may be quite complex (Eyles, 1973), and in some cases the size and composition of the reference group may depend partly on the nature of the life-domain concerned. Domains for which visual comparisons of performance levels can easily be made (housing and environment, for instance) are likely to involve wider reference groups than those for which direct interpersonal comparison is more difficult. Other things being equal, the result will be that aspirations towards the former are widely elevated and more generally comparable, while aspirations towards the latter will tend to be repressed in some subgroups.

Figure 5.7, which is based on a combination of existing perspectives Hall and Ring, 1974), Knox, 1974, 1976b; McKennell, 1971; Murray, 1974, reported in Abrams, represents an attempt to accommodate these factors in a generic model of perceived well-being. For each individual, the initial inputs to his domain satisfaction consist of his life-experience or personal history, and his current objective conditions. These are translated into a mental image of reality which is subsequently measured against his aspirations (which are themselves generated by his personal history and his reference group). The resultant feelings, which may be modified by some social psychological syndrome (e.g. anomie, alienation) or short-term mood state, represent positive or negative domain satisfaction. This, in turn, provides an input to his feelings of overall well-being. The latter is regarded as some function (as yet undefined) of the interplay of domain satisfactions, each weighted according to personal values (which, as we have seen, are themselves a complex product of both endogenous and exogenous factors). This interplay, as Knox (1976b) observes, may be subject to some form of cognitive dissonance whereby a person may

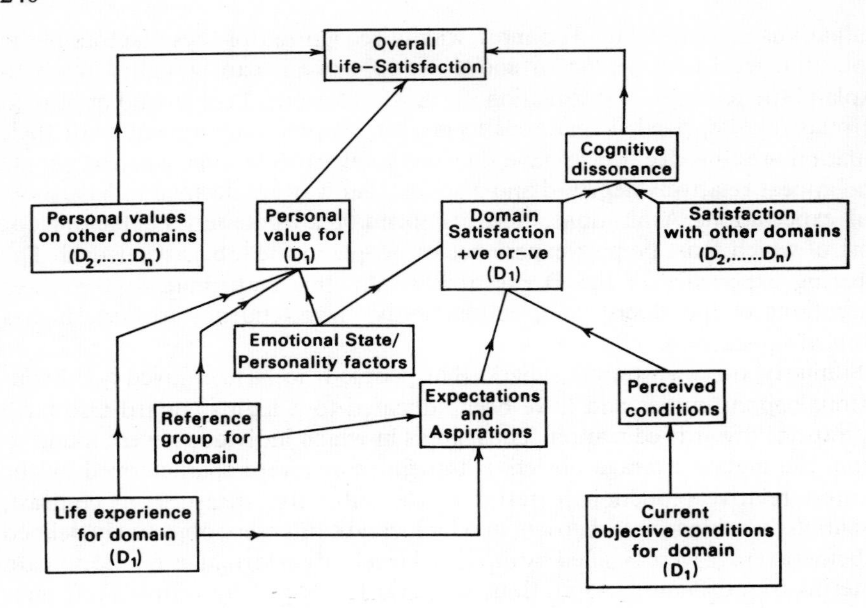

FIGURE 5.7. A model of perceived well-being

have fairly negative feelings about several particular aspects of life while feeling quite positive about their life in general, or vice versa. This kind of dissonance is a relatively common phenomenon, best known to geographers in people's ambiguous evaluations of the attractiveness of different places.

VALUES, PERCEPTIONS, AND SOCIAL WELL-BEING

The feeling of overall satisfaction is only one facet of individual well-being; the other major facet consists of a person's objective circumstances (weighted or unweighted). In any social context both must ultimately be subject to a final calibration by the consensus of various political and scientific perspectives which may decree, for example, that the satisfactions derived from cigarette smoking should be discounted because it is hazardous; that the value placed by some on pornography should be denied because it is offensive; or that the utility derived from land ownership should be negated because it is politically unacceptable.

In many ways, therefore, we do not appear to have advanced very far by introducing values and perceptions to the description of social conditions. We can, as yet, only guess at the mechanisms involved in some of the psychological processes; and in order to articulate those about which we are reasonably confident we need more data—on people's personal history, on their personality, on their expectations, and (not least) on their perceptions and valuations of subcomponents of the major domains of life. Even then, we can only give a qualified answer to the simple question of whether one person, social group, or neighbourhood is better off than another. Moreover, in view of the positive correlations we have found between objectively measured circumstances and both values and perceptions of most life-domains, we are forced to conclude that, for the purposes of generally describing or evaluating *ecological* disparities in well-being, conventional 'hard' data are as good a surrogate as any. Having said this, however, it is plain that even a crude consideration of values and perceptions can considerably enhance our appreciation of the nature and extent of these disparities. In Dundee, we find that accommodating people's values in our assessments of well-being generally serves to accentuate the relative deprivation of certain inner-city districts and public housing areas in relation to the owner-occupied suburbs; that people's attitudes towards employment varies significantly from one type of neighbourhood to another, irrespective of the prevailing material circumstances; and that accommodating people's perceptions of life in our assessments of well-being brings about an upward revision of the welfare of neighbourhoods with an aging population structure. Interpreting findings such as these prompts fundamental questions about the nature of social well-being itself and, ultimately, of distributive justice. It is therefore our contention that the values and perceptions of people whose welfare is under consideration—as well as those of the investigators—should be more generally investigated and acknowledged. One fundamental issue is represented by the simple case of people who are more satisfied than they might be if they were more fully aware of their relative position in objective terms. The problem for social scientists, planners, and policy-makers in these circumstances is whether it is a more legitimate policy objective (1) to make such people aware of their deprivation or raise their expectations and aspirations, thus making them less satisfied (and perhaps more 'revolutionary'), or (2) to focus on the amelioration of the worst (objective) conditions, thus maintaining the false consciousness of those who are ignorant but happy. Notwithstanding such ethical problems, it is our belief that simple measures of values and perceptions of the sort described in this paper can be of practical use in public policy making. To take a simple example, the results presented here suggest that any social action to be taken in favour of neighbourhoods containing large enclaves of elderly people would achieve the greatest sense of improvement if directed towards health services and accessibility to local amenities. Such an approach is by no means proposed as the basis for decision making—nor can it be regarded as being of equal importance to the conventional criteria of efficiency, safety, and 'common good'. But it would certainly help to increase the sensitivity of local government policies, and, at a time when the budgets of many cities are being severely restricted, it may seem increasingly expedient to allocate resources in this way.

APPENDIX: OBJECTIVE INDICATORS OF WELL-BEING FOR EACH LIFE-DOMAIN

Health	Disabling illness in past 6 months Visits to general practitioner due to illness

	in past 6 months
Housing	Owner occupation
	Rateable value
	Exclusive use of garden
	Shared dwelling
	Fixed bath or shower
	Electricity points in main/living room
	Outstanding repairs/modernization
	Outstanding redecoration
Employment	Fluctuating weekly income
	Shift work
	Annual increments in career structure
	Unemployed/redundant in past 12 months
Education	Terminal age of formal education
	Possession of any leaving certificates
	Participation (ever) in evening classes
	Terminal age of eldest child's education
Security	Victim of crime in past 12 months
	Possessions insured against fire and theft
	Occupational pension on retirement
Consumption/ Finance	Television
	Refrigerator
	Washing machine
	Car
Leisure	Length of paid holidays
	Average length of working week
	Obliged to work overtime regularly
	Facilities for sport, culture, and entertainment
Participation	Member of a political party
	Attendance at parent–teacher meetings
	Member of active group or tenants' association
	Canvassed (ever) at elections
	Met (ever) local councillor
Access	Travel time to: central business district
	doctor/clinic
	public telephone
	public park
	bus stop for civic centre
	convenience shops
Environmental Quality	Presence of: litter
	vacant housing
	traffic
	industrial land use
	upkeep of gardens
Stability	Neighbours (same, close/within three doors) moved in past 12 months
	Neighbours close friends
	Single-person household
	Single-parent family
	Length of present employment

A full listing of the questionnaire is given by MacLaran (1977).

TABLE 5.11. Objective conditions: domain and level-of-living scores, by neighbourhood type

Neighbourhood type	Domain											
	Health	Housing	Employment	Education	Security	Consumption/finance	Leisure	Participation	Access	Environment	Stability	Level of living
1	69	56	68	50	69	67	62	25	87	46	62	60
2	66	42	72	29	66	51	71	20	76	47	47	54
3	57	61	59	23	57	50	56	18	81	34	57	49
4	62	62	68	33	71	66	57	24	68	70	77	60
5	59	69	61	30	72	75	51	27	60	77	69	59
6	62	65	74	37	82	74	62	26	65	83	80	65
7	69	87	83	63	86	89	56	33	63	82	78	72
8	77	96	83	75	90	92	38	35	45	94	70	73
9	60	71	55	16	61	70	40	25	42	71	51	52
10	65	71	53	17	66	79	38	25	52	61	70	55
11	56	68	49	16	50	69	44	23	54	54	56	49
12	66	65	58	23	74	79	34	27	56	77	69	58
13	69	71	51	26	71	75	39	22	45	73	58	55
14	60	59	68	26	71	69	66	19	63	73	78	60

REFERENCES

Abrams, M. (1972). Social indicators and social equity. *New Society*, **22**, 454–455.
Abrams, M. (1973). Subjective social indicators. *Social Trends*, **4**, 35–50.
Abrams, M. (1976). *A Review of Subjective Social Indicators Research*. Occasional Paper No. 8 SSRC Survey Unit, London.
Allardt, E. (1973). *About Dimensions of Welfare*. Research Report No. 1, Research Group for Comparative Sociology, University of Helsinki.
Allport, G. W., Vernon, P. E., and Lindzey, G. (1970). *Study of Values: A Scale for Measuring the Dominant Interests in Personality*, Houghton Mifflin, Boston.
Andrews, F. M. (1974). Social indicators of perceived life quality. *Social Indicators Research*, **1**, 279–299.
Andrews, F. M., and Withey, S. B. (1974). Developing measures of perceived life quality. *Social Indicators Research*, **1**, 1–26.
Angrist, S. S. (1974). Dimensions of well-being in public housing families. *Environment and Behaviour*, **6**, 495–516.
Arrow, K. J. (1951). *Social Choice and Individual Values*, Wiley, New York.
Baldwin, J., and Bottoms, A. E. (1976). *The Urban Criminal: A Study in Sheffield*, Tavistock, London.
Banfield, E. C. (1970). *The Unheavenly City*, Little, Brown, Boston.
Banfield, E. C. (1974). *The Unheavenly City Revisited*, Little, Brown, Boston.
Batley, R. (1972). An explanation of non-participation in planning. *Policy and Politics*, **1**, 95–114.
Bernstein, G. (1959). A public language: some sociological implications of a linguistic form. *British Journal of Sociology*, **10**, 311–326.
Biderman, A. D. (1966). Social indicators and goals. In R. Bauer (Ed.), *Social Indicators*, The M. I. T. Press, Cambridge, Massachusetts. pp. 68–153.
Blake, J. F., Weigl, K., and Perloff, R. (1975). Perceptions of the ideal community. *Journal of Applied Psychology*, **60**, 612–615.
Bradburn, N. (1969). *The Structure of Psychological Well-Being*, Aldine, Chicago.
Bradburn, N., and Caplovitz, D. (1965). *Reports on Happiness*, Aldine, Chicago.
Bryant, B. (1975). Citizen–official perceptions of metropolitan problems: a four-city study: In T. L. Wells (Ed.), *Urban Problems in a Metropolitan Setting*, Old Dominion University, Norfolk, Virginia. pp. 5–24.
Buttimer, A. (1974). *Values in Geography*. Resource Paper No. 24, Association of American Geographers.
Campbell, A. (1972). Aspiration, satisfaction and fulfillment. In A. Campbell and P. Converse (Eds.), *The Human Meaning of Social Change*, Russell Sage, New York. pp. 441–466.
Campbell, A., and Converse, P. (1972). *The Human Meaning of Social Change*, Russell Sage, New York.
Campbell, A., Converse, P., and Rodgers, W. L. (1976). *The Quality of American Life: Perceptions, Evaluations and Satisfactions*, Russell Sage, New York.
Cantril, H. (1965). *The Patterns of Human Concerns*, Rutgers University Press, New Brunswick.
Cantril, A. H., and Roll, C. W. (1971). *The Hopes and Fears of the American People*, Universe, New York.
Cliff, A. D., and Ord, J. K. (1973). *Spatial Autocorrelation*, Pion, London.
Coates, B. E., Johnston, R. J., and Knox, P. L. (1977). *Geography and Inequality*, Oxford University Press, Oxford.
Coventry–Solihull–Warwickshire Study Team (1971). Sub-regional Study: *Evaluation*. Supplementary Report, Conventry City Council, Conventry.
Dalkey, N., Rourke, D., Lewis, R., and Snyder, D. (1972). *Studies in the Quality of Life, Delphi and Decision-Making*, Lexington Books, Farnborough.

Davidson, C., and Gaitz, C. N. (1974). Are the poor different? A comparison of work behaviour and attitudes among the urban poor and non-poor. *Social Problems*, **22**, 229–245.

Davies, B. (1976). Territorial injustice. *New Society*, **36**, 352–354.

Davies, J. G. (1972). *The Evangelistic Bureaucrat*, Tavistock, London.

Donnison, D. (1972). Ideologies and policies. *Journal of Social Policy*, **1**, 97–117.

Douglas, J. W. B. (1964). *The Home and the School*, McGibbon, St. Albans.

Eagland, R. M. (1973). Evaluation and Practice. In PRTC Seminar Proceedings, *Urban and Regional Models*, Planning and Transport Research and Computation, London.

Everitt, B. (1974). *Cluster Analysis*. SSRC Reviews of Current Research No. 11, Heinemann, London.

Eyles, J. (1973). Spatial opportunity and the concept of reference group. *Professional Geographer*, **25**, 121–123.

Eyles, J. (1976). *Environmental Satisfaction and London's Docklands: Problems and Policies in the Isle of Dogs*. Occasional Paper No. 3, Department of Geography, Queen Mary College, University of London.

Fischer, C. S. (1975). The effects of urban life on traditional values, *Social Forces*, **53**, 420–432.

Foote, N. N., Abu-Lughod, J., Foley, M. M., and Winnick, L. (1960). *Housing Choices and Constraints*, McGraw-Hill, New York.

Fowler, F. (1974). *Citizen Attitudes towards Local Government Services and Taxes*, Ballinger, Cambridge.

Gans, H. J. (1968). *People and Plans*, Basic Books, New York.

Gans, H. J. (1969). Planning for people, not buildings. *Environment and Planning*, **1**, 33–46.

Goodman, R. (1972). *After the Planners*, Penguin, Harmondsworth.

Hall, J. F., and Perry, N. (1974). *Aspects of Leisure in Two Industrial Cities*. Occasional Papers in Survey Research No. 5, S.S.R.C. Survey Unit, London.

Hall, J. F., and Ring, A. J. (1974). *Indicators of Environmental Quality and Life-satisfaction: A Subjective Approach*. Mimeo, S.S.R.C. Survey Unit, London.

Hall, P. (1972). *Forecasting the Quality of Life in Europe*. Geographical Papers No. 20, Department of Geography, University of Reading.

Harvey, D. W. (1973). *Social Justice and the City*, Arnold, London.

Headey, B. W. (1972). *Indicators of Housing Satisfaction: A Castlemilk Pilot Study*. Occasional Paper No. 10, Survey Research Centre, University of Strathclyde, Glasgow.

Heclo, H. (1969). The councillor's job. *Public Administration*, **47**, 185–202.

Herbert, D. T., and Evans, D. J. (1974). Urban sub-areas as sampling frameworks for social surveys. *Town Planning Review*, **45**, 171–188.

Hoinville, G. (1971). Evaluating community preferences. *Environment and Planning*, **3**, 33–50.

Hoivik, T. (1973). Norvège 1990. *Analyse et Prèvision, ètudes Futuribles*, O. E. C. D., Paris.

Holtermann, S. (1975). Areas of urban deprivation in Great Britain: an analysis of 1971 Census data. *Social Trends*, **6**, 33–47.

Institute for Environmental Studies (1974). *Public Services, Programs and Policy in Four North Western Wisconsin Counties*, University of Wisconsin, Madison.

Johnston, R. J. (1974). Local effects in voting at a local election. *Annals, Association of American Geographers*, **64**, 418–429.

Johnston, R. J. (1976). Areal studies, ecological studies, and social patterns in cities. *Transactions, Institute of British Geographers*, New Series, **1**, 118–122.

Kilpatrick, F., and Cantril, H. (1960). Self-anchoring scaling: a measure of individuals' unique reality worlds. *Journal of Individual Psychology*, **16**, 236–247.

King, L. J. (1969). *Statistical Analysis in Geography*, Prentice-Hall, Englewood Cliffs, New Jersey.

King, L. J. (1976). Alternatives to a positive economic geography. *Annals, Association of American Geographers*, **66**, 293–308.

Kluckhohn, F. R., and Strodtbeck, F. L. (1961). *Variations in Value Orientation*, Row, Peterson, Evanston, Illinois.

Knox, P. L. (1974). Spatial variations in level of living in England and Wales in 1961. *Transactions, Institute of British Geographers*, **62**, 1–24.

Knox, P. L. (1975). *Social Well-Being: A Spatial Perspective*, Oxford University Press, Oxford.

Knox, P. L. (1976a). *Social Priorities for Social Indicators*, Occasional Paper No. 4, Department of Geography, University of Dundee.

Knox, P. L. (1976b). Social well–being and North Sea oil: an application of subjective social indicators. *Regional Studies*, **10**, 423–432.

Lewis, O. (1959). *Five Families: Mexican Case Studies in the Culture of Poverty*, Random House, New York.

Lewis, O. (1966). The culture of poverty. *Scientific American*, **215**, 19–25.

Lichfield, N., Kettle, P., and Whitbread, M. (1975). *Evaluation in the Planning Process*, Pergamon Press, Oxford.

Lovrich, N. P. (1974). Differing priorities in an urban electorate: service preferences among Anglo, Black and Mexican American voters. *Social Sciences Quarterly*, **4**, 704–717.

McKennell, A. (1971). *Monitoring the Quality of American Life—Commentary*. Unpublished paper prepared for the SSRC Survey Unit, London.

MacLaran, A. C. (1977). *Spatial Variations in Levels of Living in Dundee*. Unpublished Ph.D. thesis, University of Dundee.

Maslow, A. H. (1970). *Motivation and Personality*, 2nd ed. Harper and Row, New York.

Minas, J. S., and Ackoff, R. L. (1964). Individual and collective value judgements. In M. W. Shelley and C. L. Bryan (Eds.), *Human Judgements and Optimality*, Wiley, New York. pp. 351–359.

Mishan, E. J. (1967). *The Costs of Economic Growth*, Penguin, Harmondsworth.

Morris, C. W. (1956). *Varieties of Human Values*, University of Chicago Press, Chicago.

Murray, J. R. (1974). *Causes of Satisfaction*. Working paper, National Opinion Research Center, University of Chicago, Chicago.

Nath, S. K. (1969). *A Reappraisal of Welfare Economics*, Routledge and Kegan Paul, London.

Newton, K. (1976). *Second City Politics: Democratic Processes and Decision-making in Birmingham*, Clarendon Press, Oxford.

Palm, R. (1973). Factorial ecology and the community of outlook. *Annals, Association of American Geographers*, **63**, 341–346.

Powell, A. C. (1973). Methodology in the strategy for the North West Region with special reference to evaluation. In PTRC Seminar Proceedings, *Urban and Regional Models*, Planning and Transport Research and Computation. London.

Raban, J. (1974). *Soft City*, Fontana, London.

Rees, P. H. (1970). Concepts of social space: toward an urban social geography. In B. J. L. Berry and F. W. Horton (Eds.), *Geographic Perspectives on Urban Systems*, Prentice-Hall, Englewood Cliffs. pp. 306–394.

Rein, M. (1973). *Values Social Science and Social Policy*. Working paper No. 21, Joint Center for Urban Institute of the Massachussetts Institute of Techonology and Harvard University, Cambridge, Massachusetts.

Robson, B. T. (1969). *Urban Analysis*, Cambridge University Press, Cambridge.

Rokeach, M., and Parker, S. (1970). Values as social indicators of poverty and race relations in America. *Ekistics*, **30**, 207–212.

Rothenberg, J. (1961). *The Measurement of Social Welfare*, Prentice-Hall, Englewood Cliffs, New Jersey.

Self, P. (1976). *Econocrats and the Policy Process: the Politics and Philosophy of Cost-Benefit Analysis*, Macmillan, London.

Smith, D. M. (1973). *The Geography of Social Well-Being in the United States*, McGraw-Hill, New York.

Smith, D. M. (1975). *Crime Rates as Territorial Social Indicators.* Occasional Paper No. 1, Department of Geography, Queen Mary College, University of London.

Smith, D. M. (1977). *Human Geography: A Welfare Approach*, Arnold, London.

Strategic Plan for the North West (1974). *Joint Planning Team Report*, H. M. S. O., London.

Stringer, P., and Taylor, M. (1974). *Attitudes and Information in Public Participation: A Case Study.* Working paper No. 3, Centre for Environmental Studies, London.

Tinbergen, J. (1956). *Economic Policy, Principles and Design*, North-Holland Publishing, Amsterdam.

Tuan, Yi-Fu (1973). Ambiguity in attitudes towards environment. *Annals, Association of American Geography*, **63**, 411–423.

Vickers, G. (1973). Values, norms and policies. *Policy Sciences*, **4**, 103–111.

Wilson, A. B. (1959). Residential segregation of social classes and the aspirations of high school boys. *American Sociological Review*, **24**, 836–845.

Zelinsky, W. (1974). Selfward bound? Personal preference patterns and the changing map of American Society. *Economic Geography*, **50**, 144–179.

Zelinsky, W. (1975). Personality and self-discovery: the future social geography of the United States. In R. Abler *et al.* (Ed.), *Human Geography in a Shrinking World*, Duxbury Press, North Scitvate, Massachusetts.

Chapter 6

Space and Environment in Interpersonal Relations

Henry W. Irving

THE INTERACTIONIST PERSPECTIVE

Very few would maintain that informal social interaction, or interpersonal relations as it is sometimes called, is the most fashionable sector of either sociology or psychology. Yet very few would deny that the field is central to both disciplines. True, some psychologists attempt to perserve the disciplinary purity of their subject by insisting on the individual as the focus of their concern, but no one has ever got very far with the individual in isolation. Sociologists, on the other hand, have usually been drawn towards the more global issues of social inquiry, focusing on structure, class, and institution, but few, if pushed, would deny that social interaction was the basic building-brick of their discipline.

For a variety of reasons, not least of which is the recently accepted legitimacy of foraging into psychology and sociology, the geographer owes some attention to interaction research. At a microlevel, issues such as personal space, the constraints of distance, and individual perceptions of space all tend to converge within the field of social interaction. At a wider scale, and perhaps more mainstream to the traditional concerns of geographers, the notion of social man interacting in, and being influenced by, a social environment has been strongly emphasized by interaction theorists from Mead and Cooley down to the present day. It is at this level, perhaps, that geographers can make their most positive contributions to interaction theory. On top of their long-standing preoccupations with settlement patterns, settlement size, residential morphology, and social segregations can be built the concept of the social environment. It is time that there was some coherent statement of the role of the environment in social interaction, and social geographers seem particularly well equipped to provide it.

There is an almost bewildering variety of approaches to the study of social interaction, and the student is confronted with a confusing array of levels of analysis and research methodologies. The most obvious way of classifying this welter of material is by discipline or profession, for the inspirational background has given rise to different levels of analysis which tend to have become reinforced by lack of interdisciplinary contact and by preoccupation with the clinical or research problems of the several professions. Clinical psychiatry, largely by dint of the efforts of Harry Stack Sullivan in demonstrating the importance of interpersonal relations in diagnosis and correction of mental disorder, has given a strong micromethodology, with an emphasis on dyadic or triadic interactional systems. Experimental psychology has extended the level of analysis to the small group (Heider, 1958; Lewin, 1976) while social psychologists such as Homans (1950, 1961) have studied groups in real-life situations to highlight the patterns of informal social activity. Sociologists interested in communities have stressed the importance of interaction in their social settings, and their perspective is perhaps best summarized in Cooley's 'looking glass self' or Mead's 'generalized other' (Cooley, 1902; Mead, 1934). All these interactionists shared the common conviction that human beings are social in their basic nature and that they have no real existence apart from existence in relation to other human beings. All of them sought to point out the limitations of psychological and sociological analysis from an exclusively individual standpoint. Only their divergent professional interests and different levels of analysis prevented the development of a coherent body of interaction theory.

Yet although such a 'genetic' classification has much merit as a way of presenting the mainstreams of interaction research, it has serious drawbacks, not least of which is the fact that it leads to a recognition of important divergences but not so clearly to any points of convergence. More fundamental is a split of the literature by research methodology, in which those striving for a holistic approach to interpersonal relations stand clearly differentiated from those who favour a strategy of abduction. In a sense, this distinction is one which can be traced throughout the whole history of psychological and sociological thought and involves the divergence of the tradition of Mead, Weber, Durkheim, Parsons, and Nadel, in search of a great system of social explanation, from that of Simmel, Chapple, Arensberg, Kimball, and Collins, a much less well-trodden track and one that has needed great determination to follow it through.

The first tradition argues, in respect of social interaction, that behavioural research is sterile and leads to conclusions which are devoid of meaning. Without consideration of cultural influences, values, sentiments, norms, personality, and a whole host of clearly interrelated social phenomena, social interaction becomes mechanistic and unworthy of explanatory attention. By emphasizing the interrelatedness of things, Weber and his followers were able to make those great generalizations about social influences which have made them masters of their discipline. Notions of class, power, bureaucracy, and religion flowed from their pens as the great social systems were formulated, elaborated, and restated. Indeed, sociology has rested, theoretically, upon this holism, this richness of explanatory thought.

To Georg Simmel, a contemporary of Weber's, such theoretical progress had a will-'-the-wisp quality. True, the systems were elegant, but precisely what was being explained, in a truly scientific sense? Holistic arguments were circular—a defect inherent in the nature of system. As elegant generalizations about great sweeps of human history, sociological thought was making great strides; as a source of hypothesis and methodology for a science of society, it was offering nothing but circularity and confusion, even in the hands of that great empiricist Durkheim. Yet Simmel was not all that successful in providing a satisfactory alternative. He struggled to abstract something that was purely sociological as distinct from cultural or idiosyncratic—'... if society is conceived as interaction among individuals, the description of the forms of this interaction is the task of science of society in its strictest and most essential sense' (Simmel, 1950)—but he could not get away from the basic notion that the individual must be the basic unit of analysis. It was left to Arensberg and Chapple, some decades later, to take the imaginative step of isolating the interaction as the basic unit of analysis.

Following a tradition of empirical research begun in 1929 by Warner in his Yankee City studies (Warner and How, 1947; Warner and Hunt, 1941, 1947; Warner and Srole, 1945), both Arensberg in rural Ireland and Chapple in industrial and institutional contexts in New England gradually forged a set of concepts and associated measuring devices which resulted, in 1940, in Chapple's formulary paper *Measuring Human Relations: An Introduction to the Study of the Interaction of Individuals.* Essentially, the paper describes how they abducted the interaction process, isolating it so that it could be formulated and subsequently measured, with no appeal to the influences or dimensions which might later be used to explain it. This was a deliberate retreat from the holism so fashionable in sociology, and one which brought the pair a certain amount of professional approbrium. First, they eliminated the physiological details which make up the interaction process. This, in sociological eyes, was not too heinous, and it was generally accepted as a legitimate clearing of confusing trivia. More daring was the exclusion of individual personality differences, for it placed their efforts firmly in the face of an academic conviction that there was no social reality outside the individual self. But when they moved to exclude culture from their formulation, they thrust their heads into a professional icebox. How could there be any meaningful social thought which ignored the complex congeries of symbols, values, and sentiments that thread human existence? It is a measure of their conviction that Chapple and Arensberg persevered in the face of such opposition. Their paper, carefully defining the basic units of the interaction process and suggesting methods of measurement, stands as a milestone in the history of social science. Largely ignored by mainstreams of sociological thought, it nevertheless provided inspiration for an ongoing tradition of scientific interactionism which has continued to hold its head high in the empirical panoply of sociology (Chapple, 1939, 1942; Chapple *et al.*, 1963; Collins and Collins, 1973; Gardner, 1945; Goffman, 1959, 1967; Whyte, 1943, 1961). In this tradition, the social geographer has a very important place.

Perhaps because of his early preoccupation with abducting the quantum interaction unit, Chapple became more fascinated with the time dimension than with space. His studies in industry and in hospitals fruitfully employed his new methodologies, but the focus of interest was on the sequencing of events. Important though this is as a dimension of interaction it is not the only one, as Chapple himself frequently pointed out. The directional components of interaction—with whom and where?—are of equal importance, but it is to the 'community' literature that one must look to get inspiration for this. Arensberg (1937) in Ireland, Warner (Warner and How, 1947; Warner and Hunt, 1941, 1947; Warner and Srole, 1945) in his Yankee City, and Lundberg in his Vermont village (Lundberg and Steele, 1938) were more naturally drawn to the spatial dimension of interaction, a dimension which almost inevitably leads away from the basic individual relationship to a consideration of wider patterns. The second section of this monograph, therefore, pays closer attention to those dimensions of social interaction which, by dint of their spatial characteristics and their evident connections with issues of traditional geographic interest, could provide a theoretical and methodological focus for a specifically geographical perspective on informal social interaction.

The process of abduction, considered so vital by Chapple in the identification of a scientific approach to social interaction, cannot remain forever the dominant motif in a field of inquiry. Chapple himself, while stressing the necessity for it, constantly avowed the ultimate goal of his field as being explanation. Having successfully isolated various facets and dimensions of interaction, he proceeded, over the space of three decades, to bring back the explanations he had originally sloughed off. In *Culture and Biological Man* (1970) he attempts an overall statement of the influences which underlie non-random variations in interaction patterns. He carefully examines the physiological background to the process—the needs for interaction and the capabilities for interaction which are rooted in man's physiological makeup—and then proceeds to indicate generalized sources of variance in interaction patterns. His broad notion is that culture shapes human groups so that they learn and practice common patterns which infinitely vary the interaction constellations that spring from mere biology. More specifically, this shaping is profitably viewed in three 'culture dimensions': space, time, and those sets of communication symbols normally regarded as the core of culture. These dimensions, in Chapple's (1970, p. 19) opinion, 'provide a means of estimating the probabilities that specific cultural settings or elements will modify or constrain the interaction'.

Chapple's own work, as previously stated, has been most copiously pitched at elucidating the time dimension. The sequencing of interactions, consequent upon structural development in society such as the division of labour and the emergence of hierarchies, has led him to develop an increasingly sophisticated set of temporal measuring devices and indices (Chapple, 1939, 1942, 1960; Chapple *et al.*, 1963). The value of this work in leading to an understanding of work-group function and dysfunction has been enormous. The symbolic dimension—the one that lies at the heart of those learned constellations of thought and behaviour commonly regarded as culture—has been less easily isolated, though Chapple makes a brave and persuasive attempt to draw together much anthropological work on rites and rituals and to tease out the interactional implications of much human activity which had previously been regarded as strictly in the realm of the mind (Chapple, 1970, chaps. 14 to 16).

It is the spatial dimension, however, which inevitably commands the attention of the social geographer. Drawing on a welter of literature of different disciplinary persuasions, Chapple carefully charts the ways in which distance, space, and position have acted as constrainers, promoters, or modifiers of interaction patterns. Essentially, interaction is viewed here as a system of control in achieving the balance between the conflicting biological requirements of avoidance and contact. The need for contact stems both from the physiological necessity for reticular arousal to facilitate the easy functioning of the biological rhythms and also from a psychological requirement for an autonomic emotional condition (Chapple, 1970, chap. 9). The need for avoidance arises when there is 'overload' in the provision of these stimuli. The interactional situation which develops in both animals and man, to strike this crucial balance, becomes institutionalized as the cultural dimension of space, a chosen set of spacing and positional arrangements which in turn serves as a constraint and influence on the subsequent interaction patterns of a particular community. In short, the need to traverse distance in the interaction process and the institutional arrangements consequent upon this need serve as a powerful conditioning force in any understanding of interaction patterns. Variations in spacing arrangements can therefore, be seen as one major influence underlying variation of interaction patterns. This relative causal role of space is one of the issues to which the third section of this monograph addresses itself.

The world 'community' is a badly bruised one. Generations of will-o'-the-wisp social theorists have sought to define it, identify it, restore it, or revile it. It has spawned semi-autonomous subdisciplines and has given rise to an almost nauseous plethora of definitional literature. It has been sought convincingly in the past, identified haltingly in the present, and promised hopefully for the future. It has flitted confusingly from the rural idyll to the urban slum, from totalitarian construct to ephemeral quest for 'alternative culture'. Yet its meaning remains elusive. It has meant all things to all men. The social geographer with the interactionist perspective stands uniquely poised to give some flesh to the gossamer bones of the community concept. Armed with a directed focus of interest—a concern to investigate the spatial dimensions and environmental correlates of social interaction—he can give descriptive and explanatory substance to the concept of community which will not only provide a provoking focus for his discipline but will also plug a nasty gap in the side of social thought. The fourth and final section of this monograph, therefore, attempts to indicate, by way of conclusion, how the social geographer can play an important role in placing the findings of much interaction research in a real-world context, thereby drawing together some strands of social thinking which have hitherto been irritatingly divergent.

THE DIMENSIONS OF SOCIAL INTERACTION

The social geographer is drawn inevitably to the directional components of an interaction or an interaction pattern. With whom? What sort of person? Where do they live? Where does the interaction take place? These are the obvious foci of interest, and the bulk of this section will be devoted to a more detailed discussion of these questions and a review of attempts to adequately answer them. Yet it is important, before doing this, to take some cognizance of the non-directional components of interaction, so as to avoid destructive insularity and compartmentalized thought. As previously mentioned, much of the research groundwork in the field involved the abduction, description, and measurement of the interaction process itself (Chapple, 1942; Collins and Collins, 1973) and this led inevitably to an interest in the temporal and sequential characteristics of individual interactions. The importance of this orientation is clear. Considerations of initiative, dominance, role, and status can be built upon such studies, and their contribution to the development of therapeutic ideas, whether in a psychiatric or more generally social context, must be fully recognized. To the researcher interested primarily in the directional characteristics of interaction patterns, however, such a research tack seems to lead in a wrong direction. Sequential characteristics are small scale and individual in emphasis. The directional interest pulls away towards a larger scale and a greater possibility of generalization. Consequently, little attention will be paid in this monograph to those dimensions of social interaction.

Non-directional underpinnings

1. *Intensity*

Not all non-directional components of interaction can be so readily isolated from the major concerns of the social geographer. In order that investigations should not be concerned with trivia, some considerable attention must be given to the notion of intensity. To measure and explain a pattern consisting of meaningless and marginal social relationships would be a fruitless exercise, and common sense dictates that, right from the start, any directional approach be tempered and complemented by some recognition of the varying value and meaning of interactions. Problems arise, of course, when this value and meaning have to be quantified. It must be recognized that an old and lonely lady whose social ambience is extremely limited will attach considerably more meaning to 5 minutes' morning chat with the postman than will the social lion with his eternal round of meetings, dinners, and convivial drinks in the tavern. Yet without the use of complex attitude measuring devices, such distinctions are notoriously intractable. We are forced to look to the more purely behavioural manifestations of intensity to construct our measures. The durability of a friendship is easily quantified. Frequency and duration are readily scaleable, and several pieces of research have successfully combined these scales into a matrix of intensity, on which any one interaction can be located and allocated a score (Irving, 1975; Irving and Davidson, 1973). The multidimensionality of a concept such as intensity makes it arguable whether such a scaling device is wholly adequate, but it is workable and has been shown to exhibit interesting distributions (Irving, 1971).

2. *Indices of intensity*

While it is relatively simple, if rather arbitrary, to score a dyadic interaction pattern with such scaling devices, the construction of an index of intensity that adequately mirrors the total interaction scenario of an individual is a much more formidable task. Caplow uses a straightforward mean 'intensity of neighbouring' score, in which the sum of the scale values of a family's relationships is simply divided by the number of relationships reported (Caplow, Stryker, and Wallace, 1964). This is easy to calculate and has the merit of indicating the average intensity of the sort of social relationships in which each respondent indulges, but it fails to distinguish between semi-recluses and social lions, a distinction which the investigation of intensity must surely be aimed at revealing. Irving goes to the opposite extreme in the search for a meaningful index (Irving, 1971; Irving and Davidson, 1973). An intensity score is given to a respondent simply on the basis of adding together the scale values for all the reported interactions. This does serve to distinguish recluses from lions, but it fails to make any distinction between those people who report one or two intense relationships from those who report many less-intense ones.

One solution to this problem has been the use of a measure of 'spread', to stand as an adjunct index to the measure of overall intensity (Irving, 1977). Essentially, this index reflects the amount of interaction intensity that is heaped upon the main interactor and, as such, is an interesting indicator of how many eggs are placed in any particular social basket. The fact that this seems to tie in with other indices of interaction in a common-sense fashion is an encouraging pointer to the value of such an index, which bridges the gap between non-directional components of interaction, such as intensity, and directional components of a type that will be presently discussed.

Another way in which the essentially aspatial intensity dimension has been profitably given directional characteristics can be found in the notion of kin orientation. The critical, if vexing, problem of how the kinship interaction network interdigitates with the non-kin network was highlighted by Irving (1975), but in a way which merely pointed towards the importance of the consideration rather than providing a satisfactory way of sorting it out. If one is trying to derive any interaction index for a given respondent, one is always faced with the problem of whether to concentrate separately on kin/non-kin relationships or whether to include kin and non-kin in an overall picture. There is no doubt that social relationships with kinsfolk often are of a very different type to those conducted with friends (Adams, 1967). These differences can be of depth, quality, intensity, frequency, duration, and durability. To concentrate on each system separately is to ignore the interesting interdigitation suggested above; to lump them together in a catch-all index is to ignore the striking contrasts which sometimes exist between them. The kin-orientation index (Irving, 1977) uses the notion of intensity to provide a set of analytical categories which can be used to circumvent this problem. In the same way as the index of 'spread' reflects the amount of intensity heaped upon the main interactor, so the index of 'kin orientation' reflects the proportion of the intensity loaded on to kinsfolk. By examining the relationships between this index and other interaction indices, one can gain some enlightening insights into the position of kin in different social situations.

3. *Interaction type*

There are certain limitations to the concept of intensity which has been presented here. As previously stated, it is a composite scale, derived from two subdimensions—frequency and duration. To concentrate entirely on the composite is to ignore the value of the constituents. Frequency and duration are important dimensions of interaction in their own right, and a scale which buries the relationships between them must necessarily be complemented by some separate analysis which gives them recognition. Most studies have supported the common-sense relationship on which the composite intensity scale is predicated—that as frequency increases, so duration tends to decrease (Caplow, Stryker, and Wallace, 1964; Deutschberger, 1946)—but the notion of 'interaction type' (Irving, 1975) suggests that no simple linear relationship exists. Rather, an interaction can be categorized, on the basis of its frequency and duration characteristics, as one of four types (Table 6.1).

Comparative study in rural and urban contexts showed striking differences in the frequency distributions of these 'interaction types' (Irving, 1975). The long and infrequent type, significantly represented in rural Dorset (13 per cent.), conspicuously absent in urban Hull, where it accounted for only 2 per cent. of the reported relationships. It is understandable that a relatively remote and thinly populated area like central Dorset, where a high proportion of the residents are retired, wealthy, well-travelled and relatively mobile, should show more of this kind of extended visiting than an urban area, but the scale of differ-

TABLE 6.1. Interaction types

Type	Durational characteristics	Frequency characteristics
1. Low intensity type	Half a day or less	Less frequently than once a week
2. Long, infrequent type	Whole day or more	Less frequently than once a week
3. Middle range type	One hour or more	Once or twice a week
4. Short, frequent type	Half a day or less	More frequently than twice a week

ence is surprising. Earlier speculation (Irving and Davidson, 1973) that protracted, rare interactions are typically middle class needs some modification. Indeed, the frequencies for each of the surveyed social areas of Hull (Figure 6.1) show that the area highest up the social scale, Kirkella, reported less of this type than any of the others. Evidently, population density and rural social norms must be considered in addition to social class. The differences in distribution of these interaction types, interesting enough between different urban areas, might prove to be critical in distinguishing the interaction patterns of town and country.

In common with other indicators of social interaction, 'interaction type' is more easily applied to a single dyadic interaction than used to characterize a person's total interaction pattern. The complete constellation of important interactions central to an individual's social life clearly contains, in many instances, relationships of different 'types'. Kinsfolk living at some remove may encourage a series of infrequent but long-duration contacts, whereas the same respondent may live in a socially cohesive, high-density area conducive

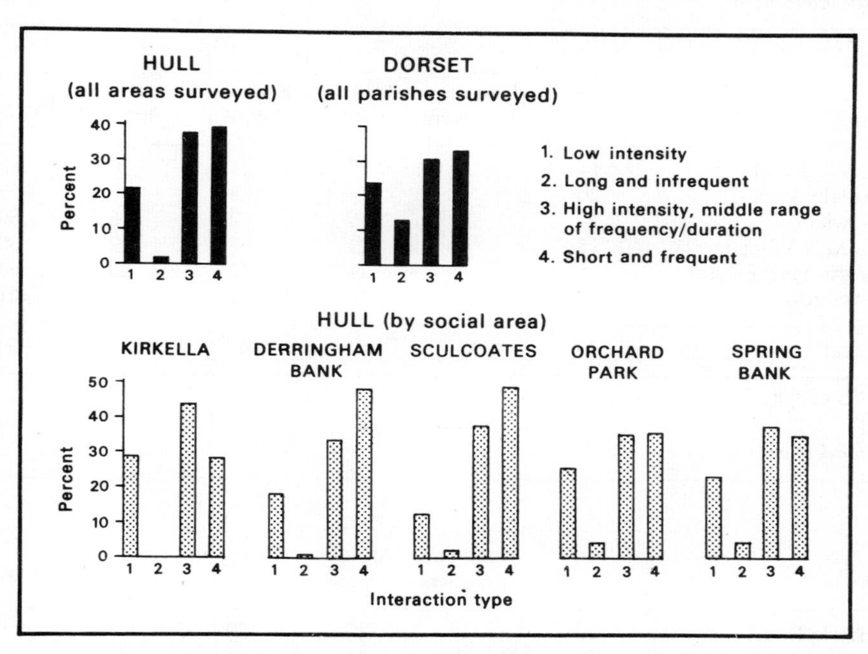

FIGURE 6.1. Frequency distributions of interaction types in survey areas

Social area types

Kirkella	A middle-class, outer suburban area
Derringham Bank	A lower middle-class area of small semi-detached and terraced housing
Sculcoates	A working-class area of old by-law housing
Orchard Park	A new council estate on the city fringe
Spring Bank	An inner-city area on the C.B.D. fringe, with much subdividing and flatting

to frequent, short, 'doorstep' contacts. Yet there is some value to be derived from characterizing, if only in a crude modal sense, the typical interaction situations of an individual. A second Hull survey did indeed reveal some interesting distributions when such an index was essayed (Table 6.2). The Avenues, an inner-city Victorian–Edwardian high-class residential area with some 'transitional' elements, but with mainly professional and managerial inhabitants, illustrated exactly the mixed situation hypothesized above. An 'interaction-type' index for kin relationships showed an overrepresentation in the 'long and infrequent' category, a situation to be expected of a residentially mobile middle-class population; a similar index for non-kin relationships, on the other hand, showed a contrasting emphasis on the 'short and frequent' category, reflecting not perhaps a situation of doorstep gossip but rather a strong middle-class neighbourhood ethic which has not been much emphasized in traditional English urban sociology literature but which might be sought in any such

TABLE 6.2. Distribution of 'interaction-type' indices for survey areas

Kin interaction

	Type					
Area	Low intensity	Long and infrequent	Middle range	Short and frequent	Bimodal	Total
Hessle Road	14	3	8	*15*	20	60
Anlaby Park	20	9	14	4	6	53
Newland	17	6	19	2	16	60
Garden Village	15	4	21	8	12	60
North Hull Estate	15	3	11	11	20	60
Avenues	19	*19*	10	5	8	61
Total	100	44	83	45	82	354

$\chi^2 = 64.7$, d.f. $= 20$, $p < 0.0001$

Non-kin interaction

	Type					
Area	Low intensity	Long and infrequent	Middle range	Short and frequent	Bimodal	Total
Hessle Road	20	0	12	20	7	59
Anlaby Park	19	3	11	8	12	53
Newland	28	2	10	2	9	60
Garden Village	15	1	11	18	15	60
North Hull Estate	16	1	10	17	16	60
Avenues	14	6	11	23	7	61
Total	112	13	74	88	66	353

$\chi^2 = 49.8$, d.f. $= 20$, $p < 0.001$

For details of the social characteristics of the survey areas see Irving. (1977).

high-density urban area that is popular as a modish retreat for outgoing professional classes. The Hessle Road area, a stable working-class neighbourhood with strong associations with the fishing industry, shows an emphasis on the short and frequent categories for both indices, reflecting, perhaps, a working-class situation associated with the Bethnal Green stereotype, with kin and friends tightly enmeshed in an extremely localized social network (Irving, 1977).

Directional components of interaction

Considerable attention has been paid, in the foregoing paragraphs, to dimensions of social interaction which are essentially aspatial. The notion of intensity is clearly important, not only as an indicator of the significance of a reported social relationship but also because it interdigitates on so many fronts with more obviously spatial dimensions. Several indices have been described, some of which are designed to measure intensity in a variety of ways and others to strengthen certain directional components of interaction. We may now, perhaps, return to a consideration of these directional components. 'With whom?' and 'With what sort of person?' are directional questions which need not necessarily have the spatial interest long associated with the core of geography. This need not worry us unduly, for, as will be shown later, the isolation of a spatial ingredient can be a sterile exercise if untempered with other, more purely social, considerations. The most obvious spatial questions are 'Where do they live?' and 'Where do the interactions take place?', and these are indeed the questions which have been given most research attention. It does not need a great deal of graphical imagination, however, to build upon these simple questions and to envisage constellations of social relationships which have strong spatial characteristics.

1. *The single relationship*

Perhaps the clearest way to review the directional dimensions of interaction is once again to build outwards from the single dyadic pattern, through the summary indices for the social field of an individual, towards broad measures for whole social groups. This is not the place to review the operational value of sociometric questions—the basic, all-important means of identifying the principal interactors in a respondent's social field. From Moreno (1934) with his captive group, and Festinger, Schacter, and Back (1950) with their homogeneous sample, through to Caplow, Stryker, and Wallace (1964) with their motley one and Lundberg with his total coverage, the interactionist research tradition has spawned a host of measuring devices of varying and controversial merit. In some cases, the respondent has been asked to identify the field (Deutschberger, 1946; Irving, 1971); in others, a field has been predesignated and the respondent asked to place the inhabitants on one or another scales of social interaction (Caplow and Forman, 1950; Smith, Form, and Stone, 1954; Wallin, 1953). Questions of friendship, feeling, and intensity have been weighted against more purely behaviourist considerations in formulating the questions, with the result that different facets of social interaction have been pinpointed in the various pieces of research. What is important, from the point of view of underpinning a discussion of the directional components of interaction, is that all these devices have been concerned with the basic question of 'With whom?'.

Only at the smallest scale of research, in experimental group or 'anthropological' situations, have the names of the interactors been of any importance. Of more interest in the quest for explanation of interactional phenomena have been their characteristics, social and residential. Where a single diadic interaction is under scrutiny, these characteristics present on real operational problems. First, it is useful, and very straightforward, to ascertain whether or not the interaction is between kinsfolk. Leaving aside the question of whether kin interactions ought to be viewed in the same manner as others, the issue of ties of blood and duty versus the ties of attraction and mutual interest have attracted a sufficient enough literature to merit the researcher's attention (Adams, 1967). A second obvious feature of interest is the class dimension. The concept of *social distance* has a long pedigree in sociological literature (Gans, 1961; Mowrer, 1958), and the most basic behavioural ingredient of the concept is, of course, the amount of interclass social interaction. Social stratification systems are, of course, almost as numerous as the students who consider them, but it is a relatively simple task to essay a consensual classificatory scheme based on educational, occupational, and income variables. From this, it is relatively easy to work out the extent to which interactions cross class boundaries, and which boundaries are the ones most rarely crossed. Some would have us believe that income convergence is leading to social convergence; others would deny this, emphasizing the normative gap that persists between manual and non-manual workers (Goldthorpe and Lockwood, 1963).

A third directional feature of an individual interaction, and one which immediately commands the attention of the social geographer, is the spatial dimension. Where an interaction takes place and the residential whereabouts of the participants are the social geographer's surrogate for traditional geographical fascinations like journey to work, journey to shop, or journey to crime. Melvin Webber and his followers have suggested that improvements in personal mobility have released modern man from the social constraints of his residential neighbourhood, in the same way that dispersal has characterized modern workplace and shopping-centre locations (Webber, 1963). Others have pointed out that social relations are far less susceptible to such liberation and that the residential neighbourhood continues to provide much raw material for social life, especially to certain less-mobile categories such as children, mothers, the aged, and the infirm (Carey and Mapes, 1972). Whatever the truth of the matter, and there seems little doubt that there are considerable variations between social types, the investigation of the spatial characteristics of interpersonal relations is a necessity if conclusive assertions are to have any validity. There are very few operational problems in finding out the loci of interactions and the locations of the residences of the participants, though it frequently becomes necessary, for purposes of further analysis, to categorize the locations. This often boils down to dichotomizing between 'local' and 'non-local', and clearly different social circumstances are productive of different thresholds. The social horizons of the Chinese peasant do not stretch meaningfully beyond the boundaries of his village (Skinner, 1964, 1965), but Webber's mobile man of the megalopolitan freeways typically seeks his social gratifications without a thought to intervening distance (Webber, 1963). Obviously what is local to one cannot be local to another, so that each definition must be seen in its own context. This becomes more than a mere technical question of frequency distributions when the concept of community is examined from an interactionist standpoint.

2. *Individual interaction patterns*

All these aspects of a diadic social relationship, interesting if unremarkable, gain both added interest and added complexity when the focus of concern shifts to the total interaction patterns of individual respondents. The problems of constructing a meaningful index of kin orientation have been discussed earlier. An index of social distance presents similar problems. Even after the key decision has been made as to what constitutes a bridging of a social gap, there remains the problem, common to all these indices, of making an adequate generalization about the respondent in this respect. One solution is to utilize the intensity dimension in precisely the same way as suggested for 'spread' and 'kin orientation', thereby making the index reflect the proportion of interactive effort that is thrown across the social distance gulf. Another solution follows the one suggested for 'intensity type'—the simple modal index reflecting the dominant interactions in a respondent's constellation.

Various solutions have been offered for the representation of the spatial facets of a respondent's social relationships. Once again, modal or intensity-based solutions can be successfully employed, but the close relationship which interaction localization must inevitably have with the concept of community

TABLE 6.3. A simple index of localization

Category	Definition
Local	More than two named interactors were local: if less than five names, then two local if only one named, then one local
Middle	Two interactors named as local: one if two to four named
Non-local	No named interactors local

Note. The definition of what constitutes a 'local' interaction will vary according to the research context. In the Hull surveys, an interaction was deemed 'local' if the residences were within half a mile of each other.

has led to the construction of an index which gives relatively more weight to those who report more interactions. A simple scale (Table 6.3) has been successfully employed to produce categories of localization which show varied and interesting distributions. Interactions with non-kinsfolk, in the Hull survey previously described, were evenly balanced between the chosen categories, and this balance was evidenced throughout all the survey areas except Hessle Road, the fishing community. Here, as might be expected from its social reputation (Horobin, 1957; Tunstall, 1962), there was a striking overrepresentation in the 'localized' category, with a corresponding shortfall in the non-local. Kinsfolk showed a rather different pattern. Overall, there was far greater clustering in the non-local category, a circumstance that might be expected, for people are always more willing or feel more obliged to overcome distance constraints in the visiting of kin than of mere friends (Table 6.4). The Avenues, a Victorian bourgeois town-house area, was particularly prone to the maldistribution, as

TABLE 6.4. Distribution of localization indices, by survey area

Kin localization

Area	Localization						Total
	Non-local		Middle		Local		
Hessle Road	14	(11.6)	12	(0.0)	34	(30.8)	60
Anlaby Park	43	(5.6)	5	(3.3)	5	(4.0)	53
Newland	40	(1.0)	17	(1.6)	3	(8.2)	60
Garden Village	26	(1.8)	16	(0.9)	18	(1.4)	60
North Hull Estate	31	(0.2)	16	(0.9)	13	(0.0)	60
Avenues	46	(3.8)	8	(1.7)	7	(3.3)	61
Total	200		74		80		354

$\chi^2 = 80.9$, d.f. = 10, $p < 0.0001$

Non-kin localization

Area	Localization						Total
	Non-local		Middle		Local		
Hessle Road	10	(5.7)	10	(2.0)	40	(11.8)	60
Anlaby Park	21	(0.3)	17	(0.7)	15	(1.5)	53
Newland	22	(0.0)	10	(0.0)	28	(0.9)	60
Garden Village	17	(0.7)	15	(0.0)	28	(0.9)	60
North Hull Estate	20	(0.0)	18	(0.3)	22	(0.0)	60
Avenues	27	(1.4)	17	(0.0)	17	(1.9)	61
Total	117		87		130		354

$\chi^2 = 28.6$, d.f. = 10, $p < 0.01$

Chi-square values are given in brackets.

was Newland, a lower middle-class Edwardian terraced suburb with a rather strange tendency towards unfriendliness right across a variety of survey indices. In these two areas, very few kinsfolk lived locally, or at least if they did they were not visited often. Hessle Road once again stands as a superb stereotype in the Hoggart (1957) mould, with kinsfolk clustered together in the tightly packed terraces, testimony to the persisting necessity of consanguineal mutual aid in the deep-sea fishing industry.

An increase of scale in the investigation of interpersonal relations does not simply involve aggregation of the characteristics of single interactions, as in the indices so far discussed. Such an increase, focusing as it does on the increasingly complex phenomenon of the total social life of a respondent or of a group, offers richer insights and a greater variety of dimensions to the investigators. Social network provides a real example (Bott, 1957). There can be no concept of network in a dyadic situation. When three or more people are considered, however, the mutual relations and strands of social contact running among them give important clues as to the cohesiveness of a group or community. Before examining the group implications of the network concept, however, it is useful to consider it as a means of representing the cohesiveness of the social situation of an individual. It is a relatively simple task to ascertain, during the course of collecting basic sociometric information, whether there are any significant links between the interactors named by the respondent. If the respondent reports that his interactors do not know or interact with each other, then he can be said to be at the centre of a loose-knit network (Bott, 1957). If, on the other hand, he reports that they all know one another and meet regularly, then we can legitimately call it a close-knit network. Admittedly, measures based on this simple idea are crude, and they fall short, in conceptual richness, of the full meaning of the network concept, but it has proved to be an interestingly discriminating variable. In a piece of comparative research involving the strikingly contrasted cities of Hull (Yorkshire) and Los Angeles (California), Irving (1977) found an astonishing similarity in the frequency distributions of respondent-based index of network density. Indeed, contrary to what Webb (1963, 1964) would have us believe about the 'non-place' freeway cities modern America, the Los Angeles sample revealed a slightly tighter-knit pat than the Hull sample. Despite the newness of development, the resid mobility, and the general youthfulness of the population, social activity d seem to have been diffused in the way Webber suggested (Table 6.5).

TABLE 6.5. Network densities in Hull and Los Angeles

City	Loose knit	Fairly close	Close	Very
Hull	168	110	57	
Santa Ana	101	128	51	

For a precise definition of network categories, see Irving (1977)

3. *Interaction patterns of groups and milieux*

The social classification of residential milieux has a long history, a history that is intimately bound up with old sociological chestnuts like '*gemeinschaft–gesellschaft*', 'urban–rural continua', and 'community' (Bell and Newby, 1971; Pahl, 1968; Thorns, 1976; Tonnies, 1957). Interactionists have given a considerable amount to these various debates, not only in providing concrete dimensions to an often-irritatingly theoretical wrangle, a contribution which will be examined in more detail in the final section, but also in providing a series of measuring devices which can be fruitfully employed to fix a particular milieu in any social taxonomy. Indeed, some of the earliest work in the great American interactionist tradition was pitched at this level of analysis. Lundberg and Steele (1938), in their study of social attraction patterns in a Vermont village, decided that groups within the village, rather than the village as a whole, were the meaningful units of study, but their indices of 'interaction' and 'cohesion' can equally be utilized at a more all-embracing community level, as evidenced by the work of Danielsson (1950) among geographically separated clusters of Jibaro Indians. Similar indices have been used to assess the social cohesiveness of urban communities. Caplow examines the way in which the 'social ambiences' of individuals interlock in various neighbourhoods of San Juan, Puerto Rico (Caplow, 1955; Caplow, Stryker, and Wallace, 1964). Deutschberger (1946) demonstrates the utility of using mean scores of a variety of respondent-based indices (friendship range, religious and racial diversity index, and location index) to characterize selected census tracts in Pittsburgh and New York. Measures of anomie (Srole, 1956), network density (Barnes, 1954), and role texture (Southall, 1959) can be seen as further attempts to characterize the basic sociology of groups and communities, though, strictly speaking, these are beginning to lead us out of our abducted world of interaction and into the fascinating but convoluted world of values and sentiments.

In attempting to study informal social relations in a real-world context, the researcher is faced immediately with the fundamental problem of group specification. Moreno (1934), Festinger, Schacter, and Back (1950), and Sherif and Sherif (1953) had no problem; their interests lay solely in the relationships which went on within their group, whether it was college dormitory, raduate housing scheme, or summer camp. There can be no frayed edges in s kind of research, and its clarity has attracted many followers. The problem, ever, lies in the extent of generality required. If one's focus of interest is on the group in question, then the method is obviously suitable; when, er, generalizations about propinquity and similarity are the aim of the e such a tight specification runs some risks. It might well happen, for sub that a substantial part of the meaningful social interaction of the situat es place outside the group or community under scrutiny. In the social embrace visaged by Webber (1963), the nearest twenty houses would not ry significant sector of a typical interaction scene. Yet Caplow,

Stryker, and Wallace (1964) have done just this in their investigation of facets of neighbourhood ambiences in Puerto Rico. Admittedly, many of their selected neighbourhoods, or barrios, are in poor tenement sections of the city where one might expect lots of informal neighbour interaction, but to so limit the scope of their work robs it of any kind of real social generality.

One traditional solution to the problem has been the predesignation of in-group and out-group. Lundberg and Steele (1938) based their index of cohesion on the relationship between the social contacts contained within the group and those coming in from outside or leaving the group to go outside. Such an approach lends itself well to community investigation, where a preconceived hypothesis about community strengths and weaknesses can be tested in basic interaction terms, but it does tend to restrict the potential of the work. Should the predesignated group prove to be sociologically meaningless, then much information has been lost. A series of village investigations in rural Dorset and rural Norfolk (Irving, 1974) have indicated that the village in many modern, mobile community or retirement contexts does not serve any meaningful community function at all. Predesignation of 'neighbourhood' in an urban context provides even more problems, for rarely will the investigator be confident that he can establish social neighbourhoods on an *a priori* basis.

Perhaps the best solution is to approach the investigation of interpersonal relations in an open, inductive fashion, at least until a substantial body of research has established a set of reasonable working norms concerning the directional characteristics of interactions. The establishment of thresholds of what constitutes a local interaction, for example, or what on the basis of frequency distributions can be reasonably considered a residentially-rooted social group, is most usefully left until the collected data can be scrutinized. It may often be the case, for example, that such thresholds vary considerably according to settlement size, homogeneity, residential density, mobility, age, and so on. Indeed, as Irving illustrates in the context of urban Hull (Irving, 1978), locational criteria that are on the whole satisfactory for that particular urban environment are inadequate discriminators when one confronts the tightly knit and highly localized interaction scene on the Hessle Road. How much more true is this likely to be when a research programme aims at taking in different settlement sizes, different mobility levels, or even different cultures within its purview? If the notion of community is under scrutiny, at least in its interactional manifestations, then it is clearly a laudable aim to attempt to circumscribe it, to work towards some locational criteria which can be applied, if not universally, then at least within a set of given circumstances. It is, however, equally important that studies should avoid meaningless predesignation, for at the best loss of information is inevitable and at the worst, tautology. The first fault has resulted in many studies of methodological note, but with no substantial social meaning. The second has spawned a whole research field devoted merely to an empty repetition of dubious initial assumptions about the nature of 'community'.

THE CORRELATES OF SOCIAL INTERACTION

Chapple and his followers, in their rigorous pursuit of a pure, abducted, and uncluttered set of interaction variables, did not wholly lose sight of the quest for explanation. Throughout the interactionist literature runs the thread of an interest in variation, and it is the explanation of 'non-random variations' in interaction patterns which is the ultimate goal (Collins and Collins, 1973). Chapple himself (1970) attempts a broad explanatory overview which has been discussed in an earlier section of this article. His threefold division of influences —time, space, and symbolic culture—is a personal one, and one with which many would quarrel, but it does at least serve to highlight, in a way unusual in the interactionist literature, the importance of place and space as powerful conditioning forces in the interaction process. It is important, however, for social geographers to guard against space determinism. In this section of the article attention is first given to space as a conditioning agent, but then, by way of corrective, the focus turns to more traditional concerns of sociological explanation, such as the conditioning role of class, status, personality, and life-cycle variables. Finally an attempt is made to aggregate these rather divergent explanatory standpoints into a gestalt, a viewpoint which recognizes the role of the social environment as a powerful backcloth to interpersonal relations.

Space and distance as conditioning factors

Chapple (1970) makes a succinct summary statement of the importance of distance, space, and position as influences on interaction patterns. The biological need for some avoidance and some contact leads to a situation in which interaction patterns serve as crucial regulating mechanisms between them. Space, therefore, can be viewed as either a constraint or as a commodity. In the former role, distance is seen to impede interaction; in the latter role, space is seen as an essential ingredient of the privacy which humans all need to avert a condition of sensory overload. The resultant interaction patterns, therefore, which become institutionalized in any human group, can be seen to owe something to those opposing requirements.

1. *Proximity and interaction*

Studies of the role of propinquity in stimulating social interaction are legion. Perhaps the clearest and most oft-quoted is that of Festinger, Schacter, and Back (1950), whose work on the friendship choices of the Second World War veteran graduate engineering students at the Massachusetts Institute of Technology highlighted the importance of both physical and functional distance in friendship formation. Admittedly the subjects of investigation were extremely homogeneous; they were all veterans, all married, and all pursuing similar aims at the same institution. Moreover, they were all recent arrivals, a circumstance notoriously conducive to *ad hoc* neighbourhood friendships. As has already been suggested in an earlier section, Festinger focused his attention purely on social relationships within two particular housing projects, Westgate and Westgate West, so that in the event of in-group interaction being an insignificant sector of subjects' total constellations, the researchers would not have known. These being the circumstances, therefore, it is rather surprising that such eminence has been given to Festinger's study. True, the situation was ideal for experimental control of variables, but as a contribution to the debate on the causes of variation in social interaction patterns its lack of generality must surely render it marginal. Festinger, Schacter, and Back (1950, p. 10) conclude:

> The most striking finding was the dependence of friendship formation on the mere physical arrangement of the houses. People who lived close to one another became friendly with each other, while people who lived far apart did not. Mere accidents or where a path went or whose doorway a staircase passed were major determinants of who became friends with this community.

It is not surprising that their work has generated controversy. Where the subjects under scrutiny were relatively homogeneous, the Festinger findings were confirmed (Priest and Sawyer, 1967). Where a more diverse, or 'real-life' situation was studied, there was at best heavily qualified agreement (Kuper, 1953) and at worst refutation. Some critics emphasized that propinquity was only of importance during the settling down of a new and raw community, such as Festinger's housing projects or brand new estates on urban fringes (Simey, 1954); another line of attack came from those who relegated the propinquity effect to the pages of history, to a time when mobility was restricted for all but the wealthiest sectors of society (Glass, 1948; Webber, 1963); yet further criticism came from those who stressed that shared interests and shared norms have always been far more potent factors in friendship formation than mechanistic distance considerations (Gans, 1961, 1967).

This battery of criticism has been only partially just. True, the impression to be gleaned from a study of controlled and homogeneous situations like the M.I.T. housing projects is one which requires so much qualification that the applicability of a great many of their key assertions to real-life interactional situations must be questioned. It is important, however, not to throw out the baby with the bath water. These criticisms, and especially those of Gans, do not do full justice to the persuasive contentions of Homans (1950, 1961), who points out the mutually reinforcing relationship between interaction and norms. Chance encounters, and here space, position, and distance must be accorded some role, do very often lead to interaction, which in turn leads to exchange of views and accommodation of views. Furthermore, it would be wrong to assume, following Webber (1963), that all sections of society were mobile to the extent that their residential environment was of no importance as an interaction 'pool'. Certain categories of person are clearly and often pathetically less mobile than others; children, the mothers of children in families with less than two cars, the aged, and the infirm are all more dependent on local sources of contact and friendship than the typical modern mobile man envisaged by Webber. Nor are these groups a numerically insignificant section of the total population. When to this is added the observation that the working classes, even though often possessed of cars in the more affluent societies, do significantly react to the costs of transport in non-essential pursuits, then it becomes clear that Webber's stereotype has only marginally more generality than Festinger's graduate students.

Perhaps most telling of all, in this argument, is the way in which urban residential situations have become steadily more segregated over the last century. Whether this segregation has been on the basis of class, life-style, family status, race, or age, the resultant tendency has been for cities the world over to become segmented into mosaic-like clusters of quite separate social groups (Johnston, 1971; Timms, 1970). This residential segregation of different social types has tended to render rather academic the argument as to whether propinquity or homogeneity of interest is the most decisive factor influencing social relationships. The two have become mutually reinforcing in a modern urban context. Mann (1955, p.134) succinctly sums up the situation when he says that the urban neighbourhood is

> ... not necessarily a primary group where all the people know all the others, as in the old village community, but rather is an area in which people can expect to find a maximum number of people with whom they would be willing and able to have personal relationships.

Residential proximity, therefore, does not force people to engage in social interaction. Indeed, all of us must be aware of circumstances in which residential proximity to someone held in low esteem has been a source of profound irritation. Yet even in our modern cities, not all of us can move about without constraint in the search for the mundane pleasures of social interaction. Our children will play with the children next door, and this will probably lead to a sharing of problems with our adult neighbours which, in the fashion so perceptively described by Homans, will haltingly but inexorably lead to some accommodation of views and sharing of common interests. Residential segregation in modern urban situations seems, despite occasional utopian planning strategies, to be a feature that is here to stay. The product of this process is a mosaic of clusters of more or less homogeneous social types which must inevitably provide satisfactory pools for informal social contacts. Admittedly, individuals can, should they wish, escape from the cloying pressures of these social clusters. Many will. But for the vast majority of people, neighbourhood interaction will remain an important thread of the complex weft of social fabric.

2. *Proximity, privacy, and personal space*

In this discussion of the constraints of space and proximity on social interaction, Chapple is careful to point out the negative as well as the positive aspects of the problem. Man needs interaction, it is true. As with many things, however, enough is as good as a feast, and there is considerable evidence to suggest that too much can be a bad thing. Interaction patterns will reflect, therefore, not merely the effect of proximity in encouraging interaction, but also the needs of individuals for a certain amount of privacy, a respite from the enervating social whirl which can, as we all know, become too much on occasions. Interaction patterns, then, ideally strike a balance between these conflicting requirements so that an individual finds himself neither deprived nor overloaded.

The need for privacy is part innate and part learned. Animal behaviourists in general and ethologists in particular have given considerable attention to innate personal space requirements (Esser, 1971). Research has shown that overcrowding and high densities lead to psychological disorders and even pathologies. Crowding produces overstimulus, sometimes called sensory overload, which in turn leads to the release of the hormone adrenalin. If prolonged, this excess of adrenalin can have severe physiological and behavioural consequences. Resistance to disease is lowered; reproductive capacity is impaired; growth is inhibited; premature senility is common. Aggression, anomie, promiscuity, and huddling have been reported. Quite clearly, crowding can have serious dilatory effects. It is wrong, however, to draw facile analogies between experimental conditions of overcrowding in rats and the conditions in which human beings typically find themselves. Yet such analogies are commonplace. Ardrey (1966), Morris (1967), and Lorenz (1966) have popularized the innate needs for personal space and territory, often to a banal degree, without due heed to the crucial differences of scale and social arrangement that exist between the two. Galle, Gove, and McPherson (1972) point out the paucity of good research on human crowding, and their study of the relationship between population density and a variety of pathological behaviours in several neighbourhoods of Chicago illustrates the difficulties of making any causal assertions when there is so much intercorrelation between density and 'structural' variables likely to be productive of pathology. Freedman (1975) makes a more positively contradictory assertion. After a thoroughgoing review of all the pertinent literature, he comes to the conclusion that high densities, at least at the level conceivably approachable in any known social context, do not have negative effects on humans. To cram people into cells, as rats are crammed into their experimental cages, may cause similar pathologies. But any known and normal condition of residence, work, or leisure does not seem to produce pathological response. Even in extreme experimental conditions, research seems to indicate that crowding simply intensifies feelings that are already there (Freedman, 1975, p. 105):

> High density makes other people a more important stimulus and thereby intensifies the typical reaction to them. Experiments have shown the complex effects of density.... Whatever the interpersonal situation, higher density will cause the individual's reaction to be stronger. We showed that positive

situations elicited more positive reactions under high than low density, while negative situations produced more negative reactions under high density.

If this is indeed the case, then it has important implications for the study of social interaction patterns in small-scale and immediate situations. If the perspective is broader, however, as that of the social geographer must necessarily be, then the importance of these innate human responses to high-density situations is only marginal. Perhaps of more significance at a broader level are the learned aspects of the privacy requirement. Hall (1959, 1966) points to cross-cultural differences in privacy thresholds: Arabs have a preference for closer conversational position and more bodily contact than a reserved Englishman would find comfortable; a crowded situation for one ethnic group or social class would not seem a crowded situation to another. When such individual cultural or subcultural idiosyncrasies are generalized to the level of group interaction patterns, then the significance of varying personal space requirements to the study of interpersonal relations becomes more clear. Social relations, especially with relative strangers, are potentially perilous. There is a serious risk of shame or even harm through behaving wrongly, and one of the most obvious safety mechanisms is avoidance through the medium of space. Sommer (1969) reports on the behaviour of newcomers towards available seats in a college library. The maximization of personal space that repeatedly occurred can be perhaps more plausibly explained in terms of social avoidance than of innate space halo requirements. When translated to a scale appropriate to the interests of a social geographer, such social avoidance can be seen as one of the main forces underlying such phenomena as residential segregation or gang territoriality. Suttles (1972) goes so far as to suggest that this segregation is a vital social mechanism for the control of aggression in our modern, role-confused society. He shows how a concern for potential social conflict exacerbates existing tensions, and generally motivates people to compartmentalize themselves into communities, localizing and intensifying their hostility. He differentiates between the responses of rich and poor to this motivation: the rich can select a residential area where the character of fellow residents is assured by the costs of living there and the presumed reputability of people so heavily rewarded by society, an area which he calls a 'community of limited liability'; the poor, on the other hand, strive to attain the same result by personal covenant among themselves to produce what Suttles has called a 'defended neighbourhood'. Whatever the generality of Suttles' views, they represent an interesting attempt to show how concepts of privacy and personal space can be extended to the group level and usefully tied in with wider social processes to provide an explanatory framework for examining social interaction patterns.

Individual social attributes as conditioning factors

It has been suggested above that different cultures and different classes can have different privacy thresholds. The same, of course, can be said not merely of personal space requirements but of interaction patterns as a whole, and the search for explanatory perspectives must not remain constrained by an over-mechanistic spatial standpoint. Central to most social explanation is the notion that behaviour varies according to social attribute, whether attribute of culture, race, class, life-style, family status, or religion, and it now behoves us to examine the literature to see what fruitful causal suggestions have been made.

1. *Culture*

Very few social interaction studies have been made which could in any sense be described as cross-cultural. Caplow's study of San Juan, Puerto Rico, recognizes the possibility that the city's Spanish Catholic heritage and its essentially 'developing' status may give rise to social peculiarities as compared to other American cities, but none of his hypotheses are designed to reveal this (Caplow, Stryker, and Wallace, 1964). Lee's (1976) study of interaction patterns and residential satisfactions in several neighbourhoods of Kuala Lumpur shows that interesting differences of social mores exist between the Chinese, Indian, and Malay communities, though the focus of his work precludes more than passing comment on these differences. Clearly, sociability norms can have their roots in the philosophical and religious value systems that underpin any society, and differences in these norms must be of considerable interest to any student of interpersonal relations.

2. *Stage of social development*

Better documented, perhaps, is the much-discussed alteration of values and norms associated with the major social upheavals consequent upon the widespread industrialization and urbanization of society that has occurred during the last two centuries. Some social commentators have seen this as a result of the change in the economic system (Tönnies, 1957), others as a response to the confusions of rural to urban migration (Wirth, 1938), but there is some consensus as to the effects, in terms of interpersonal relations. The break-up of the wider circle of kin, the segmentation of social life into separate work and residential compartments, and the consequent problems of role confusion and anomie have all attracted much comment (Frankenberg, 1966). The pattern is by no means as clear as some have implied. Vestiges of tightly-knit kin groups and highly localized social networks have continued to survive in working-class sections of our cities (Bott, 1957; Irving, 1977), whereas rural areas in modern conditions appear to have lost the social characteristics once ascribed to them (Pahl, 1965). Indeed, it has even been suggested (Meier and Bell, 1959) that anomie can be more frequently found in depopulated, demographically-imbalanced rural areas than in urban areas which, after the initial confusion of expansion, do seem to settle down to produce a variety of remarkably cohesive residential groups. There is perhaps no easy generalization to be made about the effect of urbanization and industrialization on patterns of social interaction. Increases in affluence and mobility, the loss of some social contacts, the gain of many more, the increasing economic independence of individuals, and small family units—all these have undoubtedly wrought profound changes on social patterns which had persisted unchanged for centuries. It would indeed be foolish to indulge in cross-societal comparison without due recognition of this fact. Yet perhaps the most remarkable feature at the end of the day is the way in which people's needs and potentialities for meaningful interpersonal relationships do rise above the disruptions and hardships caused by these upheavals. To most people, anomie could never be accepted as a permanent condition.

3. *Class*

Most investigations of variations in interaction patterns have naturally taken place within the confines of one society, untrammelled by large-scale considerations of the sort just discussed. In such studies, social class has naturally been a major focus of interest, since so many social phenomena can be at least partially explained in class terms. Being traditionally more mobile, in both a residential and in an immediate sense, the upper classes have long been associated with patterns of friendship that transcend the tawdry constraints of locale and instead span broad acres—a genuinely regional or even national friendship group based on shared interest. By way of contrast, the working classes have an immobile social stereotype. They live, work, and play on their own middens, with firmly circumscribed social horizons. That such stereotypes are gross overgeneralizations will be obvious to anyone. The class structure in modern society is so complicated as to make them almost meaningless. What is not so obvious is that they are more positively misleading. It behoves us to examine rather more carefully the nature of social class as a determinant of social interaction patterns.

Elizabeth Bott (1971, pp. 112–113), in discussing social network connectedness, cautions against any simple causal suggestions:

> It is only in the working class that one is likely to find a combination of factors all operating together to produce a high degree of connectedness: concentration of people of the same or similar occupations in the same local area; jobs and homes in the same local area; little demand for physical mobility; little opportunity for social mobility... (but) one cannot explain connectedness as the result of the husband's occupational or class status considered as single determinants. Connectedness depends on a whole complex of forces... generated by the occupational and economic systems, but these forces do not always work in the same direction and they may affect different families in different ways.

In her later reconsiderations (Bott, 1971, p. 264) she has a look at the other end of the spectrum:

All the research families with very loose-knit networks and joint conjugal norms were cosmopolitan/spiralist/bureaucrats of the upper middle class subculture. However, various indications in the literature suggest that, in the upper reaches of the managerial and professional class, the career of the husband may be so time consuming and involving that the marital relationship becomes segregated.

Bott does not proceed to say whether this role segregation is associated with a tightening of the social network, but Irving's (1977) investigations in Californian upper middle-class suburbs lend some support to the idea that this might be so. Professional and managerial wives seemed to be closer-knit than any others, a confirmation of the suggestion that professional work-involvement can cause segregation of the marital relationship and a compensatory increase in the supportive role of the residential neighbourhood (Table 6.6).

In general, class has been found to be a telling but complex influence on interpersonal relations. The overall intensity of interaction patterns does not

TABLE 6.6. Social class indicators as determinants of network density in Hull and Los Angeles

		Loose	Close		Loose	Close
Occupation						
	Non-manual	65	81	Non-manual	68	140
	Manual	123	105	Manual	33	59
		$Q = 0.17$			$Q = 0.07$	
Education		Loose	Close		Loose	Close
	Minimum school Leaving age	110	109	Non-	58	98
	Post-minimum	58	77	Graduates	43	143
		$Q = 0.14$			$Q = 0.32$	
Car Ownership		Loose	Close		Loose	Close
	No car	92	101	One car	25	33
	Car	76	85	Two or more cars	75	165
		$Q = 0.00$			$Q = 0.25$	

Lowest significant (5 per cent.) Value for Yule's Q with this sample $= 0.26$.

appear to be a function of class (Irving, 1971, 1975). People from all walks of life have varying social requirements which in general they strive to fulfil. Overall intensity levels are more clearly related to personality variables, with extroverts scoring high and introverts low (Irving, 1977). When one considers interaction dimensions in more detail, however, class variations do emerge. The upper and middle classes in general have less localized patterns, and, perhaps as a consequence of this, indulge in interactions of the long, but relatively rare, type. Caplow's finding in San Juan, where he reports more intense neighbourhood activity among the upper income groups, stands as the only anomaly here. The lower classes, on the other hand, adhere to their stereotype of highly localized relationships, with a preponderance of brief but frequent encounters. This pattern accords nicely with the tendency, mentioned above, for working-class people to exhibit tight-knit social networks (Tables 6.7 and 6.8). When relationships with kinsfolk are examined separately from non-kin relationships, however, some even sharper class differences are revealed. The upper classes have a markedly non-local pattern of kin interaction, reflecting the residential mobility in their educational and occupational spiral. Their

TABLE 6.7. Class as a determinant of localization indices in Hull

Non-kin localization

Social class	Localization			Total
	Non-local	Middle	Local	
Professional and managerial	27	22	26	75
Clerical	27	24	20	71
Skilled manual	17	12	16	45
Semiskilled manual	23	13	35	71
Unskilled	23	16	53	92
Total	117	87	150	354

$\chi^2 = 19.9$, d.f. $= 8$, $p < 0.01$

Kin localization

Social class	Localization			Total
	Non-local	Middle	Local	
Professional and managerial	62	8	5	75
Clerical	39	20	12	71
Skilled manual	24	7	14	45
Semiskilled manual	39	17	15	71
Unskilled	36	22	34	92
Total	200	74	80	354

$\chi^2 = 40.4$, d.f. $= 8$, $p < 0.0001$

TABLE 6.8. Class and 'interaction-type' indices in Hull

Non-kin interaction

Class	Type: Low intensity	Long and infrequent	Middle range	Short and frequent	Bimodal	Total
Professional and managerial	17	*10*	14	21	12	74
Clerical	23	0	18	13	17	71
Skilled manual	14	0	12	6	13	45
Semiskilled manual	28	2	12	21	8	71
Unskilled	30	1	18	27	16	92
Total	112	13	74	88	66	353

$\chi^2 = 42.2$, d.f. $= 16$, $p < 0.001$

Kin interaction

Class	Type: Low intensity	Long and infrequent	Middle range	Short and frequent	Bimodal	Total
Professional and managerial	20	23	22	3	7	75
Clerical	25	8	11	7	20	71
Skilled manual	8	4	17	10	6	45
Semiskilled manual	19	2	21	8	21	71
Unskilled	28	7	12	17	28	92
Total	100	44	83	45	82	354

$\chi^2 = 66.1$, d.f. $= 16$, $p < 0.0001$

non-kin patterns do not reveal this non-local tendency. Indeed, in many areas with a reasonable amount of residential stability and which have as a consequence attracted a certain ethos of community, the middle classes exhibit a heavy 'neighbouring' tendency which accords with the suburban stereotype of American sociological literature. Perhaps Caplow's findings can be accommodated here. Clearly it is in patterns of kin interaction that class makes its greatest differentiating impact. The aggressive economic and social independence of the nuclear family is best represented in those classes most able to afford it.

4. *Other personal attributes*

Common sense suggests that a great many other personal attributes could influence interaction patterns. It is odd, therefore, that findings in general have been rather negative. Caplow found no evidence of any association with migration experience, residential mobility, religious affiliation, or a variety of family status variables (Caplow, Stryker, and Wallace, 1964, p. 167). Few studies seem to have brought to light any influence from residential mobility, a factor which would, *a priori*, seem crucial in determining the strength of local ties and the development of networks. Only in the case of the *nouveaux arrivés* of Orange County, California, does this factor seem to be of any importance. Here, the most recent arrivals exhibit significantly less localized friendship patterns and significantly looser-knit networks than their more established co-residents (Irving, 1977). This is not at all easy to understand. Recently settled communities have been found to develop norms of neighbouring and cooperations as a response to shared uncertainties and needs (Festinger, Schacter, and Back, 1950; Kuper, 1953; Simey, 1954). Perhaps it is the stereotyped subculture of transience which has affected newcomers to Southern California. Only when they find, after a time, that people are similar in social needs and aspirations, after all, can they feel confident to develop local social relationships.

There is a general tendency (Irving, 1971, 1977) for age and family status variables to be associated with certain interaction dimensions, though the relationships are by no means always clear and they sometimes almost defy interpretation. Older people, and especially those who are still in larger household units rather than those who live alone, tend to have interaction patterns that are less intense, with looser networks. This suggests, therefore, that, far from encouraging the building up of an intense and close-knit web of friendship over a lifetime of social activity, age brings a slowing of the social pace in later years. Social requirements, perhaps, become more modest, and where they can be satisfied within the confines of the household there is an even more marked tendency to run down the level of outside contact which seems to characterize the younger and middle years. It must be emphasized that such suggestions are tenuous. In general, research has not pointed to the importance of variables of personal circumstances. It behoves us to take a more 'gestalt' approach.

The social environment as a conditioning factor

Although geography has a long tradition of environmentally rooted explanation, it does not provide much inspiration if the focus of concern is interpersonal relations. Legitimate and useful as the environmentalist frame of explanation has been in the past, it has long been accepted as of limited value in the quest for understanding more purely social variations. Indeed, attempts to emphasize the role of the physical environment as a determinant of social patterns played a large part in the declining popularity of such studies in the geographer's firmament (Haggett, 1965, chap. 1). Sociology, too, has paid scant attention to the environment. The primary concern of mainstream sociology has been with social structures, and only occasionally in the work of academic imperialists such as Parsons do we see attempts, albeit half-hearted, to embrace the environment (Parsons *et al.*, 1961). One noteworthy exception, perhaps, to this generalization has been the theoretical position of the community sociologists, to which more attention is devoted in the concluding section of this review. It is to social psychology, to the influential gestalt school of Kurt Lewin, that we must turn to gain a useful perspective on environmental explanation (De Rivera, 1976). Lewin's 'field theory' is too all-embracing, too complex, and too intangible to provide us with an operational device for explaining variations in social interaction patterns, but his work stands as an important source of inspiration to those who have sought to make the concept of environment much more general yet at the same time much more important as a source of social explanation.

Although concerned more specifically with formal social activity, Barker and his colleagues have given a valuable lead with their development of the idea of the 'behaviour setting' (Barker, 1968; Barker and Schoggen, 1973; Barker and Wright, 1955). Their rather mechanistic concern with the measurement of such parameters as habitat extent, habit variety, and habitat continuity, and with institutionalized behavioural responses to those environmental constraints, may not be to everyone's taste. They do, however, serve to underline in a vigorous and confident fashion that environmental factors can have a critical importance in constraining and channelling social activity. If we consider Barker's approach, and flesh it out with the more purely social ingredients of Lewin's gestalt, we are led inexorably towards a consideration of what might be called, for want of a more eye-catching label, the 'social environment'. If we accept the simple truism that social activity, by its very nature, cannot be conducted by an individual in isolation but must be acted out in the presence of at least one, and usually more, other actors, then we are led to the inescapable conclusion that the sheer availability of these other actors must be a critical explanatory variable. In more specific terms, the differential clustering of people into towns, villages, or hamlets must be a factor of some sociological importance; the differential segregation of people into residential groups of varying degrees of social homogeneity must have some effect on their social options. We are forced to seriously question the assertions of Gans (1967), Pahl (1966, 1970), and Dennis (1958) that patterns of social relationships can in no way be fundamentally affected by residential milieu. The naive social environment determinism of the 'ways of life' sociologists who suggested that urbanism (Wirth, 1938) and later suburbanism (Fava, 1956; Whyte, 1960) were great monolithic lifestyles consequent upon such loosely characterized residential situations was clearly inadequate. But rejection of the residential environment as an influence on social activity in general, and informal social interaction in particular, is an overreaction which is refuted by a number of separate research findings.

In his study of parental attitudes to education in Sunderland, Robson (1969) notes the obvious and well-documented relationships between social class and attitudes, but goes on to point out that there seem to be other forces at work influencing such attitudes—forces which seem to have a broader environmental meaning than that of the household or family unit. By using residential area as a variable, he found that attitudes which might be expected on the basis of individual or family attributes were often modified by the prevailing attitudes of the neighbourhood in general. Similar findings are reported by Bell and Force (1956) in their study of participation in formal associations; their respondents' behaviour reflected the social pressures to conform to such an extent that expectations of variation according to personal social variables were only partially fulfilled. Evidence for a neighbourhood effect has also been noted in respect of voting behaviour, delinquency, and criminal activity (Herbert and Johnston, 1976).

It is surprising that students of informal social interaction have not given much attention to this 'environmental effect'. More than with any other form of activity, interpersonal relations stand to reflect the numbers and quality of the social raw material in the background. Attitudes to education and participation in formal associations are obviously related also to broad structural variables which extend, in their institutionalized fashion, far beyond the confines and influence of the residential neighbourhood. Yet milieu was found to be importance as a variable. How much more important, therefore, it ought to be in that most disorganized and personal brand of social behaviour—interpersonal relations.

I have attempted, in several research exercises, to demonstrate this importance (Irving, 1971, 1977; Irving and Davidson, 1973). Time and time again, in a wide variety of contexts, both urban and rural, and in respect of a great many dimensions of interaction, both directional and non-directional, the effect of the residential milieu has emerged as more potent than effects from more often-considered personal attributes such as class, age, or family status. Even length of residence pales to insignificance beside the environmental variables, indicating, perhaps, that these forces and opportunities get to work very quickly and do not necessarily reflect the slow build-up of neighbourhood consensus after many years of residential stability. It is not appropriate to report here in detail the precise ways in which social areas seem to generate their own norms of social interaction. Suffice it to note that the use of area as a variable has lent support to such social stereotypes as the anonymity of the 'zone in transition', the doorstep chatter of the stable working-class area, and the more formalized entertainment routines of the middle-class suburbs (Irving, 1977; Irving and Davidson, 1973). But one finding is worthy of emphasis here, for it reinforces the theoretical validity of the environmental approach to social analysis. Those indices which would seem, *a priori*, to be susceptible to the power of neighbourhood forces (network density, localization, intensity, and 'type') have all exhibited striking variations by area—variations which three-variable analysis has shown to operate over and above the influences which might be expected for class, family status, or any other personal variables. Those which do not seem good candidates for the neighbourhood package (kin orientation and spread) have not shown areal variation. They are more satisfactorily explained in more personal terms and, indeed, the use of a personality variable in the Hull survey has lent a measure of support to this (Irving, 1977). This distinction is an interesting one. Certain dimensions of interaction seem to have a strong environmental reference; with them, family and neighbourhood norms must be seen as powerful forces, reinforcing each other on occasions and opposing each other on others, but serving to provide rich variations in patterns of social behaviour. Other dimensions of interaction are more clearly rooted in the personality of the individual. Here again, of course, such personality attributes are not necessarily solely genetic; they reflect in addition the sequence of life experiences and previous social environments which underlie the socialization of any individual. But it can be generally accepted that interaction dimensions that stem from these factors—whether or not, for example, a person feels more secure with his eggs in one social basket than with them spread around a group—are those which stand to be least affected by the more immediate influences of the social environment. When seeking explanation for variations in interaction patterns, and, in particular, when attempting to assess the importance of the social environment as an explanatory factor, it is worth bearing this distinction in mind.

LOCALITY, COMMUNITY, AND LOCAL SOCIAL INTERACTION

It is not appropriate, in this review article, to offer a lengthy discourse on the community concept. It has been done many times before, and the work of Bell and Newby (1971), as one of the most comprehensive recent critical reviews, can serve as a source of reference here. In general, the idea has come into disrepute, partly because there has been a long tradition of circuitous theoretical argument among community sociologists, with very little parallel activity geared towards the provision of tools for empirical research, and partly because it has been felt (Webber, 1968) that advances in technology in general, and in personal mobility in particular, were rendering rather redundant a theoretical construct based so firmly on locale or residential milieu. It would indeed be foolish to ignore this last point. Clearly, people are not so dependent as once they were on the locale for their livelihood, comfort, and leisure. Yet this does not mean that they have become totally independent of it. The first part of this concluding statement will be concerned with the 'residual' role of local social activity in a modern, non-local world. The second and final part will be concerned with the way in which social interactionists can offer some empirical devices to the community sociologist. By so doing, this, the only branch of sociology to offer an environmental or spatial perspective, can perhaps be blown out of the doldrums.

Two sharply divergent viewpoints can be discerned among those sociologists who continue to believe that the community paradigm remains of some value. Suttles (1972) argues forcibly that it needs a radical revamp. He agrees with the criticisms outlined in the preceding paragraph and suggests that community cohesion in the modern city stems from the 'territorial foreign policy' of residential groups. Rather than search for an arbitrarily-circumscribed internal interactional or normative cohesion, sociologists ought to be studying the external relations between communities and the wider bureaucratic society at large. Warren (1963), on the other hand, while accepting the increasing encroachment of national social structures in many walks of life formerly articulated at the local level, places much more emphasis on the persistence of 'locality relevant' functions. To Warren (1963, p. 153) it is an

> ...inescapable fact that spatial location of people's residence does affect their social relationships. Living together in close physical proximity necessitates local access to the major functions which we have listed as being 'locality-relevant'.

Furthermore (Warren, 1963, p. 154), and of even more significance to the social geographer,

> The geographical arrangement of population clusters nevertheless remains an important key to the geographic interrelationships of social units and systems.

Warren ranges widely in his enumeration of locality-relevant functions, and 'social participation' is but one of these, but he does stress the continuing functional importance of the residential milieu in this respect. Unfortunately he places most emphasis on secondary or formal associations, neglecting the continuing role of the locality in performing what Cooley (1902) regarded as primary social functions. I have already suggested in an earlier part of the paper that, even in the most modern and mobile societies, the residential milieu continues to be an interaction pool of critical importance for certain less-mobile groups, whose numerical and social significance must not be underestimated.

It would be arrogant to suggest that informal social interaction was the only useful or important perspective to adopt when shoring up and revivifying the community concept. Warren identifies locality-relevant functions in the economic sphere, in the processes of socialization and social control, and in the neglected field of mutual support. But social participation is, without doubt, a central feature of any community concept, and research has shown that formal channels of participation, although easy to identify, are perhaps not so central to the lives of most people as the attention they have received seems to indicate. Indeed, as de Tocqueville so succinctly pointed out over a century ago, the association may be a peculiarly American penchant; other societies have not shown nearly so much enthusiasm for formalism. I would like to suggest, therefore, that the study of informal social interaction, rather brusquely dismissed by Warren as belonging to another era of community sociology, provides an essential theoretical perspective for any locality-focused study.

Moreover, this article has attempted to show how this theoretical perspective can be translated into operational variables. The several dimensions of interaction which have been discussed provide some real possibilities for measuring the 'locality relevance' of the residential milieu in serving as an interaction pool. The various localization indices address themselves directly to the problem.

Measures of network, spread, type, and kin orientation, interlocked, as has been demonstrated, in a complex fashion, also provide perspectives which can be usefully attached to the themes of locality relevance.

But it would be mechanistic, and ultimately devoid of meaning, to suggest that community sociology must be reduced to a series of indices of this kind, interesting though they may be. Even Chapple, insistent as he was on the necessity for preliminary abduction of the most rigorous kind, acknowledged that interaction studies must, in the last analysis, be fed back into the complex world of social structure, social norms, and culturally-based values. Warren stresses that 'identification' remains, as it has always been, central to the community concept, and he suggests that community strength varies according to the degree that the residential locale serves as any kind of reference group for the individual. Points of reference can, of course, range widely over the behavioural and attitudinal spectrum, but it is generally felt that an important area of reference concerns the norms of interaction and privacy thought to be proper in a community. The measures of social interaction discussed in this paper provide a convenient way of assessing these norms in a variety of residential milieux. In this way, the locality relevance of the social environment in fulfilling at least one important social function can be fairly easily assessed. This function—the provision of raw material for interpersonal relations—is one which must not be overlooked in the quest for community.

REFERENCES

Adams, B. N. (1967). Interaction theory and the social network. *Sociometry*, **30**, 64–78.

Ardrey, R. (1966). *The Territorial Imperative*, Athenum, New York.

Arensberg, C. M. (1937). *The Irish Countryman*, Macmillan, London.

Arensberg, C. M., and Kimball, S. T. (1940). *Family and Community in Ireland*, Harvard University Press, Cambridge, Massachusetts.

Barker, R. G. (1968). *Ecological Psychology: Concepts and Methods for Studying the Environment of Human Behavior*, Stanford University Press, Stanford, California.

Barker, R. G., and Schoggen, P. (1973). *Qualities of Community Life: Methods of Measuring Environment and Behavior Applied to an American and an English Town*, Jossey, Bass, San Francisco.

Barker, R. G., and Wright, H. F. (1955). *Midwest and Its Children*, Harper and Row, New York.

Barnes, J. A. (1954). Class and committees in a Norwegian island parish. *Human Relations*, **7**, 39–58.

Bell, C., and Newby, H. (1971). *Community Studies*, Allen and Unwin, London.

Bell, W., and Force, M. T. (1956). Urban neighbourhood types and participation in formal associations. *American Sociological Review*, **21**, 25–34.

Bott, E. (1957). *Family and Social Network*, Tavistock, London. (2nd ed., 1971.)

Caplow, T. (1955). Definition and measurement of ambiences. *Social Forces*, **34**, 28–33.

Caplow, T., and Forman, R. (1950). Neighbourhood interaction in a homogeneous community. *American Sociological Review*, **15**, 357–366.

Caplow, T., Stryker, S., and Wallace, S. E. (1964). *The Urban Ambience*, Bedminster, New Jersey.

Carey, L., and Mapes, R. (1972). *The Sociology of Planning*, Batsford, London.

Chapple, E. D. (1939). Quantitative analysis of the interaction of individuals. *Proceedings, National Academy of Sciences*, **25**, 58–67.

Chapple, E. D. (1940). *Measuring Human Relations: An Introduction to the Study of the Interaction of Individuals.* Genetic Psychology Monographs No. 22, Princeton, Massachusetts.

Chapple, E. D. (1942). The measurement of interpersonal behaviour. *Transactions, New York Academy of Sciences*, **4**, 222–232.

Chapple, E. D. (1960). Interaction chronograph method for analysis of differences between schizophrenics and controls. *Archives of General Psychiatry* (AMA), **3**, 160–167.

Chapple, E. D. (1970). *Culture and Biological Man*, Holt, Rinehart and Winston, New York.

Chapple, E. D., Chamberlain, A., Esser, A. H., and Kline, N. S. (1963). The measurement of activity patterns of schizophrenic patients. *Journal of Nervous and Mental Disease*, **137**, 258–267.

Collins, O., and Collins, J. M. (1973). *Interaction and Social Structure*, Mouton, The Hague.

Cooley, C. H. (1902). *Human Nature and the Social Order*, Free Press, Glencoe, New York. (Reprinted 1956.)

Danielsson, B. (1950). Some attraction and repulsion patterns among Jibaro Indians. *Sociometry*, **13**, 83–106.

Dennis, N. (1958). The popularity of the neighbourhood community idea. *Sociological Review*, **6**, 191–206.

De Rivera, J. (1976). *Field Theory as Human Science*, Gardner, New York.

Deutschberger, P. (1946). Interaction patterns in changing neighbourhoods: New York and Pittsburgh. *Sociometry*, **9**, 303–315.

Dobriner, W. (Ed.) (1958). *The Suburban Community*, Putnam, New York.

Esser, A. H. (Ed.) (1971). *Behavior and Environment: The Use of Space by Animals and Man*, Plenum, New York.

Fava, S. F. (1956). Suburbanism as a way of life. *American Sociological Review*, **21**, 34–37.

Festinger, L., Schacter, S., and Back, K. (1950). *Social Pressures in Informal Groups*, Harper, New York.

Frankenberg, R. (1966). *Communities in Britain*, Penguin, London.

Freedman, J. L. (1975). *Crowding and Behaviour*, Freeman, San Franscisco.

Galle, O. R., Gove W. R., and McPherson, J. M. (1972). Population density and pathology: what are the relations for man? *Science*, **176**, 23–30.

Gans, H. J. (1961). Planning and social life: friendship and neighbour relations in suburban communities. *Journal of the American Institute of Planners*, **27**, 134–140.

Gans, H. J. (1967). *The Levittowners*, Allen Lane, London.

Gardner, B. B. (1945). *Human Relations in Industry*, Irwin, Chicago.

Glass, R. (1948). *Middlesbrough: The Social Background to a Plan*, Routledge and Kegan Paul, London.

Goffman, E. (1959). *The Presentation of Self in Everyday Life*, Doubleday, New York.

Goffman, E. (1967). *Interaction Ritual*, Adline, Chicago.

Goldthorpe, J. H., and (1963). Lockwood, D. Affluence and the British class structure. *Sociological Review*, **11**, 133–163.

Haggett, P. (1965). *Locational Analysis in Human Geography*, Arnold, London.

Hall, E. T. (1959). *The Silent Language*, Doubleday, New York.

Hall, E. T. (1966). *The Hidden Dimension*, Doubleday, New York.

Heider, F. (1958). *The Psychology of Interpersonal Relations*, Wiley, New York.

Herbert, D. T., and Johnston, R. J. (1976). *Spatial Perspectives on Problems and Policies*, Wiley, London.

Hoggart, R. (1957). *The Uses of Literacy*, Chatto and Windus, London.

Homans, G.C. (1950). *The Human Group*, Harcourt, Brace, New York.

Homans, G.C. (1961). *Social Behaviour: Its Elementary Forms*, Routledge and Kegan Paul, London.

Horobin, G.W. (1957). Community and occupation in the Hull fishing industry. *British Journal of Sociology*, **8**, 343–356.

Irving, H.W. (1971). *Pilot Investigation for the Neighbourhood Study of Hull and Haltemprice*, SSRC Research Report, London.

Irving, H.W. (1974). *Community in English Villages*. Unpublished research report.

Irving, H.W. (1975). Distance, intensity, kinship: key dimensions of social interaction. *Sociology and Social Research*, **60**, 77–86.

Irving, H.W. (1977). Social networks in the modern city. *Social Forces*, **55**.

Irving, H.W. (1978). Community in the city. Forthcoming in *Man—Environment Systems*.

Irving, H.W., and Davidson, R.N. (1973). A working note on the measurement of social interaction. *Transactions of the Bartlett Society*, **9**, 1–15.

Johnston, R.J. (1971). *Urban Residential Patterns*, Bell, London.

Kuper, L. (Ed.) (1953). *Living in Towns*, Cresset, London.

Lee, B. T. (1976). *Residential Patterns in Kuala Lumpur*. Ph.D. thesis, University of Hull.

Lewin, K. (1976). In J. de Rivera (Trans.), *Field Theory as Human Science*, Gardner, New York.

Lorenz, K. (1966). *On Aggression*, Harcourt, Brace, New York.

Lundberg, G. A., and Steele, M. (1938). Social attraction patterns in a village. *Sociometry*, **1**, 375–419.

Mann, P. H. (1955). *Community and Neighbourhood with Reference to Social Status*. Ph.D. thesis, University of Nottingham.

Mead, G. H. (1934). *Mind, Self and Society*, University Press, Chicago.

Meier, R. L., and Bell, W. (1959). Anomia and the achievement of life goals. *American Sociological Review*, **24**, 189–202.

Moreno, J. L. (1934). *Who shall Survive?*, Beacon House, New York.

Morris, D. (1967). *The Naked Ape*, McGraw-Hill, New York.

Mowrer, E. R. (1958). The family in suburbia. In W. Dobriner (Ed.), *The Suburban Community*, Putnam, New York.

Pahl, R. E. (1965). *Urbs in Rure: The Metropolitan Fringe in Hertfordshire*. Geographical Paper No. 2, L. S. E., London.

Pahl, R. E. (1966). The rural–urban continuum. *Sociologia Ruralis*, **6**, 299–329.

Pahl, R. E. (1968). *Readings in Urban Sociology*, Pergamon, Oxford.

Pahl, R. E. (1970). *Whose City?*, Longman, London.

Parsons, T., Shils, E., Naegele, K., and Pitts, J. (Eds.) (1961). *Theories of Society*, Free Press of Glencoe, New York.

Priest, R. F., and Sawyer, J. (1967). Proximity and peership: bases of balance in interpersonal attraction. *American Journal of Sociology*, **72**, 633–649.

Robson, B. T. (1969). *Urban Analysis: A Study of City Structure*, University Press, Cambridge.

Sherif, M., and Sherif, C. W. (1953). *Groups in Harmony and Tension*, Harper, New York.

Simey, T. (Ed.) (1954). *Neighbourhood and Community*, University Press, Liverpool.

Simmel, G. (1950). In K. H. Wolff (Ed. and Trans.), *The Sociology of Georg Simmel*, Free Press of Glencoe, New York.

Skinner, G. W. (1964). Marketing and social structure in rural China. *Journal of Asian Studies*, **24**, 3–43, 195–228, 363–399.

Smith, J., Form, W. H., and Stone, G. P. (1954). Local intimacy in a middle-sized city. *American Journal of Sociology*, **60**, 276–284.

Sommer, R. (1969). *Personal Space*, Prentice-Hall, Englewood Cliffs, New Jersey.

Southall, A. (1959). An operational theory of role. *Human Relations*, **12**, 17–34.

Srole, L. (1956). Social integration and certain corollaries. *American Sociological Review*, **21**, 709–716.

Suttles, G. D. (1972). *The Social Construction of Communities*, University Press, Chicago.

Thorns, D. C. (1976). *The Quest for Community*, Allen and Unwin, London.

Timms, D. W. G. (1970). *The Urban Mosaic: Towards a Theory of Residential Differentiation*, University Press, Cambridge.
Tönnies, F. (1957). In C. P. Loomis (Trans.), *Community and Society*, Harper Torchbooks, New York.
Tunstall, J. (1962). *The Fishermen*, Macgibbon and Kee, London.
Wallin, P. (1953). A Guttman scale for measuring women's neighbourliness. *American Journal of Sociology*, **59**, 241–246.
Warner, W. L., and Low, J. O. (1947). *The Social System of the Modern Factory*, Yale University Press, New Haven.
Warner, W. L., and Lunt, P. S. (1941). *The Social Life of a Modern Community*, Yale University Press, New Haven.
Warner, W. L., and Lunt, P. S. (1947). *The Status System of a Modern Community*, Yale University Press, New Haven.
Warner, W. L., and Srole, L. (1945). *The Social System of American Ethnic Groups*, Yale University Press, New Haven.
Warren, R. L. (1963). *The Community in America*, Rand-McNally, Chicago. (2nd ed., 1972.)
Webber, M. M. (1963). Order in diversity: community without propinquity: In L. Wingo (Ed.), *Cities and Space*, Johns Hopkins Press, Baltimore.
Webber, M. M. (1964). The urban place and the nonplace urban realm. In M. M. Webber *et al.* (Eds.), *Exploration into Urban Structure*, University of Pennsylvania Press, Philadelphia, Pennsylvania.
Webber, M. M. (1968). The post-city age. *Daedalus*, **97**, 1091–1110.
Whyte, W. F. (1943). *Street Corner Society*, University Press, Chicago.
Whyte, W. H. (1960). *The Organisation Man*, Penguin, Harmondsworth.
Whyte, W. F. (1961). *Men at Work*, Dorsey and Irwin, Homewood, Illinois.
Wirth, L. (1938). Urbanism as a way of life. *American Journal of Sociology*, **44**, 1–24.

Chapter 7

Housing in Latin American Cities

Alan G. Gilbert and Peter M. Ward

A society's main economic and social characteristics are clearly depicted in the form of its housing. Rich nations contain large numbers of well-built dwellings while in poor nations it is the number of flimsy dwellings which is most apparent. Unequal societies are revealed by their wide diversity of housing forms; authoritarian socialist societies by the lack of housing variety. Housing clearly reflects the economic and demographic structure of a society—its level of development, the distribution of its income, the rate of population growth, and the pace of urban expansion. Similarly, variations in the quality of accommodation reveals much about a society's social priorities, institutions, power systems, and form of government. Latin America is no exception to this pattern. Most Latin American cities contain a wide range of housing types which reflects the structural problems of those societies; for a minority the housing is as good as in most Western European countries, yet for a large proportion of the urban population it is dilapidated, overcrowded, and unserviced.

It is our intention in this paper to examine the relationship between urban housing forms and the social and economic structures of Latin American nations. We wish to demonstrate that most housing problems are a direct consequence of the process of 'dependent' development. At the same time, we do not wish to hide the wide range of urban conditions found in the region; major economic, social, demographic, and political differences exist among Latin American nations which are reflected in their respective housing conditions. In some cities flimsy shacks dominate the urban landscape; in others they are largely absent. In places squatting is commonplace; in others it is not permitted. Havana, Quito, Lima, and Rio de Janeiro are sufficiently different, as are the nations of which they form part, to warn that generalizations about Latin American housing conditions must always be qualified. If the nature of housing is multifaceted then any simple solution is unlikely. Indeed, another of the principal themes of our paper is that in the past the introduction of panaceas to housing problems has as often accentuated as cured the difficulties of the urban poor.

Our paper is divided into four sections. First, we examine the evolution of the region's economic and social structure and thereby demonstrate the principal causes of today's housing problems. Second, we discuss past misunderstandings of the term 'housing quality' and suggest how it can be made more relevant to the Latin American situation. Third, we explore the evolution, location, and interrelationships of housing subsystems, emphasizing the interdependence of those systems. Finally, we consider the potential adaptability of the urban situation: what are the dimensions of the housing problem, are conditions improving or deteriorating, what should planning authorities do to help overcome the main difficulties, and what has been tried so far in different Latin American countries? We are forced to use a fairly broad brush, but we trust that the resulting canvas will not distort the fascinating complexity of the Latin American urban landscape.

THE ECONOMIC AND SOCIAL ENVIRONMENT

Latin America's problems today are the culmination of a historical process of 'dependent' development (Cardoson and Faletto, 1969; Furtado, 1971). Put simply, underdevelopment is a consequence of the region's relationship with the world trading community. It is not an original condition; rather it is one that has evolved over time. The region's diverse pre-Columbian civilizations were radically altered by the imposition of Spanish and Portuguese rule. The most fundamental economic change was the reorientation of production so as to provide exports to Spain and Portugal—gold, silver, cotton, or sugar (Stein and Stein, 1970). This basic orientation has survived in most respects to the present day. It survived the industrial revolution when Britain replaced Spain and Brazil as the principal trading partner. It survived political independence in the nineteenth century when the new governments of the creole élites sought to expand foreign trade. It even survived the world depression of the 1930s and persistent attempts since that time to substitute foreign manufactured products. Today most governments are striving, as always, to increase their exports to accelerate the rate of economic development.

While the process of export development has been common to all Latin American countries, its impact on different countries varied widely. In Argentina the export of meat, wool, and cereals was associated with the extensive development of railways and urban infrastructure, with rapid urbanization and the massive immigration of Europeans (Ferrera, 1967; Scobie, 1964). By 1914 Argentina was a rich country. By contrast, Bolivia's tin industry never created as many jobs, never stimulated the same expansion of infrastructure, and never gave rise to an accelerated urbanization process Furtado, 1971). Bolivia has remained among the poor countries of the region as a consequence.

The impact of the slump of the 1930s, however, brought problems for both richer and poorer nations and gave rise to a similar response. The fall in world demand for the region's primary exports cut not only internal purchasing power but also, most critically, the ability to purchase manufactured imports. The more prosperous countries experienced a spontaneous process of imports substitution as local companies replaced the simpler products. The boom in exports which arose during the Second World War supported this process and by 1950 the Economic Commission for Latin America was recommending import substitution as a deliberate development strategy (U.N.D.E.A., 1949). If Latin America remained poor because the prices of the region's primary products increased more slowly than the prices of its manufactured imports then the solution was to industrialize. Most governments followed Raul Prebisch's advice: tariffs and licences were introduced to limit foreign imports, foreign investment was attracted to build both factories and intrastructure, loans and technical assistance were obtained from multilateral agencies, and government agencies were established to accelerate the modernization process.

To an extent the process worked. Brazil and Argentina were virtually self-sufficient in consumer durable and intermediate products by the early 1960s. Elsewhere the process was less advanced but had created jobs, increased industrial production, and accelerated economic growth. Unfortunately, nowhere did it resolve two key problems. It failed to resolve balance-of-payments difficulties because industrialization replaced demands for consumer products with demands for machines and parts. Nor did it resolve the problem of underemployment or raise incomes for the masses. The capital-intensive technology employed in the new industry created jobs but not in sufficient numbers to satisfy the demands of the rapidly increasing Latin American labour force. What is more, import-substituting industrialization increased the dependence of the region on the developed nations still further. Foreign investment came to represent an increasing share of manufacturing activities, financial debts accumulated as more was borrowed to accelerate the pace of growth, and imported technology had an increasing dominance over local production.

Industrialization also accelerated the rural–urban transition. Before 1930 only Argentina, Uruguay, and Chile had a majority of their population living in cities with more than 20 000 people. Elsewhere urban development had been stimulated by export-based growth and by higher rates of natural increase, but most people still lived in the rural areas. The process of import-substituting industrialization and the gamut of policies associated with it quickened the pace of urbanization throughout the region. The strategy created new investment opportunities in the urban areas and concentrated infrastructure and jobs in the major cities (Gilbert, 1974). Outside the main urban areas only limited numbers of commercial farmers responded to the increasing urban demands for food. With rural conditions failing to improve for the majority and rates of natural increase exceeding 3 per cent. in most countries, the demographic consequences were obvious. The poor and the less-poor migrated in ever increasing numbers to the major cities in search of better economic opportunities. By 1960 most Latin Americans lived in urban areas and large numbers lived in cities with more than one million people: In 1940 there were only four cities with more than a million inhabitants; by 1970 there were sixteen, three of which had between 5 and 10 millions (U.N.D.Y., 1974).

The pattern of economic development was reflected in the social structure of the cities. The expansion of industry, commerce, finance, and government created a substantial middle class. Today members of this privileged group live at standards equivalent to those of similar groups in developed nations. They have access to most forms of social services, consumer-durable products, adequate housing, and sophisticated entertainments. To a considerable extent they determine the pattern of urban expansion through their decisions on housing location, their political influence, and by their participation in the principal decision-making institutions. Urban planning is biased towards protecting their interests; the distribution of public services is strongly influenced by their commercial importance; and employment structures reflect their demand for goods and services and their choice of appropriate production technologies. Many would argue that these 'dependent elites' share the values of the elite and middle-class groups of developed societies. Certainly, their life-styles and aspirations have more in common with the middle classes of the developed societies than they do with their poorer fellow citizens.

The single most important characteristic of the poor is their limited access to well-paid, secure employment. Some do achieve regular jobs in large-scale industrial enterprise, financial groups, and commerical organizations. The majority, however, belong to what is unsatisfactorily but increasingly known as the 'informal sector' (Friedmann and Sullivan, 1974; I.B.R.D., 1975). Employment is typically small scale, employing limited sums of capital and yielding low incomes. Jobs may be found in the well-known tertiary sector but also in the artisan sector and in the construction industry. Many of these jobs are not 'traditional' but have evolved to complement and supply the formal sector. Thus lottery salesmen usually sell on behalf of state lotteries thereby helping supplement ordinary tax revenues; artisan workers produce goods for manufacturing companies on a subcontract basis; and domestic service has expanded as more families in the formal sector have been able to afford such help. The low incomes of most informal-sector workers prevent them gaining full access to the benefits of urban life. Only those workers employed by large-scale institutions tend to belong to social security and health schemes. Access to private education, car ownership, or conventional housing is limited.

Yet, it is a grave error to view the urban poor as an undifferentiated mass (McEwen, 1972; Peattie, 1975). Some poor children attend secondary school, hospital facilities are available to some, even if inconsistently, and those engaged in commerce or transport may well achieve regular incomes at some stage in their lives. As Balán, Browning, and Jelin (1973) have argued for Monterrey, there is a degree of social mobility in most Latin American cities which has guaranteed that many urban groups have achieved life-styles above those of their parents. This mobility means that a spectrum exists within Latin American cities ranging from the richest to the poorest groups. The barriers against upward mobility are very real, but they are not impenetrable. Few move from very poor to very rich, but many have moved from very poor to middle income. Most are not trapped in the 'culture of poverty' described by Lewis (1961, 1966). Rather, as Valentine (1968), Safa (1970), and Portes (1972) have argued, the poor in most Latin American cities are highly rational and cognitive in their decision making.

Most urban areas contain a polarized society where limited social mobility is permitted by rapid economic growth. Such growth enlarges the formal employment sector and thereby creates job opportunities for those in the burgeoning informal sector. Such mobility is encouraged by the favoured positions held by most cities in Latin American economies. National settlement systems reflect the underlying 'centre–periphery' relationships which exist in most of the region's countries (Friedmann, 1966). Insofar as there is a process of subsidization of the centre by the periphery, the urban centres prosper relative to the rest of the country. So long as investment resources are concentrated in the larger urban areas, the enterprising poor are likely to achieve higher material standards of living in the cities. Thus the poor in the cities face innumerable difficulties, but they are generally much better off than their rural counterparts (Gilbert, 1974). The continuance of city-ward migration testifies to this fact.

Clearly, however, urban conditions are not identical in different countries. The fact that per capita incomes in Venezuela and Argentina are between three and four times higher than those in Honduras and Bolivia makes an important difference to urban conditions. In the richer nations considerable numbers of people are employed in the formal sector; in the poorer nations only a small minority are in an equivalent position. Similarly, social and political structures vary from country to country. Some nations have experienced revolutions which have transformed social relationships; others contain social systems which can only be described as highly oppressive of the majority. Lesser differences are apparent within nations. Within the same country both rich and poor, chaotic and efficiently organized cities can be found. Medellin and Buenaventura in Colombia or Chimbote and Trujillo in Peru hardly seem as if they belong to their same respective nations. Notwithstanding the underlying economic and social similarities which we have described, important national and local differences abound. It is in the light of these variations on a common experience that the characteristics, problems, and dynamics of urban housing must be seen.

THE HOUSING RESPONSE AND THE NEEDS OF THE POOR

The social and economic polarization apparent in most Latin American cities is clearly manifest in the varied housing responses. The higher income groups have access to the same kinds of housing as most people in developed societies, the majority either buying or renting conventional housing. Such housing ranges from the luxurious, ranch-style suburban accommodation so typical of North American cities to apartments in high-rise apartment blocks. Mortgages and bank loans are available for house purchase and increasing absolute numbers of people are buying architect-designed, contractor-built housing. At the other extreme are the dwellings of the poor. This accommodation consists partly of 'spontaneous', 'self-help' housing and partly of rented facilities, both in decaying conventional housing and in spontaneous settlements.

The number of Latin American urban inhabitants who live in low-income dwellings is considerable. In some cities squatter settlers represent a majority of the population; in Maracaibo 63 per cent. of the population lived in such settlements in 1970 and in Chimbote 70 per cent. in 1968 (Peru Oficina Nacional, 1970). Throughout the region the proportion has increased during the last thirty or forty years. In Lima, the limited squatter population in 1930 had grown to represent 20 per cent. of the population in 1961 and 25 per cent. in 1972 (Collier, 1976). In Bogotá, the numbers of families living in spontaneous settlements more than doubled between 1964 and 1970—a rise from 37 to 46 per cent. of the city's total families (Valenzuela and Vernez, 1974). Similarly, the absolute numbers of people living in poor rented accommodation is also likely to have grown.

Clearly both the absolute size and the relative growth of this housing sector represents a major problem. It would be wrong, however, to assume that all forms of low-income housing provide unsatisfactory accommodation. Indeed, it may be argued that some of the mistakes which have been made by public housing agencies have stemmed from such a wrong assumption. All too often the urban literature has failed to distinguish between 'adequate' and squalid low-income housing. Such a distinction is critical for two reasons. First, it is clear that under certain conditions the poor tend to invest both their labour and their savings in improvements to their housing Consequently the low-income housing sector includes a variety of accommodation types ranging from adequate, serviced dwellings to unserviced, overcrowded slums. Second, the priorities of low-income people differ from those of architects. The wide range of housing conditions to be found in the poorer urban areas accommodates an equal diversity of housing requirements. Housing clearly ought to match individual circumstances and at different points in a personal career, with differing family characteristics and with differing levels of income and job security, demands placed upon housing vary widely. In certain circumstances what the poor require from housing has little to do with the material standards of their dwellings.

Unfortunately, low-income housing has all too often been judged only in terms of material standards, levels of service provision, design, and other quintessentially architectural criteria. The quality of low-income housing has been based on the standards of higher income people; any housing which has not matched these standards has been judged to be bad housing. Until recently few writers and still fewer government agencies questioned whether the above criteria were relevant to the Latin American situation and the current needs of the urban poor. As a result many errors were made, the principal of which was based on the assumption that the public sector was the only agent equipped to remove the housing deficit.

In an environment of plenty the application of more public resources can mitigate housing problems. Unfortunately, even in Europe it seems as if the problem is too great to be overcome by normal government housing programmes; however housing deficits are defined they always seem to be larger than the resources available to remove them. If this is true of Europe it is patently evident that Latin American governments cannot remove bad housing conditions for the majority of the population. Even to provide *basic* housing is an enormous task. U.N.E.C.L.A. (1962), for example, calculated that to provide a satisfactory home for every family in the 1950s almost one million new houses were required each year; by 1975 the revised estimate was 1.9 millions for the urban areas alone. Unfortunately, these figures did not deter most governments.

The domination of housing agencies by architects, the optimisms of so many governments in the 1950s and the 1960s when added to inaccurate information about the real nature of low-income settlement encouraged many public agencies to try build large numbers of conventional houses. Given the limited financial resources available in these countries, this required a choice between one of two alternatives. Either good housing would be provided by public agencies for limited numbers of people or the standards of construction would have to be reduced so as to provide large numbers of people with accommodation which met *basic minimum standards*. In the light of the above figures of deficits neither approach could prove satisfactory. The first approach simply provided too few homes. As we shall show below, no public housing agency succeeded in building sufficient houses even to keep up with the annual population growth. The second approach was in some respects still less successful. Poor housing was often destroyed and the inhabitants moved to minimum-standard accommodation. Unfortunately, the minimum standards did not usually match the needs of the poor who were moved. Sometimes poor housing was destroyed which had offered families support in ways not understood by middle-class architects. A common result was that the new housing was designed insensitively; material standards were invariably placed above the need for space so that the poor were unable to add additional rooms to their new dwellings; the new accommodation often occupied distant locations thereby generating long journeys to work; social networks were often disrupted; and income opportunities were limited by proscriptions on the use of housing for business activities (Ashton, 1972; Back, 1962; Bryce-Laporte, 1970; Rush, 1974; Safa, 1964). Because of such biases in housing design and administration, the new projects often failed to meet the poor's real needs.

It was the growing awareness that formal public-sector housing could never meet the quantitative needs of the expanding urban populations, and that it might not meet their qualitative needs either, which led to alternative formulations of quality criteria for low-income housing. Anthropological research in the 1960s had exposed a series of misunderstandings about squatter settlements and their populations (Mangin, 1967; Peattie, 1968; Turner 1968a, 1969). This work showed how squatter settlements often represented a satisfactory response to difficult circumstances and that the physical quality of many spontaneous settlements improved over time. Most importantly, it drew attention to the ways in which residents related to their residential environment and to their efforts at altering this accommodation to match their changing needs. Eventually Turner (1976) suggested a revised formula for evaluating the requirements of low-income populations. He suggested that the choice of housing represented a compromise between the demands for three universal housing needs: access, shelter, and tenure. It was clear that people had different priorities with respect to housing. The value of housing to its 'user' depended upon the degree to which it satisfied these priorities. Clearly the priorities of the poor were not those of the rich. Middle-income households ranked amenity and home ownership highly and usually chose to live away from the city centre and their places of work. Low-income residents fell into one of two broad groups. 'Bridgeheaders', who were often recently arrived migrants from the provinces, favoured proximity to work and sought cheap rented accommodation in downtown tenements. In contrast, 'consolidators', both city-born and migrants of longer standing, had a much stronger preference for home ownership (Turner, 1968b). They tended to occupy or purchase unserviced lots on the periphery and build their own accommodation. By trading off proximity to work in favour of a claim to land and the security which it offered, they hoped to achieve the means by which gradually to improve their housing situation.

For both these low-income groups housing quality was interpreted very differently from the criteria employed by housing agencies. While low-income residents would often have liked to live in fully serviced dwellings, the constraints associated with such housing (high rents and amortization payments, prohibitions on business occupations, etc.) made it unsuitable. The main 'quality' of spontaneous housing was the flexibility that it offered. Once the initial threat of removal had diminished, improvements were made to the physical structure of the dwellings. Such housing served, therefore, as a channel for investment and also offered a means of increasing income through the carrying on of a trade. Flexibility was also the hallmark insofar as home improvements were concerned; rooms could be added incrementally as the family expanded. Self-help reduced construction costs, made efficient use of spare or unemployed time, and in effect offered a 'freedom to build' (Turner, 1972). Therefore, although spontaneous housing did not conform with standards of quality founded upon architectural criteria, it had many other attributes which in a Latin American context could be considered of equal, if not greater, importance.

Our understanding of the term 'housing quality' has clearly been modified by Turner's and Mangin's work. No longer is it deemed appropriate to lay down high minimum standards with which all houses should be provided, especially when those standards are determined by middle-class and often foreign-trained architects. Increasingly, 'quality' is being judged in terms of the individual resident's needs within his existing socioeconomic environment. If the resident values location above good-quality materials, albeit for a temporary period, then that is the most appropriate housing, given his level in income and immediate family needs. Under this kind of definition, of course, spontaneous housing has a major advantage. By comparison with conventional public-housing solutions it is extremely flexible and can meet a wider range of residential needs. Partly for this reason, direct help for spontaneous housing has been widely advocated in recent years (Caufriez, 1972; Venezuela), Banco Obrero, 1972; World Bank, 1975.

Nevertheless, this definition of quality does pose difficulties. First, monitoring and catering for people's needs under a flexible and multiple set of criteria is very complex. The definition of what a public agency should be doing is much less easy than when it is simply building a particular form of housing. How are they to judge, for example, which section of the population needs most help? If the inner tenement slums are full of aspirant consolidators who will soon move to spontaneous housing then no action may be necessary. On the other hand, if the residents contain the old, the infirm, and the needy, intervention is required. Criteria can be established, but they require greater sensitivity on the part of administrators.

Second, the public response under this definition of quality can easily be misinterpreted. It is essential to underline the point that belief in the ability of the poor to assess their own needs is very different from believing that they have adequate means to satisfy those needs. Very often they would choose differently if their economic environment were less hostile. A spontaneous 'solution' may satisfy more families than inadequately financed public-housing 'solutions', but the former is in no sense an ideal response. The choice of a young family to live close to the city centre in an unserviced room may be the best solution to their immediate needs, even though the dwelling may be thoroughly undesirable in most other respects. What is wrong, however, is not the nature of the response but the social and economic environment which offers the poor such a limited set of choices. Quality, therefore, has been defined strictly in terms of a given social and economic environment; there is no doubt that in most Latin American cities that environment is oppressive. As we shall show below, the barriers facing the urban poor are great and in many societies many of the poor are doomed to a squalid existence for most of their lives. The governmental role, we believe, lies less in providing housing than in easing the task of self-help. Rather than trying to provide minimum-standard housing which the poor often do not want, governments should concentrate on reducing the main economic barriers to an adequate housing response. Such barriers affect large numbers of the urban population and consist of the high price of land and building materials, unemployment, low incomes, and increasingly sprawling and disorganized cities. Without such help the housing choices open to the poor will be unsatisfactory. The poor may be the best judges of their own housing needs, but without regular employment or access to cheap land they can do little to satisfy those needs. Governments ought to modify the socio-economic environment which constrains the individual housing response.

ÉLITE AND MIDDLE-INCOME HOUSING

The Iberian Conquests created a new urban system in Latin America. The city was used as a tool of colonialism, specifically for administration and for the extraction of taxes. Large numbers of new centres were founded, sometimes occupying new sites and sometimes being superimposed upon existing pre-Columbian cities (Hardoy and Schaedel, 1969; Morse, 1971b). Most of these cities exist today, and among them are numbered almost all of the region's largest urban centres. The colonial culture also generated a new and distinctive urban form. Spanish cities were planned on a standard land-use pattern; streets were laid out on a grid-iron basis centred on the *zocalo* or main square. Around this square were concentrated the principal religious and administrative buildings and the house of the Spanish élite; the poor lived nearer the edge of the city (Bataillon and D'Arc, 1973).

Political independence and foreign trade expansion initiated a process of social change which eventually modified this traditional land-use pattern. Towards the end of the nineteenth century, the landowning creole oligarchy was being displaced in many countries by a new mercantalist bourgoisie (Morse, 1971). This transformation altered the basis for judging social status; ascriptive criteria such as ethnicity and kinship were gradually replaced by more materialistic values such as the display of wealth. One vehicle for such display was housing, exemplified by the magnificent mansions constructed by the wealthiest families in Buenos Aires at the end of nineteenth century (Scobie, 1974). Gradually, the residential preferences of élite groups changed. Larger, more palatial homes required larger plots of land available only on the urban fringe; suburbanization had made a tentative beginning. Many of these élite families already owned weekend and summer residences in nearby villages—Flores and Belgrano in Buenos Aires, Chapinero in Bogotá, and San Angel and Tacubaya in Mexico City—and it was in the direction of these villages that residential expansion often occurred. New forms of transportation, particularly the electric tram at the turn of this century, and industrial and commercial expansion in downtown areas accelerated this trend. In Buenos Aires regular outbreaks of yellow fever in the downtown area accentuated the desirability of suburban life. Rapid rates of demographic growth and rising levels of car ownership encouraged élite groups to move further from the central areas. In most cities a succession of élite barrios appeared, each losing its fashionable status as architectural styles changed, population densities increased, and transport services improved.

The direction of élite suburban expansion was strongly influenced by environmental conditions. In Bogotá the areas to the north of the city centre offered an equable climate, fine views, and distance from the industrial sections of the city. Throughout the region, in fact, élites have always sought isolation, space, and the best available physical environment. Once established, élite areas influenced the land-use development of the whole city. Infrastructural provision in and around élite barrios was superior to standards in the rest of the city. Roads were built to accommodate the traffic flows caused by the use of the private car; and water, electricity, and drainage services were provided quickly by the public utilities. Private services also proliferated near such areas: luxury shopping areas, cinemas, restaurants, and private health and education facilities. Furthermore, élite residential areas affected the locations of other housing subsystems. Some aspirant middle-income groups mimicked the residential choices of their 'superiors' and occupied housing surrounding the élite barrios (Johnston, 1973). Other middle-income groups moved into vacated elite homes in the now less-fashionable areas. A similar process permitted the occupation of vacated downtown areas by commercial, academic, and professional services and in the least desirable parts by low-income families seeking rented accommodation. Spontaneous housing was also directed into areas distant from the élite suburbs, partly through the pressure of rising land prices and partly through the application of government zoning regulations (Violich, 1944). Even today élites do not generally live close to the poor in most Latin American cities.

Industrial and commerical expansion created large numbers of middle-income families. These families now occupy large areas of most Latin American cities. Despite their quantitative importance, however, little is known about the residential mobilities and preferences of these groups. That they aspire to North American and European housing and consumption styles is certain. In Turner's terms, they aim to buy fully-serviced homes located away from the city centre. The more prosperous can emulate the example of the élite and buy lots in land subdivisions where they construct architect-designed houses; unlike the subdivisions of the poor we describe below, however, these areas are fully serviced. Such subdivisions generally occupy land in the vicinity of élite barrios, but as cities expand more distant estates are developed. In Mexico City a self-contained suburb, Ciudad Satélite, has been developed beyond the urban fringe 15 kilometres north-west of the centre. Others may copy in less conventional ways; in Mexico City certain professional families recently imitated the poor and invaded land in the so-called pedregal (wasteland) to the south of the city. A more conventional response is for middle-income groups to rent or buy a ready-built house or apartment in a new 'urbanization'. For some, a further alternative is public housing. Often such housing is constructed by agencies associated with particular government workers such as the military or the police. Middle-income groups may also occupy public housing built for popular groups but which proved too expensive for most low-income families—a common situation in public-housing schemes, as we discuss below.

LOW-INCOME HOUSING

The choice of tenure

A critical choice facing low-income residents concerns tenure. Rented accommodation offers the user flexibility; compared to ownership, an individual is less tied to a particular location or to continued amortization payments. If he wishes, he can move closer to work or friends; if his income falls he can move to cheaper accommodation. On the other hand, renting usually offers little security; unless legislation prevents it, he may be evicted at short notice. Ownership, whether real or *de facto*, offers a different set of advantages. A foothold in the land market is a common motive both for purchasing land in a low-cost subdivision or for participating in a land invasion. Among a sample of squatters in Mexico City the wish 'to have something to leave one's children' was expressed more frequently than the wish to 'stop paying rent', 'for more space', or to satisfy any other single motive (Ward, 1976a). Once squatters have occupied land their principal aim is to obtain the legal title to their lot;

ownership offers security and thereby the ability to sell, sublet, or mortgage the holding. A major disadvantage is that most land available to low-income groups is located on the urban periphery or on difficult terrain. In the former case the cost of travel may reduce opportunities for 'odd jobbing'. For these reasons owners and renters often differ markedly in terms of age, occupation, family status, aspirations, and residential histories.

Low-income rental accommodation takes a variety of names and forms in different Latin American cities. They are called *inquilinatos* in Bogotá, *vecindades* in Mexico and Caracas, *casas de comodo* in Rio de Janeiro, *callejones* in Lima, and *conventillos* in Buenos Aires. They often occupy old colonial houses near the city centre which have been vacated by élite groups who have moved to more stylish accommodation in the healthier and more tranquil suburbs (Amato, 1968; Hanson, 1934; Scobie, 1974). Frequently, such houses contain rooms which look out on a central patio and may comprise one, two, or three storeys. A variation on this form of rented accommodation is the purpose-built *vecindad*. In Mexico City, for example, such buildings were constructed in the downtown district prior to rent-control legislation in the early 1940s. The design of these buildings closely resembled the central patio structure of the traditional *vecindades*. In both kinds of tenement, families occupy a single room and share water and sanitation services; the central patio serving as a communal area. Rents charged are generally low and where rent controls are in operation may be minimal. In some Mexican *vecindades* the rents may be as low as one U.S. dollar per month.

As populations expand and city centres are redeveloped the demand for tenement accommodation exceeds the supply. The surplus demand for rented accommodation is being satisfied in a variety of ways in different parts of the city. In Mexico City many small *vecindades* have developed recently in what were originally squatter settlements. These settlements, which were built during the 1940s and 1950s, are mainly located in what today constitutes the intermediate ring of the city (Brown, 1972; Ward, 1976b). Another common development is for low-income families to rent rooms to *inquilino* families. In one survey of home owners in Bogota as many as one-third of all homes had rooms sublet (Vernez, 1973b) and in another of government-built accommodation in Ciudad Kennedy 26 per cent. of the homes sublet (Reveiz and Zorro, 1976). Another kind of response is the rental shantytown. These *ciudades perdidas* in Mexico City, *favelas de quintil* in Rio, *corralones* in Lima, and rent-yards in the Caribbean are frequently located on inner-city lots. They consist of shacks which are sometimes built by landlords for rental purposes and sometimes by their occupants who pay rent to the owner of the land. These dwellings should not be confused with the shacks at the periphery built after a squatter invasion (Ward, 1976c). In the rental shantytowns rents absorb some of the investment surplus which might be invested otherwise in home improvement. The principal barrier to improvement, however, is insecurity of tenure. Services provided by the owner are minimal, and the continued existence of this housing alternative bears witness to the shortage of cheap rooms in central areas and, in some cities, the lack of public land suitable for invasion.

The relative importance of rental accommodation in major Latin American cities varies but is difficult to quantify. Morse (1971a) notes that in São Paulo the *casas de comodo* outnumber the *favelas* and in many Caribbean cities more people live in rentyards than in squatter settlements (Clarke and Ward, 1976). Clearly the essential factor determining the relative size of the rental sector is the degree to which low-income families are able to build their own accommodation. This ability depends in turn upon the availability of land, the attitudes of government, and the levels of absolute incomes among the poor. Where these factors operate against self-help 'solutions' then the rental market is likely to contain a high proportion of the urban poor.

Squatting versus land purchase

There is a considerable range of forms of 'ownership' in Latin American cities. The essential distinction, however, concerns the nature of land tenure. In many cities, the principal form is the illegal occupation of land, the so-called squatter settlement. In others, the most common pattern is the purchase from private speculators of small lots which lack building and planning permission. Settlements built on such land are known as *barrios pratas* in Colombia and *fraccionamientos clandestinos* in Mexico. Lots are laid out on a grid-iron basis by the subdivider, who may or may not install services such as sewerage or electricity but who usually promises to arrange such services once all lots have been sold and capital is available. The status of these settlements varies according to the degree of their illegality. Often the subdivider does not legally own the land. This is particularly common in Mexico where *ejido* lands, established after the Revolution and owned under usufruct rights by the community, have frequently been subdivided (Frieden, 1965–66). Alternatively, the subdivider owns the land but fails to meet the standards of service provision, community facilities, open spaces, and so on, required by the law—the common pattern in Bogotá (Vernez, 1973a). In both squatter settlements and illegal subdivisions self-help construction is the norm, while services are generally installed by the government after a long petitioning process.

Squatters are fully aware that they have no legal claim to the land. Where there is a threat of immediate post-invasion eradication, a strategy has usually been arranged previously to increase their chances of success. Careful organization and forward planning are normal among invasion communities. They tend to invade public land because the moral and potential electoral pressure on governments often guarantees continued occupancy. Invasions of private land are rare, except where there is real doubt about the identity of the owner. The prior soliciting of political help is common, as is the garnering of sympathetic publicity through the display of national flags and statements of support for the government. Their success depends upon a variety of factors which we discuss below. In many cases, however, their security is as absolute as legal ownership, so that settlers are willing to improve their dwellings. In less-successful cricumstances doubts about security limit home improvements to a minimum.

The residents of illegal subdivision normally feel very secure, even when their legal rights of ownership are somewhat precarious (Doebele, 1975). In Bogotá there also seems to be a measure of trust between the low-income residents and the subdividers. The other advantage of this form of tenure is that it offers access to credit. Unlike most conventional finance and housing agencies, subdividers will give credit to poor people who lack collateral. Nevertheless, the cost of the land is usually high, even when services are lacking. For the subdivider the risks are considerable, but if successful the rewards are large; Doebele (1975) estimated the profits from four subdivisions in Bogotá to range from 35 per cent. to more than 1000 per cent. Compared to the squatter settlement, therefore, the cost to the individual settler is high. Even though squatters frequently contribute towards the costs of providing services, their total outlay is far smaller than in the case of illegal subdivisions. This difference in outlay has important implications for low-income housing development. *Ceteris paribus*, squatters ought to have a clear advantage once some degree of security has been achieved. Faced with lower costs squatters ought to have a larger surplus from their incomes to invest in home improvements. On the other hand, squatter settlements are often less secure and are often located long distances from employment centres. Strangely, few writers have to our knowledge carried out direct comparisons between the two types of settlement.

The relative importance of each tenure form varies from city to city. The principal factors determining the mix would seem to be the structure of the land market and the attitude of government. Where land has limited alternative use values or is publicly owned, squatting tends to be more common. Around Lima, for example, the extensive desert land made squatting possible on a wide scale, especially since some of the land was owned by the state. The process of invasion, indeed, was actively encouraged by élite groups who were anxious to regain possession of the downtown tenements which they owned (Collier, 1976). If the invaded land was privately owned or was required for future land-use development, a compromise would usually be struck whereby squatters would be moved to an alternative site. In Caracas, land is less abundant, but on hillsides unsuited to conventional housing construction invasions can take place with little risk of eviction. In both Lima and Caracas, therefore, the land demands of low-income groups may be satisfied through squatting. In neither case is the value of land sufficient to threaten the interests of the private sector. Indeed, in both cities, invasions are sometimes manipulated by real estate interests. By contrast, in Mexico City, São Paulo, and Bogotá, illegal subdivisions are more common. In Bogotá, the fertile land of the surrounding *Sabana* gives it a high agricultural value. The private sector is highly resistant, therefore, to any threat of invasion, as indeed are government agencies who own extensive tracts of land; the police force in Bogotá have strict instructions about how to deal with invasions and the few attempts which have been made have resulted in conflict (Cardona, 1969). As a consequence only 1 per cent. of dwellings in Bogotá are located in invasion colonies. In such circumstances the only real alternative to renting is the purchase of illegal subdivisions.

Government attitudes towards invasion are clearly critical, even where extensive land is unsuitable for other uses. Attitudes vary considerably both between countries and between one national administration and another. Often changes of government bring major reversals or revisions of policy. The Pérez Jimenez dictatorship in Venezuela eradicated large numbers of *ranchos* in Caracas during the 1950s and resettled their populations in the now-infamous superblocks (Carlson, 1961; Dwyer, 1975). His downfall in 1958 saw the resurgence of *rancho* formation both on the hillsides and between the high-rise buildings themselves. Similarly, the restrictions on invasions which existed in Mexico City under Governor Uruchurtu (1952–1966) were removed when he was replaced. In contrast to his refusal to recognize existing squatter settlements, Cornelius (1973b) describes the spurt of legalization activities and service installation that took place under the new administration. Government attitudes to invasions may also vary between cities within the same country. Apart from differences in the local land market, governments may oppose invasions in certain cities, especially in the largest centres, as a deterrent to further inmigration. Similarly, government attitudes often vary either side of a local government boundary. In Mexico City, a prohibition upon the construction of low-income subdivisions in the Federal District imposed in 1952 led to the proliferation of illegal subdivisions beyond the urban fringe in the adjacent state of Mexico where the law did not apply. Thereafter, invasions took place inside the Federal District and are today significant in the south and west of the city.

Patterns of housing mobility and improvement

The *leit-motif* of this discussion is the manner in which different socioeconomic groups adjust their demands for housing to the available supply. The residential choices of low-income groups are highly rational, and we propose to describe briefly the grounds on which the poor choose their residential locations and how they act to improve their housing situations.

Early writing perceived squatter settlements as reception areas for incoming rural migrants. Faced with difficulties of integration into 'modern' city life these migrants were forced to live in miserable shacks located in 'marginal' areas of the city (Bonilla, 1961; Cervantes, 1968; Schulman, 1968). The changing views of squatter areas which emerged from the research carried out in the 1960s and 1970s also gave rise to doubts about this process. Research in Lima by Mangin and Turner (Mangin, 1967, Mangin and Turner, 1968; Turner, 1963) showed that most participants in squatter invasions were not newly arrived migrants but came from the downtown rental *callejones*. Turner later argued that access to cheap rented accommodation close to the sources of unskilled employment led most new migrants to prefer accommodation in the inner-city tenements. Only later, when they had gained more secure employment and 'adjusted' to city life, did the desires for more space, to own land, and to avoid rental payment persuade them to participate in an organized invasion or an illegal subdivision project. Spatial mobility, therefore, went hand in glove with socioeconomic mobility and changing household needs (Turner, 1968b). Research in other parts of Latin America gave support to this 'inner city to periphery' model for Oaxaca in Mexico (Butterworth, 1973) and for Bogotá (Flinn, 1971) and Barranquilla (Usandizaga and Havens, 1966) in Colombia.

More recently, however, the relevance of this model to the larger metropoli has been questioned (Brown, 1972; Gilbert, 1974; Lomnitz, 1975 Ward, 1976b;). Reacting to this criticism, Turner (1968b) has argued that his model is appropriate to the conditions of 'early transitional cities' such as Lima and Mexico in the 1950s, but not to today's large metropolitan areas. In the latter, a series of mechanisms blocked migrant access to the city centres—specifically, a declining central housing stock, increasing numbers of potential renters already in the city, land speculation, and artificial constraints such as rent controls. More common in such cities was a pattern whereby migrants rented accommodation or lived with kin in the intermediate ring or periphery. Brown (1972) drew attention to the fact that renters in the intermediate ring of Mexico City had a lower social status than either renters nearer the centre or 'owners' on the periphery. She explained this finding in terms of the preference of the more prosperous low-income groups to remain in the inner-city tenements. Rather than move to the periphery to build their own dwellings they preferred to take advantage of existing rent controls and the facilities of the central area of the city. This action, of course, blocked the paths of newly arrived migrants who were forced to rent accommodation in the intermediate ring. This process differed from the original Turner model, although Brown (1972, p. 17) was at pains to point out that '... the basic functional priorities of the dwelling environment—location, tenure, and amenity—continue to operate for the poor and the unskilled in the migrant population at differing stages of the urbanization and economic history of a nation in the way that the Turner theory suggests'.

Ward (1976b) also found signs of a recent breakdown in the original Turner location model. Although the dominant pattern of migrant movement in the 1940s and 1950 had been towards the centre and then to the periphery, in the 1960s and 1970s newly arrived migrants tended to move first to accommodation in the older established spontaneous housing areas. Similar findings have been found for Monterrey (Vaughn and Feindt, 1973) and for Bogotá, where new migrants have moved into rooms in the pirate *barrios* in the south and west of the city (Vernez, 1973a). Elsewhere, surveys show increasing population stability within inner-city areas (Uzzell, 1974; Valencia, 1965). One common feature of most cities through time, however, is the tendency for newly arriving families to stay with relations. Insofar as increasing numbers of these relations live in spontaneous settlements, this represents a further force modifying the original Turner location model.

As Brown (1972) argued, however, there is no question of rejecting the basic rationale of spontaneous settlement progression developed by Turner. Providing that socioeconomic conditions are not oppressive, squatter settlements offer the urban poor a means for upward socioeconomic mobility. Settlements which begin as collections of straw-mat or cardboard houses can soon develop into more solid urban areas. Providing municipal authorities do not intervene in a negative way, squatters gradually improve their dwellings. The provisional shacks are eventually replaced by one-roomed brick dwellings with corrugated roofs and concrete floors.

Improvements are predominantly the work of the owners themselves, though major jobs, such as the erection of a concrete roof, require the help of friends and/or local *albaniles* (bricklayers). Positive government intervention is critical in the process of home improvement, particularly the need for the legalization of land in the case of squatter settlements (Andrews and Phillips, 1970). Such intervention may be either explicit or implicit. Explicit action is the most effective stimulus to home improvement. In some cities, land is expropriated and sold back to the occupants at a minimum price, thereby guaranteeing tenure and compensation in the event of eradication. In Caracas, expropriated land remains in the hands of the government, but some compensation can be given to *rancho* owners in lieu of physical investments they have made prior to removal. The most common form of implicit intervention comes in the installation of services in spontaneous settlements. This form of recognition is often an effective incentive for home improvement.

In both squatter settlements and illegal subdivisions the major responsibilities for service provision results with the government and municipal authorities. Residents petition the authorities both directly and through their locally elected leaders; often a two-way cooption game evolves whereby squatters 'sell' political support in exchange for essential services (Cornelius, 1973a, 1973b; Ray, 1969). The wish of governments to control low-income population and the desire of local leaders to maintain their power help to explain why it sometimes takes up to twenty years for all services to be provided. Usually electricity is the first service to be installed and brings to an end the system of stealing power through illegal 'hook-ups'. Water hydrants are often next, installed in the street for communal use, and are followed by street paving, refuse collection, police services, and so on. The most expensive elements, drainage and private water supplies, are often the last to be installed.

The residents, as well as petitioning for services, may also improve the settlement through collective action. Such action may involve the digging of toilet pits, the levelling of streets, and the construction of a church, a school, or a community centre. In addition, they use their spare time and cash to improve their own homes—adding a new room, plastering a wall, putting in window frames, and so on.

Successful settlements which have existed for eight or nine years demonstrate a marked range of home improvements. In Caracas, where accretive squatter growth is the norm, this heterogeneity reflects differences in the length of residence of households in the *barrio*. Peattie (1969, p.19) describes the result as 'a stratigraphy which, as in archaeology, expressed evolutionary change through time by sequence and levels and forms. At the bottom of the hill the dwellings are plastered and painted masonry; just above come rough block walls; at the top are the board and tin shacks. To climb the hill is to run a development history backwards.' In communities in which all the households were formed at the same time, variations in housing quality reflects the different abilities of households to engage in home improvement (Turner, 1969). Not all spontaneous settlers, of course, are successful consolidators. A comparison of successful and less-successful squatters in Mexico City showed that improvements in squatter homes did not simply reflect length of residence but also had a positive relationship with job security, levels of income, and nature of occupation. A significant proportion of rapid consolidators were lower–middle-income groups who had been attracted to the settlements by the availability of cheap land. Many squatters, however, had scarcely improved their homes, even after ten years, and for them the settlement did not provide a vehicle of upward socioeconomic mobility but merely a means of survival (Harms, 1976; Ward, 1976a). Such improvements are clearly not inevitable. Some individuals lack the means to improve their housing due to unemployment, illness, and other difficulties, even in a generally buoyant economy. In slowly expanding economies, of course, low-income households face a more difficult task. There are also some low-income communities, as Roberts (1973) has shown for Guatemala City and Rogler (1967) for San Juan, where *barrio* organization and mutual help is extremely limited. Clearly the success of self-help is critically related to the wider social and economic environment;—a point which we develop more fully in the next section.

TEMPORAL CHANGES IN THE HOUSING SITUATION

The fact that spontaneous settlements house higher proportions of Latin American urban dwellers than ever before is open to a variety of interpretations. Many writers have argued that it demonstrates that conditions in Latin American cities are deteriorating and that the population has become increasingly 'marginalized' over time (Castells, 1973; Lazano, 1975; Pradilla, 1976; Quijano, 1971). Put as simply as this, the argument is unsatisfactory. If services such as water, electricity, and drainage are gradually extended to spontaneous settlements, if rooms are added and even a second floor constructed, then many dwellings will have more in common with conventional housing than with the flimsy shacks normally associated with the term 'spontaneous housing'. In such circumstances, therefore, a proportion, and possibly a considerable proportion, of the housing ought not to be classified with the poorest dwellings. To confuse the term spontaneous settlement with slums and to assume that a quantitative increase in the former proves that a deterioration in housing standards has taken place, negates the useful work done in Lima by Mangin and Turner. If spontaneous settlement does improve through time then perhaps different conclusions should be drawn. In any case, before the proliferation of spontaneous settlements may be interpreted either favourably or unfavourably it is necessary to consider in detail the changing conditions of those dwellings. Are more dwellings provided with services than previously? How have land-use patterns affected the locations of squatter housing? Are the real costs of building these dwellings higher or lower than previously? Without such supporting evidence the proliferation of spontaneous settlements proves little beyond the fact that Latin American cities are expanding rapidly and remain too poor to provide conventional housing for all their inhabitants.

Even if it can be demonstrated that housing conditions have deteriorated, or for that matter improved, then accurate interpretation is still difficult. If, for instance, higher proportions of urban dwellers are living in bad housing conditions than previously, this may only be a symptom of the rapid movement of people from rural to urban areas. Poor-quality self-help housing is virtually the only form of dwelling to be found in the Latin American countryside. The fact that it should appear in larger quantities in the urban areas over a particular time period may well reflect the movement of poor people to the cities and the continuance of poverty in the society as a whole. Similarly, a clear improvement in housing conditions needs to be interpreted carefully. It is possible that housing improvements in one or several cities have taken place at the expense of conditions elsewhere in the country. If, for example, governments have channelled investment resources into the major cities and neglected the smaller towns and rural areas, a not uncommon situation, then housing improvements are placed in a less-favourable light.

Changing housing conditions also have to be considered in the context of national and local circumstances. Most countries pass through periods of economic difficulty which may cut per capita incomes, raise unemployment levels, and directly hurt the poor. Under such circumstances it would be natural for housing conditions to deteriorate; services cannot be provided quickly in a slow-growing economy; rural–urban migration may accelerate if there are major economic problems in the rural areas, thereby putting further pressure on the urban housing stock; and the incomes of the urban poor will no longer allow them to improve their housing conditions. Clearly, the relationship between the state of the national economy and changing housing conditions is a close one. It is not, however, a direct or a linear relationship. The rate of economic growth is, at best, only a partial indicator of the opportunities open to different social groups for improving their housing. There is evidence from Brazil that despite a general growth in income between 1962 and 1966, the incomes of the poorest two-thirds of the population of Fortaleza declined by 13 per cent. while those of the richest one-third increased by a similar amount (Gilbert and Goodman, 1976). In Bogotá between 1972 and 1975 a construction boom increased job opportunities and incomes for many poor people. Parallel to this boom, however, went a rise in the rate of inflation of building materials and possibly the price of land, which made self-help housing much more expensive. Rapid economic growth *per se* does not guarantee the participation of the poor, and changing housing conditions are likely to reflect the distribution of benefits.

What complicates any evaluation of changing housing conditions still further is the variety of criteria which must be included and the limited statistical data available in many Latin American cities on which to base any judgement. Certainly any general empirical statement about housing conditions throughout

TABLE 7.1. Changing proportions in percentages of homes lacking water and electricity

	Running water			Electricity		
Colombia[a]	1951		1964	1951		1964
Bogotá, D. E.	15.9		10.6	19.7		12.0
Medellín	19.9		16.3	22.9		19.9
Cartagena	22.9		49.2	53.7		46.2
Pereira	30.7		60.0	29.9		58.5
Buenaventura	60.2		85.5	62.3		84.3
Venezuela[b]	1961		1971	1961		1971
Caracas D. F.	28.8		17.8	4.7		1.3
Brazil[b]	1950	1960	1970	1950	1960	1970
Greater São Paulo	46.9		41.1	20.9		7.1
Recife	71.1		46.9	49.5		14.4
Salvador	68.2		45.3	52.6		20.8
Guanabara	N.A.	23.3	17.1	N.A.	6.5	4.8
Niteroi	44.0		28.3	23.6		6.2
Mexico[b]	1950	1960	1970			
Guadalajara	55.0	27.9	21.9			
Monterrey	51.0	40.8	35.3			
Veracruz	51.4	38.1	36.5			
Puebla	69.3	N.A.	43.6			
Mérida	87.0	60.8	44.1			
Chihuahua	53.7	48.2	42.2			

[a] Without tubed water in the same building.
[b] Without tubed water in the home.
N. A. Not available.
Source. Respective National Population and Housing Censuses.

Latin America is impossible to make. This can be demonstrated by comparing the changing distributions of two service variables in different cities—the proportions of house lacking water and electricity (Table 7.1).

Table 7.1 shows that for a selection of cities of varying size and prosperity for which data are available, there is no consistent pattern. In the Brazilian and Mexican cities and in Caracas there are signs of improvement, but in many Colombian cities the contrary appears to be the case. In most of the cities an enormous rise in the absolute numbers of houses served reflects the genuine efforts on the part of many local governments to remove infrastructural problems. Despite these efforts, however, Table 7.2 shows that the absolute numbers of homes without services have increased markedly. In São Paulo, for example, although the proportion of homes without water declined from 47 to 41 per cent., the numbers of homes without water rose from less than 300 000 to more

TABLE 7.2. Temporal deficits in water supply

	Humbles of homes without water			Total number of homes		
Colombia[a]	1951	1964		1951	1964	1964
Bogotá D. E.	11 852	20 505		74 399	193 737	
Medellín	9 967	17 902		50 110	110 124	
Cartagena	5 813	15 627		15 797	31 732	
Pereira	4 712	15 081		15 373	25 122	
Buenaventura	5 349	13 134		8 887	15 357	
	1961	1971		1961	1971	
Venezuela						
Caracas D. F.	65 878	32 663		228 873	334 361	
Brazil	1950	1960	1970	1950	1960	1970
Greater São Paulo	292 784	N. A.	706 786	623 613	N. A.	1 720 556
Recife	74 485	N. A.	90 711	104 804	N. A.	193 609
Salvador	58 688	N. A.	80 994	86 065	N. A.	178 881
Guanabara	N. A.	164 913	163 438	N. A.	708 218	953 883
Niteroi	14 801	N. A.	18 816	33 666	N. A.	66 414
Mexico	1950	1960	1970	1950	1960	1970
Guadalajara	42 815	34 574	38 655	77 776	123 819	176 190
Monterrey	34 218	43 538	52 054	67 159	106 817	147 447
Veracruz	12 087	11 520	16 358	23 506	30 260	44 867
Puebla	33 950	N. A.	41 701	48 974	N. A.	95 632
Mérida	27 600	20 853	18 574	31 754	34 274	42 109
Cihuahua	12 067	16 619	20 573	22 483	34 482	48 773

[a]Without tubed water in the same building or in the home.
N. A. Data not available.
Source. Respective National Population and Housing Censuses.

than 700 000—a clear consequence of the rapid growth of the city population. Efforts are being made throughout the region to improve services, but they are rarely adequate to the task. It is equally clear from Table 7.1 that the efforts vary considerably from city to city. In Colombia, Bogotá and Medellín have clearly received many more service improvements than the smaller cities. In São Paulo, despite massive efforts, a higher proportion of people are without water than in most Mexican cities, even though by Latin American standards São Paulo is a very rich city.

These data on services suggest that we must be careful about generalizing across the continent about changing housing conditions. Because of variations in per capita income levels, rates of demographic growth, levels of government commitment and efficiency, and even topographic and climatic factors, the conditions and changes vary. What we believe is more valuable is to examine the kinds of circumstance under which housing conditions are likely to deteriorate and to discuss whether such circumstances are becoming more common in Latin American cities. One way of doing this is to consider the processes of change occurring in selected urban areas.

Most Brazilian writers have little doubt that conditions are deteriorating in cities such as São Paulo. The principal causes, however, lie outside the sphere of housing and are a reflection of the organization of society and particularly the distribution of income. Ferreira da Camargo *et al.* (1976) argue that economic growth is favouring the middle- and higher-income groups and that despite major increases in per capita income the real incomes of the poor have actually declined. Thus in São Paulo real incomes of family heads declined in real terms by 37 per cent. between 1958 and 1969, although the employment of more people in the family reduced the decline in family income to only 9 per cent. Related to the declines in income are a worsening of other social conditions. Rates of infant mortality, after falling by 30 per cent. during the 1940s and again during the 1950s, rose by 45 per cent. between 1960 and 1973. Clearly, the poor of São Paulo are suffering from the social consequences of the Brazilian economic 'miracle', and worsening housing conditions are one symptom of this situation.

In addition, the manner in which urban expansion is occurring and the land-use pattern is changing are harming the poor. Real estate speculation is leading to the destruction of the central city low-income housing areas. The poor are forced to move to the distant fringes of the city where land is available. Even here, however, spontaneous settlement is made difficult by land speculators who hold land vacant waiting for it to be serviced and thereby rise in value. The major consequence for the poor is that they are forced to move to areas a long way from the main areas of employment. Long bus journeys are therefore becoming commonplace, which poses an important time and economic constraint on family life. The efforts of local government to service the peripheral spontaneous settlements are also hampered by the speculative process; the distance from existing networks and services often complicates government efforts to integrate these settlements. Unable to control the pattern of land use, and with limited financial resources, the local government tends to provide services for those areas close to existing service lines. Since the populations of these areas tend to be drawn from middle- and upper-income groups, the distribution of services perpetuates the inequalities in the city and accentuates social segregation. Housing problems are clearly a reflection of society in São Paulo; the paradox whereby 'there is... a growth in the consumption of luxury goods and a diminution in the real minimum salary' is directly reflected in the housing situation (Ferreira da Camargo *et al.*, 1976, p. 17).

By contrast, the housing situation in Bogotá, while difficult, does not appear to be deteriorating, despite high rates of demographic growth. The reasons why this should be so are several. The Colombian economy has grown consistently during the last thirty years, which has created jobs and raised income levels. And while a repressive tax system has not helped the poor the government have not controlled low incomes, as in Brazil or Chile. This situation has allowed many poor families to improve their housing conditions by purchasing peripheral land and building their own dwellings. Local government, while not always quick or willing to service many of these settlements, has generally done so eventually, and the numbers of homes without basic services in Bogotá is relatively low (Table 7.1). In addition, while the location of housing has normally been peripheral to the city and journey-to-work distances have been increasing, this has not so far created major problems. In part this is because the distances in Bogotá are still relatively small (it is a city of only 3 millions compared to 10 millions in São Paulo). Movement is also helped by the cheapness and efficiency of the bus system; it may be overcrowded and uncomfortable but it does allow most workers to travel cheaply. There is no guarantee, of course, that this situation will continue. As Bogotá continues to grow distances will increase, and if land-use patterns are not modified to create a more decentralized employment pattern then traffic congestion will worsen (B.U.D.S., 1974). Such a situation would clearly hurt the poor. In addition, it can be argued that Bogotá has escaped a crisis to date because it has been favoured by the centre–periphery situation operating in Colombia. Resources have been invested in Bogotá while other areas have been neglected (A.N.I.F., 1974; Gilbert, 1976). It is possible that this situation may be altered in the future. If that should happen, then the effects of inefficient administration in the city would no longer be cushioned and the housing conditions might well deteriorate (Gilbert, 1977). Once again it is clear that what determines housing conditions for the poor is the wider socio-economic environment.

The cases of Bogotá and São Paulo illustrate how the housing situation varies from city to city and from nation to nation. They also exemplify some of the critical factors determining the housing situation of the poor. We cannot predict what may happen to housing conditions in Latin American cities in the future. What is certain is that the outcome will depend upon several critical variables.

First, in those cities where real incomes per capita increase, where the poorest half of the population participate in that increase, and where there is a consistent rise in the number of jobs available in the formal sector, the housing situation is likely to improve. Increasing real incomes should generate revenues with which local government can finance infrastructural improvements. The growth of incomes of the poorest half of the population should create more savings which—providing that the real costs of construction do not rise—will encourage the improvement of spontaneous housing. A consistent increase in formal-sector employment will generate additional jobs in the informal sector. These assumptions seem to have been satisfied in many of the region's largest cities during the post-war period, although the same is not true of most of the smaller centres. Economic growth rates have been sufficiently high throughout the region to create jobs and higher incomes for the populations of the larger cities. It has only been during periods of economic stress and where governments have operated regressive monetary policies that the poor have generally suffered. Whether this situation will continue is, of course, another question. As import-substitution policies become less effective (Gilbert, 1974) and as urban populations continue to soar, existing social and economic problems may be accentuated. It is also possible that poorer groups may find it harder to obtain employment for other reasons. In most Latin American countries credentialism seems to be increasing, and semiskilled jobs in either the formal or the informal sector are less open to the unqualified applicant (Balán, 1969). Increasingly, the jobs which were available in the informal sector, such as newspaper and lottery ticket vending, motor repairing, and so on, are controlled by the erstwhile newcomer poor (Peattie, 1975). It is possible, though uncertain, that future newcomers will find the employment situation far more difficult and will therefore experience major problems in obtaining sufficient funds to invest even in a spontaneous housing 'solution'.

Second, the continued access to land and building materials is critical. In those cities where invasion has been the traditional source of supply, the future situation will depend mainly upon the continued willingness of governments to allow the occupation of public or private land. In turn, government attitudes will be influenced by the availability of such land; in cities such as Rio or Caracas the topographical constraints on physical expansion are such that land suitable for invasion is increasingly difficult to find within the city limits. In those cities where land purchase is the norm, the future prospects of the poor will depend upon the cost of that land. Clearly the cost of land is likely to rise over time if the economy at large is expanding (McCallum, 1974). Providing that the distribution of income does not worsen, land should be available on the periphery at similar real prices as previously. Only if there are physical constraints on expansion, or if major efforts are made to increase land prices through speculation, are the poor likely to be threatened. On the other hand, it is possible, and clearly to be hoped, that governments will introduce reforms in the future to tax speculative land gains. The future is unclear and will clearly vary from city to city and according to the priorities of different national and local governments.

Building material costs are also a critical variable in determining the ability of the poor to construct their own dwellings. As we have already seen in Bogotá, the prices of materials rose rapidly during a period of building boom. Similarly in Mexico City, the prices of steel, wood, and cement increased by 111, 68, and 59 per cent. respectively between 1972 and 1974, a period when minimum wage rates rose by only 37 per cent. (Mexico C.N.I.C., 1975; Mexico C.N.S.M., 1975). Unless uncontrolled monopolies operate in the building supply industry there is no reason why real prices should increase dramatically in the future. Where prices do increase, however, and where governments fail to control this inflation, spontaneous housing will become more difficult.

Third, the ability of local governments to service low-income housing will continue to vary from city to city. In the future the situation may be helped in some places by slower rates of population growth. The critical factors, however, are the ability to generate revenues and to keep coasts at a minimum. The availability of finance will depend both upon the rate of economic expansion and upon the willingness of governments to increase tax levels. The question of costs is more important in certain cities than in others. In places where housing tends to occupy high or poorly drained land, providing water and sanitation services may be difficult and expensive. Similarly, in cities located in dry areas, cheap sources of water may become more scarce. Mexico City already fetches water from long distances and in Caracas water supplies will be inadequate if the city region reaches its forecast population of 9 million inhabitants in the year 2000 (Lander and Urdaneta, 1975).

Fourth, spatial segregation between social groups and the pattern of urban land use may affect the quality of housing for the poor. There are signs that in many Latin American cities social segregation is becoming more marked. One factor is the increasing size of city which is leading to greater distances between élite and poor residential *barrios*. In itself such a development may or may not be harmful. Are we entitled to assume that the poor are any keener to live near the rich than are the rich to live near the poor? But where such segregation is associated with major disparities in public services it must be seen as an undesirable trait. Equally critical is the spatial relationship between homes and places of employment. If most employment opportunities are mainly concentrated in the central business districts and spontaneous settlements continue to occupy peripheral land, the poor are likely to face longer journeys to work and higher transport costs. This may be a critical factor for some kinds of workers. Employees such as bakers or road-sweepers who start work in the early hours or *pepenadores* (scavengers) who make their living out of collecting waste paper, bottles, etc., require housing within walking distance of their 'workplace'. On the other hand, workers with stable office or factory jobs may only be mildly inconvenienced by long journeys and early starts to the day; location is not essential to their existence. At current rates of physical growth in Latin American cities travel to work represents a major problem; Bogotá, for example, more than doubled its physical area between 1958 and 1972. The hope must be that subcentres will develop which will offer jobs closer to the peripheral settlements. Planning is obviously vital in this respect and the Colombian government is striving to stimulate subcentre development in numerous cities (Colombia D.N.P., 1974; Gilbert, 1977). Certainly, unless greater order is brought to urban land use and to traffic flows all urban groups will suffer the consequences (Gilbert, 1976).

Finally, the ability of the poor to influence governments has always been a vital determinant of their housing situation (Collier, 1976; Cornelius, 1973b; Leeds, 1969). Many governments often try to buy support through infrastructural provision or through turning a blind eye to invasions. Electoral policies are closely involved in the housing situation. Currently, however, Latin America is going through a period of increasing military rule. At the time of writing only the governments of Colombia, Mexico, Venezuela, and Costa Rica can make any pretence at maintaining democracy. It would be erroneous, of course, to suggest that military governments are insensitive to public opinion or to the situation of the poor. Some military governments, such as that in Peru since 1968, have introduced important social reforms, and in the past certain populist dictators have given help to the poor. Nevertheless, recent experiences in Argentina, Brazil, Chile, and Uruguay do not bode well. In these countries economic policies have been introduced which have led to a deterioration in the situation of the poor. As long as this kind of policy continues, the housing conditions of the poor will deteriorate in line with their general economic and social situation.

ALTERNATIVE APPROACHES TO HOUSING

Most Latin American governments have intervened in the housing situation in three ways: they have established agencies to build houses for the lower-income groups; they have provided loan facilities for families wishing to buy housing; and they have provided infrastructure. Many, though not all, of these actions have been well intentioned and some of the agencies concerned with housing have been highly efficient. The basic problem facing all three responses, however, has been a basic inability to satisfy the growing demand for adequate housing and services. Construction programmes have usually been limited by the shortage of financial resources made available to the housing agencies. This financial constraint has been increased by the difficulty of acquiring cheap land. Rapid rates of population and economic growth in urban areas when allied to speculative processes have made land acquisition very expensive for public agencies. Often their task has been made still more difficult because they have concentrated their efforts in the largest cities; while the absolute numbers of housing units required in these centres has often been greatest, construction elsewhere would have been much cheaper. These various difficulties have invariably limited the numbers of units built by public agencies: in Chile the public sector managed around 20 000 units a year between 1960 and 1967 (Lozano, 1975) and in Colombia I.C.T. built an average of 12 400 units between 1962 and 1970 (C.E.N.A.C., 1975).

Similarly, although numerous public institutions have been established to provide mortgages for home purchase, the high costs of conventional housing in most Latin American cities has meant that poorer groups were automatically excluded from purchasing such accommodation. Very few efforts have been made to subsidize mortgage schemes, often for the very good reason that the financial resources were not available. Where subsidies have been offered, they have too often benefited middle-income groups. Loans have rarely been cheap, but they have generally offered a good investment to those fortunate enough to be granted credit.

To a lesser extent service provision has also favoured the more prosperous groups. Prodigious efforts have succeeded in supplying large numbers of households with water, electricity, and sanitation services, but, as Table 7.2 revealed, providing comprehensive coverage has normally been impossible. In most cities increasing numbers of city dwellers lack services and inevitably the unserviced have been drawn mainly from the poor.

Apart from these conventional approaches to the housing problem, direct government action has been limited. Nevertheless, the period since the Second

World War has been marked by some interesting interludes when governments have tried more original approaches to their housing difficulties. Frequently these actions have been only partially successful, either because the programme was shortlived or because it was misconceived. But if answers to the housing situation are possible in isolation from other reforms in society, they may well lie among the measures which we now describe. These measures reveal widely divergent social and political priorities which reflect the range of ideologies embraced by the governments concerned. The policies range from the mass production of public housing in socialist Chile and Cuba, through efforts to help spontaneous settlers, to schemes encouraging housing construction by the private building industry in Brazil and Colombia.

The Cuban (1959–present date) and Chilean (1970–1973) approaches are interesting in the sense that they were designed to directly help the poor simultaneously introducing structural reforms to society. Both the Castro and the *Unidad Popular* governments adopted rent controls and took measures against land and building speculation. In both cases the controls were successful in reducing rents. The Cuban controls were the stricter and involved the expropriation of certain kinds of rented property: slums, rooming houses, and similar kinds of low-income accommodation. The state in fact assumed the role of housing administrator—licensing housing and allocating people between dwelling units. The policy was successful in removing exploitive forms of landlordism. On the other hand, it proved difficult for people to change their accommodation and offered the state an effective means of controlling intercity and interregional migration. Both governments also participated directly in the production of housing units—in Chile with the collaboration of the private sector and in Cuba after 1963 as the sole producer (Acosta and Hardoy, 1972). In both countries more investment was directed into the housing sector than previously, and unit production levels undoubtedly increased. In Chile, for example, the 1971 budget for housing was more than double that of its Christian Democrat predecessor. Unfortunately, neither government produced as many units as it had anticipated. In Chile, severe difficulties were encountered as a result of the major economic crisis which faced the country after 1971. In Cuba, although production in the 1960s was sufficient to supply three-quarters of the demand due to natural increase, attempts to accelerate production further in the 1970s appear to have failed. The result has been to increase overcrowding in existing accommodation, admittedly at very low rents. These experiences suggest that even under socialist conditions the public sector cannot provide manufactured housing units in adequate numbers to satisfy demand. It is interesting to note, however, that despite this problem neither government embraced site and service schemes. In Cuba this was due to their total belief in mass-production methods; in Chile it was a reaction to the effect of such programmes under the Frei government (1964–1970).

Site and service projects and other forms of direct help for spontaneous settlements became fashionable as the result of Mangin's and Turner's work in Lima. The Venezuela Banco Obrero (1972) established 'popular urbanizations' for low-income populations. Individual lots were available for rent and a range of facilities ranging from a water, light, and sewerage package (U.S.$227) to a complete house (U.S.$1250) were offered for sale. In El Salvador the World Bank was involved in a site and service project with 8000 lots, and as part of the help to the Nicaraguan government after the 1972 earthquake 5 900 units were created in the Managua region. Such programmes offer a sensible way of supporting the spontaneous housing process. To be successful, however, they require reasonable locations, sympathetic administration, and sustained help from government agencies. Unfortunately, the nature of many Latin American governments suggests that they may not play such a role; several unsuccessful site and service schemes have earned the concept a great deal of criticism. In Chile, for example, the theoretically sound 'Operation Sitio' project was undermined by political expediency and a failure of administrative control. As a result there was a proliferation of 'pseudo-urbanized sites which were only lots with a legal property line.... The temporary solutions proposed for low-income groups became permanent by default, resulting in a process that institutionalized substandard conditions' (Lozano, 1975, p. 180).

A related approach has been to help the poor upgrade their existing urban areas. This is a role that has been adopted in piecemeal fashion throughout the region. In Peru this approach has been taken rather more seriously since 1968. The Velasco military government (1968–1975) interpreted its housing role as one of organizing the efforts of the private construction industry and of the squatters (Collier, 1976). The objective was both to improve the housing situation and to elicit the political support of the spontaneous settlers. On assuming power the government renamed the squatter settlements 'young towns' and established an agency to improve services and pave streets in the settlements. The government also encouraged the establishment of cooperatives and the production of prefabricated housing units by the private sector. At the same time, it strongly opposed fresh invasions of public land and has been constantly plagued by its failure to provide sufficient land for spontaneous settlement. Another major problem has arisen from the policy of channelling the political activity of the squatters through a single state agency, S.I.N.A.M.O.S. The line between state help and state control is a narrow one and it seems as if S.I.N.A.M.O.S. has often antagonized the settlers (Collier, 1976; Redclift, 1973). If such antagonism has arisen mainly because of the efforts to incorporate and restrict political activity rather than because of the housing response, it suggests that elements of the Peruvian approach may be applicable in other national contexts. Providing that adequate land is made available, services are provided, and wider economic and social policies do not undermine the ability of the poor to construct their own housing, direct government assistance to spontaneous settlers would seem to be an important partial approach to the housing problem.

In Colombia and Brazil a different strategy has been tried which has eschewed the spontaneous housing 'solution'. Although there are important differences, both governments have tried to stimulate housing construction in the private sector. The basic idea has been to offer inflation-proof loans as a means of channelling consumer expenditures into housing investment. Loans have been offered to middle- and higher-income groups who have responded to the low initial payments (compared to a traditional mortgage scheme) and who seem not to have been deterred by index-linked mortgage repayments. Both governments hoped to achieve two goals through this policy. First, the anticipated boom in housing construction would stimulate the economy by creating more jobs in the building and related industries—the key element in the Colombian (Four Strategies) Development Plan (Colombia D.N.P., 1972). Second, new élite and middle-income housing would free accommodation for lower-income groups, thereby upgrading the urban housing stock. If successful, the policy would eventually reduce the numbers of poor reliant upon spontaneous housing solutions. With respect to the first proposition, both programmes did stimulate housing construction, generate employment, and accelerate economic growth (Reynolds and Carpenter, 1975). At the same time incipient inflation has been fuelled and in the Colombian case funds may well have been diverted from other investment channels. Evidence in support of the second proposition is scarce; we simply do not know whether a process of 'filtering' has operated. Nor is there much information about other distributional components in the plans, although it is not difficult to argue that rising costs of land and building materials may have hurt spontaneous settlers. It is also probable that the approach has led to a deterioration in the distribution of income. These comments, however, refer more to the implementation of the scheme than to the basic concept. The concept of index-linked mortgage schemes is one with considerable promise for employment generation and for building middle-income housing (Reynolds and Carpenter, 1975). Strict controls, however, need to regulate the effects of such programmes, since the process creates many opportunities for speculative projects. If appropriate taxes are introduced some of these profits can be channelled into infrastructural and even low-income housing provision. Such taxes were clearly contemplated by the author of the Colombian Plan (Currie, 1971), but in the final draft taxation policies were notable for their absence. Similarly, there must be strict controls on land use so that urban diseconomies are not magnified by the pattern of urban growth. Again, while efforts have been made towards this end in Colombia, little success has so far been achieved (Colombia D.N.P., 1974; Gilbert, 1977).

CONCLUSIONS

A simple conclusion is not possible in a paper of this kind. Despite the strong similarities between Latin American cities, the diversity of housing and social conditions make generalization difficult. A hostile economic environment faces the poor throughout the region but the proportions of very poor and the nature of their housing conditions varies widely between cities. What we believe is a consistent feature is the poor's positive response to their environment. Their housing response is often highly innovative and sometimes demonstrates an ability to manipulate the political system to their own advantage. We are not wholly optimistic about the success of this approach, but do believe that spontaneous settlement offers a superior alternative to most public-housing projects. Providing land is available, that the prices of building materials do not rise excessively, that metropolitan expansion does not create major diseconomies, and that economic growth continues to create jobs in the formal and informal sectors, self-help is a viable approach to improved housing. Public authorities must help the poor's spontaneous efforts demand for improved housing. In the past, architectural myopia and vested interest gave rise to a proliferation of misguided public projects. To encourage spontaneous settlement by providing land, services, and cheap building materials seems to us a much more appropriate response.

We are aware, of course, that such a view has important ideological connotations. The viability of a spontaneous housing 'situation' depends upon one's personal assessment of several broader socioeconomic questions. Are governments capable of helping the poor or is their main purpose to increase social and political control? Will economic growth generate sufficient jobs and raise incomes sufficiently to the point where a majority of Latin Americans have access to substantial and fully serviced homes? Does the encouragement of spontaneous settlement weaken mass movements and lessen the chances for radical structural reforms? Housing policies cannot be recommended without considering questions such as these. Unfortunately, the answers to these vital questions are anything but clear. Current trends in housing and economic conditions are difficult to evaluate and clearly vary widely between countries and between cities. What may be appropriate under one political regime may be very dangerous in another. Similarly, the answers to such questions are affected by the current political mood in Latin America. During the early 1970s there was a measure of optimism as the governments of Chile, Peru, Bolivia, and Argentina followed more progressive approaches to old problems; by the middle 1970s the right-wing military reaction had removed most of that optimism. Clearly attitudes to current political, economic, and social problems vary from time to time and from individual to individual. Our belief is that spontaneous settlement is as likely to accelerate as retard structural change. In addition, we believe that partial and incremental solutions are better than none; spontaneous settlement at least gives the poor some flexibility over their own housing situations. The reader must decide if he agrees.

REFERENCES

Abrams, C. (1966). *Squatter Settlements, the Problem and the Opportunity*. Report, Department of Housing and Urban Development, Washington, D. C.

Acosta, M., and Hardoy, J. E. (1972). Urbanization policies in revolutionary Cuba. *Latin American Urban Research*, **2**, 167–178.

Amato, P. (1968). *An Analysis of the Changing Patterns of Elite Residential Areas in Bogotá*, Colombia. Latin American Studies Program Dissertation Series No. 7, Cornell University, Ithaca, New York.

Andrews, F. M., and Phillips, G. W. (1970). The squatters of Lima: who they are, what they want. *Journal of Developing Areas*, **4**, 211–224.

A. N. I. F. (Association Nacional de Instituciones Financieras) (1974). *Financiamiento del Desarrollo Urbano*, Tercer Mundo, Bogotá.

Ashton, S. (1972). The differential adaptation of two slum subcultures to a Colombian housing project. *Urban Anthropology*, **1**(2), 176–194.

Back, K. (1962). *Slums Projects and People*, Duke University Press, Durham, North Carolina.

Balán, J. (1969). Migrant–native socio-economic differences in Latin American cities: a structural analysis. *Latin American Research Review*, **4**, 3–29.

Balán, J., Browning, H. L., and Jelin, E. (1973). *Men in a Developing Society*, University of Texas Press, Austin.

Bataillon, C., and D'Arc, H. (1973). *La Ciudad de México*, Sepsetentas, México.

Bonilla, F. (1961). Rio's favelas: the rural slum within the city. *A. U. F. S. Reports*, East Coast Latin America Series No. 8(3). Also in W. Mangin (Ed.), *Peasants in Cities*, Houghton Mifflin, Boston, 1970.

Brown, J. C. (1972). *Patterns of Intra-urban Settlement in Mexico City*. Latin American Studies Program Dissertation Series No. 40, Cornell University, Ithaca, New York.

Bryce-Laporte, R. S. (1970). Urban relocation and family adaptation in Puerto Rico: a case study in urban ethnography. In W. Mangin (Ed.), *Peasants in Cities*, Houghton Mifflin, Boston. pp. 85–97.

B. U. D. S. (Bogotá Urban Development Study) (1974). *The Future of Bogotá*, Bogotá.

Butterworth, D. (1973). Squatters or suburbanites? The growth of shanty towns in Oaxaca, Mexico. In R. Scott (Ed.), *Latin American Modernization Problems, Case Studies in the Crisis of Change*, University of Illinois Press, Urbana. pp. 208–232.

Cardona, R. (1969). *Las Invasiones de Terrenos Urbanos*, Tercer Mundo, Bogotá.

Cardoso, F. A., and Faletto, E. (1969). *Dependencia y Desarrollo en América Latina: Ensayo de Interpretación Sociológica*, Siglo XXI Editores, México D. F.

Carlson, E. (1961). Evaluation of Govsira projects and programmes: a case report from Venezuela. *Town Planning Review*, **31**, 187–209.

Castells, M. (1973). La urbanización dependiente en América Latina. In M. Castells (Ed.), *Imperialismo y Urbanización en América Latina*, Gustavo Gili, S. A. Barcelona. pp. 6–26.

Caufriez, A. L. (1972). Operación Sitio: a housing solution for progressive growth. *Latin American Urban Research*, **2**, 203–210.

C. E. N. A. C. (Centro Estadístico Nacional de la Construcción) (1975). *Inversión y Construcciones del Instituto de Crédito Territorial 1942–1975*, Bogotá.

Cervantes, E. S. (1968). *Tlalnepantla: Desarrollo Metropolitano de la Zona Norte de la Ciudad de México*, México D. F.

Clarke, C. G., and Ward, P. M. (1976). *Stasis in Makeshift Housing: Perspectives from Mexico and the Caribbean*. Paper presented to the Symposium on Urbanisation, Conference of Americanistas, Paris, September 1976.

Collier, D. (1976). *Squatters and Oligarchs*, John Hopkins University Press, Baltimore, Maryland.

Colombia D. N. P. (Departamento Nacional de Planeación) (1972). *Las Cuatro Estratégias*, Bogota.

Colombia D. N. P. (Departamento Nacional de Planeación) (1974) *Ciudades Dentro de la Ciudad*, Bogotá.

Cornelius, W. A. (1973a). Contemporary Mexico: a structural analysis of urban caciquismo. In R. Kern (Ed.), *The Caciques: Oligarchical Politics and the System of Caciquismo*, University of New Mexico Press, Albuquerque.

Cornelius, W. A. (1973b). The impact of governmental performance on political attitudes and behaviour: the case of the urban poor in Mexico. In F. Rabinovitz and F. Trueblood (Eds.), *Latin American Urban Research*, vol. 3. Sage Publications, California. pp. 217–255.

Currie, L. L. (1971). The exchange constraint on development: a partial solution to the problem. *Economic Journal*, **81**, 886–903.

Doebele, W. (1975). *The Private Market and Low-income Urbanization in Developing Countries: The 'Pirate' Subdivisions of Bogotá*. Mimeo, Cambridge, Massachusetts.

Dwyer, D. J. (1975). *People and Housing in Third World Cities*, Longman, London and New York.

Ferreira de Camareo, C. P., *et al.* (1976). *São Paulo 1975: Crescimento e Pobreza*, Edicoes Loyola, São Paulo.

Ferrera, A. (1967). *The Argentine Economy*, University of California Press, Berkeley.

Flinn, W. (1971). Rural and intra-urban migration in Colombia: two case studies in Bogotá. *Latin American Urban Research*, **1**, 83–93.

Frieden, B. (1965–1966). The search for a housing policy in Mexico City. *Town Planning Review*, **36**, 75–90.

Friedmann, J. P. (1966). *Regional Development Policy: A Case Study of Venezuela*, M. I. T. Press, Cambridge, Massachusetts.

Friedmann, J. R., and Sullivan, F. (1974). Labour absorbtion in the urban economy: the case of the developing countries. *Economic Development and Cultural Change*, **22**, 385–413.

Furtado, C. (1971). *Economic Development of Latin America: A Survey from Colonial Times to the Cuban Revolution*, Cambridge University Press, London.

Gilbert, A. G. (1974). *Latin American Development: A Geographical Perspective*, Penguin, Harmondsworth.

Gilbert, A. G. (1976). The arguments for a very large cities reconsidered. *Urban Studies*, **13**, 27–34.

Gilbert, A. G. (1977). Bogotá: planning, politics and the crisis of lost opportunities. In *Latin American Urban Research*, vol. 6, Sage Publications, California.

Gilbert, A. G., and Goodman, D. E. (1976). Regional income disparities and economic development: a critique. In A. G. Gilbert (Ed.), *Development Planning and Spatial Structure*, John Wiley, London and New York. pp. 113–142.

Hanson, A. T. (1934). The ecology of a Latin American city. In E. B. Reuter (Ed.), *Race and Culture Contacts*, McGraw-Hill, New York.

Hardoy, J. E., and Schaedel, R. P. (Eds.) (1969). *The Urbanization Process in America from its Origins to the Present Day*, Editorial Instituto Torcuato di Tella, Buenos Aires.

Harms, H. (1976). Limitations of self-help. *Architectural Design*, **XLVI** (April), 230–231.

I. B. R. D. International Bank of Reconstruction and Development) (1975). *The Urban Informal Sector*. Bank Staff Working Paper No. 211, Washington.

Johnston, R. J. (1973). Towards a general model of intra-urban residential patterns. Some cross-cultural observations. In C. Board, R. Chorley, P. Haggett, and D. Stoddart (Eds.), *Progress in Geography*, vol. 4. Edward Arnold, London. pp. 83–124.

Lander, L., and Urdaneta, A. (1975). *El Desarrollo del Tuy Medio*. Mimeo, Caracas.

Leeds, A. (1969). The significant variables determining the character of squatter settlements. *America Latina*, **12**(3), 44–86.

Lewis, O. (1961). *Five Families—Mexican Case Study in the Culture of Poverty*, Random House, New York.

Lewis, O. (1966). The culture of poverty. *Scientific American*, **215**(4), 19–25.

Lomnitz, L. (1975). *Como Sobreviven los Marginados*, Siglo XXI, Mexico.

Lozano, E. E. (1975). Housing the urban poor in Chile: contrasting experiences under 'Christian Democracy' and 'Unidad Popular'. *Latin American Urban Research*, **5**, 177–194.

McCallum, J. D. (1974). Land values in Bogotá, Colombia'. *Land Economics*, **50**, 312–317.

McEwen, A. (1972). Differentiation among the urban poor: an Argentine study. In E. de Kadt and G. Williams (Eds.), *Sociology and Development*, Tavistock, London. pp. 197–228.

Mangin, W. (1967). Latin American squatter settlements: a problem and a solution. *Latin American Research Review*, **2**(3), 65–98.

Mangin, W., and Turner, J. F. C. (1968). Barriada movement. *Progressive Architecture*, **49**, 154–162.

Mexico C. N. I. C. (Camara Nacional de la Industria de la Construcción) (1975). *Indice de Costos de Construcción en México D. F., 1954–1974*. Report, Mexico Distrito Federal.

Mexico C. N. S. M. (Comisión Nacional de las Salarios Minimos) (1975). *Memoria de los Trabajos 1972 y 1973*. Report, Mexico Distrito Federal, June 1975.

Michl, S. (1973). Urban squatter organisation as a national government tool: the case of Lima, Peru. In F. Rabinovitz and F. Trueblood (Eds.), *Latin American Urban Research*, vol. 3. Sage Publications, California. pp. 155 and 178.

Morse, R. (1971a). São Paulo: case study of a Latin American metropolis. In F. Rabinovitz and F. Trueblood (Eds.), *Latin American Urban Research*, vol. 1. Sage Publications, California. pp. 151–186.

Morse, R. (1971b). Trends and issues in Latin American urban research, 1965–1970, part 1. *Latin American Research Review*, **6**(1), 65–98.

Peattie, L. R. (1968). *The View from the Barrio*, University of Michigan Press, Ann Arbor, Michigan.

Peattie, L. R. (1969). Social issues in housing. In B. Frieden and W. Nash (Eds.), *Shaping an Urban Future*, M. I. T. Press, Cambridge, Massachusetts. pp. 15–34.

Peattie, L. R. (1975). 'Tertiarization' and urban poverty in Latin America. *Latin American Urban Research*, **5**, 109–124.

Peru Oficina Nacional de Desarrollo de Pueblos Jovenes (1970). *Incidencia de la Urbanización Acelerada en Ciudades con Poblaciones de 25,000 y más Habitantes*, Lima.

Portes, A. (1972). Rationality in the slum: an essay in interpretative sociology. *Comparative Studies in Society and History*, **14**(3), 268–286.

Pradilla, E. (1976). Notas acerca del 'problema de la vivienda'. *Ideologìa y Sociedad*, **16**, 70–107.

Quijano, A. (1971). *Nationalism and Capitalism in Peru: A Study in Neo-imperialism*, Monthly Review Press, New York.

Ray, T. (1969). *The Politics of the Barrios*, California University Press, Berkeley.

Redclift, M.R. (1973). Squatter settlements in Latin American cities: the response from government. *Journal of Development Studies*, **10**, 92–109.

Reveiz, E., and Zorro, C. (1976). *Estudio Sobre los Inquilinatos en Bogotá* (Segunda parte). Centro de estudios sobre el desarrollo economic, documento No. 034, Bogotá.

Reynolds, C. W., and Carpenter, R. T. (1975). Housing finance in Brazil: toward a new distribution of wealth. *Latin American Urban Research*, **5**, 147–176.

Roberts, B. E. (1973). *Organizing Strangers*, University of Texas Press, Austin.

Rogler, L. (1967). Slum neighbourhoods in Latin America. *Journal of Inter-American Studies*, **9**, 507–528.

Rush, B. S. (1974). *From Favela to Conjunto: The Experience of Squatters Removed to Low-cost Housing in Rio de Janeiro, Brazil*. Mimeo, Harvard College, March 1974.

Safa, H. I. (1964). From shanty town to public housing: a comparison of family structure in two urban neighbourhoods in Puerto Rico. *Caribbean Studies*, **4**(1), 3–12.

Safa, H. I. (1970). The poor are like everyone else, Osca. *Psychology Today* (September), **4**(4), 26–32.

Schulman, S. (1968). Intellectual and technological underdevelopment, a case study—Colombia. *Social Forces*, **46**(3), 307–317.

Scobie, J. R. (1964). *Argentina: A City and a Nation*, Oxford University Press, New York.

Scobie, J. (1974). *Buenos Aires: Plaza to Suburb, 1870–1910*, Oxford University Press, New York.

Stein, S. J., and Stein, B. H. (1970). *The Colonial Heritage of Latin America: Essays on Economic Dependence in Perspective*, Oxford University Press, New York.

Turner, J. F. C. (1963). Dwelling resources in south America. *Architectural Design*, **33**, 360–393.
Turner, J. F. C. (1968a). The squatter settlement: architecture that works. *Architectural Design*, **38**, 355–360.
Turner, J. F. C. (1968b). Housing priorities, settlement patterns and urban development in modernizing countries. *Journal of the American Institute of Planners*, **34**, 354–363.
Turner, J. F. C. (1969). Uncontrolled urban settlements: problems and policies. In G. Breese (Ed.), *The City in Newly Developing Countries: Readings on Urbanism and Urbanisation*, Prentice-Hall, Englewood Cliffs, New Jersey. pp. 507–531.
Turner, J. F. C. (1972). Housing as a verb. In J. F. C. Turner and R. Fichter (Eds.), *Freedom to Build*, Collier Macmillan, New York.
Turner, J. F. C. (1976). *Housing by People*, Marion Boyars, London.
Usandizaga, E., and Havens, E. (1966). *Tres Barrios de Invasión, Estudio de Vida y Actitudes en Barranquilla*, Faculatad de sociologia, Universidad Nacional, Bogotá.
U. N. D. E. A. (United Nations Department of Economic Affairs) (1949). *Relative Prices of Exports and Imports of Under-developed Countries*, New York.
U. N. D. Y. (1974). *United Nations Demographic Yearbook*, Geneva.
U. N. E. C. L. A. (United Nations Economic Commission for Latin America) (1962). *Statistical Evaluation of Housing Conditions, Existing Defects and Future Housing Requirements in the Latin American Countries*, U. N. Report, Copenhagen, July 1962.
Uzzell, D. (1974). The interaction of population and locality in the development of squatter settlements in Lima. In W. Cornelius and F. Trueblood (Eds.), *Latin American Urban Research*, vol. 4. Sage Publications, California. pp. 113–134.
Valencia, E. (1965). *La Merced, Estudio Ecológico y Social de la Ciudad de México*, México.
Valentine, C. (1968). *Culture and Poverty*, University of Chicago Press, Chicago.
Valenzuela, J., and Vernez, G. (1974). Construcción popular y estructura del mercado de vivienda: el caso de Bogotá. *Revista Interamericana de Planificación*, **5**, 14–34.
Vaughn, D., and Feindt, W. (1973). Initial settlement and intra-urban movement of migrants in Monterrey. *Journal of the American Institute of Planners*, **39**(6), 388–401.
Venezuela Banco Obrero (1972). *Politica de Vivienda*, Caracas.
Vernez, G. (1973a). *The Residential Movements of Low-income Families: The Case of Bogotá, Colombia*, New York City—Rand Institute, New York.
Vernez, G. (1973b). *Bogota's Pirate Settlements: An Opportunity for Metropolitan Development*, Unpublished Ph.D. dissertation, University of California, Berkeley.
Violich, F. (1944). *Cities of Latin America*, Reinhold, New York.
Ward, P. M. (1976a). *In Search of a Home: Social and Economic Characteristics of Squatter Settlements and the Role of Self-help Housing in Mexico City*. Unpublished Ph.D. dissertation, Liverpool.
Ward, P. M. (1976b). Intra-city migration to squatter settlements in Mexico City. *Geoforum*, **7**(5/6), 369–381.
Ward, P. M. (1976c). The squatter settlement as slum or housing solution: evidence from Mexico City. *Land Economics*, **52**(3), 330–346.
World Bank (1975). *Housing*, Washington, D. C.

Chapter 8

Housing in British Cities

Pat Niner and Christopher J. Watson

INTRODUCTION

The geographer's concern with housing

Until quite recently the place of housing as a factor influencing the social and spatial characteristics of cities has received little attention in geographical work. It is true that social area analysis and factorial ecology have long enabled us to recognize and, indeed, to quantify the association of certain types of household with housing of a certain age and in certain locations. But the processes by which houses are built and allocated have tended to be regarded almost as 'external' factors, enabling the growth and social change of cities, and their influence has attracted far less attention than, say, topography or political and administrative factors such as planning policies. The geographer's growing interest in social process, however, has begun to supplement and often to illuminate a traditional concern with the physical form of urban areas. This is a fairly new dimension in geographical analysis, but one of great importance.

The contribution of the ecological school (Park, 1929) to theories of environmental determinism in residential patterns and behaviour has long been recognized and is still important today because it stressed that city growth and competition for space create differentiation in the social use of areas, leading to residential segregation. The pattern of this differentiation has traditionally been a concern of the geographer. The key question, however, is how such differentiation and segregation came about.

Economists have argued that these can be explained in terms of supply and demand factors, employment, workplace, incomes, price, and cost. One of the most important economic theories of residential mobility and change is that of 'filtering'. Briefly, this posits that, as new construction proceeds or as other vacancies arise in the housing stock, the benefits 'trickle down' the value scale to those who cannot necessarily afford a new dwelling or one of the more expensive vacant dwellings, but who nevertheless benefit from the resultant 'chain' of moves, set off as vacancies elsewhere in the system are filled. This attempt to explain the dynamics of housing has been extensively studied and commented on in the United States (Grigsby, 1963; Kristof, 1966; Ratcliff, 1949; Sands and

Bower, 1976; White, 1971), but some writers have expressed reservations about its practical benefits as a means of distributing housing resources, both in the United States (Aaron, 1972) and Britain (Murie, Niner, and Watson, 1976; Watson, 1973).

It is perhaps significant that the development of ecological and economic theories of housing and housing behaviour originate largely from the United States, where the more 'open' housing market and the *relative* absence of public intervention in housing are in marked contrast to the British situation. Robson (1969, p. 224), for example, commenting on the relevance of classic ecological approaches to the study of city structure in Britain concluded that 'the development of council housing and of town planning and the effects of a variety of social changes have had profound effects upon the urban scene and have largely invalidated many of the bases upon which the classical models have been built'. Herbert (1973, p. 119) makes much the same point. Similar problems have been encountered in attempts to develop models of residential location and decision making which are applicable in the British situation, partly because of the difficulty of incorporating 'institutional' factors, which are of such importance in Britain.

This concern with the role of institutions in the analysis of housing behaviour and social and spatial patterns has been one of the most important developments in recent years. The emphasis in the approach is on access to housing. In putting forward their theory of housing class, Rex and Moore (1967) acknowledged the influence of the ecological approaches of Park and Burgess, recognizing the importance of their emphasis on competitive processes and a 'zone of transition' as recurring urban phenomena. But they, too, emphasized the important role of local authorities in the allocation of housing.

More recently, Pahl (1975) has stressed the need to study the means of access to housing and, in particular, the role of 'gatekeepers' or urban managers who control and manage access to scarce housing resources. This has led to a developing interest not only in the place of local authorities in the housing system but also that of building societies, estate agents, private landlords, builders, and developers, and to a concern with the way in which housing is organized (Harloe, Issacharoff, and Minns, 1974).

For many geographers, current interest in housing and the urban environment is devoted to seeking explanation 'not at the level of individuals nor indeed of institutions but rather at the level of the nature of the social and economic structure of society' (Williams, 1976a, p. 61). Following Harvey (1973), much of this work is conducted from a Marxist standpoint, and whether it will be enduring in its interest or its application remains to be seen. What is certain, however, is that in focusing on questions of social justice and in challenging a preoccupation with techniques rather than understanding, Harvey and those who have followed him have heightened the concern of many geographers with the distribution of housing and housing resources. This is important in the search for explanations of spatial and social patterns which have long been recognized but remain imperfectly understood. The emphasis on processes in the urban system, which is the approach adopted in this chapter, is thus an important development for geographers and one which is helpful in improving our analysis of housing in British cities.

It will be clear from the brief introduction that interest in urban problems, particularly those of housing, is not confined to geographers. Indeed, it can be argued that in developing explanations of housing patterns and processes, geography has lagged behind work in other disciplines such as sociology, social administration, and economic and social history. Whether geographers have a distinct 'geographical' contribution to make is uncertain. What is important, however, is that they should constantly strive to avoid 'discovering' what is already well known by their colleagues in other disciplines.

The historical background to the British housing situation

The last 150 years or so have seen a tremendous growth in the British population and in the proportion of the population who live in towns. Urban development in the nineteenth century was rapid and largely uncontrolled, with the result that housing was built to very low standards, to very high densities, and without proper sanitation or water supplies. Engels (1845, p. 60) wrote:

> Every great city has one or more slums, where the working class is crowded together. True, poverty often dwells in hidden alleys close to the palaces of the rich; but, in general, a separate territory has been assigned to it, where, removed from the sight of the happier classes, it may struggle along as it can. These slums are pretty equally arranged in all the great towns of England, the worst houses in the worst quarters of the towns; usually one or two-storied cottages in long rows, perhaps with cellars used as dwellings. These houses of three or four rooms and a kitchen form, thoughout England, some parts of London excepted, the general dwellings of the working class. The streets are generally unpaved, rough, dirty, filled with vegetables and animal refuse, without sewers or gutters, but supplied with foul, stagnant pools instead. Moreover ventilation is impeded by the bad, confused method of building of the whole quarter, and since many human beings here live crowded into a small space, the atmosphere that prevails in these working-men's quarters may readily be imagined.

More than sixty years later the *Report* of the Royal Commission on the Housing of the Industrial Population of Scotland, Rural and Urban (1917) gave an equally graphic and depressing account of housing conditions north of the Border, where problems were compounded in urban areas by the use of the tenement form of building, characteristically of four stories but sometimes of even greater proportions.

Against this background, the pressure of reform was insistent and began, even earlier than Engels' account, with the concern of Chadwick and others for the 'health of towns'. But as Bowley (1945) and other writers have noted, the steps taken to try and deal with these problems were largely negative. Offending properties could be removed, after the passing of the Artisans and Labourers Dwelling Act of 1868, while building regulations, first introduced in the Public Health Act of 1875, were designed to ensure that new building would not suffer from the same insanitary and cramped conditions. Local authorities were made responsible for exercising these powers (Murie, Niner, and Watson, 1976, pp. 92–93).

It was some time before a more positive attitude to the housing problem was reflected in public policy. Though from 1875 onwards local authorities were empowered to build houses themselves, the legislation was permissive; authorities *could* build but were under no obligation to do so. Furthermore, they received no financial support from central government and most responded by doing nothing. Such 'social' provision as there was, was largely the result of initiatives by a small number of charitable housing trusts.

The first step towards more positive public intervention in housing was accidental. In 1915, rent control was introduced to prevent profiteering by landlords during wartime. Though it was promised that the control would be lifted when conditions returned to 'normal' this could not be done immediately. In fact, controls were never completely removed and they have remained as an important—though, to some, unwelcome—feature of housing policy ever since.

Towards the end of the First World War two important problems were clear. First, the housing shortage was acute because of the virtual cessation of new building during the war years. Some way of fulfilling Lloyd George's promise of 'homes fit for heroes' had to be found. Second, there was great uncertainty about whether the private sector could or would continue, as it had in the nineteenth century, to provide the majority of working-class rented housing. Signs of declining investment in housing had been noted almost since the turn of the century, partly because of more lucrative investments overseas and partly because the standards required for new building made them more expensive to build, and hence to let. There was uncertainty about whether many potential tenants could make their demand for housing effective.

Another way of providing housing for the working classes had to be found, and the task was entrusted to local authorities. The corollary was that the state had to give the financial help that had previously been denied, and Exchequer subsidies were introduced for the first time. Thus the Housing and Town Planning, etc., Act of 1919 brought about a major change in housing policy and practice, but its consequences could never have been foreseen for, like the 1915 Rent Act, it was regarded as a temporary measure, to be withdrawn when 'normality' returned.

Normality has, however, never returned, and the distinction between the private sector and the public sector of subsidized housing built and allocated by local authorities has remained and developed over the years since 1919. During this time the composition of the private sector has changed dramatically. There has been a steady decline in private renting attributable to the continuation of rent control, adverse financial conditions, extensions of security of tenure, and increasing public health action. This has been more than offset by the growth in owner-occupation, paralleled by the development of the building society movement, and aided by the stimulation of effective demand through income tax relief on mortgage interest payments, to those borrowing money for house purchase. In very general terms, these elements together represent the distinctively 'British' response to housing policy and practice.

Public intervention in housing, directly and indirectly, is all-pervasive in Britain. We must examine the broad nature and developments of housing policy as well as the other processes at work if we are to begin to understand the urban housing system and the resultant social and spatial patterns to which it gives rise.

HOUSING POLICY AND DEVELOPMENTS

The historical roots of housing policy have certain implications for its current 'style' and development. For example, the initial tentative 'temporary' steps towards intervention (until things return to normal) is still reflected in the continuing political debate about housing as a social service and the degree to which (some would argue, if at all) the state, whether at central or local government level, should intervene in housing. Critics of publicly provided housing claim that the physical segregation of council tenants and owner-occupiers is undesirable, that public-sector rents are too low, and that housing subsidies are too high. Against this are those who hold the view that by having a large public sector and by catering for 'general' needs, rather than the needs of the 'poor', the much more serious spatial segregation that characterizes public housing in, for example, the United States and France can be avoided. It is also pointed out that 'subsidy', in the form of income tax relief on mortgage repayments provides generous assistance to owner-occupiers, in inverse proportion to their needs. By contrast, the 'freedom' and 'independence' enjoyed by owner-occupiers—though true in the long term, after a mortgage has been repaid—is often said to be a burden and an ensnarement, from which many would prefer to escape if they could. It is clear there is still no consensus.

Also important is the public health origin of much housing policy. Social reformers, the government, and local authorities were all strongly influenced by the Victorian notion that, if housing were improved, the health of the population would also be improved. Moreover, 'health', to the reformers, meant not only physical health and freedom from disease but also 'moral standards'. The effect of these early influences can still be seen today in the priority given by local authorities in their allocation policies to 'health' cases; the attitude to slum clearance; and the concern with maintaining 'communities' in improvement areas and creating 'balanced communities' in new housing. The benevolent paternalism of which local authorities—through their public health, housing, and planning functions—are often accused is a criticism levelled even more forcibly against some housing associations, whose traditions also date from the period of nineteenth-century reform.

Quite fundamental to British housing policy is the 'traditional', chosen role of central government to act indirectly. While accepting responsibility for housing policy, government has neither taken nor sought absolute control of the housing system. Other bodies are responsible for implementing or responding to central policy—notably local authorities, private builders, building societies, and private landlords. It has also been relatively rare for central government to create special agencies to implement its policies, over which it might exercise more direct control. The Scottish Special Housing Association and the Housing Corporation are exceptions, but the more normal pattern has been to rely on pre-existing bodies and to develop their powers and scope as necessary. Local authorities are, of course, the prime example of this, and have been enabled and urged to extend their concern progressively towards providing a 'comprehensive housing service'. Essentially the government sets the framework (of legislation, subsidy, and influence) within which others act. Given the relative lack of control and the disparate nature of the implementing agencies, it is hardly surprising that housing policy is a far from uniform concept.

This lack of uniformity in policy stems not only from tradition but also from the nature of housing itself. It is a physical commodity, a major user of land and other resources; it satisfies both deep social needs for shelter and gives expression to aspirations; it is a major element in the budget of individuals and government; and its production, allocation, and management provides the livelihood of many thousands of people. Cullingworth (1972a, pp. 39–40) draws attention to the large number of issues which are relevant to housing policy and to housing market behaviour:

> Subsidies, tax-reliefs, statutory minimum standards, systems of amortization, deposits, eligibility rules for mortgages and for council houses, improvement grants, property taxes (rates), rent rebates and allowances, rent controls, security of tenure, slum clearance procedures, building trade practices, land controls, restraint of urban growth, regional development: a complete list of relevant issues would be very long. Some of them may not normally be regarded as being appropriately labelled 'housing' issues, but this does not lessen their significance. ... In no field more than housing is there such a multiplicity of possible objectives and such a wide range of techniques available for meeting them. One important implication of this is that the potential for conflict between different housing policies is large—much to the embarrassment of successive government.

The 'multiplicity of possible objectives' certainly exists, even at the most general level. The main objective of housing policy is usually stated in relatively uncontentious terms such as 'providing everyone with a choice in making a decent home for themselves and their families at a price they can afford'. Beneath this level of generality, at different times, different motives have been apparent or can be inferred, which can have serious implications for the rate of progress towards achieving the global objective. For example, some would argue that the introduction of council housing in 1919 'arose from the government's very real fears of revolutionary working class action both from within and outside the country' (C.D.P., 1976a, p. 12). At different times the construction industry has been used as an economic regulator, with serious implications for house building. The boost to house improvement provided by higher grant contributions between 1970 and 1974 in development and intermediate areas was not unrelated to local unemployment trends. Public housing programmes have been stepped up and down according to the philosophy and priorities of the party in office.

This, of course, is hardly surprising. Governments change and are concerned with many factors besides housing. Different policies must be adjusted and dovetailed as priorities change and as circumstances seem to dictate. In this sense, central government is by no means free from constraints in its housing policies. The most pernicious influence has been the wider economic situation and the balance of payments. At the time of writing (early 1977), public expenditure cuts, are imposed which severely limited public-sector housing activity. None of the 'policies' introduced has been initiated primarily by housing conditions or needs, but by the chosen view of, and response to, national economic circumstances.

The other significant constraint is that of political argument. Put crudely, there are votes in housing—from the number of houses built to the issue of whether council houses should be sold (Murie, 1975). Traditionally, the two main parties have been associated with different emphases between the major tenure sectors. Both parties have favoured and encouraged owner-occupation: the Labour Party is seen as emphasizing the role of council housing for general purposes, while Conservatives have tended to limit the purposes for which public-sector dwellings can be provided. Now that over half the households in England and Wales are owner-occupiers, their interests must be seriously considered by all parties.

Development in policy

So far discussion has touched on the 'style' of British housing policy and its implications. Some specific developments since 1919 must be described in more detail, since they have clear relevance for the present form of cities.

The first is usually considered under a 'planning' rather than a 'housing' heading. It includes a whole range of measures which have sought to contain the growth of urban areas and to prevent the uncontrolled spread of suburbia (Hall *et al.*, 1973), as well as those attempting to disperse population from the congested cities. Dispersal policies were first suggested officially in wartime report of the Barlow Commission on the Distribution of the Industrial Population; they were followed by the Abercrombie Plan for London which, in 1944, advocated a series of new towns as essential for the dispersal of population from the conurbation; and finally by the Committee on New Towns, whose work led to the establishment of the first New Towns, following the

New Towns Act of 1946. Residential overspill schemes were later promoted by many of the larger British city authorities, under the Town Development Act of 1952. Also important are the regional, industrial, and employment policies of the past-war years which have tried to encourage the movement of industrial concerns from the more 'prosperous' London, South-East, and West Midlands regions to the Development Areas of the North of England, Merseyside, Wales, and Scotland. At a more local level, planners have, until recently, placed emphasis on the physical separation of 'non-conforming' uses of land, in particular housing and industry.

In broad terms, these policies have been 'successful', in the sense that urban areas *have* been at least partly contained; housing and employment land uses *have* been separated; population and employment dispersal from city areas *has* taken place; and some industries *have* moved from 'prosperous' to 'development' areas. Of course, these 'successes' have not been universal, but some of the objectives which have underlain post-war planning, and industrial and employment policies have been achieved. As is so often the case, however, there have also been unintended and unfavourable consequences.

These strategic policies of regional and national importance, and the changing spatial patterns to which they have given rise, have been supported by the housing policies and programmes of individual local authorities. The most important of these have been slum clearance and new building activities, which have transformed both the social and physical character of British cities in the last fifty or sixty years. As noted previously, local authorities have had powers to demolish property 'unfit for human habitation' since the nineteenth century and have been able to build subsidized rental housing since 1919. Despite the powers available to them, however, most authorities did not begin to pursue vigorous slum clearance policies until the 1930s, when more favourable subsidies were introduced to encourage the rehousing of slum clearance families. These were made necessary because between 1920 and 1930 only about 11000 slum houses had been replaced in England and Wales with the aid of subsidy, yet over 500 000 council houses had been built. The Housing Act of 1935 added the relief of overcrowding to the statutory duties of local authorities, with the result that about 400 000 houses were provided for these two purposes in Britain before the outbreak of war in 1939.

Because of the great shortage of housing in the post-war years, partly through lack of building and partly through wartime destruction, the slum clearance programme was not officially resumed until 1954. The urgent need after the war was to build as many houses as quickly as possible, and it was at this time that the great expansion of municipal estates of the outskirts of our larger towns and cities began. This process gained added momentum as slum clearance got underway in the late 1950s and continued throughout most of the 1960s. Needs were so great that local authorities built for and gave priority in allocation to those requiring rehousing from slum clearance areas, families in overcrowded conditions, and others whose health was at risk. Waiting lists of tens of thousands were normal in most cities, and it was accepted practice to have some form of residential qualification for admission to the list—often of ten years or more. As the clearance of inner-city areas proceeded, whole communities were dispersed to peripheral estates, where the provision of housing very often preceded by several years the provision of related social, community, commercial, and educational facilities. Very often, slum clearance and new building programmes were not properly coordinated, and many residential areas near city centres were cleared years before plans for their redevelopment were finally approved and implemented. Long-term programming was made more difficult because many local authorities returned as 'unfit' only those dwellings which they hoped to be able to clear within a relatively short period. Returns by authorities in England and Wales to the Ministry of Housing and Local Government in 1965 suggested there were about 771 000 unfit dwellings, yet the Ministry's first national house-condition survey in 1967 estimated there to be about 1.8 million unfit in the country as a whole (M.H.L.G., 1968).

Despite the undoubted 'physical' success of the housing policies and programmes pursued by local authorities in the 1930s', slum clearance drive, and that of the twenty years or so following the end of the war, concern began to be voiced in the mid-1960s about the social consequences of redevelopment on such a massive scale; the failure to co-ordinate programmes; and the lack of a 'comprehensive' approach, in which local authorities would take a broader view of housing needs and potential provision in all sectors and not just that which was directly controlled and managed by them.

One of the most important changes which arose from this debate was the emphasis which began to be placed on the improvement of older housing (as an alternative to slum clearance). This was partly possible because many of the worst areas of nineteenth-century housing had been cleared, but it also reflected an underlying anxiety about the time still needed to deal with the slums which remained, and which could not possibly be replaced within ten, fifteen, and, in some cases, more than twenty years. Critics pointed out that a baby born to a family living in a house in the so-called 'fifteen-year clearance programme' could be leaving school before the house in which he had grown up would be dealt with. Longer term improvement was considered essential but so, too, was short-term ameliorative work. In fact, however, such improvement as has taken place in older housing areas has tended to be for medium or longer term periods, and often for a 'life' of at least thirty years. It has done little to relieve short-term problems and, indeed, has come to be seen as an alternative to new building by local authorities and central government alike. The achievements and inadequacies of improvement policy and practice have been well documented (e.g. Davies, 1972; Dennis, 1970; Derrick, 1976). Duncan and Cowan, 1976; Duncan and Curry, 1974; Pepper, 1971).

Improvement policies have an explicit social element. With the decline in clearance programmes, the extent of 'forced' movement from city centres to peripheral estates has been reduced. Emphasis has been placed on the need to improve 'areas' of older housing and to preserve existing 'communities'. The general improvement area approach which was introduced in the Housing Act of 1969 has been supplemented by a new emphasis on housing action areas, defined in the D.O.E. circulars which followed the passing of the Housing Act of 1974 as areas where 'physical and social conditions combine and interact to create an unsatisfactory living environment' (D.O.E., 1975a). In assessing social conditions in a potential housing action area, the Circular suggests the following factors should be taken into account:

—the proportion of households sharing cooking facilities, a bath, a water closet or other facilities

—the proportion of households living at a density of over $1\frac{1}{2}$ persons per room (or any other measure of overcrowding relevant to the area)

—the proportion of households living in privately rented accommodation; and

—the concentration in the area of households likely to have special housing problems—for instance, old age pensioners, large families, single parent families, or families whose head is unemployed or in a low income group.

All these factors can, of course, be inferred for census data at enumeration district level, and considerable work has been done to plot their incidence and distribution both nationally (D.O.E., 1975b, 1975c) and for individual cities (Mansley, 1972).

PROCESS IN THE URBAN HOUSING SYSTEM

'Process in the urban housing system' is misleading insofar as it implies that there is a single process at work or, indeed, a single urban housing system. In fact, complexity, diversity, and interrelationships are the most significant features of urban housing. A complete study of 'process' would have to encompass sales for owner-occupation of 'desirable' houses in Central London at around £ 100 000 and of less desirable houses in central Birmingham at around £2–3 000; the letting of penthouse flats at £160 a week, of houses lacking standard amenities under controlled tenancies at far less than that amount a year, and of council property where, in gaining access, the rent is secondary to the eligibility criteria adopted by individual local authorities. Process also includes all the ways in which the physical character of the housing stock is changed through new building, demolition, conversion, improvement, and deterioration. And how does improvement relate to new building and housing opportunities for low-income families? The list of dimensions involved and questions arising is almost infinite. It is useful, however, to concentrate on the processes and agencies which have direct influence on housing opportunities and access to housing. Here, three propositions can be made and illustrated: there are many and diverse actors in the housing system; each have their own motivations, aims and interests; and all are constrained to a greater or lesser extent in their action.

The main groups of actors are local authorities, private sector firms and institutions, and private households.

Local authorities

Local authorities have a wide range of responsibilities and powers for dealing with housing matters. Broadly, these fall into three categories: the direct provision, management, and allocation of council housing; concern with standards in new and existing dwellings in all sectors; and generally complementing and influencing the private sector by, for example, giving improvement grants and council mortgages, and by providing a housing aid service. Underlying all activities is the general responsibility for authorities to consider the housing needs of their areas. Within the broad objective of meeting needs, they have a great deal of discretion in the precise formulation and implementation of their housing policies. National policy and financial and political constraints limit their freedom of action.

Council house allocation procedures provide a fascinating example of the interplay between policy, discretion, and constraints—and are of special significance since they determine access to about a third of the British housing stock. Guidance in legislation to local authorities on allocation is relatively vague. There are requirements to rehouse persons displaced by clearance or other public action and to relieve statutory overcrowding. Otherwise, in the selection of their tenants, authorities 'shall secure a reasonable preference is given to persons who are occupying insanitary or overcrowded houses, have larger families or are living under unsatisfactory housing conditions' (Housing Act, 1957). Advice on allocation policies has been offered at different times through circulars, or reports of the Central Housing Advisory Committee (C.H.A.C., 1969).

Council houses become available for letting through new building, acquisition, or conversion, which adds to the stock, and through relets in the existing stock created when tenants die or move from the area or to the private sector. Demand for these vacancies comes from households displaced by clearance, the homeless, key workers, general applicants, and existing council tenants who want to move house. Clearly the first four groups mentioned are in competition; vacancies allocated to clearance families are not available for general applicants, and so on. Transfers (existing tenants seeking to move) are rather different, since such movement creates as well as occupied a vacancy. The number of transfer requests accommodated tends to be governed by the availability of suitable dwellings and the administrative costs (e.g. staff time and rent loss) of operating the system. The implications for other groups become significant when the type, size, or quality of dwellings vacated *after* transfers is considered. In most authorities, demand for council housing exceeds supply, requiring systems for determining eligibility and priorities for all groups.

Survey have shown a wide range of policies adopted by local authorities to ration available houses; each authority is unique and general statements are unlikely to apply to any particular area (Niner, 1975; Welsh Consumer Council, 1976). Policy must decide the priority given to the different allocation groups (e.g. do transfers have precedence over general-needs applicants?), the limits on eligibility for consideration (whether, for example, owner-occupiers, those not satisfying residential qualifications, or single people are excluded), and the priority between the competing claims of those deemed eligible within each group.

In practice this last point provides scope for almost infinite variety between authorities. Some operate waiting lists where priorities are settled on a first-come-first-served basis; others have sophisticated points schemes where different elements of need are given weighting points; still others consider tenant selection to be the responsibility of council or committee members. Any combination of methods can also be used.

Detailed research has shown two things having particular influence on council housing opportunities. First, despite great variations in the detail of policy and rules, in practice most authorities tend to house the same groups of people—notably young families with one or more children and the elderly. This is partly attributable to an underlying consensus that these are the people local authorities really should be accommodating (this is diversifying as the claims of childless couples and younger single people are recognized) and partly to the nature of the stock available for letting (Niner, 1975). Councils now are constrained by past building programmes which created uniform estates of three-bedroomed houses or blocks of two-bedroomed flats and maisonettes. New building can only slowly diversify the stock to accord better with current, more varied demands.

Second, research draws attention to the need to concentrate on the details of allocation procedures where it seems objectives other than simply meeting housing 'need' can become important. Authorities are responsible for managing council housing and may attempt to reduce future management problems by 'skilful' allocation; the subtle role of grading, where attempts are made to match the 'standard' of tenant and house, and the philosophies and biases of lettings staff, who may occupy relatively lowly positions in the council hierarchy but who have great influence on who gets offered which house, need close attention (Gray, 1976). Again, how does the behaviour of the applicant influence his chances? What is the significance of area preferences? How important is 'self-selection' when some accept offers that others refuse—reflecting in part the urgency of need experienced by the applicant? Findings tend to dispute any naive view that 'need' is the sole criterion and that those in greatest need will automatically be helped most rapidly or be offered the best housing solution.

A similar pattern of freedoms and constraints is discernible in other local authority housing activities—house building, urban renewal, council house sales, or mortgage loans. Faced with apparently uniform constraints in the form of legislation and finance, different authorities with differing local resources, problems, priorities, and commitment can produce vastly different results and achievements (Boaden, 1971). Underlying the policies and processes at work, and however imperfectly realized, is usually a concern with meeting housing need.

The private sector

The private housing sector is marked by the enormous number and range of institutions and bodies which operate within it. The distinguishing feature—really a truism, though it seems to have been recognized only recently by researchers—is that the private market is in business for the money, not for reasons of social conscience. The important implication of this is that 'the solutions provided will aim at maximizing profit rather than the welfare of the person seeking housing' (Karn, 1976, p. 45). This can be put more forcibly: 'every move to house workers is dictated by profit. Every failure is a failure to make money' (C.D.P., 1976b). Financial motives are equally attributable to building societies, though these are, by law, non-profit-making institutions.

The private-rented sector has been in decline since the turn of the century. Though the underlying reasons have been documented elsewhere (Murie, Niner, and Watson, 1976, pp. 179–189), less clear is the differential impact of decline on different types of property or different types of landlord. There is a suggestion that high rental 'luxury' dwellings and multi-occupation have retained some element of profitability and have therefore disappeared less rapidly. Certainly, housing quality is often low in the sector. In 1971, only 53 per cent. of tenants of unfurnished property and 35 per cent. of furnished tenants in Greater London had exclusive use of hot water, fixed bath, and inside W.C. Unless some really dramatic change takes place, it seems that quantitative and qualitative decline is likely to continue. Financial considerations make extensive new building for private renting unlikely, and it is hard to foresee any really significant increase in tenancies coming from exhortations to owner-occupiers or council tenants to let off spare rooms to 'make better use of the housing stock'.

The decline is important because the sector has traditionally provided a degree of flexibility in the housing market. Private tenancies have provided homes for young single people and married couples, immigrants, the elderly, the mobile, and others who do not want, or are not eligible for, a council tenancy or owner-occupation. The selection procedures followed by landlords are rarely formalized—some may dislike families with children and racial discrimination has been shown (Burney, 1967)—but by and large the sector is an easy access point to the housing system where there are no waiting lists. No really satisfactory alternative has yet been devised to satisfy the ease of access criterion.

Housing associations have suggested and encouraged as a substitute for the privately rented sector in the sense of providing an alternative to council tenancy or owner-occupation. As yet, the total contribution is small (0.5 per cent. of the total housing stock in 1972), and development must depend on the amount of public money made available in subsidy. Because housing associations vary widely in their objectives and functions, policies for access vary as well. Some provide accommodation for special-need groups—the elderly, or ex-prisoners, for example—others for general needs. Some adopt a conscious policy of favouring those in greatest need. How this objective can conflict with the other role accorded to housing associations for improving houses in urban renewal areas has been shown in recent research (Thompson, 1977).

The market for owner-occupation is complex, not least because different bodies and institutions operate at different stages. Thus opportunities for purchase are created by new construction undertaken by builders and developers; the transfer of property from other tenures, notably from the privately rented sector and through the sale of council houses where local policies permit; and by the vacancies created when an existing owner-occupier dies or moves house. Because of the relative levels of house prices and incomes, the majority of purchasers require a loan, so the effective allocation of owner-occupied property rests in the hands of the providers of mortgage finance: the building societies, local authorities, banks, insurance companies, or money lenders. In addition, the transactions involved in house purchase require a number of professional and semi-professional services, such as those provided by estate agents, valuers, and solicitors.

The supply of money to finance building activities is another very significant factor. Building firms' 'income comes in big lumps when the houses are sold, and meanwhile they must find the money for materials, labour and land' (C.D.P., 1976b, p. 21). Sources of finance include share capital, bank overdrafts, other borrowing, and suppliers' credit. Interest rates assume a great importance in addition to availability of credit from banks. Suppliers' credit—short-term loans from builders merchants which delay payment for materials going into a house until that house has been sold—depends on general confidence in the state of the housing market. Builders emerge as profit-maximizing firms caught between the constraints of fluctuating supplies of finance to create demand for their product and fluctuating supplies (and cost) of finance to enable them to produce at all. These fluctuations are quite outside their control, to be added to the other constraints of land availability, material and labour costs, and planning controls. It is hardly surprising that the resulting pattern of housing completions varies over time or that it bears little relationship to any concept of housing need.

In 1975, building societies provided about 82 per cent. of mortgage finance. The availability of funds and the policies and practices which determine their distribution are clearly of key importance.

'The ideals of thrift, home ownership and "personal freedom" emerge strongly as being fundamental to the building society movement' (Williams, 1976b, p. 32). Home ownership *and* thrift. Building societies borrow short-term funds to lend long term for house purchase. Therefore they must be able to attract funds in competition with other investment opportunities (shares, local authority stock, bank deposit account, national savings) available for savers, large and small. Favourable tax arrangements give societies an advantage over their competitors, but a basic inflexibility in interest rates can, at some times, prove a disadvantage. The interest rate societies can offer savers is closely related to the interest rate charged to borrowers. Changes in interest rates for borrowers are resisted, both because any increase raises the cost of housing and because any change involves the society in immense administrative costs. In line with this, savings rates also tend to be 'sticky', which can put societies at a grave disadvantage when competing rates are increasing rapidly. Conversely, rates above the 'market' level can result in a rapid inflow of funds. Variations in inflow of funds account for the fluctuations in effective demand for housing which create such problems for prospective purchasers and builders (Ashmore, 1975). Building societies also compete for savings through advertising and convenience for the investor with branch offices and agencies offering simple facilities for deposits and withdrawals.

'Investment has become the primary concern, with lending on mortgages being an outcome of it. Given this situation, building societies and the movement in general makes every effort to ensure that they are seen as thoroughly secure investment institutions' (Williams, 1976b, p. 30). 'Because they must retain the interests of their investors as a first priority, they are unlikely to grant mortgages on property where they are uncertain that prices and demand will be maintained in the future; they are also unlikely to consider people who may default because incomes may not be sustained or may not increase regularly over time' (Lambert, 1976, pp. 15–16).

The implications of lending policies designed to minimize risks have been described elsewhere, showing the types of household, property, and area favoured. Particular attention has been drawn to the contribution of building society policies to inner-city problems and urban renewal possibilities (Boddy, 1976; Duncan, 1976). The debate has assumed greater significance as local authority lending has been reduced through public expenditure controls. Building societies have not proved willing to relax their income or property rules when considering cases referred to them by local councils. In general, potential borrowers likely to be penalized by building society rules are those who can only afford, or only wish to buy, old (pre-1919) property, especially if this requires improvement or repair or is in an area with a doubtful future; those who cannot provide a 10 or 15 per cent. deposit; those whose incomes are low relative to the amount they need to borrow; and manual workers lacking skill who are thought to be particularly vulnerable to redundancy or loss of overtime and who lack assured incremental salary scales. The chances of all 'marginal' cases are worse when funds are scarce and 'safe' lending opportunities exceed the potential supply.

Estate agents act to bring together purchaser and seller for house sales. This is not their sole function; house estate agents may also be surveyors, valuers, auctioneers, property managers, commercial property agents, and frequently insurance and mortgage brokers too. Any estate agency may offer several of these skills. Since payment for services connected with a house sale takes the form of a percentage commission on the purchase price when a sale is completed, the agent is interested in encouraging sales and maintaining or raising price levels.

Part of the skill in negotiating sales is seen to be 'matching' purchaser to area.

Race, income, and social class have been mentioned as factors for discrimination. Williams argues that current residents in an area represent potential clients for an agent. If an agent is seen to be acting against their interests by encouraging coloured or low-class purchasers, he may suffer both by being denied any future custom and through any fall in prices which might result from mass selling. 'Thus the safest response is to keep like with like and to deter persons from moving to areas occupied by persons "unlike" themselves' (Williams, 1976b, p. 58). Deterrence may be by warnings about clearance, mortgage problems, or general adverse comments on the area or neighbours. Encouragement can take the form of stressed advantages or positive assistance with a mortgage. Certain agents may also become more directly involved in the housing market, particularly through links with property companies.

Links are important. So far, each institution has been considered as a separate entity, whereas research has been particularly concerned to discover and chart the networks of connections between different bodies and individuals, and to assess the effect of these on housing opportunities.

There are many different forms that links can take. Most intangible of all are the shared values and attitudes of those active in the private market. More positive and formal are 'guarantee' mortgages for new developments. The professional network in sales transactions works to the mutual advantage of those participating: 'estate agents make money selling a house and a buyer is much easier to find if they can arrange building society finance. Solicitors depend on new clients for a substantial part of their conveyancing work and it helps if they are recommended by estate agents or can themselves arrange building society finance. Building societies need investors and it helps if solicitors channel trust funds their way' (C.D.P., 1976b, p. 5). The Benwell and North Tyne C.D.P. team have produced a chart of the 'Tyne-Wear connection' showing common directorships, family, or servicing links between a number of building societies, solicitors, property companies, accountants, and estate agents operating locally. Less formal links—flows of commission and 'favours'—must be still more extensive.

The links between values and building society managers—the reliance placed on the valuer's report when considering the suitability of a property for mortgage security—have been shown particularly in renewal areas where adverse reports can lead to a self-fulfilling prophecy as property becomes unsaleable and deteriorates or is occupied by those willing to pay the high costs of finance company loans—again perhaps to deteriorate as money for repairs is not available.

Local authorities and voluntary organizations offering housing aid may attempt to break into these networks to achieve social ends. For example, clients may be advised to invest with a building society, channelling their funds through the aid centre, so that this becomes a recognized source of savings comparable to a local solicitor or accountant. Rather than commission, the aid centre seeks in return a better bargaining position when a 'marginal' mortgage is urgently needed. Playing the system in this way demands a sensitive approach and a clear eye for the social objective. For the potential owner-occupier threading his way through the maze, and particularly for those lacking the qualities which recommend their claim to profit-maximizing, risk-minimizing bodies, the prospect can be bleak. Social need as such has no bargaining power.

Private households

The final group of actors identified within the housing system are the households who occupy and exchange houses. Trends in housing research over the years have tended to diminish the importance accorded to household choice and behaviour in understanding the housing system. From theories where changes in family life-cycle and aspirations to preferred life-styles provide the motivation for movement and change in the housing system, the household has been effectively demoted to a mere pawn, without effective choice, at the mercy of the urban managers who control access to housing, themselves subject to inexorable constraints on their activities set by government intervention and the capitalist system.

Certainly there is an air of unreality about studies based purely on household aspirations. Some attempts at deciding the future desirable tenure split fall into this category. Figures are repeatedly produced which show that 'most people' want to be owner-occupiers, but the possibility of this being achieved or the amount they would be willing to pay and the type of house they might be willing to buy are not always specified. 'To state that "most people want to own their own home" begs the important question of on what terms and at what cost' (Murie, 1975).

Accepting that choice is constrained to a greater or lesser degree, Murie's suggestion of using simple decision space models is useful. 'The total decision space of individual households is *reduced* prior to the exercise of choice or preference by eligibility factors, job factors, shortages and previous housing experience' (Murie, 1974, p. 121). It is useful to suggest very briefly some of the relevant factors. Eligibility factors include those of the local authority, private landlord, building society, or estate agent already mentioned. Job factors include occupation, location, and the spatial area within which housing must be sought. Examples of shortages in the housing stock might include few very large houses in the council sector, cheap houses in some parts of South-East England, or privately rented dwellings. Previous housing experience is significant for the ways in which it may predispose a household to look in one direction rather than another because one course of action is familiar and because entry to the housing market in one way can limit future actions—if, for example, the purchase of a substandard house excludes the new owner-occupier from consideration for a council tenancy. The household's characteristics will determine what combination of constraints is to be experienced and how much individual choice remains to satisfy preferences and aspirations. A whole spectrum from a black, unemployed, single teenager to an existing owner-occupier in an area of high house prices with a professional job and earnings of over £ 10 000 a year might be imagined.

A particular area where the choice/constraint issue arises is the concentration of Asian immigrants into owner-occupied houses in certain areas of older housing. Asians are conspicuously under-represented in council housing. To some extent their absence from the public sector can be explained through ineligibility under residential qualifications or initial tenure if this was owner-occupation. Again, family structure—either incomplete households where men are waiting to bring over wives and children, or large or extended family units—are not of the type for which most council housing is designed. Because few Asians are council tenants, there is no body of shared experience. On the other hand, there is the claim that Asians prefer to buy, have the tradition of ownership, and that therefore any constraints they might experience in gaining access to local authority housing are irrelevant. Perhaps the more fruitful area for concern is whether or not the owner-occupied housing market will allow Asians to move from older, substandard housing when this is desired.

The actual balance between what must be ascribed to constraints and what is left free for choice is an unresolved area; nor are there really satisfactory research methods for elucidating the problem. One approach is to use social survey techniques which painstakingly ask the respondent to describe his housing history, detailing at every step what actions were taken and with what result. Recent movers or newly formed households provide samples for such questionnaire surveys, but there remain problems of forgetfulness and of rationalization after the event. To overcome these, action research within community groups or housing advice services can trace each step of a client's housing career as it happens. But here, of course, distortions can arise through the 'intervention' of the researcher himself.

Unanswered questions remain in considering the role of households in the housing system. Do higher vacancy rates in poor-quality property (with a low rateable value) reflect consumer choice in rejecting the older housing as obsolescent or the lending policies of financial institutions which have the effect of making older substandard property unsaleable? Are the levels of under-occupation found in some owner-occupied housing, where elderly single people or couples continue to live in their family home when children have grown up and left, evidence of conscious choice or lack of realistic alternatives? Choice, and the extent to which it can and should be legitimately exercised, may well grow in public and political importance if the present apparently paradoxical situation of rising vacancy rates in both the public and private sectors is accompanied by continuing problems of homelessness. Public expenditure restrictions may encourage a more limited and 'hardline' attitude to the role of council housing, still further limiting the scope for individual households to exercise such choice as they have in determining their housing circumstances.

Implications and tenure 'choice'

Leaving aside for the moment the relative degrees of choice and constraint, it should now be clear that the housing system is structured in such a way as to favour some households and to discriminate against others. Patterns of access do exist and households with certain characteristics are more likely to have the opportunity to become owner-occupiers, *or* council tenants, *or* private tenants. With different characteristics, a different tenure solution would be more probable.

It is possible to 'predict' characteristics of households likely to enter the major tenures, given an understanding of the objectives and policies of the major controlling institutions and the constraints they are likely to face in practice when implementing these policies. The following predictions are adapted from an analysis of institutions and access to housing (Murie, Niner, and Watson, 1976, pp. 224–231).

Access to council housing

From a knowledge of usual eligibility and priority rules adopted by local authorities, among entrants to council housing we would expect to find relatively large numbers of households which are:

1. *Small families.* While applicants may be able to register an application before marriage, they are seldom actively considered for housing before marriage takes place. A number of factors combine to make it more probable that allocation of a tenancy will occur when children have been born—e.g. by increasing potential overcrowding, the birth of children will increase priority, and many authorities lack dwellings considered 'suitable' for offer to childless couples. As the role of council housing is extended and the stock diversified, we would expect the relative over-representation of small families to decrease.
2. *Small elderly households.* Old-age pensioners are eligible to apply for a council tenancy, and may receive priority because of illhealth and poor existing housing conditions. Much recent building has been devoted to accommodation particularly suitable for the elderly.
3. *Households from slum clearance and redevelopment areas.* Councils have a statutory obligation to ensure that accommodation exists for those displaced by clearance or other demolition. As clearance programmes are completed and as improvement increases in importance, the number of households rehoused can be expected to decline.
4. *Households previously living in overcrowded conditions.* Overcrowding and the sharing of accommodation, which are often related, attract the greatest number of points and thus the highest priority in many allocation schemes. Shortage of space is one of the most widely accepted aspects of housing need and has the advantage of being relatively easy to measure.
5. *New households.* The points scheme or eligibility rules of most authorities give priority to applicants who lack accommodation of their own and are living perhaps as lodgers with parents or in-laws.

The entrants to council housing could be expected to include relatively small numbers of households which are:

1. *Former owner-occupiers.* Owner-occupiers are often deemed ineligible for

a council tenancy unless severe illhealth or social need is claimed. Clearance areas mostly involve rented rather than owner-occupied property. Recent recognition of the problems of underoccupation in privately owned houses may lead to some relaxation of rules excluding owner-occupiers—particularly the elderly.

2. *Single persons under retirement age.* Young single people without dependants are often considered ineligible for council housing; even when they *are* eligible, they may receive low priority, compared with competing claimants for small accommodation. Again any widening of the traditional role of council housing can be expected to help young single people.
3. *Newcomers to the local authority area.* Because of residential qualifications, people moving into the local authority area are often regarded as ineligible for council housing for some minimum waiting period. Even where residential qualifications are not applied, greater priority is often accorded in practice to 'local' residents.

Access to owner-occupation

Rather fewer hypotheses can be made in relation to the owner-occupied sector, because eligibility criteria are less well specified. Only the policies and rules followed by the building societies are known in sufficient detail to allow analysis. From these, we would expect entrants to owner-occupation to include relatively large numbers of households:

1. *With average or above-average incomes.* House price levels and repayment requirements suggest that those with higher incomes will find it easier to obtain mortgage finance.
2. *Headed by non-manual workers.* The white-collar occupations are distinguished by security of earnings and incremental salary scales. These features, as much as the absolute level of earnings, are viewed favourably by building societies.

Entrants to owner-occupation can be expected to include relatively few households:

1. *Headed by people in unskilled or semiskilled manual occupations.* While not necessarily subject to very low wage levels, these occupations can be insecure, which makes it unlikely that a building society will favour an application from such a worker, particularly when demand for funds outstrips supply.
2. *With a household head aged* 45 *or over*. Building societies usually require that a new loan should be repaid before retirement age. Since the maximum repayment period is often twenty-five years, a *new* borrower aged over 45 would be at a disadvantage. (This does not affect existing owners to the same extent, as they have the considerable asset of their present house in any transaction.)

Access to the privately rented sector

There are problems in predicting the type of household expected to be entering the privately rented sector. There is an apparent lack of common eligibility requirements in the sector as a whole. One of the most important features of the privately rented sector is the poor quality of its housing stock. Many tenants lack, or have to share, basic amenities; accommodation is often not self-contained; and most dwellings are old. Because of these poor conditions, it can be assumed that households able to exercise choice will generally try to avoid private renting. Those most likely to become private-sector tenants will, therefore, be those who are excluded from entry to other sectors. Thus, entrants to the privately rented sector can be expected to include relatively few households:

1. *With average or above-average incomes.* Those with higher incomes are likely to be able to raise a mortgage for entry to owner-occupation, and are not necessarily barred from the public sector.
2. *Which are small families.* Households of this type are particularly likely to be eligible for a council tenancy. The heads of small family households are often young, and those with sufficient incomes may have little difficulty in attracting mortgage finance.

Entrants to the privately rented sector can be expected to include relatively large numbers of households which are:

1. *Single persons under retirement age.* Young single people are often considered ineligible or receive low priority for council housing. At the same time, mortgage lenders favour more 'orthodox' family structures. Single persons are often mobile, and thus likely to find some positive advantage in the relatively free access conditions for private tenancies.
2. *Newcomers to the local authority area.* Recent migrants may be excluded by residential qualifications from local authority tenancies, and some households which ultimately intend to become (or to continue as) owner-occupiers may take a private tenancy as a temporary measure.

Such survey material as is available seems to support these contentions. The expected groups are over-represented or under-represented among entrants to the different tenures as predicted (Murie, Niner, and Watson, 1976, pp. 227, 229, 230).

Of course, the discussion so far has been extremely general. Access to the different tenure sectors is important, but these very broad factors by no means wholly explain just what house a household is likely to receive *within* the tenure. Once again, the rules of the different institutions are important. Council housing, being allocated *chiefly* in terms of concepts of need, is usually matched to family requirements in that house size reflects family size. Owner-occupied housing is *chiefly* allocated through money-bids, therefore price becomes the important variable (associated as it may be with size and quality), to be matched by income or other measures of financial resources the household can devote to housing. The privately rented sector is so diverse that even very broad generalizations are impossible. In all sectors intangible 'social' or 'class' elements can be important; grading can affect the quality or desirability of a house offered to a council house applicant and the social intangibles may influence estate agents in 'steering' potential purchasers towards one area rather than another. Equally, aspirations and desires linked to education and social class will affect the alternatives considered by applicants where some exercise of choice is possible.

SPATIAL CONSEQUENCES AND PATTERNS

At national and regional level

In Britain as a whole, the twentieth century has seen continuing growth in population, households, and dwellings; consistent changes in the tenure structure of the housing stock; and greatly improved housing conditions. But these trends have varied in their impact, and present housing 'problems' and 'benefits' show significant social and spatial variation.

Since the Second World War, about 8 million dwellings have been built in England and Wales and 1.3 million slums have been demolished. Taking account of other losses, this has resulted in a net gain to the housing stock of 6.5 million dwellings. House building has made a very important contribution to the growth of towns and cities through the expansion of urban areas and the spread of suburbia. In 1900, less than 4 per cent. of the total land area of Britain was in urban use; by 1950, the proportion had risen to 7.2 per cent (Best and Coppock, 1962, p. 229). Today, it may be as high as 8 per cent. in Britain as a whole and 12 per cent. in England and Wales (Cullingworth, 1972b, p. 87). In functional terms, the area of urban influence—where population depends on the urban concentration for its livelihood—is very much larger than this (D.O.E., 1976a, p. 1):

> If both physical (i.e. land use) and functional criteria are considered simultaneously, it is readily apparent that one of the key characteristics of urban change in Britain, especially since 1945, has been the increasing divergence of these two facets of urbanization. In the nineteenth century, the physical, functional and also political boundaries of towns generally coincided. Today, many people living in seemingly rural areas work in non-agricultural activities, located in physically urbanised areas, while even the agricultural population depends on the city for a widening range of services. Indeed, much of the physical growth of towns has occurred in settlements beyond the continuously built up areas.

This spread of urban areas and the separation of physical and functional 'boundaries' of cities has been influenced by many factors. These include conscious dispersal policies; the 'realities' of land availability where large areas for new development are to be found on peripheral sites or around the smaller towns which surround larger cities; and the increased personal mobility and apparent willingness of many people to live at a considerable distance from their work.

The increase in the number of dwellings since 1945 has exceeded the growth in the number of households, and figures now suggest that, in Britain as a whole, there is a 'crude surplus' of dwellings over households. This simple comparison, however, ignores the number of people who would like to live separately but who cannot, for one reason or another, form a household of their own, as well as the regional imbalances in the supply of housing which still exist: e.g. the crude deficit of dwellings found in Greater London cannot effectively be offset by surpluses in the North or the North-East of England.

Regional differences are also apparent in the tenure composition of the dwelling stock. Nationally the pattern has been one of net gains for owner-occupation and public-sector renting, and net losses to private renting and other tenures (Table 8.1).

TABLE 8.1. Tenure of dwellings in the United Kingdom

Stock of dwellings (in thousands)	1960	1965	1970	1971	1972	1973
Owner-occupied	6 967	8 243	9 567	9 810	10 098	10 359
Rented from local authorities or New Town corporations	4 400	5 023	5 848	5 976	6 032	6 094
Rented from private owners and others	5 323	4 535	3 768	3 674	3 551	3 438
Total	16 600	17 801	19 183	19 460	19 681	19 891

Source. Social Trends No. 5, 1974, Table 131, p. 162.

As percentages of the total stock, dwellings in owner-occupation rose from 42 to 52 per cent. between 1960 and 1973, dwellings rented in the public sector rose from 26 to 31 per cent., and private rented dwellings declined from 32 to 17 per cent. In 1973, the share of owner-occupation varied between 60 per cent. in the South-West and the South-East outside Greater London and 32 per cent. in Scotland. Public-sector tenancies were highest in Scotland (53 per cent.) and the Northern Region of England (38 per cent.) and lowest in the Outer South-East (20 per cent.). Over a quarter of dwellings are still privately rented in Greater London, compared to only 13 per cent. in the West Midlands. Such variations reflect differing economic, social, and political histories in the regions. Given the different access rules for the sectors, they also suggest that different patterns of housing opportunity obtain in each region.

Housing quality has many dimensions. Successive censuses show a decline in the number of households sharing a dwelling, living in overcrowded conditions, and lacking amenities. Since 1967 the total number of unfit dwellings in England and Wales is estimated to have fallen from about 1.8 million to 800 000. Regional differences were again shown in the second National House Condition Survey (D.O.E., 1973).

At city scale

In practice, regional patterns may be of little significance in influencing housing opportunities, since most households are constrained by the need to work to a rather narrower scale, usually related to employment opportunities in towns, cities, and conurbations. It is at this scale that policies of new building, clearance and improvement, and the policies and processes of allocation have created distinctive patterns of social and residential segregation. Policy and process have interacted to produce results which have not always been intended.

The post-war drive for council house building, both to meet known shortages and for slum clearance, took place on 'green field' sites on the edge of built-up areas. Because these new peripheral estates were catering for those 'in need', who, in general, lacked effective housing choice or opportunity in the owner-occupied sector, they housed mainly the unskilled and semiskilled, and contained a disproportionate number of young families, whose needs invariably took priority over those of older people. The needs of single-person households were hardly catered for at all. Distinctive communities were created in this way, including many people who, through low personal mobility, found living in peripheral areas unsatisfactory, especially before local services such as shops and schools could be provided. As clearance programmes have proceeded, so local authority housing has been brought into city centres on the cleared sites. In some inner-city wards the proportion of council housing is now very high. The 'choice' facing a prospective tenant may now be the offer of a house on an estate far from the city centre, or a flat or maisonette in a high-density redevelopment scheme.

With continuing new building, those who could afford to become owner-occupiers were often attracted to such new housing as they could find within the city boundaries (though this was limited, since many authorities retained the largest green-field sites for their own estates). Even more were led to seek housing beyond the cities themselves, in the expanding suburban towns. Others, particularly skilled workers, were attracted to the growing New Towns. An additional and important supply of houses for owner-occupation has come from the sale of privately rented houses, either to sitting tenants or (at greater profit to the landlord) with vacant possession. This practice has contributed to the growth in the number of older properties for owner-occupation in the inner ring of cities, an area which has proved significant in the housing of immigrants in many places, and which is also now a prime target for renewal or improvement policies.

Because of these trends, there is growing concern about the structural changes which have taken place in British cities and the contribution to them that has been made by strategic planning and industrial and employment policies, as well as local housing policies and processes. In the present idiom this is referred to as the 'inner-city problem'. From 1961 to 1971, all the British conurbations (Greater London, Merseyside, South-East Lancashire, Tyneside, West Midlands, and Clydeside) lost population, though decline was concentrated in the inner areas of the conurbations. In general, the proportion of working-age adults declined throughout the decade, despite a rise in the proportion of younger adults. The decline was generally more marked in the inner areas than in the conurbations as a whole. The proportion of retired people in the populations of both central areas and conurbations rose over the decade, but at a higher rate in the inner areas. The rises in the proportion of young people in the inner areas was not uniformly reflected in the conurbations; overall the inner areas showed relative increases (D.O.E., 1975b, p. 2).

Housing conditions, too, show an important variation between the conurbations as a whole and their inner areas. Differences between and within conurbations reflect the links between the level of publicly and privately rented housing and the standard of basic amenities and overcrowding. Greater London, with its high proportion of privately rented property, has a much greater incidence of bad housing conditions (in terms of basic amenities and overcrowding) than the West Midlands and Tyneside, where the proportion of public housing is much greater (Table 8.2) (D.O.E., 1975b). Nevertheless, in Clydeside, where the proportion of public sector housing is the highest in Britain, extremely bad housing and social conditions persist (Cullingworth and Watson, 1971; D.O.E., 1975b; Mansley, 1972), some of them being concentrated in public housing estates (English, 1976).

TABLE 8.2. British conurbations: percentage of households by tenure, 1961 to 1971

	Owner-occupied			Public rented			Private rented		
	1961	1966	1971	1961	1966	1971	1961	1966	1971
Greater London	36	39	40	18	22	25	42	37	34
Merseyside	32	36	40	27	29	33	38	33	27
South-East Lancashire	44	48	51	22	25	30	31	24	19
Tyneside	28	30	32	33	37	42	36	30	26
West Midlands	38	42	45	35	38	40	23	18	15
Clydeside	20	23	25	45	51	59	33	24	16

Source. Census.

At the level of individual cities, rather than conurbations, the disparities between inner and outer areas are much more pronounced, particularly in the 'inner ring' which surrounds the central business district. This, of course, has been recognized for many years (Edwards, Leigh, and Marshall, 1971; Robson, 1969) and is a characteristic of cities in most Western industrialized countries (Johnston, 1971). Increasing attention is being focused on these problems and the measures which might be taken to deal with them, largely through the inner-area studies commissioned by the Department of the Environment in the early 1970s and (at the time of writing) now nearing completion. These studies were undertaken in Liverpool, Birmingham, and the London Borough of Lambeth.

The summary report of the Birmingham study defines the problems of inner areas as characterized by (D.O.E., 1977, p. 19):

(i) A large loss of population—down from about 50,000 in 1951 to about 32,000 now.

(ii) An increasing concentration of lower skilled families (many of them coloured). This is the result of selective migration into and out of the area, rather than of a cycle of deprivation within families already established in the area. The better off and more skilled have moved out leaving the more unskilled behind. The mean household income in Small Heath is two-thirds of that in the West Midlands; the disparity in incomes is even greater.

(iii) A declining economic and industrial base. The loss of jobs is outstripping that of population. Rates of unemployment are rising relative to the city as a whole. The rate of decline in manufacturing jobs is double that in the city as a whole.

(iv) Particular vulnerability to changing trading and labour market conditions with high rates of unemployment at times of recession.

(v) Very little public or private investment in the area in the recent past—whether in homes, shops, schools amenities or workplaces—except in areas of comprehensive redevelopment, which we have found to have their own special problems....

Clearly, far more than bad housing conditions characterize decline in the inner city. Indeed, one of the most important lessons to have been learnt in all the work that has been carried out in the last ten years or so is the inextricable relationship *between* housing, employment, industry, investment, planning, education, social service provision, and many other factors, in contributing to the patterns of growth and decline that characterize different parts of our cities. At one level, the inner-city problem today exist because planned programmes of dispersal of population and industry were too successful; because clearance programmes disrupted local communities and destroyed small firms; and because council house building and allocation policies were geared to particular concepts of need and priority. Those who remain in the inner city can face what the Lambeth inner-area consultants call the 'housing trap'. The less skilled and affluent—those who most need to move for new jobs—have little choice of doing so. 'The choices available to them are owner-occupied houses, which they cannot buy, and public housing, to which they are denied access. Few can go to Outer London boroughs because the authorities there have discouraged public housing for Inner Londoners and, lacking the skills in greatest demand, they have been largely excluded from the new and expanding towns' (D.O.E., 1977, p. 44).

Local consequences and patterns

So far, we have examined spatial and social consequences and patterns at regional and city level. But it is also useful to examine process in the urban housing system at a 'micro' scale, e.g. at the level of individual local authority estates or areas of private housing where particular groups of households are concentrated or are in the ascendancy. The general trends and patterns already described have important local variations which cannot be ignored in attempting to explain the consequences of housing policies and practice.

As English (1976, p. 319) observes 'many generalisations are made about the local authority sector in Britain but, in reality, council housing is highly stratified, providing accommodation and environments which range from excellent to appalling. At the same time, the socio-economic characteristics of residents, even if they are largely working class, vary profoundly between estates'. Critics of the British housing system who point to the segregation between tenure sectors often ignore the segregation *within* sectors and the social differentiation to which this gives rise.

Once again, an historical perspective is helpful in explaining some of the patterns which can be seen today. Reference was made earlier to the subsidies introduced in the Housing Act of 1930 to encourage the rehousing of slum clearance families, and many new, often flatted, estates were built under the provisions of the Act entirely for this purpose. As a result, they acquired a social character markedly different from that of the 1920s estates, which has been sustained in the popular imagination, if not always justified in practice. Thus, a change of building form (from 'cottage-style' semi-detached houses to three-or four-storey flatted blocks), coupled with allocation policies which gave priority to those from slum clearance areas, have had a great influence on public attitudes—not least, those of potential council tenants (S.D.D., 1975; S.H.A.C., 1970). The opportunities for architectural experiment were not lost, however, and these, too, played their part in reinforcing views which led certain estates or developments to acquire 'unpopular' and 'popular' reputations (Ravetz, 1974).

The same pattern was repeated after the war: first, with the large estates built to meet the great post-war shortage of housing, often using non-traditional building materials, since these were all that could be obtained; and then with the development of multistorey housing and maisonette blocks, which reached its heyday in the 1960s.

There is considerable evidence that the amenity, physical characteristics, and 'social reputation' of local authority housing estates greatly influences their relative popularity (among both waiting and transfer list applicants) and the characteristics of their population (Damer, 1974; English 1976; S.D.D., 1976). And though much of this evidence comes from Scottish work, the English report *The Needs of New Communities* (C.H.A.C., 1967) provides useful support.

Of course, every local authority housing department knows which its 'problem' estates are. They are characterized by high tenant turnover, a large number of transfer applicants, and a concentration of the 'deprived'—the unemployed, those with low incomes, single-parent families, and large families. To try to change and improve the social balance of such an area is difficult through allocation policies, since those in greatest need who have no effective choice elsewhere cannot afford to wait for more 'popular' areas and must take the first house or flat offered to them. Because turnover is highest in 'unpopular' areas, that is where vacancies most often arise. Thus the character of such areas is self-perpetuating. In one 'deprived' Scottish estate, 44 per cent of allocations in 1974 were made within one year of application, compared with 16 per cent. for the town as a whole (English, 1976, p. 322). In another, the average waiting period for council housing in 1973 was 9 months for a 'popular' estate, 3 months for an 'intermediate' estate, and 1 month for an 'unpopular' estate (S.D.D., 1976, p. 48).

Since it is largely the perceived social character of estates that determines their popularity, the measures that can be taken to deal with those that are unpopular are difficult to determine. They range from demolition, which is a physical solution to what is really a social problem, to some form of comprehensive improvement in which physical, social services, education, employment, and many other factors would need to be considered. Once again, 'housing problems' cannot be dealt with by conventional housing policies alone.

Microscale variations in urban private housing are also important. The problems of the inner city have already been discussed, but it must be emphasized again that the policies of lending institutions, in particular building societies, are very influential in determining access to owner-occupied housing in what are generally regarded as declining inner areas (Boddy, 1976; Duncan, 1976; Karn, 1976; Lambert, 1976; Williams, 1976b). The 'mortgage famine' in the inner city, particularly since the restrictions on local authority mortgage lending, have limited the availability of public funds for lending in these areas.

There are, however, examples (particularly from London) of developments against this general trend. The phenomenon of 'gentrification', 'the process by which a predominantly working class area of residence becomes increasingly middle class' (Williams, 1976a, p. 1), though recognized at least ten years ago (Donnison, 1967), has become increasingly apparent since the 1969 Housing Act. The availability of more generous improvement grants and the prospect of local authority expenditure on environmental improvements certainly speeded the process and caused considerable alarm about what proved to be an unintended 'side effect' of improvement policy in the early 1970s. The opportunities were considerable for the speculative improvement and sale of what were previously rented properties. The Report of the Expenditure Committee on *House Improvement Grants* (1973, p. xxiii) refers to the spectacular case of a converted house in Camden which was sold for a total of £112 000, two years after having been bought for a sum variously estimated at £7 000, £14 000, or £24 000. Though the costs incurred by the owner in converting the house into eight units were in dispute, the Expenditure Committee was informed that an improvement grant of £9 000 had been given by the local authority. Cases such as these are now less likely, since the more restrictive grant code introduced in the 1974 Housing Act was intended to limit the opportunities for what can only be regarded as public subsidy of private profit.

But a change in the law, and in the availability of improvement grants, though it may reduce the opportunities for speculation, cannot remove them.

It is unlikely that it will significantly reduce the demand for 'middle-class' housing in the central areas of cities (though it may affect its supply), and such demand—which is often for owner-occupied housing—can be met only at the expense of the privately rented sector, which is so often the sector of last resort for people who need to live in inner areas but have no prospect of becoming owner-occupiers and only limited prospects of a council tenancy.

It would be wrong, however, to conclude that changes in class structure in certain urban areas were due entirely to speculation and to the harassment or 'winkling' of tenants. The natural turnover in the housing market through the death of old people and the movement of others creates vacancies which will be filled by other households—often younger and often better off than previous residents.

Roberts (1976, p. 92) notes that for gentrification to occur, there must be a 'gentry': 'In many areas... there is a distinct shortage of people in the relevant social groups. Frequently, too, these groups have ample opportunities to enter the other parts of the housing market. The capital involved in buying and improving an old house is not so different from that required to by a new one on mortgage.' Though one might question the existence of 'ample opportunities' for access to other parts of the market, the fact remains that it is in places where pressure for housing is greatest and where the function—often of quite small areas of housing—is finely balanced that the competition for housing resources is seen most clearly. Gentrification, though it achieves the worthwhile objective of improving existing housing, has often done so at the expense of those least able to compete in the housing market.

THE FUTURE

The current emphasis on the 'inner-city problem' is likely to remain, at least in the immediate future. The spectre of American experience is now presented as a warning against allowing processes of social segregation and multiple deprivation to 'go too far'. Appropriate policies have not yet been proposed, but it seems inevitable that they must have important spatial implications, not just for the inner areas but for other areas too. Positive discrimination in favour of some areas implies negative discrimination elsewhere. The future of major public investment in the new and expanding towns is already being questioned. Regional policies of industrial dispersal are other candidates for reconsideration. Once-proud policy initiatives—hailed as major British contributions to planning philosophy and practice—now seem in jeopardy. How successful ameliorative action can be is debatable. The conclusions of the Community Development Projects, if not of the Inner-Area consultants, suggested that relative deprivation would be cured only through fundamental changes in the organization and structure of society. It is unlikely that such fundamental changes would be forthcoming as part of any government's 'package' for the inner city.

A second, and closely related, consideration for the future is the growing certainty that public funds will be severely restricted for many years to come.

This means that concentration of public resources in the inner city *must* imply less spent elsewhere. Public expenditure restrictions relevant to housing are likely to have various effects. Local authorities have often in the past been urged to take a comprehensive view of their housing responsibilities. This will be much more important (and persuasive) if authorities no longer have the resources to meet housing needs directly, having to rely to a greater extent on the private sector. Such reliance, of course, entails many uncertainties. How can an authority be sure the private sector will respond as expected as appropriate? What powers, control, or influences exist locally and nationally to ensure the desired response? Might we, for example, expect controls over building societies to be increased?

Limited public funds *should* mean clearer definitions of priorities in relation to needs and objectives. The new system of housing investment programmes, where local authorities must justify claims for spending in different policy areas, is intended to foster such increased clarity. Certainly there is an implication that more information will be required about local housing situations, which could provide a basis for more rational (and realistic?) planning and policy making.

Finally, limited funds in the public sector and lack of confidence and effective demand in the private sector have implications of a very unpleasant kind. If local authorities are to build and private builders are unwilling to do so, the prospects for new households and those not yet established in the housing market are bleak. If restricted funds for new building lead to the adoption of lower standards of space or amenity, problems of management and maintenance will be increased for the future. If improvement policies are urged just to save money, there will be an immense backlog of houses requiring clearance—giving a house a thirty-year life in the 1960s and 1970s will extend that life to a date coinciding with the end of the 'financial life' of council houses built in the inter-war years. The conflict of time scales is always an important factor, and never more so than now.

Spatial consequences follow. A tighter definition of need for public-sector housing could lead to greater social segregation in council estates. Lack of local authority mortgages could mean an increase in the extent of older housing areas where finance for house purchase is unavailable or difficult. Continued restrictions on incomes and rising transport costs may restrict the willingness or ability of people to live far from their work.

Perhaps the most important lesson from this brief analysis is that, to understand the social and spatial patterns of British cities, still more attention must be given to the wide variety of policies and processes at work in the housing system and—even most important—to the interrelations between them.

REFERENCES

Aaron, H. J. (1972). *Shelter and Subsidies: Who Benefits from Federal Housing Policies?*, The Brookings Institution, Washington, D. C.

Ashmore, G. (1975). *The Owner-Occupied Housing Market.* Research Memorandum No. 41, Centre for Urban and Regional Studies, University of Birmingham.

Best, R. H., and Coppock, J. T. (1962). *The Changing Use of Land in Britain*, Faber, London.

Boaden, N. (1971). *Urban Policy Making*, Cambridge University Press, Cambridge.

Boddy, M. J. (1976). The structure of mortgage finance: building societies and the British social formation. *Transactions of the Institute of British Geographers*, New Series, **1**(1).

Bowley, M. (1945). *Housing and the State, 1919–1944*, George Allen and Unwin, London.

Burney, E. (1967). *Housing on Trial: A Study of Immigrants and Local Government*, Oxford University Press, London.

C. D. P. (Community Development Project) (1976a). *Whatever Happened to Council Housing?*, C. D. P. Information and Intelligence Unit.

C. D. P. (Community Development Project) (1976b). *Profits Against Houses: An Alternative Guide to Housing Finance*, C. D. P. Information and Intelligence Unit.

C. H. A. C. (Central Housing Advisory Committee) (1967). *The Needs of New Communities.* Report of a Sub-Committee of the Central Housing Advisory Committee, H. M. S. O., London.

C. H. A. C. (Central Housing Advisory Committee) (1969). *Council Housing: Purposes, Procedures and Priorities.* Ninth Report of the Housing Management Sub-Committee, H. M. S. O., London.

Cullingworth, J. B. (1972a). *Problems of an Urban Society*, Vol. 1, *The Social Framework of Planning*, George Allen and Unwin, London.

Cullingworth, J. B. (1972b). *Problems of an Urban Society*, Vol. 2, *The Social Content of Planning*, George Allen and Unwin, London.

Cullingworth, J. B., and Watson, C. J. (1971). *Housing in Clydeside*, H. M. S. O., London.

Damer, S. (1974). Wine Alley: the sociology of a dreadful enclosure. *Sociological Review*, **22**(2), 221–248.

Davies, J. G. (1972). *The Evangelistic Bureaucrat*, Tavistock Publications, London.

Dennis, N. (1970). *People and Planning: The Sociology of Housing in Sunderland*, Faber, London.

Derrick, E. F. (1976). *House and Area Improvement in Britain.* Research Memorandum No. 54, Centre for Urban and Regional Studies, University of Birmingham.

D. O. E. (Department of the Environment) (1973). *Housing Condition Survey 1971, England and Wales*, Housing Survey Reports No. 9, D. O. E.

D. O. E. (Department of the Environment) (1975a). *Housing Act 1974:* Parts IV, V, VI. *Housing Action Areas, Priority Neighbourhoods, and General Improvement Areas*, Circular 14/75, D. O. E.

D. O. E. (Department of the Environment) (1975b). *Study of the Inner Areas of Conurbations*, Vol. 1, *Summary and Conclusions;* Vol. 2, *Detailed Studies*, D. O. E.

D. O. E. (Department of the Environment) (1975c). *The Use of Indicators for Area Action, Housing Act 1974*, Area Improvement Note 10, H. M. S. O., London.

D. O. E. (Department of the Environment) (1975d). *Housing Land Availability in the South-East*, H. M. S. O., London.

D. O. E. (Department of the Environment) (1976a). *British Cities: Urban Population and Employment Trends, 1951–71*, Research Report No. 10, D. O. E.

D. O. E. (Department of the Environment) (1976b). *Housing Policies for the Inner City*, Inner Area Study, Birmingham, Report by the Consultants, D. O. E.

D. O. E. (Department of the Environment) (1971). *Inner Area Studies: Liverpool, Birmingham and Lambeth*, Summaries of Consultants' Final Reports, H. M. S. O.

Donnison, D. V. (1967). *The Government of Housing*, Penguin Books, Harmondsworth.

Duncan, S. S. (1976). Self-help: the allocation of mortgages and the formation of housing sub-markets. *Area*, **8**(4), 307–316.

Duncan, T. L. C., and Cowan, R. H. (1976). *Housing Action Areas in Scotland.* Housing

Improvement Policies in Scotland Research Paper No. 3, The Planning Exchange, Glasgow.

Duncan, T. L. C., and Curry, J. (1974). *Housing Improvement Policies in England and Wales.* Research Memorandum No. 29, Centre for Urban and Regional Studies, University of Birmingham.

Edwards, J. R., Leigh, E., and Marshall, T. (1971). *Social Patterns in Birmingham 1966: A Reference Manual.* Occasional Paper No. 13, Centre for Urban and Regional Studies, University of Birmingham.

Engels, F. (1845). *The Condition of the Working Class in England*, Panther Books, St. Albans, Herts. (Reprinted 1969.)

English, J. (1976). Housing allocation and a deprived Scottish estate. *Urban Studies*, **13**(3), 319–323.

Expenditure Committee (1973). *House Improvement Grants*, Tenth Report from the Expenditure Committee, Vol. 1, Report, H. M. S. O., London.

Gray, F. (1976). Selection and allocation in council housing. *Transactions of the Institute of British Geographers*, New Series, **1**(1), 34–46.

Grigsby, W. G. (1963). *Housing Markets and Public Policy*, University of Pennsylvania Press, Philadelphia.

Hall, P., Thomas, R., Gracey, H., and Drewett, R. (1973). *The Containment of Urban England*, George Allen and Unwin, London.

Harloe, M., Issacharoff, R., and Minns, R. (1974). *The Organization of Housing: Public and Private Enterprise in London*, Heinemann, London.

Harvey, D. (1973). *Social Justice and the City*, Edward Arnold, London.

Herbert, D. T. (1973). Residential mobility and preference: a study of Swansea. In *Social Patterns in Cities*, Institute of British Geographers Special Publication No. 5, pp. 103–121.

Johnston, R. J. (1971). *Urban Residential Patterns*, Bell, London.

Karn, V. A. (1976). *Priorities for Local Authority Mortgage Lending: A Case Study of Birmingham.* Research Memorandum No. 52, Centre for Urban and Regional Studies, University of Birmingham.

Kristof, F. S. (1966). Housing policy and housing market behaviour: experience in the United States. *Urban Studies*, **3**(2), 89–111.

Lambert, C. (1976). *Building Societies, Surveyors and the Older Areas of Birmingham.* Working Paper No. 38, Centre for Urban and Regional Studies, University of Birmingham.

Mansley, R. D. (1972). *Areas of Need in Glasgow.* Second Review of the Development Plan, The Corporation of Glasgow.

M. H. L. G. (Ministry of Housing and Local Government) (1968). House condition survey in England and Wales. *Economic Trends* (H. M. S. O.), **175**, 24–26.

Murie, A. (1974). *Household Movement and Housing Choice.* Occasional Paper No. 28, Centre for Urban and Regional Studies, University of Birmingham.

Murie, A. (1975). *The Sale of Council Houses: A Study of Social Policy.* Occasional Paper No. 35, Centre for Urban and Regional Studies, University of Birmingham.

Murie, A., Niner, P., and Watson, C. (1976). *Housing Policy and the Housing System*, George Allen and Unwin, London.

Niner, P. (1975). *Local Authority Housing Policy and Practice: A Case Study Approach.* Occasional Paper No. 31, Centre for Urban and Regional Studies, University of Birmingham.

Pahl, R. E. (1975). Urban processes and social structure. In *Whose City?*, 2nd ed. Penguin Books, Harmondsworth. pp. 234–264.

Park, R. E. (1929). *Human Communities*, Glencoe Free Press New York. (Reprinted 1952.)

Pepper, S. (1971). *Housing Improvement: Goals and Strategy*, Architectural Association Paper No. 8, Lund Humphries, London.

Ratcliff, R. (1949). *Urban Land Economics*, McGraw-Hill, New York.

Ravetz, A. (1974). *Model Estate: Planned Housing at Quarry Hill, Leeds*, Croom Helm, London.

Rex, J., and Moore, R. (1967). *Race, Community and Conflict*, Oxford University Press, London.

Roberts, J. T. (1976). *General Improvement Areas*, Saxon House/Lexington Books, Farnborough, Harts.

Robson, B. T. (1969). *Urban Analysis*, Cambridge University Press, Cambridge.

Royal Commission on the Housing of the Industrial Population of Scotland, Rural and Urban (1917). *Report*, Cd. 8731, H. M. S. O., London.

Sands, G., and Bower, L. L. (1976). *Housing Turnover and Housing Policy: Case Studies of Vacancy Chains in New York State*, Praeger Publishers, New York.

S. D. D. (Scottish Development Department) (1975). *Housing and Social Work: A Joint Approach*, Report of the Morris Committee on Links Between Housing and Social Work, H. M. S. O., London.

S. D. D. (Scottish Development Department) (1976). *Local Housing Needs and Strategies: A Case Study of the Dundee Sub-Region*, H. M. S. O., London.

S. H. A. C. (Scottish Housing Advisory Committee) (1970). *Council House Communities: A Policy for Progress*. Report by a Sub-Committee of the Scottish Housing Advisory Committee, H. M. S. O., London.

Thompson, A. P. S. (1977). *The Role of Housing Associations in Major Urban Areas: A Case Study of Merseyside Improved Houses*, Centre for Urban and Regional Studies, University of Birmingham. (Forthcoming.)

Watson, C. J. (1973). *Household Movement in West Central Scotland: A Study of Housing Chains and Filtering*. Occasional Paper No. 26, Centre for Urban and Regional Studies, University of Birmingham.

Welsh Consumer Council (1976). *Council Housing: A Survey of Allocation Policies in Wales*, Welsh Consumer Council.

White, H. C. (1971). Multipliers, vacancy chains and filtering in housing. *Journal of the American Institute of Planners*, **XXXVII**(2), 88–94.

Williams, P. R. (1976a). *Change in an Urban Area: The Role of Institutions in the Process of Gentrification in the London Borough of Islington*. Unpublished Ph.D. thesis, University of Reading.

Williams, P. R. (1976b). *The Role of Financial Institutions and Estate Agents in the Private Housing Market: A General Introduction*. Working Paper No. 39, Centre for Urban and Regional Studies, University of Birmingham.

Index

BIBL. UNIV. LAUR. UNIV. LIB.
3 0007 00186373 6